THE ART OF
BECOMING INFINITE

The Art of Becoming Infinite

Mou Zongsan's Vertical Rethinking of
Self and Subjectivity

Gabriella Stanchina

https://www.openbookpublishers.com

©2025 Gabriella Stanchina

This work is licensed under the Creative Commons Attribution-NonCommercial 4.0 International (CC BY-NC 4.0). This license allows you to share, copy, distribute and transmit the text; to adapt the text for non-commercial purposes of the text providing attribution is made to the authors (but not in any way that suggests that they endorse you or your use of the work). Attribution should include the following information:

Gabriella Stanchina, *The Art of Becoming Infinite: Mou Zongsan's Vertical Rethinking of Self and Subjectivity*. Open Book Publishers, 2025, https://doi.org/10.11647/OBP.0442

Further details about the CC BY-NC license are available at http://creativecommons.org/licenses/by-nc/4.0/

All external links were active at the time of publication unless otherwise stated and have been archived via the Internet Archive Wayback Machine at https://archive.org/web

Any digital material and resources associated with this volume will be available at https://doi.org/10.11647/OBP.0442#resources

ISBN Paperback 978-1-80511-477-2

ISBN Hardback 978-1-80511-478-9

ISBN PDF 978-1-80511-479-6

ISBN HTML 978-1-80511-481-9

ISBN EPUB 978-1-80511-480-2

DOI: 10.11647/OBP.0442

Cover image: A close up of a painting of purple and red, 12 January 2023. Photo by Susan Wilkinson, https://unsplash.com/photos/a-close-up-of-a-painting-of-purple-and-red-6EKbwxKcacs

Cover design: Jeevanjot Kaur Nagpal

Table of Contents

Introduction   1
   A Vertical Rethinking of the Self: The Significance of This Study   1
   Mou Zongsan's Life and Works   13
   Chapter-by-Chapter Overview   20

1. The Question of Subjectivity   39
   1.1 The True Face of Mount Lu   39
   1.2 Contemporary Perspectives on Self   45
   1.3 Comparative Perspectives   59

2. Mou Zongsan and the *Critique of the Cognitive Mind*   69
   2.1 Towards a New Philosophy of Mind   69
   2.2 Structure and Significance of the *Critique of the Cognitive Mind*   72
   2.3 Perception and Apperception   79
   2.4 Self-Consciousness and Psychological States   83
   2.5 The Problem of the Self   86
   2.6 From the Physiological Self to the Logical Self   88
   2.7 Self-Consciousness and Meaning   92
   2.8 The Oscillation between Self-Limitation and Springing Out (跳起)   96
   2.9 The Mind of the Quiet Shining (*Jizhaoxin* 寂照心)   103
   2.10 Toward the Transcendent Mind: The Meaning and Use of *Zi* 自   108

3. The "Diaphanous Subject" in Daoist Thought   113
   3.1 Daoism as the Metaphysics of the State of Mind   113
   3.2 *Jingjie* as Spiritual State and Hodological Space   121
   3.3 Withdrawing and Progressing: Western Subject versus Daoist Subject   134
   3.4 The Three-Step Dialectics of Daoism   144

3.5 The Daoist Subjectivity According to Mou	153
3.6 The Diaphanous Subject	157
3.7 Self-Awareness and Trans-consciousness	160
3.8 Priority of the Sense of Sight	166
3.9 Subject, Ancestor, Host	175
3.10 Diaphanous Subject and Thin Subject	179
4. *Constitutive Mind and Constitutive Nature*: The Moral Subject in Confucianism	189
4.1 Confucianism and "Authentic Subjectivity"	189
4.2 Freedom and Indeterminacy	197
4.3 The Performative Subject	204
4.4 The Subject as Incipience and Origin	209
4.5 Constitutive Mind and Constitutive Nature	221
4.6 Subjectivity and Interiority	232
4.7 Conclusion: The Child in the Well	242
5. Self-Limitation of the Moral Self as *Kenosis*	247
5.1 *Kenosis*: History of a Concept	247
5.2 Paradoxes of Self-Limitation	256
5.3 Abyss and Sinkhole: Self-Limitation as Sinking	263
5.4 *Kenosis* as Alienation: Hegel and Mou	270
5.5 *Kenosis* as "Making Space for the Other": *Tzimtzum* and Lévinas	282
5.6 Tremor and Awakening: Mou and Lévinas	287
Conclusions: Facets of Self across Cultures	301
The Contemplative Subject in Western Culture: Interiority, Reflection, Solitude	301
The Confucian Moral Subject in Mou's Thought: Rethinking the Concepts of Interiority and Reflection	311
Loneliness and "Vigilance in Solitude"	326
Differences between Chinese and Western Culture: From "What Is a Self?" to "How to Become an Authentic Self?"	331
Bibliography	335
Index	351

Introduction

A Vertical Rethinking of the Self: The Significance of This Study

In the early winter of 1619, stranded by war events in a German location with no contact whatsoever, and able to enjoy only a bare solitary room, René Descartes enacts the most dizzying mental experiment attempted by humankind. Applying methodical doubt, he virtually erases every element of reality of which he cannot have clear and distinct certainty. He erases the changing impressions of the senses, the body that appears to him as separable from the mind, mathematical truths that might be inspired by an evil demon, daily existence that is no more certain than dreams, and finally, after snuffing life to the bone, he arrives at that consciousness of himself as a thinking and doubting substance that alone cannot be bracketed. In the winter dreariness of a room, the modern subject is born—lonely, worldless, floating between dreaming and waking, who must keep himself alive with the feverish monologue of self-consciousness. The man capable, as Plato wrote, of seeing the world through the eyes of the dead was born.

When Descartes, having arrived at the elementary core of the "I think," has to step outside himself to start building the world again, he discovers that he needs the "God hypothesis," a transcendent perfection that man in his wretched frailty does not possess. The philosopher George Berkeley (1685–1753) also argues that every creature that exists does only in the instant we perceive it. To avoid the disturbing flicker of a world that continually appears and disappears, only God's omnipresent eye remains to ensure the world's uninterrupted and stable being. Later, post-Kantian idealism would attempt to replace the God hypothesis, i.e. the assumption that only the existence of a perfect Being guarantees the truth and certainty of our knowledge, by recognizing the ego as having constitutive power over reality. Johann Gottlieb Fichte (1762–1814), in his daring speculative enterprise to penetrate the nature of the self-consciousness that, in its source and native state, grasps itself and generates the world, finally arrives at a singular definition of self-consciousness as "an activity in which an eye is inserted."[1] This unsettling metaphor is simply meant to put an end to the irresolvable dilemma of the self, the separation of acting from knowing, of spirit from body, of inner and outer realms, by imagining an eye that sees everything by seeing itself, a kind of perfectly transparent witness, the radiant and impossible center of the labyrinth of mirrors that is consciousness.

"The being of Spirit is a bone," Georg Wilhelm Friedrich Hegel (1770–1831) wrote provocatively in the *Phenomenology of Spirit*.[2] It only takes one step further for Descartes' solitary room to take the shape of a skullcap. An inner space wallpapered with impressions and images of the world. The motto inscribed on the temple of Apollo at Delphi, which is at the origin of Western thought, "Know thyself" (*gnōthi seauton*), seems to have brought us circularly back to the starting point. Since the twentieth century, neuroscience has offered us a glimpse into the the brain's role in shaping our conscious experiences, revealing its extraordinary complexity and efficiency. Philosophies of mind and cognitive sciences have again placed the self and subjectivity center stage. However, any attempt to conceptualize the world as existing within inner space as a representation, or to view inner space as merely an emergent property of our neural circuits, runs into insoluble contradictions. One wonders if we have ever really emerged from Plato's cave. That is, whether Descartes' lonely room or the skullcap of neuroscience is but a reproduction of that kinematic device envisioned by Plato, in which the simulacra of things projected as shadow-play on the walls of our minds ensnares us until we forget the possibility of a world outside.

---

1   Johann Gottlieb Fichte, "Darstellung der Wissenschaftslehre. Aus dem Jahren 1801–1802," in: *Fichtes Werke*, ed. by Immanuel Hermann Fichte, 11 vols, II, Berlin: Walter de Gruyter, 1971, p. 150. For further insight into the concept of self-consciousness in Fichte see: Dieter Henrich, *Between Kant and Hegel. Lectures on German Idealism*, Cambridge, MA: Harvard University Press, 2003, pp. 263–276.
2   Georg Wilhelm Friedrich Hegel, *The Phenomenology of Spirit*, Cambridge, UK, and New York: Cambridge University Press, 2018, p. 433.

If we try to look to other cultural models for novel solutions—examining, for example, the millennia-old tradition of Chinese thought—we sometimes seem to find our own echo. Does not Mengzi 孟子 (372–290 BCE), the greatest disciple of Confucius 孔子 (551–479 BCE) say, "The myriad things are all within me. To turn inward and discover the authenticity: There is no greater joy than this!"? Does the Neo-Confucian Zhang Zai 張載 (1020–1077) not repeat, "All things are within me. Under heaven, there is nothing that I am not"? Or are we in danger of falling too easily into what Stéphane Mallarmé called "the demon of analogy"?[3]

In *Nineteen Lectures on Chinese Philosophy*, the most influential Chinese philosopher of the twentieth century, Mou Zongsan 牟宗三 (1909–1995), seems to assert that Western thought has failed precisely in its attempt to define the subject: "We often say that Chinese culture and Western culture develop in different directions. Chinese culture does not deny the objective aspect, but sets aside the objective aspect for the moment and opens the door of the subject from the perspective of the subject, this is true not only for Confucianism, but also for Daoism and Buddhism."[4] The greatest contribution of Chinese philosophy according to Mou is to have "opened the door of subjectivity." To do this, it has shifted the focus of thought from knowledge to moral action, in which the answer to the question of what is human is the practice and effort of becoming human.

This book explores Mou Zongsan's thinking about the self and subjectivity, with a focus on the comparative approach in the Western tradition, whose paradigmatic thinker, in Mou's eyes, is Immanuel Kant (1724–1804). Kant's thought, often recomposed in ontological terms in the wake of Martin Heidegger (1889–1976), represents for Mou the most rigorous and coherent expression of knowledge-centered Western thought. Mou contrasts this "horizontal" model, based on the separation of subject and object and aimed at cognitive enhancement, with the "vertical" view dominant in the Chinese tradition.

---

3 The title Mallarmé gives to his prose poem, written in 1864.
4 Mou Zongsan, *Nineteen Lectures on Chinese Philosophy: A Brief Outline of Chinese Philosophy and the Issues It Entails*, Scotts Valley, CA: CreateSpace Independent Publishing Platform, 2015, p. 454.

The vertical model has, at its core, a practical-performative interpretation of the subject based on the spiritual and moral self-cultivation that enables the finite human being to "become infinite," rediscovering and embodying that original unlimited moral mind that constitutes him. The manifestation of such a moral mind entails the unveiling of a reality that is structurally processual, dynamic-generative, in which each entity is related to and resonant with other entities. It is worth noting that, in Mou's terminology, the word "moral" does not refer reductively to ethics, understood as a branch of philosophy that deals with good and evil, free will and the will, and the possibility of action tuned with virtue. In Mou's thought, morality is the primary philosophy that grounds and determines the nature of metaphysical reflection. The "moral metaphysics" that Mou proposes starts from the manifestation in practical life of an absolute reality that is mind and principle together. The full unfolding of such mind coincides with its actualization and concretization in human action and requires a process of self-perfection and self-transformation. The endeavor of becoming authentically human is not limited to interpersonal ethical judgment and acting, but it involves unraveling the meaning of reality and recognizing the irreducible and universal value of every element in the universe. It is, therefore, a matter of removing things and other human beings from their reduction to mere instruments and revealing them in their absolute value as "thing-in-itself."

In Kant, the "thing-in-itself," or noumenon, is the unattainable background of that reality which is given to us always and only filtered through our cognitive schemes. Noumenon cannot structurally become the object of our knowing and is conceivable only as drawn from a divine intellect, which, in knowing things, creates and gives birth to them. This "intellectual insight," which for Kant is precluded to a finite mind, for Mou is instead realized in the action of the saint, that is, of every human being striving to rise to the highest authenticity and perfection.[5] For this

---

5   With the term "saint" I translate the Chinese concepts of *shengren* 聖人 or *zhenren* 真人. In both cases, they refer to a human being who is fully accomplished in her spiritual self-realization. Other scholars legitimately adopt the word "sage"; however, I prefer the use of saint in order to highlight that this path to perfection goes beyond the acquirement of a knowledge or wisdom, and entails a transformation of the body-mind totality. In any case, it should not be interpreted as a religious term, like for example the Catholic saint.

accomplished human being, every moral action is the embodiment of the infinite in everyday circumstances, the revelation of the universe as a living and interconnected unity, in which even my self as an acting and creative subject is included. This vertical thinking, which Mou believes is the great legacy that the Confucian tradition delivers to the world, does not reduce things to a masterable and exploitable object but elevates them to a subject, that is, an active and creative node.

This work aims to investigate how this "subjectivization" of the real that takes place in everyday moral effort can restore to us an alternative view of the self than that of modern philosophies of mind. The latter often represent the pinnacle of Western investigation based on the primacy of scientific knowledge, the fragmentation of things into single, separate objects, and the problematic communication between the inner realm of the mind with its bundles of representations and the objective world from which it emerges. Although the moral paradigm is dominant in Mou, we may ask whether the dimension of scientific knowledge, with its undoubted advancement in the understanding of the ego, retains a role in this view. Are practical-moral knowledge and logical-cognitive knowledge somehow related?

For a philosopher of Mou's generation, heir to the thought that had attempted to show how science and democracy were compatible with the Chinese tradition, but at the same time tending to reaffirm the superior efficacy and originality of the Confucian moral and metaphysical approach, establishing the nature of the relationship between these two forms of knowledge was crucial. Mou solves this problem with the concept of *ziwo kanxian* (自我坎陷), which has been translated in many ways, such as self-limitation or self-constraint. The word *kanxian* (坎陷), as is often the case with Chinese words, retains the vivid materiality of the experience from which it arises, and speaks to us of a sinking, a ravine carved out by the presence of water, which nevertheless is not an abyss, a breaking through of reality with no return. The moral mind's willingness to fall implies the ever-present possibility of rising again, traveling upward along this curve, leaving the impervious narrowness of the bottom of the ditch to find the wide expanse of the sky. The moral mind cares for every tiny thing; its vigilance is unbroken, so that nothing of the whole is lost, and nothing can be said to be external or foreign to it. The anxiety of knowledge, exploration, and analysis of the logical-scientific self arises from this moral urgency, drawing its unsatisfiable dynamism from it, but at the same time, it is oblivious to it in its limitedness.

It is as if the moral mind becomes two-dimensional from being three-dimensional, moving along a space-time plane that it tries to exhaust, but with the blindness to the whole that comes with it. The moral mind traps itself, attaches itself to things, divides itself internally into subject and object, observer, and observed. The cognitive subject moves from within a universe, which, because of self-limitation, is now spatio-temporally limited, constrained to a perspective point of view that shifts, leaving traces of its own psychological experience in its memory and gathering them into a coherent narrative. The "I think" of Descartes and Kant is also the narrative "I" that is conscious of its own inner states and the "I" that must reconcile the inside of the fold, the *qualia*, with the outside of the fold, the world of phenomena, without being able to abandon that fold that it is. The *kanxian* is this fold or inflection that the moral mind originates by folding over reality to make it the object of knowledge, and this generates the division between observer and observed. Borrowing the language of physics, this cognitive folding is a measurement.

In the stimulating book *The One: How an Ancient Idea Holds the Future of Physics*, particle physicist Heinrich Päs argues that, from the entanglement-based perspective of quantum physics, the universe is an interlaced oneness, a correlation of everything with everything, while from the perspective of the finite self, it looks as it does in classical physics—a series of separate objects evolving over time, linked by determinable causal relations. "[...] the emergence of matter and possibly even space and time itself isn't a real process in the fundamental quantum universe. It only describes the impression an observer located in space and time gets about this fundamental reality."[6] For a measurement to be possible, in fact, the universe must be divided into observer, object, and environment.

The problem remains unsolved as to how the limited self that explores reality by walking through it from within can rise to "God's viewpoint," that is, the one in which all things are a perfect unity, and the observer experiences their being one with all things. In Mou's

---

6   Heinrich Päs, *The One: How and Ancient Idea Holds the Future of Physics*, London, Icon Books, 2023, n.p.

proposed system, this is possible because the human being can rise to the divine through moral cultivation; they are a finite being who can make themselves infinite. Therefore, it is not a matter of moving to a different cognitive hypothesis about the universe, nor to a different ontology generated by the demands of observation, measurement, and epistemic accretion. For Mou, it is necessary to move from the cognitive self, which is a moving focal point, to the moral self. The moral self does not relate to the world by deciphering it from another perspective but by embodying the world, experiencing it as a part of the self that requires care, actively participating in its vital transformations. This shift is, in Mou's terminology, a rising from the curved to the flat, from the attached ontology to the detached ontology, from the mental state of the self that wants to cognitively appropriate things to that of the authentic self, which embodies the silent belonging of all things in every action.

How can this tension toward an "authentic self" that fuses subject and object in its totality provide an alternative viewpoint to that of contemporary research on the self and its biological premises? According to David Chalmers, the "difficult problem of consciousness" is to explain the relationship between inner, subjective experiences (*qualia*), and neural correlates, that is, the material structure of the brain that makes them possible.[7] In Mou's thinking, the self that in its own confinement (seclusion) auscultates itself and the inner echo of its mental states is the illusory self of attachment to self and things. To seek a correlation between what in the mind is purely subjective, inner, and private, and the brain, that is, the aspect of it that appears objective and quantifiable, represents an attempt to match the two sides of the fold. In doing so, we forget that the very possibility of moving from the inner to the outer domain reveals to us the most basic fact that the self is the inexhaustible act of transcending itself. The subject is that which at every moment is capable of going beyond itself, of awakening to its co-partnership with the world. The self, for Mou, is a dynamic and creative process of expansion.

The closest we come to what we now call "philosophies of mind" is reached by Mou in his first production, culminating in the work *Critique of the Cognitive Mind*. In it, Mou follows a Kantian model, that is, he

---

7 David Chalmers, "Facing Up to the Problem of Consciousness," *Journal of Consciousness Studies* 2:3 (1995), 200–219.

describes the structuring of the self from its perceptual entanglement with the world to reflective self-consciousness. Already in this work, however, the most basic activity of the human mind, which Mou calls perception (*jue* 覺), contains a clue that allows us to recognize that, amid the anonymity of objects, a subject—that is, something radically different and irreducible—has come into being. Within epistemology, *jue* is usually translated as "perception," but its older meaning is "to be awake, to be vigilant." The self then is an awakening that repeats itself incessantly. Whenever it seems to make itself objectifiable and experienceable in its psychological states (as Chalmers would say, of *qualia*), the self immediately distinguishes itself from them, jumping out of all its affective reverberations to assert itself as a pure act, which in no way can become an object or harbor a passivity within itself. In its creative capacity, the self discloses further dimensions, such as imagination or intellect, but it does not allow itself to be arrested and solidified in these expressions of itself. The self is always already beyond its own embodiments, like the jet of a spring that is always new, even as the water that flows from it becomes visible by gathering in different forms.

If the self is a process, should we understand it as a Heraclitean river in which our experiences flow, and which only by mnemonic retrieval work can we temporarily fix into a coherent narrative? This hypothesis, which in contemporary thought gives rise to the theory of the "narrative self," also stems from a search for knowledge. In contrast, Mou, reworking the Confucian tradition, emphasizes how the becoming of the self is that of a practical self-constitution. What we call the self is first and foremost the ever-renewing tension to become the highest and most authentic form of self. Mou often notes how, in the transition from the horizontal-constructive to the vertical-transformative plane, many nouns—and thus defining concepts—must be rethought as verbs, that is, as actions. In this way, Mou exploits one of the peculiarities of the Chinese language, and particularly of classical Chinese, whereby, in the absence of conjugations and declensions, a noun and its verbal form can appear identical. In his texts devoted to Daoism, for example, Mou emphasizes how the idea of emptiness (*wu* 無), which originates all things, is not to be understood as a static non-being but as a verb, a practice of spiritual cultivation that aims to empty oneself of all particular determination and return to the original, unconditioned openness that is proper to the mind of the infant. For Mou, therefore, the self is not merely an object of thought, but it holds within itself a verbal value. Being self implies a practical and active project of becoming oneself, of arriving at one's most authentic state. This practical-performative idea of the subject has often been neglected in the Western tradition. From Descartes' concentric doubt to grasp the indisputable core of one's identity to modern neuroscience, which seeks to locate precisely the place of self-awareness in the brain, the same paradigm is at work— that thirst to know and define the world that Mou sees personified in Goethe's Faust. The universality to which it tends is, according to Mou, the false infinity of a consciousness that proceeds from object to object, toward an unlimited horizon that is necessarily beyond its reach. The true infinity, for Mou, is the moral mind, which intersects with everyday reality and realizes itself concretely by recognizing to every event the infinity of its value.

If we want to understand what is at stake in this "vertical reversal" of the self operated by Mou on the back of Confucian values, we have to start from degree zero, from that primary scene we have in our minds when we question things. In the Western tradition, the primary scene can be depicted as a subject encountering an object that is placed in front of them. It may be that the subject seeks to cognitively assimilate the object through the faculties of its spirit or that the object (Heidegger's *ob-jectum*) is projected by the subject, as in early idealism. It may be, with Edmund Husserl (1859–1938), that the subject exists only in its being intentionally directed toward the object or that it is the mysterious contact of an inner realm with the outer realm, where the boundary membrane irrevocably permeates or separates. Conversely, in Mou's moral metaphysics, the primary scene is the example proposed by Mengzi to show that human nature has the bud of benevolence within it. The subjects here are two: a child who is on the verge of falling into a well and each of us who, upon seeing the child, is shot through with a thrill of apprehension and spontaneously extends a hand to stop them. This scene implies no time for perception or reflection. Everything happens in an instant, sharp as the edge of the well. The child is not the object of our knowledge, but we and they are part of an event in which danger, thrill, and saving action are simultaneously consummated.

Mou skillfully elaborates on the insight of Neo-Confucian Cheng Mingdao 程明道 (1032–1085), who recalls how, in the Chinese language, the expression for "non-benevolence" (*bu ren* 不仁) is synonymous with the numbness of a paralyzed limb. To refrain from acting morally is to disown that we are one body with each other, to reject a part of ourselves. The shudder is not mere dismay but is, for Mou, an ontological shaking, a reawakening to the truth of us, that is, to the infinite extent of our moral consciousness. We do not grasp ourselves reflexively, re-presenting the subject-object pair, fictitiously placing ourselves before the image of us in a mirror. If any knowledge exists, it is what Mou calls "retrospective verification" (*nijue tizheng* 逆覺體證). We know ourselves by twitching as that twitching and action bring us back to our original state, which we forget in daily cares. This too is a *jue*, an act in which we are able to transcend ourselves, to tear through the torpor of the mind of habit, to know the other and the world as a living and sensitive part of us. We reboundingly discover that a perfect vigilance has always been within us, the unquenchable light of our innate moral consciousness (*liangzhi* 良知). This luminous mind is us, but it is given to us solely in the action by which we reach out to the other by claiming them as part of us, in which we extend the horizon of our being without limit. Spiritual self-perfection is that action that makes us progressively authentic, that is, without distinction between outside and inside, and vigilant even in the smallest thing. If self-awareness is a reawakening to us, is it not, in this, similar to the hyperbolic certainty of Descartes' "I think"? No, Mou tells us, as that is a punctiform intuition that I am compelled to repeat endlessly to feel firm in certainty. The moral mind is a permanent presence and manifests itself in the world in which we act, with absolute concreteness. It is our original nature that is actualized in every worldly affair.

Nature and mind are, for Mou, the warp and weft of the borderless fabric that is the self. Through these two concepts, he reconstructs with skillful weaving a new model of interiority that is not founded on the self-exclusion of the self from the world. Nature (*xing* 性) is the substance of all that exists, and Mou inherits, from the most ancient Chinese text, that *Yijing* (易經 *Classic of Changes*) to which he dedicated his first juvenile essay, a vision of reality as a changing, dynamic forge of transformations. Metaphors related to textile art, from which many concepts in

Chinese thought are derived, are particularly appropriate here. The inherent nature of the world is a dense fabric of interrelationships and correspondences that reconstitutes itself at every moment. Already in the *Critique of Cognitive Mind*, reality appears to the mind not as a dispersion of unrelated things but as meaning. The condition of this unveiling is a mind participating and active in the world. We saw above the example offered by quantum physics, in which the nature of things appears related to the state of mind. The universe structured in space-time, and dominated by the causal relationship, is our everyday evidence as subjects with limited perspective focus. The quantum universe is perfect unity, where everything is relatable to everything, and this infinite density of correlations and dimensions nested within each other is God's dizzying point of view. In Mou, the correspondence between the state of mind and reality is first and foremost practical and performative, for the subject is not only perspective and measure but is an active participant in the structuring of things. For Mou, the world of fragmented and uncommunicating objects, such as that found in David Hume's (1711–1776) empiricist thought, is the objective correlate of a mind that has a specific moral stance, that of detachment and analytical gaze that eschews all interest (in the Latin sense of *inter-esse*, being in relation). To the moral mind that is instead care, participation, and active involvement, the world manifests itself as meaning and wholeness. This is not simply a shift in perspective but a more advanced level of human becoming, in which mind and reality are inextricably intertwined.

What Mou proposes to us with his moral metaphysics, which he regards as the most faithful expression of perfect Confucian teaching, is to radically rethink reality as something that is first and foremost given to moral consciousness and that is fully actualized only in moral effort. Reconstructing the world along the vertical axis means no longer thinking of it as a cognitive field but as a performative field, hinged in action and transformation. In the morally accomplished human being, the processual and dynamic nature of reality is brought to fruition. In his works, Mou outlines a new conception of the subject by completely redefining the horizon within which to understand it and the tools of that understanding. The only way to manifest the nature of things is not to enunciate it or strive to know it but to actualize it through my actions. By paying attention to every single event and every human being,

I concretely realize the universality of mind that nothing has outside itself and nothing abandons; I transform every occasion into the point of falling and realization of that vertical dimension that intersects the horizontal succession of things.

How can this redefine the inner self, which in the Cartesian subject involves a retreat into one's own solitude, like a hermit in exile from the world? Whereas the Cartesian subject comes to self-consciousness in a centripetal motion, which leaves out everything that appears uncertain and unfounded to them, for Mou, the self manifests itself in a dual motion, centripetal and centrifugal. On one hand, the self is capable of internalizing, that is, having in itself as its own law the actualizing principle of all things, their source of life and value. On the other side, this being law unto itself can only manifest itself as an infinite expansion of vigilance and care, whereby nothing is foreign or external to me. Mou retrieves from the Chinese tradition the idea of *ganying* (感應), that is, of universal resonance and correspondence between all things. This dynamic unity in which everything communicates with everything comes to full manifestation through my being, as responsivity and responsibility to every person and every thing. The self is a task. Accomplishing myself in reality, I discover, with a retrospective gaze, the infinite power of expanding myself and participating in the life of the world that is my spiritual consciousness. I restore what is fragmented and extraneous to its full value as an absolute end, that is, to its being thing-in-itself, when I discover that everything is for me, endowed with meaning, and one with my active and creative being.

In 2018, as I was gathering materials for this book, the 24th World Congress of Philosophy was taking place in Beijing. The first International Congress of Philosophy was held in Paris during the *Exposition Universelle* in 1900 and gathered eminent thinkers and academicians from Europe and the United States of America. The 24th World Congress was held 118 years later in China, manifesting the global and cross-cultural nature that philosophy has acquired or proposes to acquire. The title given to the congress was particularly significant: *Learning to Be Human*. The Chinese title *Xue yi cheng ren* 學以成人 can be more properly translated as "studying to become human," and effectively summarizes the Confucian idea that being human is actually a lifelong process of becoming human through study and self-cultivation.

Tu Wei-Ming, in the concluding reading of the World Congress, stated, "Humanity as awareness assumes a transcendent significance. Since we are inseparable from and holistically interconnected with all things, we have found a common source. It is not the objective reality of the common source alone, but the human awareness and capacity to participate in it that enables us to assert greatness as human beings. Subjectivity is critical in this connection"[8] and "Our spiritual transformation is not a departure from where we are but a journey to the interiority of our being. Paradoxically, the innermost core of our being, the source of self-knowledge, is none other than the macrocosmic reality ingrained in our existence."[9] Rethinking the self and the subject from a comparative and cross-cultural perspective, this book aspires to be a fruit of this vision and hope that gathered more than 6,000 philosophers from all over the world in Beijing in 2018.

Mou Zongsan's Life and Works

Mou Zongsan is one of the most original and influential Chinese philosophers of the twentieth century. His work, which is of impressive value and depth, is collected in thirty-three volumes, thus testifying to the multifaceted evolution of his thought. His works range from early texts devoted to logico-epistemological issues, to texts in which he proposes a reinterpretation of crucial moments in China's rich philosophical tradition in its three schools (*daotong* 道統), Daoism, Buddhism, and Confucianism, from translations of Ludwig Wittgenstein and Kantian critiques, to socio-political texts and interventions around the role of China and its thought with respect to the challenges of modernity. The more mature metaphysical essays in which Mou—distilling and critically reworking China's rich heritage of thought, and placing himself in constant confrontation with Western thought, particularly Kant—develops his "moral metaphysics" are the theoretical centerpiece. Mou argues that, despite its complexity of which Mou is fully aware, Western thought finds its paradigmatic exponent in Kant, because he is able to lead such thought systematically and rigorously back to its

---

8   Wei-Ming Tu, *Spiritual Humanism: Self, Community, Earth, and Heaven. 24th World Congress of Philosophy, Wang Yangming Lecture*, n.p.: 2018, p. 26.
9   Ibid., p. 28.

distinctive character, namely the horizontal approach to the world. By the term "horizontal," Mou means a model of thought grounded in logic and epistemology and determined in its genesis and purpose by the exigencies of knowledge enhancement. The result is a representation of the world characterized by the hegemony of speculative-theoretical thinking, and the separation of subject and object. Even where morality becomes the object of thought, as in Kantian practical reason, a "metaphysics of morality" is arrived at, that is, a search for the metaphysical presuppositions of free will and its orientation to the good. Through a thorough reinterpretation of Neo-Confucian thought, Mou instead proposes a vertical approach based on the practical self-cultivation of the subject, the dynamic tension to "human becoming," and the metaphysical dimension of a creative moral mind that pervades and vivifies the universe, and that reveals itself to intuition at the very heart of moral action.

In conducting my research, I focused on the main works containing references to Mou's idea of self and subjectivity. The chosen texts are among the pivotal works in Mou's lifelong research path, and they allow for a comprehensive understanding of Mou Zongsan's philosophical endeavor.

Mou conducted his early studies at Peking University, where he became interested in Bertrand Russell's (1872–1970) logical thought and the dynamic, processual view of reality developed by Alfred North Whitehead (1861–1947), as well as in the *Yijing* (易經 *Classic of Changes*), in which he glimpsed a similar representation of the universe determined by mathematical rules and transformative processes. His encounter with Xiong Shili 熊十力 (1885–1968) is a crucial event in this early period. In his *Xin Weishi Lun* (新唯識論 *New Treatise on the Uniqueness of Consciousness*), Xiong Shili fuses the refined Buddhist interpretation of mind with the onto-cosmological principles of the Confucian tradition. As a result of his teaching, Mou felt reconfirmed in his belief that Chinese thought has an autonomous value and creative force that puts it on par with Western thought, and is also capable of responding in original ways to the crisis of meaning induced by modernity. A second theoretical gain derives from an episode that Mou would later recall in his autobiography *Wushi zishu* (五十自述 *Autobiography at Fifty*) as a moment of spiritual enlightenment. It is the icastic response with which Xiong rejects Feng Youlan's 馮友蘭 (1895–1990) idea that the foundations of morality are mere assumptions:

> You say that innate moral knowledge is a hypothesis. How is it possible to speak about a hypothesis! Innate moral knowledge is something truly real and, moreover, a manifestation. It is necessary to be immediately conscious of this, to affirm it immediately.[10]

Moral law cannot be an abstract hypothesis generated by thought, but it is present and evident to human intellectual intuition as it contains an enlightening and self-manifesting force. What Mou developed in the most mature phase of his thought, namely, that the source of moral law must be both and active principle and creative, self-enlightening mind, is visible *in nuce*. Mou's most important work at this stage of his thought is *Renshi xin zhi pipan* (認識心之批判 *Critique of the Cognitive Mind*). From a close comparison with Kant, Russell, Hume, and Gottfried Wilhelm Leibniz, Mou develops a kind of constitutive phenomenology of the mind, the essential features of which are dynamism and the capacity for self-transcendence, and demonstrates how the logical self contains within itself the necessity of a higher instance, namely, an infinite moral mind, capable of realization as concrete universality. In 1948, Mou moved to Taiwan in dissent with the emerging communist regime. His work as a university lecturer took place from then on between Taiwan and Hong Kong, and he never set foot in the People's Republic of China again.

In the Taiwanese period, Mou wrote a number of works inspired by Hegelian dialectics such as *Lishi zhexue* (歷史哲學 *Philosophy of History*) and the collection of articles *Daode de lixiangzhuyi* (道德的理想主義 *Moral Idealism*). In these works, Mou addresses one of the fundamental themes of the discourse of the New Confucians, namely the compatibility between Chinese thought and new ideas of progress, including scientific development and democracy, developed in the West and linked to the Enlightenment and the primacy of scientific rationality. Mou's position was critical of the May Fourth Movement and Marxism, which viewed the Confucian tradition as an obstacle to China's

---

10 Mou Zongsan, *Wushi zishu.* 五十自述 (*Autobiography at Fifty*), Taipei: Ehu Chubanshe, 1989, p. 88. Translated by Sébastien Billioud, *Thinking through Confucian Modernity. A Study of Mou Zongsan's Moral Metaphysics*, Leiden: Brill, 2012, p. 7.

historical development and uncritically absorbed elements of Western thought. According to Mou, Confucian thought is not only compatible with scientific and democratic progress, but can also provide superior moral and spiritual guidance to their application. In doing so, Mou uses the Hegelian concept of "dialectical self-negation," which would be a mainstay of his more mature production, to justify the possible coexistence of a transcendent moral mind and a rational, cognitive mind that, while hierarchically inferior to it, has a structural relationship with the moral mind while preserving its space of autonomy. In 1958, together with other leading intellectual figures such as Tang Junyi 唐君毅 (1909–1978), Xu Fuguan 徐復觀 (1902/03–1982), and Zhang Junmai 張君勱 (1887–1969), Mou signed the *Wei Zhongguo wenhua jinggao shijie renshi xuanyan* (為中國文化敬告世界人士宣言 *A Manifesto for a Re-appraisal of Sinology and Reconstruction of Chinese Culture*). This declaration reaffirmed a desire to revitalize Confucianism by means of a comparative discourse with Western philosophical tradition, as well as further ushering in a third phase of Confucian thought, following the Confucianism of the classical age of Confucius and Mengzi, and the Song-Ming Neo-Confucianism. The need to recover the Chinese doctrine of mind and nature (*xinxingxue* 心性學) is especially emphasized, thus freeing it from the misunderstandings operated by Western sinologists.

After his move to Hong Kong in 1960, Mou wrote his most complex and refined work, *Xinti yu xingti* (心體與性體 *Constitutive Mind and Constitutive Nature*). This work is a masterful three-volume reconstruction of the three fundamental schools of Song-Ming Neo-Confucianism, to which *Cong Lu Xiangshan dao Liu Jishan* (從陸象山到劉蕺山 *From Lu Xiangshan to Liu Jishan*), published in 1984, must be added as a virtual fourth volume. The originality and fertility of the inseparable concepts of mind (*xin* 心) and nature (*xing* 性) represent the warp and weft of the complex historical-philosophical tapestry woven by Mou. As analyzed in the third chapter of this book, the emergence of the moral subject is at the heart of the work. The subjective element, that is, the autonomous moral creativity represented by the mind, and the objective element, that is, the dynamic and holistic structure of the universe represented by nature, find their living intersection precisely in the practical moral subject, capable of self-cultivation and spiritual self-elevation.

During the elaboration of his *magnum opus*, Mou devoted himself to rethinking two other great Chinese traditions. *Foxing yu Bore* (佛性與般若 *Buddha-Nature and Wisdom*) and *Caixing yu xuanli* (才性與玄理 *Physical Nature and the "Profound Thought"*) are respectively devoted to Chinese Buddhism and the writings of the two leading neo-Daoist commentators of the Wei-Jin era, Guo Xiang 郭象 (c. 252–312 CE) and Wang Bi 王弼 (226–249 CE). They should be juxtaposed with cycles of historical-comparative lectures such as *Zhongguo zhexue shijiu jang* (中國哲學十九講 *Nineteen Lectures on Chinese Philosophy*). Mou writes extensively around Buddhism and identifies the Tiantai school and the text *Awakening of Faith* as the most coherent realization of "Perfect Teaching." Mou believes that all three Chinese traditions, Daoism, Buddhism, and Confucianism, arrive during their historical development at a paradigmatic and eminent model by progressive approximations, which Mou designates as Perfect Teaching (*yuanjiao* 圓教), and which represents the essential theoretical contribution that the Chinese tradition delivers to world thought. It includes the belief that alongside and above the finite mind based on empirical knowledge ("the mind of seeing and hearing") human beings possess an infinite and transcendent mind, capable of intuitively grasping the essential or "noumenal" level of reality, having unlimited meaning and value. For Mou, the "Perfect Teaching" in which the Confucian tradition culminates is the most accomplished. This is because it recognizes a capacity for moral creativity in the human subject, through which it can, in moral cultivation and action, actualize the nature in itself of things, imbuing every concrete circumstance with infinite value. In all three traditions, there is a positive view of the human being who is finite but can become infinite through what Mou, adopting the Kantian term for divine knowledge, calls "intellectual intuition." That is, man possesses direct and intuitive access to the transcendent and life-giving core of "reality-in-itself."

Mou's more mature works, in particular *Xianxiang yu wu zishen* (現象與物自身 *Phenomenon and Thing-in-Itself*), *Zhi de zhijie yu Zhongguo zhexue* (智的直覺與中國哲學 *Intellectual Intuition and the Chinese Philosophy*), and *Yuanshan lun* (圓善論 *On the Supreme Good*), bring "moral metaphysics"—the landmark of Mou's thought—to full and coherent expression. Here, the critical confrontation with Kantian thought that runs through much of Mou's work comes to full maturity and resolution. The very interpretation of Kantian philosophy, filtered through the Chinese translation of the *Three Critiques*, changes. The purely "logical" Kantianism, based on *a priori* knowledge and "I think," which was the term of comparison in *Critique of the Cognitive Mind*, gives way to an "ontological" interpretation indebted to Heideggerian thought. A cornerstone of this mature phase of Mou's thought is the articulation of two distinct ontological levels, that of the unattached ontology proper to the moral and transcendent mind, and that of the attached ontology, in which the cognitive enterprise of the empirical mind is accomplished. From the Buddhist classic *Awakening of Faith*, Mou extracts the idea of "a mind that opens two doors" (*Yi xin kai er men* 一心開二門). Whereas in Buddhist thought this expressed the coexistence in human beings of an "authentic mind" or "Buddha Mind" and a "mind of being born and perishing", in Mou's original appropriation, "a mind that opens two doors" implies the bifurcation of two ontological levels in the self, the moral self and the cognitive self. Mou's theoretical enterprise reaches its climax in finding a paradigm that defines the complex relationship of derivation and inclusion between these two levels of the self. The Hegelian dialectic and its idea of "self-denial" are the basis for the development of the idea of self-limitation (*ziwo kanxian* 自我坎陷) of the moral mind, which Chapter 5 of this book deals with extensively. Through it, Mou not only justifies the compatibility between his moral metaphysics and logical-scientific thought, but also demonstrates its internal derivation and the dialectical necessity of transcending logical thought to reinstitute the superior completeness and perfection of the moral mind.

Mou is one of the main representatives of New Confucianism in twentieth-century China. From a historical-philosophical viewpoint, the coalescence of a self-defined "New Confucianism Movement" is a tardive phenomenon; therefore, according to John Makeham, the existence of a unitarian lineage should be considered a retrospective creation.[11] However, Mou Zongsan is usually indicated as belonging,

---

11 According to John Makeham, "Although scholars outside of China (principally those in Taiwan and Hong Kong) had, since the mid-to-late 1970s, begun to identify phases in the historical development of New Confucianism, it was not until the mid-1980s that mainland scholars first began to articulate the notion

with other disciples of Xiong Shili like Tang Junyi and Xu Fuguan, to the second generation of this movement. Mou's treatment of the concepts of "mind" and "subject" stands out for its systematicity and depth among his contemporaries. However, note that some themes are common heritage, albeit with different nuances of meaning, of the entire New Confucianism Movement. First and foremost, the distinction between two levels of knowledge, that from seeing and hearing (*jianwen zhi zhi* 見聞之知) and of the virtuous nature (*dexing zhi zhi* 德性之知), derives from Song-Ming Neo-Confucianism and is common to most modern Confucian philosophers. From this premise, many exponents of New Confucianism infer the existence of two modes of mind. Xiong Shili distinguishes between the habituated mind, which analyzes things through discernment, and the original mind, which is one with fundamental reality, that is, the all-encompassing totality that transcends all distinctions: "When we reflect within, brilliantly, in a thought-moment, there is clear awareness. This is precisely the awareness of self-nature […]."[12] This self-nature, as mind that transcends material conditionings is "[…] an aware, illuminating, pure and Clear Reality that stands by itself, relying on nothing."[13] His disciple Tang Junyi distinguishes a transcendent self (*chaoyue ziwo* 超越自我), or moral self (*daode ziwo* 道德自我) from an empirical self (*jingyan ziwo* 經驗自我) trapped in space and time and therefore mutable and illusory. Only the moral self, to which we must strive by overcoming the finite empirical self, is true and permanent. Xu Fuguan believes that the priority given to knowledge, which arises from wonder, curiosity, and the will to control, is the basis of Western scientific progress. The Chinese tradition, which is based on the bud of goodness that Mengzi believes is present in every man, privileges the moral self-concept. However, Xu does not believe that it corresponds to a transcendent subject. The contribution that Chinese thought can make to world culture lies precisely in its ability to locate the source of all value, excluding any metaphysical assumptions, in the human mind. The cognitive and the moral self are therefore not

---

of a philosophical school called New Confucianism." John Makeham, "The Retrospective Creation of New Confucianism," in: J. Makeham (ed.), *New Confucianism: A Critical Examination*, New York: Palgrave Macmillan, 2003, p. 33.

12   Xiong Shili, *New Treatise on the Uniqueness of Consciousness*, New Haven, CT and London: Yale University Press, 2015, p. 21.

13   Ibid., p. 24.

mutually exclusive, but mutually imply each other as two sides of the same coin. Fang Dongmei 方東美 (1899–1977) also does not separate the different levels of the mind but interprets the human mind as an ascending continuum. For Fang, "Humans and the universe are a continuum, and intimately bound together. From this togetherness with all beings, humans are in the position to slowly raise their selves and reach a realm that is above the world of the myriad of beings."[14] As we have seen, Mou Zongsan instead establishes that the cognitive self and the moral self stand on two distinct ontological levels. According to Jana Rošker, "Mou Zongsan was the only second-generation theorist who, due to his belief in the need to establish an empirical, free self that could meet the requirements of Asian and Chinese modernization, tried to modify the traditional complementary unity in the relationship of inner sage/external ruler and formulated it in a dualistic form, defined by a distinction between the moral and empirical self."[15]

Chapter-by-Chapter Overview

Chapter 1

The first chapter of this volume is devoted to a critical overview of the modern and contemporary theories about the self. The aim of this overview is to highlight the centrality of this question in the modern scientific and philosophical discourse, as well as to provide a background for a better appreciation of the originality and specificity of Mou's thought on self. Thanks to the development of the neurosciences, with its research into the neural correlates of our mental life, as well as the emergence of the cognitive sciences, the question of the self has acquired an unprecedented centrality in the philosophical debate. The method and scope of such debate are moreover often determined by requests for theoretical clarification that have arisen in the scientific field, and therefore present a marked gnoseological character. I individuated three

---

14　Umberto Bresciani, *Reinventing Confucianism.* Taipei: Taipei Ricci Institute for Chinese Studies, 2001, p. 287.
15　Jana S. Rošker, *The Rebirth of the Moral Self. The Second Generation of Modern Confucians and their Modernization Discourses*, Hong Kong: The Chinese University Press, 2016, p. 148.

main topics running through the discussion, and tried to synthesize the state of the art in the philosophy of mind around these three questions.

The first question examines the necessity of the idea of self, intended as an "ego," i.e., a stable and persistent fulcrum of self-identification in mental life. Some scholars argue that we need a fixed and centralized point of perspective embedded in our thought or hovering above it, in order to maintain in our mind order, continuity, and sense of "mineness." Other scholars, starting from Husserl and Jean-Paul Sartre (1905–1980), theorize that one's flux of representation is self-ordering and self-structuring, and possesses therefore coherence and meaning even before an "ego" is reflexively constructed.

The second topic is self-consciousness. In what way do I become aware of myself? Some thinkers argue that the knowledge of myself is not essentially different from the knowledge of any outer object. Self-consciousness emerges when I look at myself in an objectifying manner, like through an ideal mirror. Other thinkers object that the process of self-recognition seems to require a preventive acquaintance with oneself, and therefore the phenomenon of self-consciousness presents itself as a familiarity and intimacy with oneself that precedes and makes possible any act of reflection.

Finally, I investigate the relationship between the self and the outer reality, starting from the body and extending to the consciousness of other human beings. Some scholars represent the self as structurally embodied or constituted in the sight of the others. The question is to which degree can I admit a "transcendentality" of the self, thinking of it as an *a priori* scheme making my experience possible. Furthermore, can I attribute to the self an autonomy, i.e., a capacity of detaching itself from its neural conditions, for example as an "emergent property" new and irreducible to the brain which is its corporeal basis? May I legitimately represent my mental life as an inner and secluded domain, or should I locate my self outside of me, in the contact membrane between consciousness and the world?

I finally provide an overview of the scholarly work attempting to answer to this question through a comparison between Western and non-Western ideas of self, highlighting that these kinds of comparative attempts are still very limited in numbers and in their capacity to challenge the epistemological-oriented mainstream of contemporary philosophy of mind. However, these works are advocating for a paradigm shift from the cognitive self to a performative, dynamic, and multidimensional idea of self which could impart an unexplored and groundbreaking turn in studies of self. In my literature review, I did not find monographs that systematically approach these aspects in the wider horizon of contemporary research about philosophy of mind, nor works which recognize the original contribution that Mou can offer on the debate about the question of "I" and self-consciousness. For these reasons, in my research I tried to follow the red thread of the question of subjectivity throughout the development of Mou's thought, sometimes using the conceptual tools of philosophy of mind to highlight the similarities and differences between Mou's idea of subjectivity and some of the most debated theories about the notion of "I."

Chapter 2

The second chapter analyzes in depth Mou's *Critique of the Cognitive Mind*. As the most mature work characterizing his earlier fifteen years of endeavor in logic and epistemology, it embraces the works of Russell, Wittgenstein, and Whitehead as reference points. Furthermore, even the title itself implies a close commitment to Kant's *Critique of Pure Reason*. The work serves as a bridge between Mou's early interest in logic and language and the subsequent moral metaphysical development of his thought. In describing the inner life of the human mind, Mou skillfully interweaves Chinese and Western thought, which is a feature of the rest of his philosophical writings. In *Critique of the Cognitive Mind*, Mou shifts his attention toward the internal and subjective processes of the mind, maintaining the search for an objective and universally valid foundation as a tension that runs through the entire process of ego formation. The method Mou adopted to forge his original philosophy of mind distances itself from the multilayered architecture of Kant's first *Critique*. Rather, it recalls a phenomenological quest, starting *in medias res* from the interdependence of perception and reality and accompanying the living autopoietic evolution of the mind.

Given this mutual connection between mind and the world, Mou affirms that, even at the most basic level of cognitive interaction, reality is not scattered as autonomous fragments waiting to be set in order by the mind through the law of causation. On the contrary, it reveals itself as a unified whole, with a cohesive structure and an inherent meaning. According to Mou, the most basic expression of the mind is perception, that is, a self-aware dynamism of manifestation, structurally intertwined with the flux of the universe. We can perceive the originality of Mou's approach here, reminding us that the majority of previously discussed Western theories of mind share an unformulated assumption—knowledge is the primary modality of our relationship with reality. According to this assumption, we learn about the world through basic mental operations of grasping, defining, and exploring its nature. Therefore, the primeval approach to reality is a disengaged inquiry into an object that appears in its otherness and externality. Mou challenges the elementariness of this experience by arguing that the human mind is always practically engaged in reality. Active participation and interest in the world imply that cognitive endeavors are only complete when guided by a moral, practical, and holistic approach to reality. Through this lens, the mind reveals itself as an unceasingly active dynamism. The prominence conferred on activity, dynamicity, and creativity is the cornerstone of Mou's investigation of the mind and subjectivity.

According to Mou, the mind is not an objective entity that we can examine and locate inside our brain, but a self-transcending movement of manifestation. The strict interrelation between the flux of the phenomenal world and the mind, as the creative locus of its manifestation, defines the task and responsibility of the mind. Its lively function is to preserve the integrity of this manifestative event and provide an ultimate place for its object to settle and disclose itself as an objective and universal totality of meaning. To provide an objective foundation for the perceived phenomenal word, the mind is able to spontaneously emanate structuring frames, such as space and time at the level of imagination, and finally the logical self, which synthesizes and produces all categories. The self-reflection of the logical self through which the mind, returning to itself, possesses and guarantees its own objectivity, is the supreme achievement of a cognitive mind. For Mou, the dynamism of the mind is a rhythmic succession of self-limitation and transcendence over those very limits. In the search for objectivation, the mind molds and fixes content through spatio-temporal and logical frames. This graspable, solidified content, which is the product of the self-limitation of the mind, should be liquefied. This is because the mind transcends and dissolves its partial cognitive products to restore its structural dynamicity and creativity. This capacity of mind to continuously emerge from its self-limitation is termed "intuition" by Mou.

However, from his previous studies on logics, Mou derives that "the cognitive mind, both in self-limitation and in springing out, cannot obtain a final principle through which the system of knowledge can be completely verified."[16] The faculty of understanding, through the emanation of forms *a priori*, becomes progressively wider but cannot achieve full verification without exception, that is, a concrete universality. Only intuition, in the very instant of eliminating any boundary, accomplishes full verification in a flash, leaving us with a glimpse of the infinite completeness of the universe. Depending on the self-limitations from which it emerges, intuition is transient and elusive. This is the final and unsurpassable boundary of the cognitive mind. However, the possibility of infinite self-realization adumbrated in intuition allows us to hypothesize the existence of a higher level of the mind. This mind should have a trans-cognitive, ontological character, being simultaneously both subjective and substantive. It will be able to unfold itself in everything and its self-knowing will be the same as that of its infinite being. The conclusion of Mou's cognitive research is, therefore, that epistemology is ultimately incomplete and unsatisfying because it cannot find in itself the universal principle and motive of the mind and universe. In the rest of his works, Mou searches in Chinese tradition for another way to pursue truth. The exploration of this vertical, moral-metaphysical approach represents Mou's greatest and most original contribution to philosophy of the mind.

The mind cannot be reduced to an object of knowledge because it is an ever-flowing process of manifestation. What is manifested through one's mental process is the world as a meaningful and interrelated totality. The mind can evolve through the rhythmic processes of self-limitation and self-transcendence. The ultimate aim of our inner life—realizing the

---

16 Mou Zongsan (牟宗三), *Renshi xin zhi pipan*. 認識心之批判 (Critique of the Cognitive Mind), 2 vols, II, 560, in *Mou Zongsan xiansheng quanji*. 牟宗三先生全集 (Complete Works of Mou Zongsan), vols XVIII–XIX, Taipei: Lianhe baoxi wenhua jijin hui, 2003.

full synthesis of mind and reality, subject, and object—is unattainable at the mere cognitive level.

Chapter 3

In *Critique of the Cognitive Mind*, Mou moves toward a comparative approach, establishing a similarity between an ephemeral intuitive mind and Daoist thought. This chapter investigates Mou's interpretation of Daoist subjectivity. In addition to his treatise on "Neo-Daoist" intellectual developments during the Wei-Jin dynasties entitled *Physical Nature and the "Profound Thought"*, Mou's philosophical engagement with Daoism is evident throughout his entire body of work. The model of the Daoist saint, emerging from classics such as *Daodejing* and *Zhuangzi*, represents the first step in the elaboration of a practical-performative paradigm of the self. This paradigm has a vertical orientation; it is based on the possibility of ascending to a higher level of spirituality through the practice of self-improvement. In contrast, as argued by Mou, the main currents of Western thought adhere to an epistemological horizontal paradigm pivoting around a progressive increment in theoretical knowledge. I will argue that the key concept in the definition of a performative model of subjectivity is *jingjie* 境界, which can be translated as "state of mind" or "inner landscape." By adopting this concept, Mou demonstrates how overcoming the boundary between subject and object, which could not be satisfactorily accomplished in *Critique of the Cognitive Mind*, can be attained in spiritual practice. The subject is an uninterrupted dynamism, and through the idea of *jingjie*, it acquires a vertical dimension rooted in practice, thereby becoming the "performative self." Subjectivity is something that can be molded, reconfigured, nurtured, and perfected through lifelong spiritual practice, and in correlation, reality will manifest itself at different levels of accomplishment, purity, and meaning. If I elevate myself, the entire universe is elevated in me. Conversely, if I plunge into attachment, the entire universe is chained and spoiled in me. What I try to demonstrate through a thorough analysis of the evolution of the concept of *jingjie* in Chinese literature, art, and philosophy, is that *jingjie* is an original conceptual model of the interdependence, indissolubility, and mutual self-transformation of mind and world. It goes beyond

Husserl's phenomenological idea of intentionality and the correlativity between noesis and noema—or the relationship between the mind and manifested objects. Husserl's theory of intentionality is based on a horizontal cognitive model; in contrast, *jingjie* implies that the subject is not an epistemological, self-defining entity but an active, operating, self-refining performative subject. Here, I introduce a characteristic adopted and modified by Mou throughout his work: the use of spatial metaphors, instead of abstract categories, to interpret mental processes. I suggest understanding *jingjie* as a hodological space, that is, a place that can be reached, entered, experienced, and vertically elevated through the self-realization praxis.

The ideal of a fluidification of the self, outlined in *Critique of the Cognitive Mind*, is more suitably embodied by a performative self, which, like in Daoist thought, is always in the act of making or becoming oneself through a progressive self-cultivation. According to Mou, the specific creative practice performed by the Daoist saint is "generating without generating." This practice requires the subject to renounce every effort to dominate and define the world, instead striving to be void of bias and to reflect on the universe as an ideal mirror. The self molded through this practice is what I call a "diaphanous" or "evanescent" self. Through voiding itself from any attachment, the "diaphanous self" transparently reveals the "nothingness," that is, the inchoate common root of mind and reality, at its authentic core. Embodying this inchoate origin, the Daoist self ignites the process of manifestation. Letting all names and boundaries go, the Daoist subject allows them to grow autonomously. Retreating quietly into the silent clarity of the beginning, they create a space for the world to emerge and flourish.

The rhythmic movement of self-limitation and self-transcendence, which, in *Critique of the Cognitive Mind*, punctuated the development of the mind, reappears in this way in Mou's analysis of the Daoist self as a circular dialectic of backward and forward movements. First, the concept of nothingness, which plays a pivotal role in Daoist works such as *Daodejing* and *Zhuangzi*, is interpreted by Mou in verbal form as the action of *wu*-ing, that is, self-voiding. The performative subject renounces the effort of grasping and attaching itself to the thing, and through this withdrawal, it turns around and moves back to the root. This backward movement can be interpreted as a detachment from a limited and fixed ego and the restoration of a pre-egoic state. Second, the Daoist self, having reached the mental state (*jingjie*) of nothingness, is now able to become the locus of the manifestation of the universe, letting myriad beings burst forth and effloresce without obstacles. This gushing forth is the forward movement of the mind, called by Mou "directionality." Directionality is the projection of a mental space of clarity in which myriad beings are welcomed into their spontaneous, unconditioned "being-so." Finally, one must endlessly repeat this back-and-forth process to avoid the ever-resurgent temptation to make nothingness an object of one's knowledge. Even if directionality does not coincide with the progressive attempt to increase knowledge and dominance, it bears the risk of the mind plunging again into attachment to the ego, losing its original unbounded openness, and becoming completely absorbed by the thing. If this happens, the mind and thing are ossified in their role as viewer and viewed, and we fall again into the horizontal mode of the epistemological ego. Therefore, the practices of self-detachment and self-transcending should remain uninterrupted.

The philosophical gain in introducing the ideas of *jingjie* and performative subject lies therefore in a more coherent foundation of the equivalence between subjectivity and activity. What Mou calls the "metaphysics of the state of mind" is the conceptual frame for a new idea of self. Being a self implies the practice of becoming a self, that is, performing an unceasing effort of dynamization, fluidification, and detachment. Self-reflection and self-possession of the cognitive subject are lower-level subordinate processes of attachment. Emancipating from its byproducts—that is, the concretion of the ego and the polarity of the inner realm versus the external world—requires a vertical trajectory of practice and spiritual training. The more we recede from any attachment, the more fluid, metamorphic, and brimming with life is the universe unfolding in front of us.

The Daoist saint does not substantially produce the world; however, at any spiritual level, her mind and the universe are mutually and concurrently revealed. However, according to Mou, the lack of the "metaphysics of being"—that is, an objective foundation—precludes the Daoist subject from realizing itself in the concreteness of the objective world. For the Daoist self, every descent into the level of concrete and multifarious things represents a risk of being entrapped in a world of boundaries and determinations, and therefore requires a constant spiritual practice of transcendence and unfettering. Although the dynamicity of the subject is continuously reaffirmed in this way, what is missing is the second character of the self—its agency. Agency refers to the possibility for the self to positively and objectively actualize itself through involvement in the world of beings. Full autonomy of the self is accomplished only if its intrinsic dynamicity is the simultaneous unfolding and realization of an objective principle. According to Mou, only the Confucian tradition, identifying this principle of actualization with moral consciousness, can restore the agency of the self. Only by finding the trace of its own action in all things does the subject lose its evanescence and realize itself in the concreteness of the objective world. Meanwhile, the object is no longer pure exteriority; it discovers within itself the trace of the acting subject in the form of meaning.

Chapter 4

The fourth chapter is devoted to uncovering Mou's idea of "authentic subjectivity." According to Mou, this new paradigm of subjectivity was inaugurated by Confucius and Mengzi and reached its zenith in specific currents of Song-Ming Neo-Confucian thought. Through an original reformulation and systematization of this inheritance, Mou develops his "moral metaphysics," in the framework of which his conception of subjectivity finds its definitive foundation. The "authentic subject" should not be confused with one of the poles of the dyad subject/object operating in Western, horizontal and knowledge-based mainstream philosophy. By contrast, it represents the culminating point of the vertical reorientation of the idea of the self.

The previous chapters identify some distinguishing characteristics of the vertical self: dynamism, performativity, and self-transcendence. Moral metaphysics aims to bring any of these characteristics to full completion. Regarding dynamism, the moral self or authentic subject manifests itself as a process of uninterrupted liquefaction of any concretion and attachment. Mou distinguishes between a "little self" and a "great self." The little self is the mind of habit, an inner domain constituted by psychological states, and it is constantly construed through a narrative interweaving of our memories. This inner domain is the province of *qualia*. In contemporary philosophy of mind, *qualia* are the subjective and qualitative aspects of our mental lives, the inner side of phenomenal experiences. They are echoes and traces passively produced by sensorial contact with the external world and are directly accessible only to privately experiencing subjects. In *Critique of the Cognitive Mind*, Mou called them "psychological states," contrasting them with perception, that is, the ever-present ability of the mind to emancipate itself from any passive reverberation and affirm itself as pure dynamical act and ever-resurgent new beginning. Translated in a performative and practical dimension, Mou understands the little self or the unauthentic subject as a conglomerate of attachments and habits residually left behind in our attempt to dominate and control the objective world. The great self attainable in our moral deeds is a higher spiritual state that overcomes the distinction between the inner and outer worlds. The dynamism of self-transcendence actualized in my moral agency is a constant awakening from selfish slumber to the infinitude of my being one with all things. As Mengzi expresses it, "All things are already complete in us."[17]

The unparalleled contribution of the Confucian tradition lies in the primacy of morals. It is critical to highlight that in Mou's thought "morals" has a more comprehensive semantic spectrum than in Western philosophy because it is not a specific branch of knowledge dealing with ethical virtues and freedom of will, as epitomized in Kant's *Critique of Practical Reason*. Morals and the moral self possess a performative and metaphysical dimension, including the ability to decipher the meaning embedded in reality, the action of conferring value to things, respecting them as end-in-itself, and avoiding the reduction of the world to a mere instrument, and finally the intuition of the universe as one with the self. The Western horizontal paradigm, in which ethical principles are deduced from the knowledge of being, is unable to explain phenomena such as moral failure and objectively justify the freedom of will. Therefore, Mou suggests that we begin our philosophical inquiry with the moral experience of value, rather than the relation between the mind and external objects. Confucian tradition offers a prime example

---

17   萬物皆備於我矣 (Mengzi 4.1) See James Legge (trans.), *The Chinese Classics: Translated into English with Preliminary Essays and Explanatory Notes by James Legge. Volume 2. The Life and Teachings of Mencius*, London: N. Trübner, 1875, p. 326.

of moral experience in Mengzi's apologue of the "child by the well." When I see my child about to fall into a well, Mengzi argues that my feelings of compassion are immediately awakened. What I perceive in my emotional intelligence is a sense of urgency and concern that results in the spontaneous and immediate action of grabbing the child. In this archetypal experience, the self emerges as a vital vibration of urgency and agency, witnessing my being-one-body with the child. The infinitely irreducible value of the world possesses a force of self-manifestation and actualizes itself in my all-embracing responsiveness. According to Mou, I become retrospectively aware of my moral mind as a universal, active interconnectedness of all that exists, preceding any separation between subject and object.

With respect to the Daoist subject analyzed in Chapter 3, the conception of the performative subject that aims for self-realization is reconfirmed, as is the idea of *jingjie*. However, Mou's assertion that the full meaning of the subject is inaugurated by Confucianism reveals that the characteristics of the self (i.e., dynamism and reflexivity) can be fully appreciated only when the moral self comes to the forefront. According to Mou, the merit of orthodox Confucian teaching is to have placed something maximally positive and attainable through human freedom, that is, the moral self and the supreme spiritual level attainable through my effort of self-cultivation. Daoism's diaphanous subject maintains structural passivity. The *jingjie* of the Daoist saint, reached through a systematic withdrawal from any purpose or concrete engagement with reality, is a mental landscape in which the self and nothingness, that is, the inchoate origin of the cosmos, merge into one. From this point, the Daoist self can only contemplate the exuberant gushing out of myriad things from the origin, being careful to constantly efface itself to avoid obstacles to the endless metamorphosis of things. In Mou's moral metaphysics, the moral mind replaces nothingness as a creative inception. The self is required to actively participate, embodying and actualizing the moral principles in minute objective circumstances, without letting anything out of the sphere of concern and responsibility.

In addition to dynamism and performativity, reflexivity and self-awareness are the third characteristic of the self. The Daoist diaphanous subject, in attending to the multifarious manifestation of beings, can look back at itself and become aware of the unity between the universe and the transparency of the self, which is the condition for this manifestation. However, because of the necessity of avoiding attachment to the self and constantly restoring the transparency of the mind, it is nothing more than an ephemeral gleam. In contrast, Mou's moral self, in performing ethical deeds, realizes and actualizes the principle that it embodies every single thing. The specific circumstances are not given through a visually based detached contemplation but are concretely actualized in their value and meaning through active participation and concern. In "bringing things to realization without any of them being lost" (*ti wu er bu ke yi* 體物而不可遺), the "mind of benevolence" concretizes the moral principle by penetrating into the infinite particularity of situations. Through my moral activity, I come to realize myself as one with the moral mind, which is the highest spiritual state. Here, I operate at the ontological level that Mou identifies with the Confucian idea of inherent nature (*xing* 性). Nature is brought to perfect manifestation through creative efforts to reach the spiritual state of the moral mind. Nature is not a static substance but a living principle that possesses the ability to self-actualize. Mou valorizes the idea, stemming from the very beginning of Chinese thought—the *Yijing* (Classic of Change)—that reality is a living, dynamic flux of transformation and an interacting web of mutual responsiveness. As Mou declared in *Critique of the Cognitive Mind*, reality in itself is holistic, interconnected, and pervaded with meaning. However, in the absence of a manifesting mind, this organic order of things, which is their principle and value-in-itself, remains only a latent ontological property. Only in self-perfected human beings are the mind and nature, manifestation and content, inseparable. The manifestation proper to the moral mind is not merely a symbolic expression, but is the concretization of the moral principle into the infinite particularity of situations. The distinctive power of my human self is the ability to embody the moral principle of my specific nature so that the principle of my action is not outside me but comes from the heart of my being. In this way, I acquire autonomy and freedom and am able to preserve and nurture them by extending the horizon of moral care to the entire universe. Saying that "All things are already complete in us," Mengzi endows the finite human mind with an infinite capacity for moral extension and elevation. Building on the Confucian teaching of *ren* and Mengzi's theory of mind and nature, the Song-Ming era of Neo-Confucianism gradually brought to fruition the unification of the metaphysical plane of moral practice and the creative energy of the universe. Realizing my moral mind, I awaken myself to be one with the cosmos. Everything is in me, because by expanding the field of my concern and vigilance to the universe, I do not consider nothing external to myself. The authentic self redefines the idea of interiority as autonomy, that is, the capacity to embody the principle of being and acting and having nothing outside that can dictate or obstruct actions.

Though posing moral practice as the culminating point of human endeavor, Mou recognizes the necessity and value of any epistemological effort, particularly scientific knowledge. The reason lies just in the fact that moral activity is spontaneously actualizing in the specificity of phenomena and circumstances. If even the smallest thing must not be forgotten or left out of the sphere of meaning, then cognitive activities are embedded in the circular movement of the moral mind. Facts and events that occur in the performative field have an objective aspect at their core. When moral action encounters difficulty in its scrupulous accomplishment, the mind should stop and analyze this obstacle as a thing contraposed to a knowing subject. The final aim is to restore the ever-flowing circular dynamism of the absolute mind. Eliminating any obstruction through apprehension of the objective thing is subordinated to the unavoidable task of the self. This temporary arrest and entrenchment in the horizontal multiplicity of things is called by Mou *ziwo kanxian* 自我坎陷 that is, self-limitation of the moral self.

Chapter 5

Chapter 5 is devoted to the dynamism of self-limitation (*ziwo kanxian* 自我坎陷) of the moral self—that is, a paradoxical dynamism of entanglement that produces an ontological bifurcation between the moral self and cognitive self. From the viewpoint of the self, the question is how knowing, limited egos, scattered through the multiplicity of our brains and intentionally related to an exterior world, can be produced by an all-embracing and inexhaustible moral self, and ultimately contribute to its full realization. Now we have reached the key point of Mou's definition of the human being as a "finite being that can become infinite." My methodological proposal is to take advantage of the centrality of space and spatial metaphors in Mou's thought. In Chapter 3, we outlined the hodological nature of *jingjie*, that is, the mental landscape shaped by our effort to reach and move through it. The word *kanxian*, which is difficult to translate, is employed by Mou to designate the self-limitation of the moral self, and is etymologically related to "sinking" and "descending." Furthermore, Mou affirms that the knowing self is characterized by a "curved" or "twisting" thought. This suggests that the difference between absolute and finite selves is not representable as an abyss, a catastrophic fall without return, but as an inflection, a dynamism of descent that, in its curvature, allows the possibility of a recollection and an ascensional return to the straight level of the infinite mind. To unravel the paradox of self-limitation, we should bear in mind that any dynamism can be seen from two spatial viewpoints: that of the finite self, characterized by fragmentation and dialectical opposition, and that of the moral self, which transcends fixed separations through a circular dynamism that intersects the finite world only to elevate it to the origin and source of life.

In addition to the topological interpretation, I think that another fruitful approach to the dynamism of "self-limitation" is represented by the Western-Chinese comparative approach. The reason is that Mou himself, in developing the idea of self-limitation in his later works, such as *Phenomenon and Thing-in-Itself*, or *Intellectual Intuition and Chinese Philosophy*, is constantly operating in a comparative way. In pursuing this cross-cultural contrast, I adopt the term *kenosis* as a frame of reference. The relevance of this concept, originally derived from theology, lies in the fact that it can indicate any process in which a higher metaphysical substance voluntarily renounces the fullness of its width and power to manifest and act on a lower plane.

The first kenotic model is presented in Hegel's *Logic* and *Phenomenology of the Spirit*: the dialectical unfolding of the Absolute that, passing through the travail of the negative, returns progressively to itself, discovering the truth of its absoluteness concealed in the beginning. The point of maximum similarity between the Hegelian approach and that of Mou lies in their shared conception of the Absolute as subjective— that is, as an organic unfolding of life that reflexively returns to itself. Analyzing the two ways of self-limitation in Hegel, that is, alienation (*Entfremdung*) and exteriorization (*Entäusserung*), I highlight the similarities between this kenotic movement and Mou's *ziwo kanxian*. In both cases, the self is not given from the beginning but realizes itself in the process of becoming. This process of self-construction requires commitment and continuous mediation with concreteness, as well as the force to transcend every partial embodiment. However, two significant differences can be observed between the Hegel and Mou groups. The first is the different consideration of horizontal finite reality, which, in Hegel, does not possess any autonomous positivity but should be continuously annihilated and conserved only in his logical truth. In Mou, finite contingences are the places of manifestation and realization of the moral mind; thus, they possess a specific ontological and metaphysical value. The separation between the cognitive ego and the world as objects of knowledge is instituted only through attachment. This temporary and illusory division in the cognitive mind must be overcome, but the concreteness of any moment should be recovered through moral action. Hegel's dialectical self develops on a purely cognitive level, and its longing for completeness is projected toward the final stage of the Absolute Spirit. In contrast, Mou's moral self is accomplished at every instant through concern for other beings. The vertical axis of action intersects the horizontal axis of reality. The point of intersection between the verticality of moral endeavors and the horizontality of finite things is not to be found only at the end of the process, but is a fulfillment and a truth that can take place at any instant.

The second kenotic model is offered by Emmanuel Lévinas' (1906–1995) "philosophy of the Other" and is rooted in the kabbalistic idea of *tzimtzum*, that is, the voluntary self-withdrawal of God in order to free a void space in which the finite creature can autonomously consist and flourish. What appealed to Lévinas was the primacy of ethics, which seems to recall the basic tenet of Mou's moral metaphysics. According to Lévinas, in my everyday life, I am immersed in the anonymity of being, enthralled by my search for enjoyment and self-fulfillment. The only event that can draw myself out of this circle of entrapment is the appearance of the face of another fellow human being who, in his vulnerability, draws me out of my horizon and calls me to my moral responsibility. I wake up from my selfish and dream-like plenitude only when I am attracted to this new barycenter, and I experience disruption and irreducible otherness. If we recall the Mencian example of the child about to fall in a well and the alarm and urgency shaking the roots of my being, we may notice here a common vital experience that is spontaneously produced by the appearance of the other. However, if we thoroughly analyze this experience, we may perceive a noticeable difference between Lévinas and Mou, which is based on a different idea of the self. In Lévinas, the subject is structurally centripetal and immersed in its egotistic jouissance; therefore, the disruption of radical otherness is required for me to be passively and forcibly drawn outside myself in the space of ethics. In contrast, in Mou, the human being may be immersed in the mind of habit and traverse his everyday world with the distraction of a somnambulist; however, the core of one's being is the moral mind, which is always vigilant, living, and responsive. The innate moral consciousness that operates in my luminous core is a space for ethics. Despite the attempt to elaborate on metaphysics based on moral duty, Lévinas' ethics remain at a cognitive level, that is, bound to an insuperable exteriority and distance between the finite self and the other. Mou's self-limitation of the moral mind does not withdraw to let finite beings exist autonomously, as in the hypothesis of *tzimtzum*. Mou's moral self accepts restraining itself, cognitively penetrating the phenomenal details of the world, and subsuming them in its action. In this way, the subject is able to fulfill its authentic nature, which is an infinite dynamic responsiveness to which nothing can be external.

Conclusion

In the concluding chapter, I address in a systematic way the challenge posed to us by the contraposition between a vertical and a horizontal self. The key argument raised by Mou Zongsan, i.e., that it is Confucianism that opens the door to the subjective universe, may seem controversial. Indeed, since its foundation, Western thought seems to have revolved precisely around the subjective dimension. It is therefore necessary to analyze the three main characteristics of self—interiority, solitude, and reflection—and to see how these characteristics present themselves in Western epistemologically-oriented thought, and in that moral-metaphysical dimension which is Mou's original contribution to the philosophy of self.

Interiority: starting from Plato and Descartes, the realm of the self is presented as a kind of fortified citadel, an ideal refuge for spiritual hermitage and contemplative life. The premise for the constitution of this inner space is that the subject withdraws from any relationship with the universe outside itself, and this operation of radical isolation and detachment causes the subject to play the role of spectator rather than of participant in the world. The "hard problem of consciousness," i.e., the enigmatic connection between the subjective *qualia* and the objective structure of the brain, is the latest formulation of this topological divide between interiority and exteriority. According to Mou, interiority can be reformulated as inherence. Human beings possess in themselves an autonomous principle of actualization and concretization. If the mind's interiority represents its structural capacity to embody the creativity of heaven and earth and extends this creative capacity to all things, giving them meaning and value, then interiority is both centripetal and centrifugal. The Chinese traditional concepts of "inner resonance" (*ganying* 感應) or "inherent connection" (*gantong* 感通) efficaciously condense human's ability to extend the sphere of their own mind-body oneness to all things, experiencing others and the universe as a sensible part of themselves.

Solitude: analyzing both philosophical and poetical rendition of the singularity of individual self, we may conclude that the loneliness of the contemplative subject is an inevitable consequence of the withdrawal, isolation, and rupture of all relations wrought by the subject. On the contrary, the solitude pursued by Confucians through the practice of "vigilance in solitude" (*shendu* 慎獨) is positive and revelatory of the common origin of the self and the universe. The state of solitude in a vertical dimension is no more a condition of aloneness and seclusion, but a return to the auroral and silent state of mind, when subjective understanding and objective universe have not been yet divided and contraposed. Paradoxically, in a moral-metaphysical dimension, solitude as silent resonance makes possible maximum alertness and responsivity.

Reflection: how can we formulate the idea of self-reflection in a way that avoids a reduction to the centripetal tension, self-objectification, and self-enclosure that we have seen to be dominant in Western thought? According to Mou, the mind, through its being implicated in and morally participating in the affairs of the world, reveals itself to itself and becomes self-conscious. Thus, the "self" already contains the dynamism of resonating with the things of the world and responding and corresponding to them. Bringing myself to completion implies bringing all things to completion; through turning back, I go back to the origin of the co-creation of mind and world. This unity of the human heart and the universe is not the mystical contemplation of a static One but the timely practical realization of becoming one body shared by self and universe. Indeed, the second responsibility of the moral mind is to emancipate things from the domain of the useful and the exploitable and to look at them as an absolute finality, that is, as that "thing-in-itself" which Kant could not attain through his merely cognitive quest.

Finally, Mou Zongsan's moral metaphysics implies that "self" is only fully realized in a vertical dimension, which means that absorbing and processing information is not the primary function of the subject. When I speak of a "self," I mean a dynamism of uninterrupted self-transcendence and a desire to ascend to a higher level of realization. Furthermore, it is not the will to knowledge that unlocks the dimension of interiority, but the manifestation of the all-encompassing moral mind through my practical action.

1. The Question of Subjectivity

1.1 The True Face of Mount Lu

The question of self and of subjective identity is so original and pervasive that it marks the threshold between an unexamined life and a philosophical mode of existence. "Who am I?" is not merely a question, but the first jolt of awakening of a mind that returns to itself, and through this act allows the universe to become aware of itself. The motto "Know thyself" (*gnōthi seauton*) was said to have been inscribed by the seven sages of ancient Greece in the forecourt of the Temple of Apollo at Delphi. Carved in the stone, it was the most fundamental answer people received when they reached Delphi in order to interrogate the gods. The exhortation to self-knowledge is deeply rooted in Chinese traditional thought as well. In the thirty-third chapter of the *Daodejing*, it is written "He/She who knows others is intelligent; he/she who understands himself is enlightened; he/she who is able to conquer others has force, but he/she who is able to control oneself is mighty" (知人者智, 自知者明。勝人者有力, 自勝者強). Interestingly, the illuminating character of self-knowledge is paralleled with the ability to restrain oneself. Domination over others manifests the possession of a power that is occasional and exterior, whereas the bright knowledge of the essential and constitutive core of our self provides us with a permanent inner capacity of self-mastery and self-control.

An analogous concern for the practical aspect of the self may be found in Plato's dialogues. In *Charmides*, Critia, referring to the Delphic motto, establishes an equivalence between self-knowledge and temperance (*sophrosyne*): "When a worshipper enters, the first word that he hears is 'Be temperate!' This, however, like a prophet he expresses in a sort of riddle, for 'Know thyself!' and 'Be temperate!' are the same."[1] In *Republic*, Socrates further substantiates the concept of temperance as self-mastery. The knowledge of the true spiritual core of oneself is not merely a theoretical pursuit, but a practical commitment of self-identification with our authentic essence, which spontaneously produces an ability to control unruly pleasures and desires:

> Temperance, I replied, is the ordering or controlling of certain pleasures and desires; this is curiously enough implied in the saying of "a man being his own master;" and other traces of the same notion may be found in language.
> No doubt, he said.
> There is something ridiculous in the expression "master of himself;" for the master is also the servant and the servant the master; and in all these modes of speaking the same person is denoted.
> Certainly.
> The meaning is, I believe, that in the human soul there is a better and also a worse principle; and when the better has the worse under control, then a man is said to be master of himself; and this is a term of praise [...].[2]

It is indeed deeply meaningful that if we go back to the *fons et origo* of both Chinese and Western thought, we find an exhortation to self-knowledge that cannot be reduced to an epistemic appraisal. To know ourselves is a practical process of discernment and cultivation, which implies an ethical evaluation of the different aspects of our ordinary identity and the ability to transcend them in moving toward a harmonic state of both self-mastery and self-realization.

If we fast forward to the philosophical research of the twenty-first century, we may notice a renaissance in the study of self and consciousness. In the last twenty years, the question of self has stimulated a debate that is impressive for the quantity and quality of the contributions and for the complexity of the multidisciplinary approaches involved. Compared with the ancient textual background, the question "Who am I?" may take advantage of how much we now know about both the mind and the brain. The neurosciences provided us with a previously unthinkable comprehension of the physiology

---

1   See Kosman Aryeh, *Virtues of Thought. Essays on Plato and Aristotle*, Cambridge, MA: Harvard University Press, 2014, p. 239.
2   Plato, *Republic*, New York: Simon and Schuster, 2016, ch. IV, 430D–431E.

and structure of our brains, prompting a discussion about the "neural correlates" of the subjective features of self-consciousness. Psychology and phenomenological psychopathology refined the stratigraphy of our mind, including the subconscious and unconscious states, and assessed how the structures of subjectivity that underpin the experience of ourselves and the external world are modified in patients suffering mental and neurological disorders. Cognitive science, on the basis of a vast array of experimental data, aims to translate our mental and linguistic functions into computational procedures and circuitry, challenging the evolutionary singularity of the human mind and hypothesizing the reproducibility of self-consciousness in artificially intelligent models. Given this astounding increase in cognitive instruments and knowledge paradigms, could we say that the Delphic task "Know thyself!" is closer to being accomplished? Has the question "Who am I?" finally lost its enigmatic elusiveness? May the brightness of our screens and diagnostic imaging technology successfully replace the enlightenment of self-understanding? We may detect that the advance in knowledge seems to happen at the expense of the ethical and practical significance of self-understanding. The loss of the moral dimension of the self seems to be required in order to attain linguistic disambiguation and scientific reproducibility. The question of the self is highly relevant in modern philosophical discourse. The methodology and scope for such a thorough investigation of the mind are moreover often determined by requests for theoretical clarification that have arisen in the scientific field, and therefore present a marked epistemological character.

To convey the peculiar entanglement underlying the concept of self, and the challenging nature of its interrogation, we may recall a poem by the Song dynasty scholar Su Dongpo 蘇軾 (1037–1101):

> Viewed horizontally a range; a cliff from the side,
> It differs as we move high or low, or far or nearby.
> We do not know the true face of Mount Lu,
> Because we are all ourselves inside.
>
> Su Shi (Dongpo), "Written on the Wall of the Temple of West Woods"

This is one of the most well-known and widely quoted Chinese poems. It deals with the problem of knowledge and calls into question the accessibility of an objective, comprehensive truth through or beyond the multiplicity of subjective perspectives. The visual background of this interrogation is rooted in Chinese landscape painting. The mountain painted by a Chinese painter is generally not a real mountain, but rather an integration of different parts and perspectives of the mountain, which the observer can recognize moving in the painting and thus appreciate the various views and distances. A pictorial representation with shifting focus presupposes a living apprehension of the landscape and the subsequent fusion of mnemonic images from different views. This attitude is quite distinct from the scientific attention to detail and geometrical rendition of perspective characteristic of the classic Western painting. Su Shi's description echoes the three distances that in the Chinese painting actually replace linear perspective: the *gao yuan* (高遠), which emphasizes verticality and directs the gaze toward the impending mountain, the *yuan shen* (深遠), which absorbs the viewer in the vastness, and the *ping yuan* (平遠), which reproduces the horizontal expansion of the mountain range. However, Su Shi introduces an interesting torsion here, since the viewpoint adopted is not that of the external onlooker who appreciates the nuances of the painted landscape, but the wanderer walking through cliffs and ravines in the middle of the mountain, unable to decipher the global structure of the landscape. This is a very meaningful rendition of the puzzling position held by any of us when we question the nature of our self or self-consciousness. We are immersed in our ubiquitous identity, and irrevocably trapped in the boundaries of our mental horizon. We are deprived of the privilege of setting a step aside and contemplating ourselves from an external angle. We may indeed consider the self as an object of knowledge, conjecturing, for example, the possibility of mapping a locus of self-consciousness in the neural web of the human brain. In this case, however, we are abandoning our subjective and living "me" in order to acquire the detached and objectifying approach required by the methodology of the positive sciences. To verify the accuracy of any statement about this objectively thematized self, we have no alternative but to turn the gaze inward and compare it with the subjective experience of "being ourselves here and now." This back-and-forth movement is highly problematic, since the dimension of the self-as-a-subject of my inner life seems not to tally with the self-as-an-object of the detached apprehension. On the contrary, we assist in a veritable epistemological bifurcation. Drawing on Su Shi's imagery, if Mount Lu is our self, we are structurally embedded in it. Wandering through the mountain is not only our inescapable ontological condition, but, from a certain point of view, our wandering through and enjoyment of the mountain in its different aspects also constitute the mountain itself.

The irreducible certainty that survives René Descartes' methodological doubt—*cogito ergo sum*—may as well be expressed as *cogito, sum*, since I do not infer my existence from the evidence of my thinking, as the discursive conjunction *ergo* would suggest. Rather, the reality of the self is fully expressed in and exhausted by the activity of thinking, and *cogito* and *sum* are contemporaneously given, not as a logical consequence, but in an intuitive, self-manifest manner. So, how could the wanderer cognitively explore the landscape that surrounds her, given that she and the mountain are mutually transforming and exchanging? As Franz Brentano (1838–1917) and Edmund Husserl (1859–1938) claim, this mapping of the inner landscape requires the application of a specific methodology, i.e., a phenomenological description of the phenomena of the inner self as they appear in their immediacy. In contemporary philosophy, the phenomenological approach as developed by Jean-Paul Sartre, Maurice Merleau-Ponty (1908–1961), Max Scheler (1874–1928), and more recently by philosophers of the mind like Dan Zahavi, is the prevalent methodology adopted by researchers, aiming to reproduce the paradoxical "view from the inside" of the self that precedes and is implied as the condition of possibility of any duality of subject-object. The phenomena of our self—like attention, inner flow of time, stream of consciousness, and different degrees of self-awareness—reveal our psychic focus as an experience we are performing and living through, just like the cliffs and ranges of the mountain are not an objective property of the mountain, but merely another modality of the manifestation of our vertical and horizontal sight.

As we will see more extensively below, two crucial questions can emerge in the inner horizon of this phenomenological description: in this stream of first-person experience, can we actually grasp Mount Lu in its distinctive identity, or are we merely involved in a shifting, ever-changing, living flux, lacking any synthetic focus? Going back to the metaphor, does a recognizable "ego" or "self" really exist, or are our mental phenomena explainable without reverting to an egoic perspectival center? The second question is related to self-consciousness. Are the wanderer and Mount Lu one and the same reality, capable of knowing itself through their intertwining existence and inseparability, or is the true face of Mount Lu cognizable only if the self of the wanderer can extricate itself from this seamless experience of unity and contemplate Mount Lu, in a way analogous to a viewer looking at an external object? If we abandon the intricacy of this perspective-from-inside and adopt the point of view of the external onlooker, embracing the epistemological paradigm of the neurosciences and thematizing the self-as-an-object, are we in a better position to grasp the "true face of the Mount Lu"? If we represent the self as an emergent property of the brain or as a functional network of computational processes through which we gain access to the information of the universe, how do we then reconcile these third-person descriptions with the specificity of the self as disclosed in our personal awareness, namely that of always being accompanied by a subjective-experiential aspect, a sense of "what-it-is-like-to be-me"? Are we in danger of losing the structural dimension of our living stream of consciousness, instantiating what Ludwig Wittgenstein (1889–1951) wrote in his *Tractatus Logico-Philosophicus*: "We feel that even if all possible scientific questions be answered, the problems of life have still not been touched at all"?[3]

Before introducing a synthetic examination of the modern and contemporary philosophical research on the self, it is worth remarking that a vast amount of the critical works on self-consciousness are devoted to the analysis of the questions revolving around the "neural correlates of the consciousness," i.e., how consciousness, as a mental phenomenon, is related to the brain. Several explanatory hypotheses have been introduced in the last twenty years, and their predictions variously verified through neuro-diagnostic or computational models. Some aspects of these models imply wider philosophical and metaphysical frames, concerning the possibility for a physical causal chain in the brain to produce or determine non-physical mental states or, on the contrary, for the mind to produce the neural correlates of consciousness. The latter can be expressed as the physicalist or Idealist stance. More radically, is it better to simply get rid of the delusionary belief that consciousness

---

3   Ludwig Wittgenstein, *Tractatus Logico-Philosophicus*, trans. D. F. Pears and B. F. McGuinness, London: Routledge, 1961, p. 73.

exists as an independent phenomenon, like in eliminativist theories? Or, should we consider consciousness a fundamental and ubiquitous feature of the universe, as panpsychist theorists propose? In any case, despite the fact that these questions play a hegemonic role in the debate, they derive their origin and methodology from a neuroscientific background. The philosophical thought here may accompany and contribute to clarify some epistemological tenets, but nevertheless plays an ancillary role. If we want to address the problem of self in a philosophical way, we should remember that the generative moment of philosophy lies in the discovery of oneself, the illuminating power of this intuition, and the imperative to unceasingly return to this critical awareness. Becoming conscious of our stance and of the linguistic, ontological, and hermeneutical background in which our cognition is deeply rooted is a never-ending task, and the critical discernment—as Su Shi's poems says "we are all ourselves inside" —serves as an irrevocable and inescapable foundation for philosophical thought. This does not necessarily imply that a philosophy of consciousness should adopt a phenomenological methodology, nor that a third-person apprehension is unattainable, but philosophical investigation possesses an autonomy and specificity in critically examining its own position and boundaries, and cannot eradicate self-consciousness from the conditions of its original manifestation.

1.2 Contemporary Perspectives on Self

It is a widespread conviction among researchers in the field that the problem of self, like a two-headed Janus, presents itself in two different ways, which are mutually irreducible, and therefore require specific theoretical tools and two different methodological and terminological reference frames in order to be approached appropriately. One of the most quoted versions of this puzzling epistemic bifurcation is offered by David Chalmers.[4] He distinguishes between an "easy problem" and a "hard problem" regarding self-consciousness. The "easy problem" involves the explanation of the cognitive functions of the mind,

---

[4] David Chalmers, "Facing Up to the Problem of Consciousness," *Journal of Consciousness Studies* 2:3 (1995), 200–219.

namely reacting to stimuli from the physical world, discriminating and categorizing, increasing and integrating the network of information it beholds, using its cognitive contents as a paradigm for action. Ned Block encapsulates these mental abilities under the term "access consciousness," specifying that a state is access-conscious if, by virtue of the mind being in that state, its content can 1) serve as a premise in reasoning, 2) be poised for rational control of action, and 3) be ready for elaboration in speech.[5] Why is this constitutive ability of the mind to turn on itself and access its own representational content deemed by Chalmers "easy" to explain? Despite the complexity involved in the everyday execution of these multifold functions, we can notice that all these features are already more or less satisfactorily explained by neurosciences and cognitive sciences. The reason is that they can be represented as sequences of neural functions or computational processes. Further research is required; we still lack a fine-grained vision of the globality of neural connections, and more detailed models of the multifold interference between different areas of the brain will in the future provide us with a deeper understanding of the neural correlates of reason, behavior, and language. However, there is an elusive aspect of these mental phenomena that seems to be irreducible to the objectifying approach of neuroscience, i.e., the subjective experience accompanying all these conscious functions.

This subjective and unique way the mental process appears to me forms the core of Chalmers' "hard problem of the consciousness," and has been defined in several ways, as "phenomenal consciousness" (Block), "the way it feels like to be" (Nagel), or *qualia* (Nagel)—the experiential properties (e.g., colors, sensorial impressions, pain) through which the world is revealed to my subjective awareness and thereby constitutes my inner world. Whereas the other cognitive properties intentionally refer to a common world, can be quantified or expressed as a divisible sequence of function, and therefore clearly and unambiguously defined in a scientific language, this subjective aspect seems to resist any reduction. I can obviously generalize and thematize these experiences, categorizing them, for example, as pain, but I cannot simply access them in the same way I know an external object, for example, the structure of the brain,

---

[5] Ned Block, "On a Confusion about a Function of Consciousness," *Behavioral and Brain Sciences* 18:2 (1995), 227–247 (p. 231).

without losing the peculiar way they are given to me and constitute my subjectivity. The examination of the inner structure of this phenomenal consciousness and the analysis of the "mineness" of this phenomenal inner world is the specific challenge posed to the philosophy of self. It is required to turn the gaze inward and to describe the living experience, accepting the first-person account as a primary source. Even then, this rhythmical intertwining of the two directions of knowledge, the one proceeding from inside toward a conceptual thematization and the one constantly returning to the inside in order to interrogate the self and verify the fidelity of the conclusions to the inner experience, does not satisfy the requirements of positive sciences.

I will synthesize three of the questions that animate the debate in this philosophical field. The first is the question of the actual existence of the "ego" itself: does my stream of consciousness reveal at its fulcrum the presence of a substantial ego, or can I adequately describe my inner experience in a non-egological way? The second question focuses on self-consciousness: is it essentially a reflective, mirror-like knowledge or does it presuppose a more intimate self-acquaintance? The third problem is relative to the person, i.e., the self as realized and operating in the world: can we think about the self and the mind prescinding from its manifestation through the body or is a structural unity of body-mind a necessary premise for the apparition of a self? These three questions play a pivotal role in the philosophy of self because they reflect the three meanings of the self: the perspectival, possessive, and personal viewpoints.

The most influential critique of the idea of self as a distinct autonomous substance is the so-called "bundle theory of self" exposed by David Hume in his *A Treatise on Human Nature*. If I plunge into my inner world trying to catch my own conscious self, what I find is always a specific sensation, a perception, a memory, an image, and the only interconnections these perceptions display are the external relations of resemblance, succession, and causation. No perspectival focal point seems to internally unify my stream of consciousness; my mental life seems to be "nothing but a bundle or collection of different perceptions, which succeed each other with an inconceivable rapidity, and are in a perpetual flux and movement."[6] A similar, albeit more detailed and refined theory is posited by Husserl in *Phenomenology of the Internal Time-Consciousness*. The founder of phenomenology argues that the flux of consciousness possesses an inner structural self-organizing pattern that is intrinsically temporal and can be highlighted through an analysis of our perception of time. Whereas Descartes' self is contracted in the punctiform instantaneous self-identification of the "I think," Husserl claims that this kind of perpetual presence to myself, which epistemically realizes itself in the exclusive apprehension of the "right-now," is inadequate in explaining our ability to perceive temporally extended phenomena like a melody. The conclusion of Husserl's analysis is that the width of this conscious presence has to be enlarged to involve duration. If we magnify the seemingly instantaneous act of apprehension, we will discover a threefold structure: the retention of the past, the primal apprehension of the now, and the protention toward the future horizon. The microstructure of inner consciousness is given to itself as a temporal stream and not as the distinct, perpetual presence of a substantial autonomous ego. Furthermore, this stream manifests an innermost structure that is self-organizing and self-illuminating and does not require the singular spotlight of a hovering ego. It is worth noticing that Husserl's early position evolved substantially after the so-called "transcendental turn," acknowledging that a pure, transcendental ego is the necessary correlate of our stream of consciousness. However, this pure ego should be considered as a mere "ego-pole": "[The ego as an identical pole for all experiences] is no "being," but rather the counterparts of all beings, not an object (*Gegenstand*) but an *Urstand* for all objectivity. [...] It is something nameless... not something which stands or hovers above everything, something which is, but rather a functioning something."[7] This functional correlate "is nothing peculiar, floating above many experiences; it is simply identical with their own interconnected unity (*Verknüpfungseinheit*)."[8] Sartre, in *The*

---

6   David Hume, *A Treatise of Human Nature*, ed. by David Fate Norton and Mary J. Norton, Oxford: Oxford University Press, 2005, p. 165.

7   Edmund Husserl, *Die Bernauer Manuskripte über das Zeitbewußtsein (1917/18)* (Husserliana: Edmund Husserl—Gesammelte Werke 33), Dordrecht: Kluwer Academic Publishers, 2001, pp. 277–278.

8   Edmund Husserl, *Logische Untersuchungen*, Vol. II (Husserliana: Edmund Husserl—Gesammelte Werke 19/2), The Hague: Nijhoff, 1984, p. 262. Dan Zahavi argues that the two different versions in Husserl's work may coherently coexist:

Transcendence of the Ego, argues that when our attention is plunged into an action, like reading a book, no ego as owner or inhabitant of the mind is present. Only when we reflect upon our action, an ego is retrospectively sedimented and apprehended: "I was reading a book." However, this ego is an objectified self, not the subject of the living action. This brief overview reveals that the non-egological position may be underpinned by two different degrees of negation; one that totally refuses the necessity of an ego as a transcendental unifying principle, highlighting the self-organizing structure of the stream of consciousness, and another that endorses what we can call a "weak" interpretation of the self, rejecting only the illusion of an autonomous, substantial free-standing ego. This second stance is akin to Immanuel Kant's notion of the "transcendental apperception," or Cogito, which necessarily accompanies any representation as an overarching synthetic principle. It is worth differentiating the nuances of meaning involved in the idea of self or ego. In contemporary philosophy of the mind, some influential scholars such as Thomas Metzinger and Daniel Dennett adopt a radical exclusionary position, denying the idea of self as an unchanging ontological substance, and therefore labeling the self as an illusion.[9] This radical rejection is rooted in the neuroscientific vision of the mind and neglects the possibility of other non-reified understandings of the ego. A researcher like Galen Strawson, albeit departing from the physicalist problem of the neural correlates of consciousness, and refusing that the experience of ego could be located in a specific zone of the brain, nonetheless endorses the idea of a "minimal subject," which is present and alive only in the living moment of experience and cannot exist above or apart wholly from the field of experience.[10]

"When Husserl speaks of an egoless streaming, the term "egoless" [...] is meant to indicate that the ego is not participating or contributing to the (self-) constitution of this fundamental process in any active way. [...]. It is not the ego which unifies the experiences. This is taken care by the very process of temporalization. But although the passive syntheses are not initiated by me, they still happen to me, not to somebody else or to nobody." Dan Zahavi, "Unity of Consciousness and the Problem of Self," in: Shaun Gallagher (ed.), *The Oxford Handbook of the Self*, Oxford: Oxford University Press, 2011, pp. 316–335 (p. 323).

9 Thomas Metzinger, "The No-Self Alternative," in: S. Gallagher (ed.), *The Oxford Handbook of the Self*, Oxford: Oxford University Press, 2011, pp. 279–296. Daniel Dennett, *Sweet Dreams: Philosophical Obstacles to a Science of Consciousness*, Cambridge, MA: MIT Press, 2005.

10 Galen Strawson, *Selves: An Essay in Revisionary Metaphysics*, Oxford: Oxford University Press, 2009.

The neuroscientist Patricia Churchland[11] justifies her brand of exclusionary theory, observing that several questions throughout the history of science did not receive a solution; on the contrary, they simply dissolved when the physical phenomena they were meant to elucidate found a more adequate scientific explanation. She draws an analogy between the self and the concept of aether, the non-existent fluid thought to be necessary as medium of propagation for electromagnetic or gravitational forces in previous centuries. Churchland argues that due to the advancement in our knowledge of brain structures, self-consciousness may reveal itself to be like aether: an unnecessary hypothesis for successfully explaining reality. Using a metaphor, we could resume this argument, saying that the Gordian knot of the self, which seems to be hopelessly entangled thanks to the physicalist reduction of the mind as a mere product of neuronal activity, could reveal itself as a vanishing slipknot that is easily undone by pulling the tail. Reconnecting to the previous distinction between scientific and philosophical approaches, I think that even if the genesis of our ego could be satisfactorily reduced to brain activity (which at the actual level of research is far from being the case), the philosophical question about why the experience of an ego is given in us, would still remain unsolved. Developing the analogy with the concept of aether, we are reminded that Kant, in his *Opus Postumum*, despite negating that aether is an objective substance in the universe, deduces that its appearance and persistence in the history of thought requires a philosophical explanation, redefining aether as a transcendental necessity of human thought, which could retain a theoretical significance as a medium between the *a priori* realm and the world of matter.

If we search for images on the internet correlated with the words "self" or "self-consciousness," we will very easily come across numerous drawings or photographs depicting mirrors or plays of reflections on mirror-like surfaces. An image that often appears on the cover of books devoted to the question of self-consciousness is the so-called "mise-en-abyme" or "double mirroring" effect. The infinite regression in depth of two mirrors reflecting one another, and the labyrinth-like recursion of any subject placed between the mirrors, seems to vividly represent, with

---

11 Patricia Churchland, *Touching a Nerve: The Self as Brain*, New York: W. W. Norton & Company, 2013.

its uncanniness and baffling indecisiveness, the elusiveness of a mind trying to grasp itself in the void created by the absence of the world. For neuroscientists like Dennett, who reject the self and label it as an illusion, it may as well represent the paradoxical outcome of the misuse of knowledge, when we stop to direct our cognitive acts to the world and force the cognitive apparatus to apprehend itself. Is it, however, adequate to use the imagery and concept of self-reflection in order to describe the intimate awareness we have with ourselves? If I look at myself in the mirror, am I recognizing the core of my identity beyond the external somatic trait of my face?

If we go back to the Cartesian germinal certainty of myself, the Cogito, it seems that every time I think on myself, I rediscover in a flashing experience my undoubtable being-here, and I recognize myself as myself, like I was contemplating me in the mirror. This is different from the knowledge of the external universe I derive through my senses or the certainty through which my intellect acknowledges the abstract truths of mathematic and logic. All these cognitive experiences, argues Descartes, have the form of a subject apprehending an external object, and all of them can be distorted by my bodily boundaries or maliciously inserted in my mind by an evil genius. The "I think, I am" focal experience structurally differs from all the other acts of apprehension, in as much the subject and the object are here one and the same thing, and the pure act of thinking is the self-affirmation of the absolute reality of the self, so that we can summarize this coincidence-in-itself saying that in the self (and only in the self) thinking and being, or knowing and being, are one and the same. As Güven Güzeldere remarks, the uniqueness of the self resides exactly in this overlapping: "if all there is to (the reality of) conscious states is their appearing in a certain way to subjects, and if they have no existential status independent of their so appearing, the ontology of consciousness seems to collapse into its epistemology."[12] One way to interpret this singular and baffling imbrication was offered by Sartre in *The Transcendence of the Ego*, in the example given above. When I'm absorbed in reading, claims Sartre, I am in an egoless condition of total self-oblivion. Only when someone calls my attention to what I

---

12 Güven Güzeldere, "The Many Faces of Consciousness: A Field Guide," in: Ned Block, Owen Flanagan and Güven Güzeldere (ed.), *The Nature of Consciousness. Philosophical Debates*, Cambridge, MA: MIT Press 1997, pp. 1–67 (p. 10).

am doing, I am reminiscent of myself and able to formulate the word "I." Sartre's interpretation is that when I am focusing the attention on me, I am actually "producing" my ego, so that the ego intermittently coagulates and vanishes in my act of reflection. This reading brings us to the "reflective consciousness hypothesis," often referred to by contemporary theorists as the higher-order theory of self-consciousness. Supporters of this theory argue that self-awareness requires the ability to detach oneself from the busy flux of living and observe oneself "from above," in order to have a representation of oneself—diverting attention away from overarching interests in the world to pause and reflect, as if standing before a mirror, recognizing one's image and becoming an object of one's own knowledge. We may notice that this reflective consciousness is not structurally different from our intentional knowledge of things: a higher-order self-as-a-subject thematizes and ascertains a lower-order self-as-an-object. However, there is a further requirement, which Carlos Castañeda[13] calls "de se constraint". I do not merely represent the self-as-an-object, but I should in the same act recognize myself as myself. How can I recognize this object-self as myself, if this is the first time that I discover and represent it in my knowledge? One of the more debated problems about the higher-order theory is that it seems that I should already possess a knowledge of my own self in order to reflectively recognize it, in the same way as I should already have obtained an image of myself if I want to recognize that the person staring at me from the surface of the mirror is nothing else but me. To avoid the risk of getting entangled in an infinite recess, some scholars claim that the original sprout of self-awareness should not be a form of knowledge, but on the contrary a form of self-acquaintance, a familiarity and intimacy with the self preceding any subject-object division. Several Western scholars expressed this intuitive, quiet awareness of being at one with yourself. German Romantic philosopher Novalis (1772–1881) calls it "self-feeling," remarking that "What reflection finds, appears to have already been there before."[14] Johann Gottlieb Fichte (1762–1814) in his *Doctrine of Science* attempts to formulate several definitions of

---

13 Hector-Neri Castañeda, *The Phenomeno-Logic of the I: Essays on Self-Consciousness*, Bloomington, IN: Indiana University Press, 19999.
14 Novalis, *Schriften*, ed. by R. Samuel with H.-J. Mahl and G. Schulz, Stuttgart: Kohlhammer, 1965, p. 112.

self-consciousness, and concludes that the Cogito is the perfect oneness before active and passive, subject and object appear and is therefore that "intellectual intuition" that Kant ascribed only to God's mind. The twentieth century phenomenologists developed in depth the condition for this self-acquaintance, namely that the ego is not a monadic substance, but a self-disclosing activity. Husserl writes that the experiential stream is characterized by a *"für-sich-selbst-erscheinen,"* that is a tacit permanent self-manifestation, and that "to be a subject is to be in the mode of being aware of oneself."[15] Martin Heidegger (1889–1976) highlights that any intentional act directed to the world implies a co-disclosure of the self, so that the self is ubiquitously present and permeating all of my intentional comportments. Sartre, in the introduction to *Being and Nothingness*, claims that while being-in-itself (*en-soi*) refers to the self-sufficient, contingent existence of ordinary things, self-givenness is the original mode of being of intentional consciousness. This consciousness, defined as for-itself (*pour-soi*), exists prior to any act of self-reflection. Recalling the primary nucleus of the Cogito, he highlights that only because of syntactic rules are we forced into formulating it as "I am conscious of myself," inserting a linguistic divide in the core of self-consciousness. Therefore, he proposes to put the "of" (French "de") in a bracket, and to simply say *"conscience (de) soi,"* in order to avoid objectifying the self and to maintain the constant self-adherence within the flux of experience.[16]

The same-order theory, which asserts that one possesses an intuitive self-awareness before any reflexive act, was explicitly formulated and developed by the so-called School of Tübingen, with major exponents including Dieter Henrich and Manfred Frank. Departing from Fichte's definition of the self as a self-posing dynamism, they develop the idea of pre-reflexive consciousness as living familiarity (*Vertrautheit*) with the self that is always present in an athematic way, i.e., without implying a detached and objective knowledge about the content of the self. This pre-reflexive being-present to myself is aimed to solve another weakness of the higher-order theory (HOT), namely that the reflection about my mental stream and the mental stream itself are two

---

15   Edmund Husserl, *Zur Phänomenologie der Intersubjektivität. Texte aus dem Nachlass. Zweiter Teil: 1921–1928*, ed. by Iso Kern, The Hague: Nijhogg, 1973, p. 151.
16   See Jean-Paul Sartre, *Being and Nothingness: An Essay in Phenomenological Ontology*, London: Routledge, 2018, p. 13.

numerically distinct acts, neither of which is self-conscious, unless I climb to a further level and reflect on my reflection *ad infinitum*. How is it possible for the sum of two non-conscious mind states to produce the event of self-consciousness? The answer of Henrich and Frank is that one's mental acts are always self-conscious in an implicit way, since the defining feature of any of my mental acts is to be there for myself, disclosed to and familiar with myself. As synthesized, pre-reflective consciousness—like all pre-reflective mental states—can be described as being "non-propositional, not states of explicit knowledge, non-thetic, not objectifying, not intentional, non-identifying, not language-based, not relational and not based on any knowledge of rules."[17] This may imply that the capacity of being self-conscious can be extended to other animals, even if they are not capable of reflective conceptual knowledge, which has far-reaching ethical implications. It also implies that self-consciousness can develop to a higher degree of clarity, not through conceptual processes, but through bodily proprioception.

This reference to body perception can act as a bridge toward the third aspect of the self that is investigated in modern philosophy of mind: the wide-ranging idea of personal identity. This dimension transcends the inner horizon of self-consciousness in order to embrace other constitutive aspects of our identity, which is given to us in the everyday experience as rooted in a physical and social world. Strawson invites us to re-evaluate the complex tissue of experience, which is made of a sensorial awareness playing in the background of our palpitating inner life: "[...] those who think that the sensations and feelings that give us experience of the world are like invisible glass, so that we are generally wholly unaware of them, utterly falsify the extraordinarily rich, rapid, nuanced, complexly inflected, interdipping flow of everyday experience."[18] This stratified and interrelating experience in which our self-awareness discloses itself reminds us that our ego is never isolated in an inaccessible interiority, but in our experience is always embedded in a world and actively responding to a physical and social environment. Maurice Merleau-Ponty (1908–1961) highlights that our

---

17 Marc Borner, Manfred Frank, and Kenneth Williford, "Pre-reflective Self-Consciousness and the *De Se* Constraint: The Legacy of the Heidelberg School," *ProtoSociology* 36 (2019), pos. 383.
18 Strawson, *Selves*, p. 26.

being intentionally directed to an outer world is the condition of being conscious of oneself as a bodily, world-immersed subjectivity: "There is a world for me because I am not unaware of myself, and I am not concealed from myself because I have a world."[19] Twentieth-century philosophy of consciousness, based on the concept of intentionality—in which my noetic acts and the perceived world are seen as two coessential aspects of the same phenomenon—has been increasingly directed toward an "exteriorization" and "mundanization" of the self. It theorizes that the essence of self-awareness is not found in a secluded inward dimension, but in its living, embodied capacity to constitute the world and its meaning. As Zahavi writes, "the constitution of the world implies a mundanization of the constituting subject,"[20] implying a re-evaluation of "the necessity of [the subject's] concrete and contingent existence in the midst of the world."[21]

This is not the first time in philosophy that a world-embedded subjectivity plays a pivotal role in the definition of the self. Novalis, for example, suggestively expresses the idea that the border between mind and the world and their dynamism of mutual relation and implication is the proper place of the self-manifestation of the I: "The seat of the soul is the point where the inner and the outer worlds touch. Wherever they penetrate each other—it is there at every point of penetration."[22] However, the phenomenological turn in the twentieth century lays the foundation for a reappraisal of the world-immersed self as embodied subject. I will summarize two of the many problematic fields arising from the acknowledgment that the subject structurally belongs to the world: first, the question of the body; and second, the role played by other selves in the constitution of self-awareness. While Descartes adopts a dualist stance, claiming that the relationship between my Cogito (*res cogitans*) and the physical body (*res extensa*) can be reduced to an external and highly controversial connection, phenomenologists like Husserl and

---

19   Maurice Merleau-Ponty, *Phenomenology of Perception*, London and New York: Routledge, 1962, p. 347.
20   Dan Zahavi, "Philosophy, Psychology, and Phenomenology," in: Sara Heinämaa and Martina Reuter (ed.), *Psychology and Philosophy: Inquiries into the Soul from Late Scholasticism to Contemporary Thought*, New York: Springer, 2009, pp. 247–262 (p. 260).
21   Sartre, *Being and Nothingness*, p. 359.
22   Novalis, *Philosophical Writings*, trans. and ed. by Margaret Mahony Stoljar, Albany, NY: SUNY Press, p. 26.

Merleau-Ponty depict the self as structurally embodied, emphasizing the distance between the objective physical body (*Körper*) and the subjectively lived body (*Leib*), or, as Husserl formulates it, the paradoxical coexistence of my "being in the world" and my "being a subject for the world." The two main questions developed by the researchers are: am I able to detach self-consciousness from the body using it as a mere transparent dispositive of knowledge or is the living experience of my being in a body permeating my subjective consciousness like a background foundation? Am I actively structuring my body as a hierarchically detached fulcrum of agency, or is the possibility of self-cognition itself dependent on some basic bodily processes (like proprioception, orientation, or the perspectival limitation of my own body)?

The problem of the relation between the body and our mental self undergirds the first question: given that we are embedded in a world through our physical functions and appearances, should we think of ourselves as merely embodied subjects—mental structures that contingently possess a body and receive through its sensorial organs information about the world—or are we bodily subjects, shaped and structured by our body in such a way that the emergence of our ego-awareness is made possible through our embodied nature? From an epistemological viewpoint, this bifurcation mirrors the previously examined question of the ego: is our stream of experience fundamentally ego-less and able to function even if we are not present to ourselves, or on the contrary, is our ego something we are always aware of, so that we cannot mentally operate in the world without being conscious of ourselves? In the first case the body or self-consciousness are like a transparent medium or a frame we can detach from. Sydney Shoemaker advocates for this transparency of the body: "We are not presented with ourselves in introspection as bodily entities,"[23] therefore "when one is introspectively aware of one's thoughts, feelings, beliefs, and desires, one is not presented to oneself as a flesh and blood person, and one does not seem to be presented to one as an object at all."[24] Michel Henry in *Philosophy and Phenomenology of the Body*[25] presents a more

---

23 Sydney Shoemaker, "Introspection and the Self," *Midwest Studies in Philosophy* 10:1 (1986), 101–120.
24 Sydney Shoemaker, "Personal Identity: A Materialist's Account," in: S. Shoemaker and R. Swinburne (eds), *Personal Identity*, Oxford: Blackwell, 1984, pp. 67–132 (p. 102).
25 Michel Henry, *Philosophy and Phenomenology of the Body*, Dordrecht: Springer, 1976.

elaborate development of this sharp division between the transparent subjective body and the inessential material body. Inheriting from Maine de Biran (1766–1824) the idea of self as an active force and pure agency, Henry contrasts the mentally internalized subjective body, which is deprived of any materiality and belongs as a fundamental "I can" to the sphere of the absolute immanence of subjectivity, and the biologically lived body, which lacks noetic transparency and, in its passivity, can only be the external object of my ownership.

The idea of bodily subjectivity, implying that no self-consciousness can prescind from its embodied nature, is advocated by phenomenologists such as Husserl and Merleau-Ponty, and more recently by scholars such as Shaun Gallagher. Gallagher, adhering to the "theory of embodied cognition"—promoted by several philosophers such as Andy Clark (1997) and Alva Noë (2004) and by neuroscientists such as Francisco Varela (1991) and Antonio Damasio (1994) among others—affirms that body, mind, and world cannot be separated like in Descartes' pure spiritual Cogito, since the body shapes the mind at a fundamental pre-noetic level. The phenomenological school highlights that our apprehension of the world requires a bodily experience and investigation performed by our living embodied self (the subjective body: *Leib*). Husserl claims, for example, that a crucial aspect of the self, its perspectivity and its ability to locate itself at the zero-point of any worldview, is anchored in the voluminosity and orientation of our experienced body and in its kinesthetic ability to disclose the continuity of our self-perspective throughout variations. Merleau-Ponty, in *Phenomenology of Perception* and *The Visible and Invisible*, analyzes in depth the phenomenon of "double sensation"—when my right hand touches my left hand, perceiving itself alternatively as object and subject—anchoring my self-consciousness in a more fundamental corporeal "reflection":

> When my right hand touches my left, I am aware of it as a "physical thing." But at the same moment, if I wish, an extraordinary event takes place: here is my left hand as well starting to perceive my right, *es wird Leib, es empfindet*. The physical thing becomes animate. [...] Thus, I touch myself touching; my body accomplishes "a sort of reflection."[26]

---

26 Maurice Merleau-Ponty, "The Philosopher and His Shadow," in: *Signs*, Evanston, IL: Northwestern University Press, 1964, p. 166.

Sartre in *Being and Nothingness* criticizes this attempt to find a bodily root for reflectivity, claiming that touching oneself cannot be the adequate foundation for self-identification, and arguing that I exist for myself as a body known by the other. The necessity of the gaze-from-outside by another subject in order to acknowledge myself fully leads us to the final question analyzed in this chapter, the problem of other selves. The structural difficulty Husserl faces in providing an account of how I recognize that the other person, physically present in front of me, possesses self-consciousness is clearly evident in his *Cartesian Meditations*, where Husserl writes: "neither the other Ego himself, nor his subjective processes or his appearances themselves, nor anything else belonging to his own essence, becomes given in our experience originally."[27]

The existence of other selves, given the inaccessibility of their inner stream of experience to me, cannot be directly apprehended in an intuitive way, as this would imply a fusion and indiscernibility between my mind and the other subject's mind. However, argues Husserl, a direct cognizance structurally embedded in my experience becomes possible if I turn my attention to the world, which, as the totality of intentional objects, is always co-constituted by the agency of other subjects. Though the world of my experience is a world molded, modified, and oriented by the operative engagement of others, the meaning of this intervention is necessarily precluded by the inaccessibility of their minds, so that the only way to verify my hypotheses about others' intentions is everyday concrete intersubjective life, in an endless process of corroboration. Husserl's attempt, albeit widely discussed and criticized in the subsequent developments of phenomenological thinking, marks the acknowledgement of the secluded loneliness of the Cartesian self, echoed by the Kantian "I think." The "I," as the generating force of the first idealism, lacks a structural interpersonal and relational dimension. In his *Phenomenology of Mind*, Georg Wilhelm Friedrich Hegel (1770–1831) theorized that others are the only adequate mirror through which I can know myself, and that a self-consciousness can be properly given only to another self-consciousness. In the contemporary philosophy of consciousness, some scholars brought to full accomplishment the

---

27 Edmund Husserl, *Cartesian Meditations: An Introduction to Phenomenology*, Dordrecht: Kluwer Academic Publishers, 1991, p. 109.

intuition that self-awareness requires a previous basic "reflective doubling" mediated by social experience. In particular, we can mention George Herbert Mead (1863–1931), who proposes a reversal of the traditional relationship and hierarchy between self-consciousness and other consciousnesses. He posits that social interaction is a prerequisite for my self-awareness, because I can acknowledge myself only by catching the reflections of myself thrown back at me by other subjects. Jürgen Habermas, through his entire body of work, promotes a decisive shift to inter-subjectivity with a pragmatic-communicative turn. Not the solitary self-apprehension of the Cogito, but a social interactive context is the germinal ground of the experience of self. The self emerges only in acquiring "communicative competence," i.e., in being able to move between a first-person and second-person perspective, entering a dialogical system of reciprocally interlocked perspectives among speakers and hearers. The primacy of this socially-constituted self, which implies the necessity of a mutual mirroring, is, not by chance, criticized by scholars supporting a pre-reflexive theory of self-consciousness. As Roger Frie summarizes, "the subject possesses a pre-reflective 'being-familiar-with itself' which can neither be derived from, nor reduced to intersubjective relations."[28] Individual subjectivity is therefore an original phenomenon. As Manfred Frank aptly states: "talk of inter-subjectivity stands or falls with the ability to provide the term subjectivity a meaning."[29]

1.3 Comparative Perspectives

The philosophy of consciousness has evolved predominantly within the horizon of Western traditions of thought. Hume's theory of the bundle of perceptions, Descartes' Cogito, Kant's transcendental apperception, and the attempt of German idealism to transcend its abstract and formal nature toward an active self dynamically engaging with the world are the foundations upon which contemporary scholars construct or defy

---

28　Roger Frie, *Subjectivity and Intersubjectivity in Modern Philosophy and Psychoanalysis. A Study of Sartre, Binswanger, Lacan, and Habermas*, Lanham, MD: Rowman and Littlefield, 1997, p. 11.
29　Manfred Frank, *Selbstbewußtsein und Selbsterkenntnis: Essays zur analytischen Philosophie der Subjektivität*. Stuttgart: Reclam, 1991, p. 452.

a model of the self. We may wonder if other non-Western traditions of thought could provide a source of alternative, challenging, or creative images of the self. Only in the last two decades has scholarship started to welcome and critically debate contributions from other cultural horizons, with a meaningful attention paid to approaches deriving from Buddhist philosophy. The progressive permeation of Buddhist spiritual methods and practices in the West fostered a positive attitude among scholars, leading to the recognition of the complex, rich, nuanced, and sometimes paradoxical heritage of the Buddhist philosophy of mind. However, it is necessary to remark that this openness did not overturn the hegemony of Western paradigms, nor did it erode its epistemologically-oriented roots. We may adopt as an example a representative anthology of essays, *The Oxford Handbook of the Self*. Among thirty-one essays devoted to various aspect of the problem of subjectivity, only two derive a significant inspiration from non-Western models of thought; in both cases, the focus of debate is centered on the Buddhist idea of the non-self. In "Witnessing from Here: Self-Awareness from a Bodily versus Embodied Perspective," Aaron Henry and Evan Thompson, discussing the foundation of the sense of "mineness" and ownership in the self, introduce a cross-cultural comparison with Miri Albahary's treatise *Analytical Buddhism: The Two-Tiered Illusion of the Self*,[30] in which, according to the authors, "drawing on a novel and controversial interpretation of early Indian Buddhism, Albahari argues that the self we habitually take ourselves to be is an illusion."[31] The aim of the essay is to verify if this Buddhist-inspired non-egological view of consciousness casts, on the whole concept of the self, a shadow of deceptiveness and illusoriness. Or, as the authors contend, a minimal version of the self should subsist in the form of a bodily pre-reflective self-awareness. In particular, Albahary claims that the Buddhist theory of no-self entails a sharp distinction between "perspectival ownership" and "personal ownership." In "perspectival ownership," the subject merely witnesses reality from a specific spatio-temporal perspective, being no more than

---

30 Miri Albahari, *Analytical Buddhism: The Two-Tiered Illusion of the Self*, New York: Palgrave Macmillan, 2006.
31 Aaron Henry and Evan Thompson, "Witnessing from Here: Self-Awareness from a Bodily Versus Embodied Perspective," in: Shaun Gallagher (ed.), *The Oxford Handbook of the Self*, Oxford: Oxford University Press, 2011, pp. 228–250(p. 229).

an impersonal presence or awareness. In contrast, "personal ownership" involves the subject reflexively identifying with the psychophysical features of awareness, regarding itself as their substantial owner. This identification leads to the emergence of a bounded personal self, driven by the emotion of craving to appropriate all experiences as an ontologically distinct "mineness." "If one could remove the deep-seated psychological "craving" for me and mine that drives the experience of identification," the authors summarize, "one would thereby remove the illusion of selfhood and realize the inherently ownerless structure of experience."[32] Through an analysis of the "bodily" versus "embodied" character of the self, the authors argue that the perspective-holding, witnessing self, which should provide the basis for a liberated state of Nirvana, is necessarily constituted as a bodily subject preceding any act of desire-led "identification" and reification. In the second essay, "Buddhist Non-Self. The No-Owner's Manual," Mark Siderits adopts a more explanatory methodology, presenting what he calls "Buddhist Reductionism," i.e., the philosophical conviction that there is no enduring self and that the person is a conceptual fiction, whose truth is purely conventional. Siderits reconstructs the debate between different schools inside the Buddhist tradition, defending the Reductionist view against several theoretical objections. In the end, the author presents the paradoxical idea of a blind-sight "Robo-Buddha," a fully-enlightened being who acts effortlessly to help beings overcome suffering, without needing a consciousness, and defends its epistemological coherence, claiming that "There being nothing for which things appear in a certain way, there is no longer the basis for a sense of 'I am'. There is just a causal series of psychophysical elements, interacting with its environment in such a way as to maximize overall welfare."[33]

A distinguishing feature that emerges from both of the essays is that the Buddhist concept of non-self, while being fully acknowledged as a philosophical argument and afforded respectful attention and critical appraisal, is considered merely in its epistemological significance and outcomes as a non-egological theory of self-consciousness, akin to other

---

32 Ibid., p. 230.
33 Mark Siderits, "Buddhist Non-Self. The No-Owner's Manual," in: Shaun Gallagher (ed.), *The Oxford Handbook of the Self*, Oxford: Oxford University Press, 2011, pp. 297–315 (p. 314).

non-egological stances rooted in Western traditions that are discussed at length throughout the entire volume. The pivotal role played by value-imbued emotions, like desire and craving, in the constitution of the self, are the practical and performative actions posed as dynamic roots of subjectivity, instead of the Western logical and cognitive processes. Finally, the subordination of the theoretical aspects of the self to the preeminent moral and metaphysical tension toward spiritual accomplishment and liberation receives only peripheral consideration. The heterogenic nature of Buddhism as a spiritual and existential path with respect to the Western philosophical, psychological, and neuroscientific pursuit of a cognitive truth, which runs as an implicitly accepted and undiscussed red thread throughout the anthology, is not adequately perceived in its challenging potential. While some concepts such as the Buddhist non-self are welcomed as thought-provoking, the prevailing theoretical-epistemological horizontal trend remains unchallenged in its partiality. Instead, this trend is further sharpened to peruse and assimilate the "outsider."

A further examination of the literature on comparative philosophy of self-consciousness brings to light three aspects that significantly diverge from Western approaches to the question: the stratification of consciousness, the vertical-metaphysical tension, and the moral-performative dynamism inside the self. I will offer some examples of these three aspects, which may represent the inchoate unfolding of an alternative path of thought. First, these works frequently suggest the existence of neglected layers of the self. In *The Self. Naturalism, Consciousness, and the First-Person Stance*, Jonardon Ganeri accurately examines the evolution of the concepts of the self, the mind, and the body throughout the entire course of Indian philosophy, highlighting how several themes and hypotheses formulated by contemporary philosophy of mind were actually anticipated in Indian thought millennia ago. Synthesizing and elaborating the intuitions scattered throughout the work, Ganeri suggests a tripartite structure for the self:

> My own view is that in full account of human subjectivity, three distinct dimensions in the self are equally in play [...]. There is an underself, the sub-personal monitoring of the mental states, autonomous or alienated, that one embodies, "ownership" here implying a relocation of unconscious access to the content of one's states of mind. There is an

immersed self, the element of first-person presentation in the content of consciousness, "ownership" now referring to a phenomenologically present sense of mineness. Finally, there is a participant self, the inhabitation of a first-person stance, "ownership" involving the relations of involvement, participation, and endorsement.[34]

What is relevant here is that the self is accomplished only if grounded, lived, and engaged. Ownership here is not reduced to the cognitive aspects of self-ascription and agency, but extends itself to a voluntary act of choice and inhabitation in oneself, implying a moral horizon of values, the possibility of endorsing or refusing the content of the mind with which I identify. This active self-position could, however, lead to detachment and depersonalization if it would not be embedded and immersed in the living flux of my emotional presence to the world, and rooted in the inexhaustible depth of the subconscious mind, which cannot be known but only embodied. I live myself, I am engaged with myself, and I am therefore ultimately responsible for the self I become.

The philosopher of mind Evan Thompson, in *Waking, Dreaming, Being: Self and Consciousness in Neuroscience, Meditation, and Philosophy*, derives from the *Upaniṣad* a further stratification of the mind as enacted in its states of being: waking, dreaming, and sleeping. Though the neurosciences in the last twenty years displayed a growing interest in the brain's function through oneiric states, the self in philosophy is primarily interpreted as the awake self. Descartes' Cogito, reached through the dream argument—the acknowledgement that our perceptions are not reliable as the source of truth because we cannot exclude the possibility that we are immersed now in an illusory lifelike dream—could be represented as the apex of wakefulness,[35] providing incontrovertible and undeceiving evidence of my presence to myself. Indian philosophy, from its early roots in the Vedic literature, shows an interest in the definition of the states of consciousness, without necessarily privileging the awakened state. In the oneiric state, the self reveals itself as being able to create its own world and illuminate itself with its own light. The deep sleep, according to the *Māṇḍūkya Upaniṣad*, is not absence of awareness,

---

34 Jonardon Ganeri, *The Self: Naturalism, Consciousness, and the First-Person Stance*, Oxford: Oxford University Press, 2015, pp. 328–329.
35 See Jacques Derrida, *Writing and Difference*, London and New York: Routledge, 1978, pp. 36–76.

since self-consciousness is a flame that cannot be extinguished, but only the absence of the witness-consciousness and its subsequent separation between subject and object. There is, therefore, a subtle, latent, and pervasive modality of being-a-self, which is a hint of a fourth state of the mind, the pure nondual awareness beyond limitations of the cosmic self. "Unseen, inviolable, unseizable, signless, unthinkable, unnamable, its essence resting in the one self, the stilling of proliferation, peaceful, gracious (*śiva*), without duality (*advaita*)," this pure awareness reveals the authentic nature of self as light, standing apart from attachment to fleeting experiences, serving instead as "the constant, underlying source for these changing states."[36] This analysis of the states of mind not only provides us with a different articulation or taxonomy of the meaning of the self, which doesn't necessarily allow us to transcend the Western epistemologically rooted paradigm, but gestures toward a metaphysical dimension of the self. This illuminated, nondual self has an ontological significance, since it distills the pure substrate of any emergence of the experiential mind. This cosmic self goes beyond the boundaries of human consciousness and bears a moral value, since it represents the authentic nature of the mind, which can be reach through meditation and practice.

The existence of a superior state of mind, which transcends the subject-object divide in the cognitive self, reveals itself in a quiescent and mysterious way in the everyday experience of the continuum of consciousness through dream and deep sleep, and this hint can be singled out and expanded, sharpening our mind in meditation exercises. Ramesh Chandra Pradhan, in his *Metaphysics of Consciousness. The Indian Vedantic Perspective*, claims that "the contemporary theories of mind have not been successful in unfolding the truth of consciousness because of their naturalist and physicalist or materialist commitments. These theories have denied to the mind and consciousness [...] their autonomy and creativity and their propensity to evolve into higher mind and consciousness."[37] Outlining the major theories that have impacted

---

[36] Evan Thompson, *Waking, Dreaming, Being: New Light on the Self and Consciousness from Neuroscience, Meditation, and Philosophy*, New York: Columbia University Press, 2014, Fourth Section.

[37] Ramesh Chandra Pradhan, *Metaphysics of Consciousness. The Indian Vedantic Perspective*, Singapore: Springer Nature, 2020, pos. 37.

the contemporary Western understanding of mind and consciousness, the author highlights how physicalist reductionism and research into neural correlates of consciousness do not fulfill the ceaseless quest for a higher level of mind visible in the Western history of thought, from Plato to Hegel, from literature to religion. This framework set aside the moral and spiritual dimensions of the self, denying or neglecting the superstructures of consciousness, which embody values and meanings of life. Taking advantage of the Indian Advaita Vedanta tradition, the author suggests we consider the intuition of an absolute cosmic consciousness, which is transcendent and immanent to the universe. The immanence of this higher dimension should be interpreted in a dynamic way, thinking of the human self as an evolutionary process aiming for a higher metaphysical stage.

The practical and methodological path to a wider horizon of self is depicted in the volume *The Oxford Handbook of Hypo-egoic Phenomena*,[38] which expounds and analyzes the experiences that arise when the dominance of a self-focused, egocentric, heteronomous understanding of consciousness is diminished. These include states such as flow, equanimity, mindfulness, compassion, and mystical experiences. These phenomena can be reached only if we abandon the idea of a cognitive ego-pole as a spotlight directing the beam on a field of more or less obscure fixed elements in favor of a broader sense of self characterized by an active involvement in the world. The editors of the anthology present the emergence of scholarship and science about hypo-egoic phenomena as an underdeveloped yet highly promising field of research. Significantly, the first essay of the volume, "Moderating Ego in East and South Asia: Metaphysical Habits of the Earth" by Owen Flanagan and Philip J. Ivanhoe is devoted not to Western traditions of thought, but on Early Buddhist and Chinese ideas of "no self" and "oneness" instead. If in Buddhist thought the self is deflated once it is seen as an impermanent manifestation of the ever-changing flux of the cosmos, in Chinese Song-Ming Neo-Confucianism, it is ethically enlarged to become coextensive with the universe, seeking to actively experience itself as one body with heaven, earth, and all things. In both cases, the atomism and individualism often involved in the Western

---

38 Kirk Warren Brown and Mark R. Leary (eds), *The Oxford Handbook of Hypo-egoic Phenomena*, Oxford: Oxford University Press, 2016.

tradition cannot be addressed and challenged only through a theoretical perspective. According to the authors, Buddhist and Neo-Confucian teachings require a practice of self-cultivation in order to acquire a new, all-encompassing habit or tendency of the heart. The apex of this practice in life is to gain evidence of cosmic oneness, in which I am a responsive and creative part of the universe, which unfolds itself, and which is embodied in the interdependence and shared fate of all sentient beings. The emphasis on preserving the dynamicity of the principle and the idea of thought as the path of self-realization is efficaciously expressed in the concept of the performative self. Elaborating on Buddhist Yogācāra sources, Thompson suggests that the statements based on the constellation I-Me-Mine are not referential or descriptive of a substantial identity, but on the contrary are "performative utterances," the practice itself of becoming a self: "[...] the function of the term 'I' is to enact a self. To think or say 'I' is to engage in a self-individuating and self-appropriating form of I-making. [...]. Again, the self isn't an object or a thing: it's a process—the process of 'I-ing' or ongoing self-appropriating activity."[39] This performative paradigm that refuses the concept of the self as an independently existing thing is radically different from the eliminativist theory, which denies the existence of an ego because it is deemed as irretrievable in the neural background of the brain, what Thompson calls "neuronihilism," stigmatizing its tendency to "overintellectualize our experience." This "I," conceived not as a substantive but as a verb, requires us to inhabit this activity of "making-I" without attachment to any fixed "I"-image or model. It is a praxis conducive to a process of enlightenment, because it entails that we uninterruptedly wake up from the reifying illusion of the self-as-object, in order to realize our authentic self.

Summing up, the contribution of these comparative essays to the contemporary debate about the self constitutes more of a paradigm shift than an alternative epistemological frame. Some suggestions, like the value accorded to specific states of mind, like dreaming and sleeping, as the bearers of a truth about the self, or the idea of a performative self, could be isolated, adopted, and subsumed in several contemporary theories of self. However, it would be reductive to consider non-Western philosophies as a mere reservoir of tantalizing intuitions, which can

---

39   Evan Thompson, *Waking, Dreaming, Being*, pos. 7404.

be drawn upon in order to solve some baffling conundrums posed by Western debates on consciousness. The most valuable insight they provide us is the challenge to the centrality of epistemology in our idea of the self. Is it universally true that "Ontology collapses in epistemology," or is this merely the inevitable outcome of our pristine and unquestioned reliance on the Cogito as the foundation of our inner life? From this viewpoint, the scattered clues emerging from these limited comparative attempts resemble cracks in the vault of the cognitive self's seclusion, faintly revealing a neglected fourth dimension shining through.

2. Mou Zongsan and the *Critique of the Cognitive Mind*

2.1 Towards a New Philosophy of Mind

In the first chapter, we analyzed three major questions raised by contemporary philosophy of mind research. These questions epitomize the most challenging aspects of the conundrum called "self" or "I." Firstly, is the idea of ego as a permanent core of mental life necessary to explain our inner experience, or can we consider our mental life as a spontaneously self-organizing process preceding or substituting the emergence of an ego? Secondly, in which way do we recognize and know ourselves? In the same way that we know any other being—i.e., by objectifying and contemplating ourself through an ideal mirror—or do we perhaps possess a pre-reflective non-objectifying acquaintance with ourself? Finally, is my own self a secluded inner domain, or is it structurally interconnected with the world? All these questions are formulated in a philosophical reference frame characterized by the primacy of epistemology, and the often-conflicting answers they received share at least one premise: the most basic relationship between the self and the world is knowledge.

This book has a dual aim: first, to elucidate in a comparative and critical manner Mou Zongsan's view on the question of self; second, to propose his theorical contribution as an alternative way, deeply rooted in Chinese tradition of thought, of approaching this challenging question. This chapter is devoted to analyzing a pivotal work of Mou Zongsan, *Critique of the Cognitive Mind*. The choice of this work as a departing point for my research is not trivial. From a biographical viewpoint, *Critique of the Cognitive Mind* represents the most systematic outcome of the earlier phase in Mou's philosophical path, which is focused on logical and epistemological questions. From a methodological viewpoint, this work is very suitable for comparative analysis. As the title suggests, this work precedes the elaboration of the "moral metaphysics," which Mou will consider to be his original and distinctive contribution to the philosophical debate, and still revolves around the development of the cognitive self. For this reason, it may aptly work as a bridge, joining the Western epistemologically-oriented paradigm, and the process of "verticalization," i.e., the performative and metaphysic reorientation imparted by Mou in his developed understanding of the question of self. The first two main questions raised in contemporary philosophy of mind, i.e., the nature of ego and the problem of self-consciousness, find here a preliminary solution, which sets the stage for later developments.

However, in this attempt to pursue an epistemologically-driven philosophy of self, we may easily detect an inner tension which cannot be satisfyingly solved inside this horizontal framework. The human self, in this work, emerges first and foremost as a self-constituting and self-transcending process. It is a living and organic force aiming beyond itself. The cognitive ego with its reflexive self-consciousness is a logical structure produced by this flowing, pre-reflexively self-aware processual mind in order to acquire objectivity and universality. If this attempt is doomed to fail, it is because there is an insoluble oscillation between the fixed logical structure and the dynamism of self that brims over and exceeds its self-limitation. The only possible solution that Mou foreshadows in the final part of this work, is the passage to a different, moral-metaphysical dimension. Only through this reassessment can the need for objectivity and universality be finally satisfied through the practical actualization of the moral self, and the intuitive discovery of its infinite resonance with the universe.

Another question which is worth mentioning here is the translation of the key term *xin* 心. In sinological studies, the term *xin* 心 is often translated as "heart-mind." The aim is to transmit the specificity of the idea of mind in Classical Chinese thought. The character for *xin* 心 graphically represents a heart, and the rendition "heart-mind" emphasizes that *xin* is not reducible to an abstract faculty of understanding, but is at the same time the seat of cognition and feelings, emotions, and desires. In opposition to Western mainstream philosophy, which often highlights the dyadic opposition between mind and body, the term "heart-mind" is meant to express the inseparability of mind and body in Chinese philosophy, as well as its moral and practical character. In this book, I prefer to consistently translate the word *xin* as "mind." There are three reasons for this:

1. Mou in his works employs the word *xin* not only in referring to Classical thought (where the translation "heart-mind" could be perfectly suitable), but also in pivotal expressions which are usually translated by scholars simply as "mind." Some examples are: *xinxue* 心學 (the Neo-Confucian School of Mind), *xin ji li* 心及理 ("mind is the principle," the fundamental tenet of the School of Mind), *xinxingxue* 心性學 ("the doctrine of mind and nature"), *yi xin kai er men* 一心開二門 ("one mind opening two gates," the main teaching of the Buddhist scripture *Awakening of Faith*).

2. In Mou's works *xin* as an isolated word refers primarily to the moral mind. However, Mou's thought is based on a dualism between a "cognitive mind" (認識心、識心) or "finite mind" (有限心) and a "moral infinite mind" (本體之心、本心、无限智心). Any comparison between the two, as well as the derivation of the cognitive mind from the self-limitation of the moral mind, would be impossible without a general underlying concept of mind preceding the distinction. The aim of this book is to contrast Western knowledge-based philosophies of mind and Mou's vertical moral-metaphysical idea of mind. I suggest that Mou's moral metaphysics, with its effort of verticalization, may represent an effective response to some insurmountable conundrums embedded in contemporary philosophy of mind. This implies a semantic continuity and comparability between Chinese and Western ideas of *xin*/mind as the spiritual faculty of knowing, feeling, and acting. The possibility of such a comparison is at the core of Mou's philosophical endeavor itself, as Mou passionately states in *Nineteen Lectures on Chinese Philosophy*: "In the development of the vision of Western Philosophy, Kantian philosophy moved Western philosophy one step forward. However, if we wish to move Kantian philosophy a step forward, we must allow it and Chinese philosophy to mutually agitate, combine,

and harmonized. In addition, if we want to enrich Chinese philosophy by moving it forward, thus ensuring that it has a future, we must allow it to connect to the Western, Kantian philosophy. This kind of communication between cultures will reveal the importance of the Buddhist framework of 'one mind opening two gates.'"[1]

3. I consider therefore Western "mind" and Chinese "heart-mind" not as two separate concepts, but as two gates opened by the same *xin*. In this work I constantly emphasize the embodied, practical, performative, and holistic nature of Mou's mind. I do not feel it necessary to introduce a separate word for this "vertical mind," since I think that, at least in the context of this work, the specificity entailed in the expression "heart-mind" can be preserved through the medium of conceptual distinctions.

2.2 Structure and Significance of the *Critique of the Cognitive Mind*

Critique of the Cognitive Mind (*Renshixin zhi pipan* 認識心之批判)[2] is a critical essay by Mou Zongsan devoted to epistemological questions. The thrust of the argument describes the bottom-up process of constituting the logical self. This process starts from the basic physiological contact and mutual exchange between things and the percipient kernel of the self, and follows the development of this percipient mind through

---

[1] 就西方哲學理境的發展,康德哲學確實使西方哲學往前推進一步,可是若要使康德哲學再往前推進,則必須與中國哲學互相摩盪,互相結合;同時,要使得中國哲學更充實,更往前推進,亦必須與西方康德哲學相接頭,如此才能往下傳續。這種文化的交流,正顯出佛教「一心開二門」這一架構的重要性。Mou Zongsan (牟宗三), *Zhongguo zhexue shijiu jiang*. 中國哲學十九講 (Nineteen Lessons on Chinese Philosophy), *Mou Zongsan xiansheng quanji*. 牟宗三先生全集 (Complete Works of Mou Zongsan), vol. XXIX, Taipei: Lianhe baoxi wenhua jijin hui, 2003, p. 311. Translated by Esther C. Su in: Mou Zongsan, *Nineteen Lectures on Chinese Philosophy: A Brief Outline of Chinese Philosophy and the Issues It Entails*, Scotts Valley, CA: CreateSpace Independent Publishing Platform, 2015, p. 323.

[2] Mou Zongsan (牟宗三), *Renshi xin zhi pipan*. 認識心之批判 (Critique of the Cognitive Mind), 2 vols, *Mou Zongsan xiansheng quanji*. 牟宗三先生全集 (Complete Works of Mou Zongsan), vols XVIII–XIX, Taipei: Lianhe baoxi wenhua jijin hui, 2003.

the stages of intuition, imagination, and understanding. Reaching the intellectual level of understanding, the mind is finally able to constitute the a-priori structure of the phenomenal world as opposed to its reflexive self-awareness, the logical self. Although the epistemological foundation of the cognitive self is attained, Mou Zongsan argues that it is precisely the nature of the mind as a dynamic, self-transcending process that ultimately determines the structural incompleteness of the cognitive realm. Since the horizontal incrementation of knowledge can only endlessly repropose the issue, this incompleteness provides us with a hint of the existence of a third dimension, that vertically transcends the effort of the logical self and brings it to accomplishment through the all-permeating power of the moral self. From the viewpoint of the logical self, since our knowledge is rooted in the finite world of phenomena, we can only foreshadow this uppermost dimension, speaking about the ultimate substance of moral self in a tentative and apophatic way.

The methodology adopted by Mou Zongsan—following and illuminating from within the development of the cognitive mind—is distinctive. Though he starts from the basic layer of sensibility, he does not adopt a reconstructive method like Immanuel Kant, tidily arranging, layer by layer, faculties of the mind in an architectonical way. Though inheriting the terminology of Kant's transcendental thought, Mou is aware that the mind is in flux, an evolving dynamic process, in which the phenomenal world as a manifestation is indissolubly intertwined with the increasing complexity of the mind as the locus of manifestation. This strict interrelation is frequently depicted, as we will see, as a task and a responsibility of the mind, which aims to preserve the integrity of this manifestative event, and to provide an ultimate place for its object to settle down and disclose itself as an objective and universal totality of meaning. The percipient activity of the mind (xinjue 心覺) and the flow of things and events are represented as two interacting streams proceeding forward. In both, perception plays a transcendental role, extracting and refining the meaning of the phenomenal world, making it more and more universal and linguistically shareable. The cognitive mind, produced by the inflection and self-limiting of the moral mind, is not a secluded compartment ruled only by abstract logical principles and with the restricted scope of increasing knowledge. It is like a two-dimensional horizontal section of the all-including sphere of the mind of Dao, lacking its ultimate perfection, but at the same time retaining and displaying some of its characteristics. Mou adopts two metaphorical clusters to express these features that exceed the pure epistemological and descriptive domain: the stream and weaving. The imagery of the stream and liquidity conveys the never-ending dynamicity of the mind, whereas the imagery linked to weaving expresses the interlace of subjective and objective dimensions, and the relentless search of a thread that penetrates and runs through the tissue of reality. Both images suggest that perception (*jue* 覺), as the general cognitive activity of the mind, is a lively and dynamic process, which is interwoven with reality and aims at valuing and preserving its permanent meaning. Though the cognitive mind is primarily oriented toward knowledge, and cannot transcend its logical boundaries, it nonetheless retains a trace of the moral nature of the transcendent mind, produced through its inflection and self-limitation. This trace manifests as a task entailing a moral-like effort. The main driving force and goal pursued by the mind is the "objectivation" (*keganhua* 客觀化) of reality through the attainment of self-objectivation (*ziwo keguanhua* 自我客觀化) in the reflexive self. Objectivation here is not a synonym for objectification or reification: the scope of the mind is not subjugating and reducing reality, and itself, to a passive and static object; on the contrary, it is guaranteeing a heuristic validation and a stable foundation for meaning, i.e., for the universal quintessence of the world in the cognitive realm. The subsequent passages in the evolution of the mind are expressed through verbs rather that nouns: the mind limits itself, springs out, assimilates, illuminates, emanates formal frames in order to preserve, refine, grasp, stabilize, and settle the flux of things. The architectonic structure of the Kantian "critique of pure reason," subdivided into faculties and hierarchical layers, is replaced by an ever-changing ebb and flow of activities and tasks. The self-constitution of the logical self as the disclosure of meaning is not an endpoint; rather, it flows back to permeate and illuminate the entire process, weaving a unifying thread through the tissue of reality.

    A word that vividly expresses connection and interrelation as a tidal movement is *gantong* (感通). Mou uses this word at the beginning of *Critique of the Cognitive Mind* to remark the two-sided dynamism of stimulus-and-response, which is the primal elementary relationship between the self and reality. The starting point of knowledge is this living contact and fluid exchange that precedes any separation between subject and object. We will see in further chapters the full significance acquired by *gantong* and *ganying* (感應) in the context of the theoretical history of Confucianism according to Mou. In this early context, *gan* (感) generally means the cognitive state of "sensation" or "affection." However, in contrast to passivity and receptivity, which is usually the distinguishing feature of sensation in Western epistemology, *gan* 感 in Chinese philosophy is endowed with a wider spectrum of meanings, highlighting the active and transitive nature of sensation. As a verb, *gan* 感 expresses the co-occurrence of activity and passivity in the sense of touch, in which "moving" and "being moved" coalesce in an inextricable correspondence. The sense of "being responsive" and "being open" to the contact with the other is involved too, and clearly illustrates how Chinese thought represents reality as a harmonious interrelation between earth, heaven, and human being. The presence of the radical of "heart" or "mind" in the character *gan* 感 reveals that reality, already in its inchoate manifestation, is not a lifeless object contraposed to the spirit (like in the German word *Gegenstand*). On the contrary, it always entails the spiritual resonance between things and the mind, made possible through the flow of spiritual energy *qi* 氣, which constitutes things and sentient beings.

Furthermore, Huaiyu Wang writes: "[In the Ancient Chinese texts], the major meanings of *tong* are 'to reach,' 'pass through,' 'open,' and 'transmit,' and 'to correspond,' 'communicate,' and 'interact,' as well as 'to comprehend.' As a noun, *tong* refers to 'a passage,' 'a thoroughfare,' or 'a hole'—an opening or orifice that runs through and discloses the internal body of a thing. The core meaning boils down to an open way of transmission among different bodies and locations."[3] Placing *gantong* 感通 at the outset of his inquiry, Mou Zongsan implicitly declares that we are always in the midst of the compenetration of mind and reality. After the event of self-limiting the moral mind, the gaze from above is precluded, and the only way to reconstruct the evolving path of the cognitive mind is to dwell in the dimension created by this inflection of the moral self. This dimension is limitless in width, allowing an incremental advancement of the double fluxes of reality and mind,

---

[3] Huaiyu Wang, "Ren and Gantong: Openness of Heart and the Root of Confucianism," *Philosophy East and West* 62:4 (2012), 463–504 (p. 464).

which are without end. We can only identify a point of departure in the act of sensorial contact, adopt a phenomenological perspective from inside the living experience, and proceed forward.

The germinal condition of the experience is rooted in the indissoluble relationship between physiological facts and the physiological self. Mou Zongsan distances himself from naïve realism, according to which, at the core of the cognitive experience, there is a contact between the human mind and an already existing and structured thing. On the contrary, he places in the event of sensation the point of mutual constitution of mind and facts. Any specific thing arisen (*shengqi* 生起) by the physiological sensation manifests itself in the horizon of the physiological self, or percipient kernel. As we will see, Mou, in making use of the term "self" to indicate the subjective pole of perception, explicitly declares that this terminology is tentative and evocative. At this primary level, an independent self does not exist, because in the sensorial cognition the self is merely an aggregate of physiological facts, and the concrete thing is an aggregate of physical facts. In the event of contact and perception these aggregates coalesce and manifest themselves at the same time as a mutual compenetration. My sensorial cognition cannot transcend the general horizon of this fleeting manifestation in order to become a transcendental principle of actualization. Mou thoroughly compares his position and George Berkeley's idealistic tenet *esse est percipi* (to be is to be perceived), remarking that the simultaneous emergence of mind and thing in sensation represents a merely epistemological proof of the coincidence between existing, in the sense of becoming apparent and perceiving. The insuperable limit of our cognitive process resides in the fact that in the mutual exchange of the contact, we have only an ability to manifest things, but not a metaphysical creative power. We are therefore not allowed to transcend the cognitive dimension in order to hypothesize an ontological coincidence of being and knowing. We can only recognize that the cognitive mind develops gradually, starting from this node joining the simultaneous manifestation of me and the thing.

From here, the structure of the cognitive mind is articulated in three stages: intuition, imagination, and intellect. All the cognitive acts performed at every level are called, in a general way, "perception" or "apperception" (*tongjue* 統覺). The defining characteristics of intuitive apperceptions are passivity and receptivity, as they are intended to assimilate directly and without deviation: "straight and no curve" (*zhi er wu qu* 直而無曲). They do not involve any dialectical process of thought, nor can they actively generate space, time, or the *a priori* structures of concepts. The function of intuition is to faithfully assimilate and preserve the object that arises through sensorial contact. The thing grasped through intuitive apperception does not have transcendental conditions, nor new, concrete content, but only receives and preserves the dynamic homogeneous flux of things. Though the arisen thing is fleeting and instantaneously appears and disappears, a shadow or imagination perdures in the perception. Through this image (or representation, *biaoxiang* 表象), intuitive apperception can assimilate and illuminate (*zhaoshe* 照射) this fleeting thing, and therefore is able to autonomously provide us with its enduring significance. Since intuition lacks argumentative/predicative (*bianlun* 辯論) deviations and can faithfully receive the process of the thing, this meaning does not rely on the necessity imposed by the intellect. It possesses, however, the adequacy/determinacy (*quedingxing* 確定性) of intuition—allowing us to preserve the enduring meanings that run like a thread through the uninterrupted flux of things. In order to accomplish this activity of preservation and formal conservation through the representation/image, the cognitive mind aims at prolonging and extending them (*pingpu er wei yi guangyuan zhi yi duan* 平鋪而為一廣延之一段), or in other words, spatializing and making the representation perdure in time. The meaning is subordinate to the immediate perception, but is limited to the subjective viewpoint, and cannot become objective and universal. In order to objectivate itself, perception should become active and productive, generating the *a priori* condition of space-time.

In the cognitive process, fleeting things can perdure in the mind as permanent meaning. "Imagination is collecting together the things and synthesizing them in the apperception in the shape of a memory."[4] Imagination has two modalities, empirical imagination and transcendental imagination. Empirical imagination does not create or emanate anything; it passively follows the flux of memories, collects them in form of a memory (recollection), assimilates them in a static manner, and constitutes an imaginative apperception in the mind. If

---

4   Mou Zongsan, *Critique of the Cognitive Mind*, I, 89.

we want that these acts of passive assimilation, moment for moment (*yi hu yi hu* 一忽一忽), become a capacity freely extended in space and time, our imagination should restore its creativity/productivity and emanate the *a priori* forms of spatio-temporality. Transcendental imagination is the source of space and time. Not only does the *a priori* structure of space-time emanate from transcendental imagination, but this imaginative force actively compenetrates and molds our experience as well, providing real beings with their fundamental spatio-temporal character. However, these spatial and temporal forms only determine the exterior aspect of the relationship between things; they cannot penetrate or reveal the genuine internal connections between representations (*shixiang* 示相) or fully objectivate themselves. Intuitive apprehension halts at the preservation of the arisen things, and then crystallizes, so that the human mind must ascend to a broader level. As for intuitive apperception, transcendental imagination, after generating the formal determination of space-time, condenses and stiffens. Moreover, perception must leap beyond this blockage or cessation, to penetrate the intellectual apperception of conceptual thought. On the level of intellect/understanding, to perfectly accomplish its self-objectivation, the intellect must objectivate and universalize its object.

In the dynamic process of the intellect, we have an empirical and a transcendental aspect as well. The empirical concept accompanies and aligns itself with the concrete content of the stream of real beings. This empirical mind has objective content, but the mind itself is still in a subjective state. In this not yet active stream, the content of the mind may have an objective meaning, but the mind itself has not yet objectivated itself.[5] Only when the mind emanates a pure principle can it objectivate itself, and endow imagination or phenomena with an objective and universal aspect (*biaoshi* 表示). It should emanate from itself the logical system of rules, forms, and concepts, in order to control its own *a priori* dynamism. Pure concepts are not determinative rules emerging from the external world, but the inner dynamic structure of the cognitive mind grasping itself. Only at this point does the mind start becoming the objective mind, or the logical mind. The system of pure concepts of rational thought (*lijie sikao* 理解思考) represents a dialectical deviation

---

5　認識心, 若只視之為一順曆的動用之流, 或只自經驗一面而觀之, 則無不意象之紛紜, 識神之恍惚。變滅無常, 漫無定準. Ibid., I, 95.

(*sibian* 思辨). Through this curvature, the mind returns to itself, firmly possesses itself. It is not only "in itself" but "for itself," i.e., it becomes a logical self. In this absolute subjectivity, mind and principle are the same, and subject and object are the same, because it has the pure principle of itself as content. In the act of becoming a logical self, the mind penetrates through the exterior forms of space and time, and enters the inner relation of the phenomenon. In this way, the phenomenon finally becomes an objective substance of the real world. From the intuitive apperception to the apperception of intellectual thought, the cognitive mind fully manifests the oneness and all-compenetration of the spirit: "Mind (*Xinjue*) only when it reaches the final objectivation can become the starting point of the objective use. From this mind can descend and collect together layer after layer, retrocessing to the intuitive apperception and collecting it together. Actually, there is only one mind, and only in its being connected with the object and manifesting its transcendental ability, can it manifest itself in every stadium/layer and modality."[6]

2.3 Perception and Apperception

In the third chapter, Mou formulates for the first time his theory of apperception, remarking that "Perception and apperception are synonyms." This expression plays a pivotal role in Mou's epistemological system. Contrary to the transcendental apperception theorized by Kant in *Critique of Pure Reason*, Mou's apperception does not represent the apex of an epistemological system or the purest outcome of understanding, but it is from the very beginning strictly correlated with the fundamental concepts of the theory of knowledge. First of all, we should briefly analyze the use and significance of "perception" or "mental perception" in Mou's *Critique*. This is one of the terms that occurs more frequently in the text of the *Critique*. The reason is that it plays a role that is very elementary and at the same time all-embracing, because it denotes the life of the cognitive mind in its quintessence. Mou previously claimed that the cognitive mind has perception as its essence and "reaching the thing and knowing it" as a function. Given that the

---

[6] 心覺, 至其終極的客觀化時, 始可作為其客觀運用之起點, 由之以層層下貫, 直貫至『直覺的統覺』而後止。原來只是一心, 唯在其關涉於對象, 而顯示其超越的機能時, 才顯為種種階段與形態。Ibid., I, 93.

cognitive mind is a dynamic process, essence and function are not two separate and contiguous dimensions, like a substance and its attributes in Aristotelian logic, but they compenetrate to restore the holistic life of the mind. From the very beginning, in the physiological sphere, and throughout the stages of intuition, imagination, and understanding, perception always represents the active manifestation of the mind. It should however not be interpreted as a subjective function separated from perceived reality, because as we saw before, mind and reality are always mutually echoing, responding, and interacting. Writing that the function of the mind is to reach and understand reality implies that perception is structurally endowed with intentionality and directionality toward the thing. It means that, from a phenomenological viewpoint, perceptual dynamism precedes the separation and opposition of subject and object. Perception illuminates the outline of things (*zhaoshe* 照射), and synthetically absorbs their determined characteristics. In the intuitive mode of the mind, it truthfully grasps and safeguards the flux of reality in its suchness (*ruru* 如如), i.e., in its pure being, what it is without any external addition. Things rise and fall, are produced through causes and fleetingly exist as a row of impermanent events. In order to preserve its ontological meaning and provide it with a place to dwell, perception emanates space and time. Extended in space and lasting in time, the meaning, the perceived semantic backbone of reality, still lacks a necessary reason (*liyou* 理由) and a guiding principle that justifies its objective value, and perception emanates therefore the pure logical undergirding of everything that exists.

The logical self, which synthesizes and identifies all categories, is the supreme achievement of the cognitive mind, and at the same time, the ultimate enactment of perception. It is noteworthy that in manifesting meaning, perception reveals itself not as a single act, but as an oscillating process, because to extricate and retain the meaning of reality, perception must simultaneously return on itself. Indeed, grasping the meaning of the thing necessarily implies that the scattered stimulations received through experience are collected, ordered, and harmonized through the unifying activity of the mind. Perception is not passively subjected to physical causes and effects in order to manifest a meaning, but, on the contrary, has an autonomous and self-manifesting ability and power of spontaneity, i.e., perception is a faculty with inner dynamism. Through provoking the phenomenon, perception grasps its meaning, so that the object of perception is not a chaotic plurality without inner relations, but a unitary relational complexity bound together through the dynamic of the cognitive mind actively unifying and synthesizing. Mou calls this dynamic function "apperception." It is worth noting that apperception's dynamism of "living spiritual perception grasping intentionality and returning on itself" does not add any concrete content. Not only is the meaning revealed through apperception not an additional new conceptual implication in meaning, but it does not entail any supplementary *a priori* condition or boundary either. Perception is from its germinal manifestation, before the emanation of the *a priori* forms, related and aimed at the meaning. If the object of perception is meaning and not real things, as Mou highlights several times, perception should necessarily be an apperception, because the realm of meaning can only be perceived in self-aware dynamism.

The pivotal significance of the merging of perception and apperception (i.e., self-awareness) in Mou's text requires reference to the Western epistemological tradition. In the *Critique of the Cognitive Mind*, Mou constantly confronts authors who have worked with this epistemological concept, sometimes in an explicit way, as is the case with Gottfried Wilhelm Leibniz, David Hume, and Kant, and sometimes in an implicit way, adopting and creatively reshaping its terminology. The word "apperception" was introduced in the philosophical dictionary by Leibniz to indicate the reflexive act through which I become aware of my perceptions, which in themselves can also remain unnoticed. My apperception of a specific sound is composed of many small perceptions of which I am unaware. The apperception is a specific form of perception characterized through its clarity, distinctness, and its self-consciousness. While perceptions also belong to animals and plants, apperception is unique to the human being. Every perception is accompanied by the peculiar ability of paying attention to and reflecting on perception. As a reflexive "perception of perception," apperception is, for Leibniz, the ultimate foundation of consciousness and the ego. In the Kantian epistemological system, transcendental apperception, or "I think," is the supreme unifying function of the intellect: "It must be possible for the 'I think' to accompany all my representations: because otherwise something would be represented within me that could not be thought at all, in other words, the representation would either be impossible, or at least would be nothing to me. [...]. I also call the unity of apperception the transcendental unity of self-consciousness, in order to indicate that *a priori* knowledge can be obtained from it. For the manifold representations given in an intuition would not one and all be 'my' representations, if they did not all belong to one self-consciousness."[7] According to Kant, having a representation implies that I can add the "I think" before this representation. Only if I can coherently form the phrase "I think X" can I say that X is my representation. Compared to the Kantian formulation, we notice, first of all, that apperception, in Mou's thought, does not belong to the faculty of understanding as its synthesizing vertex; neither does it imply the production of an *a priori* condition, because at any stage of the cognitive mind—intuition, imagination, or understanding—perception is apperception, i.e., it possesses an autonomous unifying power and entails the self-conscious activity of the mind: "In this homogeneous flux, in every modality of apparition, sensation or perception, imagination or intellect, always there is an apperceptive function."[8] Apperception cannot be reduced to a formal *a priori* condition, but it is the activity of the mind itself in its functionality, usefulness, and appearance (*dongyong* 動用; *biaoxiang* 示相). Apperception is the modality through which the object manifests itself in the knowing mind. The expression "functionality" (*dongyong*) highlights that apperception is actually useful and a dynamic structure of the mind. Mou carefully demonstrates that in the mind, substance and function are one and the same. Apperception is not the external appearance or concrete quality of a subject already existing, but it indicates the act through which the world undergoes a unifying process, through which a meaning luminously discloses itself. At the same time, since the cognitive mind is this act itself, apperception means that the mind too in this unifying movement reveals and illuminates itself. In apperception, the mind, like a lamp, illuminates itself in illuminating its object. If apperception denotes a form of self-awareness, does it imply

---

7 Immanuel Kant, *Critique of Pure Reason*, London: Palgrave Macmillan, 2007, pp. 152–153.
8 在此同質的等流上, 有種種變形, 如感覺或知覺、想像、理解, 些是其變形。在此, 不論其變形如何, 總是一個統覺之用 [⋯]。Mou Zongsan, *Critique of the Cognitive Mind*, I, 86.

that the cognitive mind is necessarily conscious of itself in every single act, and therefore possesses a double object, i.e., the meaning and itself? Are we allowed to say that, like in Kant, apperception entails a reflexive movement, so that perception can be the object of itself? Is a "self" or an "ego" operating in every activity of the mind? And if not, why are we easily induced into this error?

2.4 Self-Consciousness and Psychological States

One of the greatest differences between Mou and Kant is that for Mou, apperception is not limited to the level of intellect, because at any stage perception is structurally apperception: "Elevating from the stage of physiological sensation, we meet intuitive apperception, memory, and imagination (empirical and transcendental) that jump out (*tiaoqi* 挑起) and transcend, and they are apperceptions. In transcending the imaginative apperception, we reach the conceptual thought of the intellect, which is as well apperception. The entire dynamism of mental perception (*xinjue*) is apperception."[9] Before introducing the question of self and reflexive self-consciousness in the *Critique of the Cognitive Mind* we should pay attention to a decisive distinction made by Mou between perception/apperception and psychological states. Mou further distances himself from Kant here. In *Critique of Pure Reason*, besides introducing the idea of transcendental apperception, Kant uses the expression "sensible apperception" in order to describe the object of inner sensibility, which is the psychological subjectivity. Mou elaborates an interesting distinction between apperception and psychological states, which implies that what is given in my inner sensibility, for example a state of pain, cannot be confused with apperception. This leads ultimately to a formulation of the self-consciousness in apperceptive acts that exclude any reference to self-reflection. This has decisive implications for the idea of self in the *Critique*. In our experience, argues Mou, it is very easy to confuse perception with the psychological states associated with it. My perception of pain, for example, is at the same time both perception and psychological state. Since the pain is not an

---

9 [...] 順生理感而起者, 亦名直覺的統覺。自此而跳起之記憶與想像 (經驗的或超越的), 亦名統覺。自想像之統覺而跳起者為理解之概念的思考, 此亦名統覺。自心覺活動言, 些名統覺。Ibid., I, 97.

external phenomenon, the word "pain" would be meaningless if pain does not manifest itself in the psychological horizon of the mind. Only in the dynamism of mental perception can pain appear as an internal phenomenon and an object of the inner sensibility. Mou claims that pain is a trace and a shadow: a trace that perception leaves in the inner sensibility as well as the shadow projected by the object of perception in the mind. Given the embodied nature of sensibility, there is an inner direct relation between the phenomenal world and the psychological effect it produces in my inner sensibility. Pain, just like the thing that elicits it, is a concrete event emerging from causes. There is, therefore, an ontological homogeneity between the flux of things and pain as the object of inner sensibility. To explain this psychological state, I should use the inner *a priori* form of time and the *a priori* relationship of causality. On the contrary, the act of perceiving in the "perception of pain" represents a rupture in the homogeneous flux of the caused events, and it is therefore heterogeneous and cognitively transcendent with respect to reality.

Perception, as we said, is the dynamic substance of the mind, a pure activity disentangled from any web of causation. Perception is not subordinate to temporality nor explainable through a chain of causes and effects; in the stages of imagination and understanding, it is perception that actively produces and emanates the transcendental conditions of space, time, and categories. Perception in the cognitive process cannot play the rule of object, because it is necessarily an "ultimate subjectivity." A perceptive act can never become an object for the inner sensibility, but it is, on the contrary, the transcendental condition of possibility of the inner sensibility. Perception evades any attempt to grasp it as an object, and it is therefore structurally elusive. However, what is given through perception can be echoed in the psychological realm, and it can leave a trace on inner sensibility. If, however, apperception implies a kind of self-awareness, should we deduce that perception, reflecting on itself, can at least be an object to itself?

This question provides us with the opportunity to deepen our understanding of the word apperception. Apperception for Leibniz and Kant is a reflective and redoubling "perception of perception," and it represents a cognitive dynamism that structurally entails self-reference. Mou inherits this vision in allowing that perception constitutes a pure activity that returns to itself in its very act of intentionally reaching the meaning. Does this mean that we can unfold and fully express the activity of the "perception of pain" as "perception of the perception of pain"? Can I say that, through apperception, I perceive my perception of pain? The risk involved in this movement is, according to Mou, that we may interpret the relationship between the two hypothesized acts of perception as a reflexive self-awareness. We can erroneously sustain the notion that the first "perception" has an active and subjective function, whereas the second "perception" is a passive object of the first perception. This use would be in manifest contradiction with the nature of perception, which can only play the role of an "ultimate subjectivity." "I perceive" represents a transcendence that eludes any attempt of cognitively grasping and controlling it. (This transcendence is obviously operating in the cognitive horizon and does not have a metaphysical sense.) Given that the stream of perception is always above the perceived objective world, this stream, from an ontological viewpoint, cannot crystallize in an object, and from the linguistic viewpoint it cannot absolve the function of the predicate. We should therefore discard any reflexive higher-order theory of self-consciousness. Though Mou Zongsan sometimes uses terminology that seems to refer to reflection, like retrospective manifestation (*fanshi* 反示) or "returning to itself," we should provide another interpretation of these metaphorical expressions.

As I said before, perception is like a source of light: in revealing other things, it simultaneously reveals itself as a source of irradiation. Strictly speaking, a lamp does not illuminate itself, but since it is the light itself, in irradiating the light it reveals its nature. In the same way, the mental perceptive activity through the act of perceiving manifests its own nature, or as Mou writes, "Perception has a self-revealing ability." It means that in exercising its function, it simultaneously completely discloses itself. The perception in the word "apperception" does not entail a subject-object divide, but a pure activity, a reaffirmation of an absolute subjectivity, which exists and consists in itself. Perceiving a perception is not a cognitive dynamism, but an instantiation, i.e., I cannot know "perception," but I can only actively embody and perform the act of perception. From this point of view, "perception of a perception" can be reduced simply to perception.

Why may I still fall into the trap of reflexivity? The reason for this error is, for Mou Zongsan, the confusion between perception and psychological state. We can refute that perceiving pain is the same as the psychological state of receiving the perceived thing in the inner sense. In other words, since perception is the absolute activity of emanating time, it can be instantaneously performed, but cannot be traced or leave a trace. On the contrary, the psychological state projected by perception belongs to temporality and can be "dilated to a string," traced back in memory and grasped through knowledge.

2.5 The Problem of the Self

Mou claims that in every modality of the flux of mental perception, we experience apperception and therefore self-consciousness. "In this homogeneous flux, we have different modalities (*xingtai* 形態) like sensibility, imagination and intellect, but no matter in which modality we are, the function is always apperception."[10] Though perception in its entire developmental process has the characteristics to be self-aware, why does not Mou use the expressions "sensible/intuitive self" or "imaginary self"?

Before engaging in depth with Mou's early theory of the self, we should synthesize the debate on the question of the self in Western philosophy. In the Western history of epistemology, we can distinguish two heuristic models of the self: the reflexive and the pre-reflexive model. John Locke, Leibniz, and Kant are the most eminent theorists of the reflexive model. Locke offers us a very clear version of the reflexive paradigm. He claims that human knowledge derives from only two possible sources: sensibility and reflection. When we receive the impression of an external phenomenon through our sensitive organs, we are at the same time able to perceive our self. The relation between these two cognitive processes is not only one of simultaneity, but also necessity, because in the context of cognitive dynamism, sensibility and self-consciousness of sensibility are indivisible. Reflective ideas are the original act of representation and this ability to represent means that we are able to objectivate

---

10 在此同質的等流上，有種種變形，如感覺或知覺、想像、理解，有些則是其變形。在此，不論其變形如何，總是一個統覺之用，此即所謂統覺一般。Ibid., I, 86.

the stream of consciousness, making it an object of inner knowledge. Leibniz calls "apperception" the reflective awareness of the mental act, but, as opposed to Locke, he claims that apart from sensible and introspective apperception, there also exist small perceptions, which are undetectable and devoid of consciousness. Despite refusing Locke's and Descartes' equivalence of self-consciousness and perception, he nonetheless admits that self-awareness entails a relation between a subjective and an objective consciousness. Kant inherits this reflective model. Since self-consciousness is the basis for the transcendental use of our mind, we cannot use these same transcendental conditions to define it. Self-consciousness cannot receive a representation through categories. On the contrary, the possibility itself of the categories of thought presupposes the existence of pure self-consciousness. The self here is therefore a void, a synthesizing and unifying structure; it cannot become a substantial object of self-knowledge. Articulating his theory of transcendental apperception, Kant claims that the possibility of "I think" is rooted in the separability of a subjective and objective pole in the self. "The thought of being aware of myself implies a double layer of the self, self as a subject and self as an object. When the 'I think' become object of the self, inaugurating a scission of the self in two halves, it is an undeniable fact."[11]

After Kant, Johann Gottlieb Fichte advances several critiques with respect to the internal contradiction of this reflexive model, stressing that using a reflexive model leads us into a vicious circle. We may synthesize the vicious circle of self-reflection by adopting the metaphor of the mirror. When I am reflected as an image in the mirror, in order to acknowledge the identity shared by me and the objective image reflected, I should already possess some form of knowledge of my aspect, and this seems to require a previous reflective acknowledgment, and so on. In the reflexive model, self-consciousness is the outcome of the activity of self-objectivation performed by the subjective self. The re-appropriation of itself through the acknowledgment of a perfect identity between the subjective and the objective self presupposes the existence of a standard of judgment, i.e., a familiarity with myself which, if I want to avoid an infinite regress, can only be acquired in a pre-reflective way. The quest

---

11   Immanuel Kant, *What Real Progress Has Metaphysics Made in Germany Since the Time of Leibniz and Wolff?*, New York: Abaris Books, 1983, p. 69.

for a solution to this logical conundrum led some scholars to elaborate a pre-reflexive theory of consciousness. Manfred Frank, one of the most eminent representatives of the "School of Tübingen," claims that prior to reflexive self-awareness, a sense of familiarity with ourselves should exist. This acquaintance is not a form of knowledge and does not imply a conceptual mediation, but is a form of immediate intuition. The self or ego produced in the act of self-reflection is rooted in a form of self-awareness that precedes the distinction between the subjective and objective view. Using the words of Martin Heidegger, we may call this pre-reflective awareness *sich-selbst-vor-sich-selbst-haben* ("the self possesses itself before itself").

2.6 From the Physiological Self to the Logical Self

Mou Zongsan uses the term "self" twice in his text. At the beginning of the work, he introduces the "physiological self," highlighting the characteristics and boundaries of the immanent epistemological horizon. In this horizon, we can abstractly distinguish a subjective and an objective polarity, but this distinction is not adequate in explaining the specificity of the cognitive act. We can interpret knowledge as a relation between two polarities, granted that we do not refer to an exterior relationship between two substances separated and independently subsisting, but rather an inner relation of mutual arousing and exchanging. According to Mou, the basic core of knowledge is sensibility, which should not be confused with the first level of knowledge in Kant's *Critique of the Pure Reason*. In Kant's system, sensibility could be divided into an empirical and a transcendental sensibility. Kant transcends a phenomenological description of cognitive dynamism in order to establish the *a priori* conditions of the phenomenal world. On the contrary, Mou, in his attempt to clarify the primeval level of knowledge, adopts a phenomenological method. He does not presuppose any opposition between subject and object, but attempts to illuminate the germinal state of the "contact and response" in our experience. From this viewpoint, sensibility represents an event having a spontaneous and constituting power. Not only "every specific thing manifesting itself in the core of the self is arisen by the physiological sensibility," but the self too appears (*tuxian* 凸 顯) in the dynamism of sensibility. It is worth noting that sensibility is not a transcendent principle of actualization, but only an immanent principle of manifestation. The "core of the self" provides the thing with a space of manifestation, and it is defined by this manifestative force. This space of manifestation does not equate with a subjective polarity or a transcendent substance, but denotes a living relationship between receptivity and responsivity. Mou highlights that in this relation, both physiological subjective facts and physical facts lack unity, because sensibility does not entail any synthetic process. A physical fact, like, for example, a table, is actually a bunch of physical facts and physical properties entangled together, like the subject is a bunch of psychological events. Physical facts and psychological events, in the very instant of manifestation, receive a provisional and fleeting unity. This complex subjective fact, though Mou calls it the temporary self, is actually not a proper self, because it lacks structural unity. "The physiological self is a bunch of physiological facts, called subjective facts. Imagine calling it a self, it is not actually a self. The physiological facts, from the viewpoint of the self, are subjective facts. The external things like the table, I call them physical facts. The table is a bunch of physical facts, like self is a bunch of physiological facts. There is not a stable permanent thing called table or a proper self."[12] Therefore, what Mou calls the "physiological self" it is not an authentic self but, using a tentative language which cannot assume the division of subject-object, it represents the function of the subjective polarity. Using "self" is a linguistic necessity, and Mou, in the rest of the work, does not go back to this concept.

On the contrary, Mou very often mentions the concept of the "logical self." The logical self is the apex of the self-objectivation of the cognitive mind. Perception, having emanated space and time in the transcendental imagination, transcends and becomes apperception of the conceptual thought. In purely intellectual objectivation, perception is not only a dynamism of understanding, but for the first time becomes an objective mind, a pure intellectual substance. Only if the intellect (*lijie*) emanates concepts/categories and objectivates itself can perception reach its ultimate scope and become a logical self. In *Critique of the Cognitive Mind*

---

12 生理自我即一聚生理事。此一聚生理事, 名曰主體事。假名自我, 實無所謂我也。[…] 生理事從自我方面說, 故曰主體事。外物(虛說), 譬如桌子(實說), 以對我而言, 曰物理事。桌子為一聚物理事, 亦猶自我為一聚生理事。實物無所謂桌子一常物, 亦猶無所謂自我也。Mou Zongsan, *Critique of the Cognitive Mind*, I, 3–4.

the use of "self" is very rigorous. Self-consciousness as a property is not enough for fulfilling the requirement implied by the word "self," because self is a structure based on reflexive thought. We can see that Mou adopts an "egological theory" of the self, because reflexive self-awareness is always called "apperception" but not the "self." The ineludible characteristic of the self is the inner relation between a subjective self and an objective self: "Firstly, from the viewpoint of the self-awareness, it is a single homogeneous stream, from the prescriptive viewpoint, it is an objective self-sufficient principle. Secondly, it is an absolute subjectivity containing the subjective and the objective modality, i.e., it is in itself and for itself."[13] In the cognitive horizon, the self represents an endpoint, a culmination, the last product of a process of objectivation, starting from intuitive apperception. (Obviously, from a metaphysical viewpoint, we cannot stop at this point; we have to penetrate through the logical self and ascend to a transcendent authentic self.)

In the intuitive and imaginative apperception, perception returns on itself, and is therefore "in itself," but is not yet manifestly "for itself." Apperception is a pure subjective function, and it is not able to give to itself an inner and pure principle. This pure principle cannot derive from the outer world of phenomena, otherwise there will not be an inner relation between principle and perception, and the principle will belong only to the flux of the phenomenal objects. Only when the intellect transcends imagination and emanates the pure principle, producing its own *a priori* standard, can perception objectivate itself and its object. In the horizon of the intellect, the subject is the source of the inner dynamism of the principle, fusing together the activity of the mind and the prescriptive structure of the principle. This subject does not passively correspond to the flux of things, but actively produces its objective norm, ascending and becoming an absolute cognitive subject. This is the reason why perception should reach the intellect level for becoming a logical self, because the "in itself" and "for itself" levels are reached when perception wins the ability to abstract itself from the object. The most important outcome of the intellectual process is that perception receives the character of being contraposed to the thing (*yuwuweidui* 與物為對). Since perception, in emanating the pure principle, draws the

---

13 [...] 一、自心覺方面言, 它是一個單一的同質流, 自規律方面言, 它是一個客觀的自足的理。二、它既是主觀的又是客觀的一個絕對主體, 既在自己而又對自己。Ibid., I, 100.

dividing line between objective world and subjective (logical system) world, so it is the first time that perception can objectivate its own content, having in itself the division between subject and object: "If it does not have both the subjective and the objective, it cannot accomplish itself. Subjectively, from the viewpoint of capability (*dongyong* 動用), objectively, from the viewpoint of the pure principles. If it is possible to harmonize subject and object, mind and principle, it can be in itself and for itself. In itself is the subjective side, for itself is the objective side. All what is in itself and for itself is an absolute subject, and at the same time an objective subject."[14]

Mou Zongsan, in order to express the characteristics of a self-objectivating thought, adopts the spatial metaphor of curvature. The dialectical dynamism of understanding is "curve and reaching," whereas intuition is "straightforward and not a curve." The relation between perception and thing is straight and not a curve, or *rurude* 如如的, in the Buddhist sense of conforming in a plain way (*pingdengbuer* 平等不二), i.e., perception passively follows and conforms to the stream of the thing, without any transcendental creativity. The curvature of understanding does not add any specific content, but adds the reflexive ability of producing *a priori* structures in order for the mind to return to itself, or objectivate itself. Perception, in order to reach the condition of being a self, should fulfill three requirements: 1. it should be an apperception, i.e., it should be self-aware, 2. it should possess the active ability to create/produce, and 3. it should perform a reflexive dynamism. Starting from the intuitive stage, perception meets the requirement of being self-aware, and in the stage of imagination acquires the ability to produce space and time, but only in the intellectual stage does it fulfill all the requirements. Mou posits that the logical self requires self-consciousness and productive ability as inescapable conditions. We can say that Mou upholds a "reflexive model" and an "egological theory," but through his concept of apperception, he is able to avoid the vicious circle of the reflexive self-consciousness. Self has self-consciousness as its root, but it is not identical to it. Therefore, the pre-reflexive dynamism

---

14 若非『既是主觀又是客觀的』,必不能圓滿其自己。主觀的,自其動用一面言;客觀的,自其純理一面言。在它能所合一,心理和一,故能『在自己而又對自己』。若分拆言之,『在自己』是它的能;『對自己』是他的所。凡『在而又對自己』者些為絕對的主體,同時亦即為客觀的主體。Ibid., I, 96.

of apperception represents a necessary step in the process of formation of the self. Perception turns itself to becoming this objective subject through self-consciousness. In this process, intuitive and imaginative apperception guarantee that the logical self, in the act of returning to itself in a curved and reflexive mode, already possesses a pre-reflexive standard in order to recognize and objectivate itself. The self is not a static concept, but a dynamic process, entailing that the self possesses itself before itself.[15]

2.7 Self-Consciousness and Meaning

The key concept in *Critique of the Cognitive Mind* is "meaning." Through this concept, Mou tries to overcome the traditional Western dualism between form and matter. Starting from the germinal phase of the physiological mind, mind and facts, subjective and objective, have a single cause/origin (*yuan* 緣). What the mind grasps through intuitive apperception are not scattered facts or events, or a meaningless chaotic matter, but a whole that manifests itself in the core of living experience. Diverging from Kant, in the cognitive process we do not have a transcendental subjectivity with synthetic function. This subjectivity uses an *a priori* form to provide a vital, ever-changing matter with unity and understandability. In the basic cognitive stage of the intuitive apperception, the world of things already possesses an intertwining dynamism and a cohesive force. According to Mou, reality is not constituted by the determined sum and the casual succession of facts, but is a tissue with warp and weft, or an ordered

---

15 Mou Zongsan, in *Critique of the Cognitive Mind*, usually uses self-consciousness (自覺) in order to express the dynamism of apperception:. There is only a line which seems to contradict the idea that perception and apperception are synonyms: "When one hears a sound and perceive it as a sound, we still don't have a synthesis between subject and object. Though I am not necessarily self-aware of my perception (i.e., that I am perceiving the sound), however this does not imply an inseparability between the self and the thing" (當其聽一聲二覺其為一聲, 已不是能所圓融矣。我雖對我之覺(覺一聲之覺)不必有自覺, 然亦不是物我不分也). Mou Zongsan, *Critique of the Cognitive Mind*, I, 10-11. Actually, the dyad subject/object or self/thing adopted here by Mou refer to the level of the intellect. Saying that "I am not necessarily self-aware of my perception" (我雖對我之覺不必有自覺), self-awareness means here reflective consciousness. Apperception implies a not-reflective self-consciousness, since it still does not belong to the level of the logical self.

structure. In other words, reality has an inherent meaning. Reality has perception as a manifestative principle; therefore, perception and reality constitute an indissoluble whole. On this basis, we can deduce a significant difference between Mou and Kant. In the *Critique of Pure Reason*, Kant claims that sensibility has a biological and transcendental aspect and transcendental sensibility produces space and time as *a priori* conditions. On the contrary, Mou Zongsan denies that sensibility has a transcendental aspect capable of emanating space and time, because this *a priori* formative capability belongs only to the transcendental imagination. This apparently secondary aspect is actually hinting at a deeper epistemological divide, because Mou negates the notion of the more basic state of the cognitive mind, i.e., intuitive apperception can have transcendental productivity. Since intuitive apperception is straight and not curved, it has the function of assimilating the meaning as it is. The meaning belongs to the facts, not to mental perception, and is therefore objective and not subjective. Meaning is not the product of a formal principle of the mind that molds an amorphous reality; it is the authentic structure/pattern of the perceived object. The real world manifesting itself in perceiving the mind possesses already a causal relationship emerging in accord with the patterns (*suiyuanqi* 随缘起), and therefore an ordered meaning. Intuitive apperception, being straight and not curved, has the determinate task of preserving and manifesting reality. It should see reality not as fragmentary, piecemeal, and lifeless matter, but as a physical and dynamic process, a causal relation and a semantic thread.

Mou Zongsan thinks that there are two different theories of meaning, which can be dangerous: Hume's empiricism, and the spiritual tenet and outcomes of Daoism and Buddhism. Hume denies that there is in things an inherent structure and connection on the basis of his epistemology, which is based on an extreme sensationalism. In 1740, in *An Enquiry Concerning Human Understanding* (1.3.6.15, SBN 93), Hume wrote: "We have no other notion of cause and effect, but that of certain objects, which have been always conjoined together, and which in all past instances have been found inseparable. We cannot penetrate into the reason of the conjunction." According to Hume, the sensation or memory/impression of any single thing is the apex of truth and reality, is evident and living, whereas the correlation between cause and effect is based only on an empirical conjunction. We only retain that a thing is followed by another thing. Mou claims that the outcome of this theory is that the "sensation is given to me only as scattered, but does not convey to me any meaning. The things arisen by our physiological sensibility are seen as fragmentary, not as a process. Advancing further and extending it, they are seen only as quantitative things, because we can isolate and fragment it without finding any exchange/communication."[16] For Hume, every perception is a *chana*, an instantaneous perception, i.e., any single thing is a momentary *chana*-thing without any correlation with other things, so that network, relation, and meaning does not belong to the real world. Mou claims that Daoism and Buddhism have philosophical worldviews that begin from a different basis and lead to the same outcome. Their point of intersection resides in a detached observation without care or participation. But this detached, secluded, and alienated view is limited only to the super-rational cognitive mind, and is unable to grasp the moral mind (*tianxin* 天心), where the intuition of the causal correlation does not have rational necessity.

Mou claims that, in order to transcend this worldview, we should return to the traditional Confucian benevolence of the heavenly moral mind (*tianxin zhi ren* 天心之人), i.e., we should not only perform a theoretical examination, but also let the thing return to the living process of things, to the practical life of the heavenly moral mind, and verify it. Only if there is a subject engaged through humanness with the concrete world can we effectively grasp and follow the inherent dynamicity and meaningfulness of reality and understand the connecting red thread of the tissue of reality. It is worth noticing that the cognitive process for Mou Zongsan is not only an epistemological enquiry, but also a practical and active value. Perception has the responsibility to preserve the immutable meaning of worlds, and through self-objectivation, to bring this meaning into objectivation within the flux of things. To affirm that in the cognitive process we can find a practical moral call guarantees the nexus between the moral mind and the cognitive mind. Only if the heavenly moral mind subsists can the process of examination of the cognitive mind reach and fulfill its aim. For Mou, the meaning

---

16   […] 感覺只給吾以雜料, 而不給吾以意義, 視生理感所引起之緣起事只為點之雜料而不視之為一歷程, 復進而外延化之而只視之為量的事, 因而可以孤零而星散之, 而全無交涉 […] Ibid., I, 25.

is not only a semantic or linguistic structure, but the indissoluble connection between human mind and the world of things. Only if the mind penetrates and permeates the world and takes responsibility for the phenomenal whole, can it reveal its significance.

On this basis, we can deduce what influence the key concept of meaning has on the theory of apperception. Mou claims that the real object of apperception is not the things but the meaning: "The intuitive apperception has actuality (*you zhenshisuode* 有真實所得), because this apperception is able to autonomously provide us with meaning. If we are looking without seeing, hearing without listening, there would be no meaning, and also no intuitive apperception. If I have apperception, I have meaning. Meaning and intuitive apperception is a relationship between equivalent."[17] That apperception gives me meaning does not mean that apperception is independent of physical things, but only that it is independent of the intellect. Only if we have the conceptual system of the intellect can our cognitive mind preserve the objective necessity of the meaning; but the possibility of the meaning itself does not wait until the cognitive process reaches the level of intellect for having a fundamental effect. Saying that if we have apperception, we have also a meaning, implies that I do not need the dynamism of reflection or the logical self constituted in the reflexive curvature in order to grasp the meaning of reality, and that pre-reflexive apperceptive intuition is enough. The difference between looking and seeing, hearing and listening, consists in the fact that seeing and listening entail a self-aware grasping, and so a self-conscious capacity of attention: "This kind of obtaining something, I call them apperceptive grasping. This apperception arises in things like an instantaneous process and grasps it."[18] As I wrote before, Mou aims to guarantee that, even in the most elementary stage, we already find meaning, we already have apperception, and they both are the necessary precondition of the self-constituting and self-objectivating of the logical self. In criticizing Daoism and Buddhism, Mou claims that an indifferent, uncaring, and detached spiritual attitude prevents the

---

17　直覺的統覺有真實所得，故知此統覺能獨立給吾意義。設若視而不見，聽而不聞，則無意義，亦無直覺的統覺矣。有此統覺即有意義。意義與直覺的統覺為等價關係。Ibid., I, 15.

18　此種取著吾人即名為此統覺之『把住』。此統覺如現起事如為一忽之歷程而把住之。Ibid., I, 16.

human mind from perceiving the meaningfulness of reality. Only if the subject has an actively participatory approach to the world, engaging with it through praxis, can the meaning of reality manifest itself. On this basis, we can infer and summarize that the characteristics of the pre-reflexive self-consciousness of apperception consists in an active participation in reality, which becomes the principle of manifestation embedded in the network or tissue of processual reality. If there is not a subject actively entangled in the world, the process of constitution of the self is ultimately impossible.[19]

2.8 The Oscillation between Self-Limitation and Springing Out (跳起)

As previously mentioned, *Critique of the Cognitive Mind* describes the function and inner development of the cognitive mind. This development, starting from the most simple and elementary stage, the physiological sensibility, ascends to the reflexive dimension of the logical self. The force that promotes this evolutionary process is the tension of the cognitive mind toward a perfect objectivity of the perceived reality, which can be reached and verified only through the self-objectivation of the self. At the physiological stage, since real things are perceived and arise through our sensory organs, they still have a subjective connotation. In intuitive apperception, we are able to conform to the flux of reality and assimilate its permanent meaning. However, the manifestation of this meaning is subordinate to our instantaneous act of perception. In order to objectivate, stabilize, and universalize this grasped meaning, our mind should emanate the *a priori* forms of space, time, and categories, i.e., the human mind should progressively exteriorize and objectivize the conditions of its inner functional dynamicity. The logical self represents the apex of this process, because through the dialectical curvature of reflection,

---

19 Analyzing Buddhist's worldview Mou writes: "遁空山, 作禪堂, 捨棄一切生活, 而以靜引靜, 遂覺山河大地, 連同自心, 無有不靜, 無有不寂。且亦無有山河大地可言, 無有自心可言。" (Living as a hermit, constructing temples, refusing life, use silence to induce silence. Then you will feel that the mountains, rivers, and earth, together with your own mind, are all peaceful, and everything is still. Moreover, there are no mountains, rivers or earth to speak of, and there is no self-consciousness to speak of." Ibid., I, 28. This conclusion is very similar to Hume's philosophical outcomes.

the mind becomes its own objective standard and acknowledges itself as a synthesizing movement, reaching the aim of fusing mind and principle. If the logical self effectively embodies the final stage, the cognitive mind comes full circle and accomplishes its responsibility, so that epistemology does not need to have a metaphysical self-closing or completing system as its foundation. Nevertheless, Mou claims that the human mind has no firm position in this reflective curvature, because it does not attain an ultimate completion, and cannot find a resting point or foothold. In order to demonstrate this thesis, Mou emphasizes that the dialectical mind, or the curved mind, presents two shortcomings, of which the first concerns Mou's epistemological system in its totality, and the second concerns a problem apparently without solution.

1. In Mou's epistemological theory, the dynamism of the cognitive mind is a ceaseless oscillation. Every time the mind accomplishes a cognitive stage, it "condenses" or "solidifies," i.e., it cannot avoid the risk of coagulating in the reached result. To transcend this static interruption, the mind should spring over from its self-limitation (*kanxian*) and restore its structural dynamicity and productivity. The oscillation between self-limitation and springing out guarantees the inexhaustible fluidity of the mind. Though the logical mind is the ultimate stage of rational thought, it too is trapped in the contraposition between subject and thing: "Because in the cognitive relation involving the object (the mind) arrests itself in this logic self, which is contraposed to the object, like a liquid at every reached target condensate and stiffen itself, in order to reveal its objectivity. Stopping and limiting itself, it reveals its lack of foothold in forward direction. Stopping and stiffening, it reveals that it should jump over this solidification."[20] At one extremity I have the object, connected through physiological sensibility, as a dwelling place. At the other extremity, if we follow the homogeneous stream of the understanding in order to search for what does not stop, does not limit, does

---

20 此因在關涉對象之認識關係上而停於此之與物為對之邏輯的我猶如流動之液體在達成莫種目的上凝固其自己因而顯示其客觀性者同。[…]。停於此, 即限於此, 其限於此, 亦即表示其前尚有不停於此者。停於此, 即靜於此, 其靜於此亦表示尚有越呼此靜者。Ibid., I, 102.

not stiffen, we discover that this research movement happens inside understanding itself. I cannot reach something that authentically transcends this static point, and so I should necessarily look through and hypothesize a standpoint belonging to another vertical level, namely the metaphysical true self.

2. Our understanding, as an objectivation process, requires us to absorb and unify everything, leaving nothing outside its scope. However, the understanding in itself is incapable of fully accomplishing this totality without some form of leakage. Mou introduces here the logical problem of the verifiability of universal affirmative propositions. If we acknowledge the truth of a universal sentence like "all human beings are mortal," it seems that in order to verify this proposition, I should rely on the empirical understanding of every individual, i.e., we should verify the truth of the proposition for any human being. But in the progressive advancement of our "understanding based on experience," this kind of verification becomes an active and inexhaustible process. However, in the sphere of understanding and experience we can only verify the truth of the proposition in a separate way, step by step, for any single subject belonging to the "all human beings" class. Since the gradual advancement of this knowledge has no endpoint, we cannot reach absoluteness, but only produce a passive, inexhaustible progress. Moreover, if we use inductive inference, what we reach is only an inductive generalization, not an absolute truth. Given this, in the sphere of understanding, we cannot exhaustively demonstrate the universality "all the human beings are mortal." Thus, our certainty should be founded on a meta-rational methodology of verification, namely meta-rational intuition: "The completeness (*yuanmanxing* 圓滿性) and faultlessness without exception of a logical proposition implies its intuitiveness."[21] We said above that for Mou the cognitive process is not a mere epistemological investigation, but possesses what we may call an ethic-like responsibility to

---

21　邏輯陳述之圓滿性與無漏性, 即函有此陳述之直覺性 [⋯]。Ibid., II, 599.

preserve and realize the dimension of meaning. In order to reach this scope, we have to found/establish the specificity of every single thing in the network/tissue of the known world. To completely realize/actualize the meaning, the cognitive mind should possess the capacity of thoroughly permeating the cognitive mind, and an inexhaustible dynamicity. From this, we can see that putting meaning at the core of his system ultimately led Mou to acknowledge that the cognitive process cannot arrest or pause itself. Instead, it serves as a hint of its existence as a foundation that transcends the level of rational thought.

According to Mou, I spontaneously admit/acknowledge the truth of a general principle (like "all human beings are mortal") and I have the ability to ask for a "complete verification" of this general principle. This demonstrates that the mind should have another modality of knowledge that is not submitted to the limits of intellectual thought. Before all else, Mou investigates the necessary, inherent, and unavoidable limitedness of intellect, affirming that every formal condition emanated by the cognitive mind, from space-time to categories, has a double function, since they are the necessary preconditions of the cognitive process, and at the same time they represent an inner boundary of the knowledge itself. Mou Zongsan calls this dialectical process "self-limitation" (*ziwo kanxian* 自我坎陷). In his later works, Mou claims that the cognitive level is constituted through the self-limitation of the moral metaphysical mind. In order to give a response to all the specific moral questions of human beings, the authentic self transforms itself into a cognitive self. Through the dynamism of self-limitation, the moral mind is able to know the particularity and concreteness of the real circumstances. When the moral mind arrests itself and attaches to itself, its imbued and permeating luminosity stagnates, becoming a limited self. The cognitive level reveals, therefore, a structural twistedness. This twisting movement, since it implies a self-restraining and self-limiting activity, produces an ontological bifurcation between the attached ontology of the cognitive self and the unattached ontology of the authentic self. In *Critique of the Cognitive Mind*, Mou explains that the cognitive mind itself requests a self-limitation in order to acquire full knowledge and objectivate itself and the known meaning. The full manifestation of self-limitation is the reflective process of the logical self, which allows human beings to become "for themselves and in themselves." Since the logical self is not only the ultimate endpoint, but retrospectively permeates the entire development of the cognitive mind, so this reflexive curvedness structurally belongs to human nature, and is at the same time the line of demarcation between the finiteness of the cognitive level and the infiniteness of the transcendent/metaphysic level: "If we took this curvature, then what is under this curvature arrests itself in this logical self, the objective mind in an epistemological way, what is above this curvature does not arrest to this and transcend this. This is the metaphysical transcendent self I wanted see through and hypothesize. What arrests itself here is in the contraposition to the thing in order to know it, what does not arrest itself here is no more contraposed to the thing and make a step to the metaphysic level."[22] Compared with the self-limitation of the moral metaphysical mind, the self-limitation of the cognitive mind has an all-encompassing value, because it determines the fundamental condition of the cognitive process. In the self-limitation, since there subsists a contraposition with the thing, so there is a separation between the fact and the principle, and knowledge cannot accomplish its quest toward a complete actualization and verification.

We run here into the problem of dialectical negation and the reversal of self-limitation. In his later works, Mou does not explain in a thorough way why the cognitive self should ultimately negate and transcend itself and restore the "plainness" and unattached ontology of the authentic self. These works pivot around the problems of philosophical nature and the modality of experience of the authentic self and stress that the cognitive self is merely a fleeting phenomenon produced by the dialectical dynamism of the authentic self. According to its own rhythm, the flux of the moral mind uninterruptedly limits itself, and then re-assimilates the cognitive self in order to restore its transcendence. On the contrary, in *Critique of the Cognitive Mind*, the analysis proceeds from the cognitive to the metaphysical level, placing the logical self in the paramount position. Developing the two arguments based on the

---

22 如果吾人把住此曲折, 則此曲折以下者為靜於此之邏輯的我, 認識上之客觀的心, 此曲折以上者即為不停於此而為越乎此者。此即吾人所欲透視而預定之形上的超越的真我。停於此者與物為對而為認識的, 不停於此者不與物為對而為形上的踐履的。Ibid., I, 103.

structural dynamicity of the mind and the impossibility to satisfy the verification requirements of the universal propositions, Mou attempts to demonstrate that the reason why the cognitive mind has an inner tension to free itself from self-limitation and constantly ascend, can be found in its structural inability to fully realize itself.[23]

In general, the cognitive mind should limit itself in order to reach knowledge, and therefore understanding produces the formal conditions of a cognitive act. At the same time, this process in its entirety reveals in this curvature both the condition and the structural limit of knowledge. The curvature necessarily limits and affects the cognitive horizon in its essence. I think that the reflective logical self is the most evident embodiment of this curvature, which characterizes the entirety of the cognitive process as constituted by self-limitation. The curved finite mind reaches the intellectual comprehension of reality, or as Mou writes, "through this curvature accomplishes itself," but this finite nature is what ultimately acts as an obstacle to the completeness and absoluteness of this cognitive process itself. To overcome this obstacle, the mind should spring out from this curvature, acquiring a straightforward and direct modality. In the intuitive apperception, we already obtain this directness and immediacy, but this germinal intuition, albeit straightforward and not curved, comprises a passive conformity to reality and a mere preservation of its meaning. This happens, explains Mou, because its directness and intuitiveness produce themselves inside the self-limitation of the cognitive mind. To acquire completeness of knowledge, I therefore need an intuition that can emerge from self-limitation, i.e., not an empirical intuition, but an intellectual intuition.[24] Mou claims that this intellectual intuition, just

---

23   Similar to the oscillation of the moral mind between self-limitation and restoration, the entire activity of the cognitive mind is constituted by this alternation between self-limitation and transcendence.

24   Some Chinese scholars questioned the correctness and validity of Mou's borrowing Kantian concepts like "intellectual intuition," "thing-in-itself," "transcendental," arguing that Mou detaches himself from the original Kantian meaning of these concepts. I fully agree with Lee Ming-huei, finding that Mou's reinterpretation of the aforementioned words is fully intentional and explicitly declared by Mou himself. Furthermore, this reinterpretation is a hermeneutical process which underlies the entire history of philosophy as the expression *Begriffsgeschichte* (history of the concepts) reveals, and make progress possible in the conceptual sphere. Even Kant in adopting, for example, the Platonic term "Idea," remolds it substantially in order to make it meaningful in

because it is aimed at the full accomplishment of understanding, cannot totally transcend the cognitive mind, but should emerge in it, providing us with a hint of what is beyond the logical self.

The intellectual intuition ascribed by Kant to the divine *intellectus archetypus* or, by Berkeley, to the omniscient divine mind, does not meet this requirement. On the contrary, they imply that verification, foundation, and the truthfulness of the logic system are unreachable for human beings, so that our knowledge is ultimately not fully established or rooted. However, Mou's cognitive mind is able to grasp the self-evident truth of the universal principle and to spontaneously acknowledge the flawless completeness and universal truth of logical concepts. This means, for Mou, that every time we apprehend a logical concept, we intuitively grasp its evidence: "Every logical concept elicits a full demonstration. Realizing this demonstration/verification is disclosing it in the spiritual light. The foundation of the spiritual light resides in its ability to elicit a logical concept without exceptions. I recognize the irradiation of the spiritual light, and I have the inherent capability of spontaneously producing categories. The irradiation of the spiritual light is where the intuition dwells. When I understand and spontaneously emit categories (*gedu* 個度), there is the subtle use of the intuition behind."[25] Every act of eliciting a concept leaves the shimmering of spiritual light behind it, but in the sphere of understanding and experience we cannot perfectly grasp and master this "sparkle" of intuition. Through the logical concept, we cannot grasp this subtle, transient, elusive, and difficult to ascertain intuitive capacity, because this intuition is not in the domain of the intellectual curvature, but in the sparkle following behind, i.e., it has a strict relation

---

his own system. In this frame, Mou's appropriation of the Kantian concept of "intellectual intuition" is not different from that operated by post-Kantian Idealist philosophers, like Fichte and Schelling, in the attempt to ascribe intellectual intuition to the human mind. See Lee Ming-huei (李明輝), "How to Inherit Mou Zongsan's Legacy?". 如何繼承牟宗三先生的思想遺產? in: *Xin ruxue lunwen jingxuan ji Li Minghui xin ruxue lunwen jingxuan ji*. 新儒學論文精選集李明輝新儒學論文精選集 (Selected Works of Lee Ming-huei on New Confucianism), Taipei: Taiwan Xuesheng Shuju, 2019, pp. 178–179.

25 是以每一邏輯概念誘發一滿證。滿證之實現, 在乎靈光之透露。靈光之根據在其與邏輯概念之提出而俱起。吾人承認靈光之照射, 如承認理解有自發格度範疇之內能。靈光之照射, 即為直覺之所在。理解於自發格度範疇之時, 即有直覺之妙用在其後。Mou Zongsan, *Critique of the Cognitive Mind*, II, 595.

with the process of emergence of the logical concept itself. Mou claims that this intuitive image (*zhijue xiang* 直覺相) (related to Buddhism) is "the retrospective endpoint of my investigating the understanding."[26] In fact, intellectual intuition illuminates the germinal dynamism of the concept and the production and emanation of its formal conditions. The origin of the concept is ungraspable for my thought, because it happens before the understanding itself is born. From a certain point of view, the phase of emanation of space, time, and categories, produces the limit of the thought, determines its insuperable finiteness. From another viewpoint, it reveals that the cognitive mind, from the beginning to the end, possesses an inherent creativity/productivity. If the *a priori* frame of the intellectual thought represents the condensed state of the cognitive process, intuition represents its fluidifying capability, and the possibility of liberation from its boundaries. Mou calls this kind of mind the "mind of the quiet shining."

2.9 The Mind of the Quiet Shining (*Jizhaoxin* 寂照心)

In order to describe the features of this mind, the use of poetic language is not casual, since the poetic inspiration represents far better our intelligent capacity to become one with the universe: "The mind of the quiet shining rises and invigorates, so that nothing remains latent and hidden. It really is very light rain and wind, the wind swells sails of painted boats in vain. Vast and hazy, everything is permeated by the life-giving spring breeze and rain."[27] The mind of quiet shining cancels the boundaries of intellect, saturating and pervading, reinvigorating and harmonizing. This mind cognitively penetrates through the entire universe; all the differences are given in the luminosity and intuition of this mind. After being absorbed and enveloped, they receive their full verification, but this accomplishment is at the same time a liberation from any finite condition. The entire manifestation of the "mind of the quiet shining," since it implies an act of freeing oneself from these conditions, possesses only a negative function and a transient force of penetration. The faculty of understanding, through the emanation of forms *a priori*,

---

26 [...] 吾人考察理解活動之後面的截斷處。Ibid., II, 643.
27 如是,寂照心起而振舉之,絲絲縷縷無毫髮隱藏。是真雨絲風片,煙波畫船,蒼蒼茫茫,無所不在春風化雨中也。Ibid., II, 653.

becomes progressively wider, but cannot achieve a full verification without exceptions; it does not possess an absolute all-encompassing power, but it is only capable of an inferential partial verification. Intuition, in the very instant (*chana*) of getting rid of the boundaries, in a flash accomplishes these requirements and possesses an authentic universality. The mind of the quiet shining, since it manifests itself in getting rid of the self-limitation of the conditions emanating from intuition, is complete in every step. This entails that in every step of the verification, the cognitive mind exhausts the entire universe. Springing out from self-limitation, the mind of the quiet shining instantaneously catches a glimpse of the entirety of the universe, but because intuition reveals itself only in the act of eliminating self-limitation, self-limitation is its fundament and the condition from which it originates. Using the metaphor of the web, Mou writes that for every act of knowledge "There is a main thread you can infer in the universe." This main thread stands out and catches my eyes in the knowledge. The mind of the quiet shining "in the emersion of this clue appears in its entirety. The mind of quiet shining should have as root this emerging clue/extremity. It cannot overflowingly suffuse and illuminate everything. It cannot only expose/reveal its totality following the glimpse. This luminous glimpse is therefore its root and its limit."[28]

As I wrote above, "cognitive mind" is a broad term, dynamically involving two different modalities: curved mind and straight/intuitive mind or the mind of the quiet shining. What are the different features that display the subjectivity of the "curved mind" modality and of the "quiet shining mind" modality? Are these modalities of the mind self-conscious? What do they reveal to us about Mou Zongsan's theory of self? The ultimate epitome or realization of the curved mind is the logical self. The logical self is not only the vertex of the faculty of intellect, but also the result of the entire processual development of the mind. Though intuitive apperception and imaginative apperception are, by definition, two self-aware modes of knowing, only when the cognitive mind reaches the final stage of self-objectivating does a "self"

---

28 測宇宙之一點頭緒。這個頭緒在知識中凸出於吾人之眼前。[…] [寂照心] 順凸出之一點端倪而全體呈露之。是以寂照心之照射必以此凸出之端倪為跟，它不能漫然泛照。它只能順此曙光一點而全體暴露。所以這曙光一點是它的跟隨是它的限制。Ibid., II, 652.

based on reflective thought appear. The reflective act of turning on itself perfectly epitomizes the curvedness of the intellect, allowing the mind to reach the ultimate synthesis between objective self (being-in-itself) and subjective self (being-for-itself). Since in the logical self the cognitive mind becomes capable of finally recognizing its own dynamism, we can say that the mirror-like reflection of the self-consciousness is the highest expression of the curvature of the mind. On the contrary, the most important function of the mind of the quiet shining resides in the uninterrupted elimination of the *a priori* conditions, emancipating the cognitive mind from the boundaries emanated by the mind itself. We can infer that the reason why Mou does not use the expression "self" in presenting this intuitive mind is because the goal of it is to liquefy all the fixed boundaries, and the reflective logical self as well. The mind of the quiet shining, since it is based on an intuitive activity, could be self-aware as the empirical intuition. However, different to empirical intuition, this kind of intuitiveness is not a pre-reflexive consciousness. The paramount shortcoming of the reflective self resides in its absolute subjectivity. In recognizing its own reflective activity, the logical self merges an objective and a subjective aspect. However, the process of constitution of this logical self necessarily constitutes itself in contraposition with things. The task of the intuitive mind is to cancel the line of demarcation between the self and thing. The mind of the quiet shining intuitively penetrates the universe, i.e., it does not reject the characteristics of being-in-itself and for-itself, but freeing itself from the boundary of the contraposition to things, it uninterruptedly becomes the place of manifestation of the universe.

In my opinion, we have to draw support from the metaphorical language adopted by Mou in describing the features of the mind of the quiet shining. Particularly worth our attention is the recurrent metaphor of the web in Mou's work. Mou relates this image with Leibniz' vision of the monad as the living mirror of the universe. "In any step of the verification, the cognitive mind exhausts the universe in its entirety, so any verified knowledge represents a total knowledge of the universe. It does not have a delimited boundary, because it represents an autonomous all-including universe, and so the cognitive mind acquires in every step of the verification an absolute self-sufficiency."[29] In *Monadology* (1714), Leibniz claims that the universe is constituted by numberless spiritual substances called monads. The nature of monads is thought. Every monad mirrors and represents the entire universe, but every monad necessarily embraces this universe from its own specific viewpoint.

What Mou wants to demonstrate with this analogy is that every human mind has the ability to cognitively encompass the entire world, but in the domain of self-limitation the perfect reflective capability of this mind is concealed and latent. Only if the mind springs out from self-limitation can it acquire the ability of manifesting the entire universe. Mou uses the metaphor of the web in order to illustrate the same theoretical content: "Every knot of the web encompasses all the web, this is logically already established, but in the self-limited modality the knowledge cannot completely reveal it, so only the mind of quiet shining is able to gather and illuminate it."[30] We could overlap and fuse together both these metaphors, imagining the world of knowledge as an infinite web, and in every knot of this web, there is a spherical pearl-like mirror. In this frame, every pearl mirrors all the universe, including the other mirrors. Though every mirror is the reflected image of all the web, there cannot exist two perfectly identical mirrors, because every mirror has its specific place in the web, and its peculiar reflecting point. The reflective self we reach through the curvature of understanding possesses both the characteristics; it potentially penetrates the entire reality, but its act of cognitive encompassing is limited by the ineliminable subjectivity of the reflective self. In the sphere of self-limitation, the logical self represents the entire universe as a collection of objects of knowledge. However, since it is structurally contraposed to things, the logical self coagulates and stiffens in a limited perspective and is always incomplete, unable to reach the ultimate sum of the step-by-step verification. Since the self already represents everything and manifests the whole, the intuitive mind that springs out "cannot increase my knowledge."[31] It can only,

---

29   在每步滿證中,認識之心將窮盡宇宙之一切,是以每得滿證之知識是表像一全宇宙之知識。因為它此時是一個無限制無封域者。既無限制封域,故表示一窮盡無漏而自足之宇宙。它每一步滿證是如是之宇宙,故認識之心於每一步滿證即獲得一絕對之自足。吾人可於此予萊布尼茲反映全宇宙之思想以新說明。Ibid., II, 646-647.

30   然而每一個網函其全面之網是邏輯上所已決定者,唯因坎陷中的知識不能盡露之,所以寂照心才起而照射之。Ibid., II, 653.

31   [...] 不能增益吾人之知識。Ibid.

in the act of freeing itself, restore the originary infiniteness and the all-embracing opening of the self. In accordance with the metaphor, we can imagine this act of "springing out" (*zhenju* 振擧) and "freeing" of the mind of the quiet shining as it uninterruptedly jumps or plunges from one mirror to another, transcending every ossified viewpoint, eliminating the boundaries of subjectivity, restoring the ability of the self to mirror all reality. Nevertheless, the mind of the quiet shining, despite possessing intuitiveness, cannot produce and establish a stable self, it can only appear as a fleeting apprehension that embraces everything. Mou thinks that this is the peak of Buddhist and Daoist thought.

We can take as an example the parable of the dream of the butterfly narrated in chapter 2 of *Zhuangzi*:

> Once Zhuang Zhou dreamt he was a butterfly, a butterfly flitting and fluttering around, happy with himself and doing as he pleased. He didn't know he was Zhuang Zhou. Suddenly, he woke up and there he was, solid and unmistakable Zhuang Zhou. But he didn't know if he was Zhuang Zhou who had dreamt he was a butterfly, or a butterfly dreaming he was Zhuang Zhou.[32]

At the beginning, Zhuangzi possesses a stable self-awareness and a definite subjective viewpoint. Through the oneiric experience, Zhuangzi jumps out from his self and spiritually moves to the subjective viewpoint of the butterfly. Like Leibniz's monad, the subjective sphere of both Zhuangzi and the butterfly are sealed and self-sufficient, and therefore the subjective viewpoint of the butterfly does not lean on Zhuangzi to exist. After waking up, Zhuangzi discovers that the demarcation line between these two subjective perspectives is blurred. The condition of awakening bears a similarity with the mind of the quiet shining: Zhuangzi frees himself from the seclusion and the boundary of his own subjectivity, and spontaneously and freely shifts to the butterfly's self and back. However, this experience of "liquefaction" of the subjective standpoint is not durable, because the logical thought reinstates the difference between the two selves. The "free and easy wandering" experienced in the state of the mind of the quiet shining is the philosophical ideal of Zhuangzi. Mou writes: "in this illuminative intuition, I accomplish the

---

32 Burton Watson (ed.), *The Complete Works of Zhuangzi*, New York: Columbia University Press, 2013, p.18.

task of being 'entirely alike and entirely different.' This task implies the quest for 'The alikeness without any difference.' The myriad things are entirely alike and entirely different in the mind of Dao, and I realize this in a perfect way in mind of the quiet shining. However, in the curved mind of the self-limitation, I cannot say this. The ideas of 'entirely alike and entirely different' and 'the alikeness without any differences' cannot be verified through the dialectical knowledge."[33]

The reason resides in the constitutional negativity of the intuitive mind. The intuitive mind depends for its manifestation on the negation of subjective boundaries and on the act of freeing itself from the viewpoint of the reflective self and is therefore subordinated to the curved mind. As the metaphor of the web suggests, there is another possible solution to the problem of "solidification." If I could transcend every limit and grasp the design of the entire web, I could reach the comprehension of reality in its infinitude. But "the cognitive mind, both in self-limitation and in springing out, cannot obtain a final principle through which the system of knowledge can be completely verified."[34] In order to reach the final settling point of the universe, I should ascend to the metaphysical absoluteness of the authentic self in the mind of Dao.

2.10 Toward the Transcendent Mind: The Meaning and Use of Zi 自

In the final chapter "The logical structure of the cognitive mind toward its transcendent aspect," Mou aims to deepen his search for absoluteness and authenticity. The cognitive mind, examining its lacks in a critical way, hopes to transcend its finiteness, and to finally reach an ultimate foundation for the process of knowledge. Though attaining this goal exceeds the use and capability of the cognitive mind, nevertheless Mou believes that we can, through a negative-apophatic way, determine the formal features of this ultimate ground. We should

---

33　在此直覺照射中, 吾人成就『畢同畢異』一主斷。此主斷即函有『無異之同一性』一主斷。萬物畢同畢異, 在道心上吾人予以最終之成就, 在認識之心上吾人予以寂照之成就。而在坎陷之曲屈心, 則不能說。是即明『畢同畢異』與『無異之同一性』些不能由辯解知識以證之。Mou Zongsan, *Critique of the Cognitive Mind*, II, 651.

34　認識之心, 無論在坎陷中或躍出中, 些不能得到一最後之原則以完整知識之系統。Ibid., II, 647.

negate all the inevitable boundaries of our knowledge, in order to reach a full verification: "In the empirical apperception, from the causally generated thing I receive the concept of 'mutable, not durable.' Through the intellectual understanding, I achieve the concept of 'impossibility to fully verifying the system of logical principle,' in the intellectual intuition I reach the concept of 'infiniteness in a merely subjective meaning.' Reversing all these concepts I can reach the idea of an absolute truthful substance."[35]

We can obtain only the logical structure and outline of this substance, without actualizing and verifying the truthfulness of this concept. In the epistemological domain, the human mind cannot directly grasp and experience the abstract concept of the substance. According to Mou, through this negative method I obtain a substance that is purely dynamic, purely subjective, and purely spiritual. In the substance, there is no separation between the essence and the existence. Substance is sovereign over everything, permeates everything, sees itself in itself, and seeing itself it contemplates the entire universe. There is not a concrete being that can separate itself from the substance and exist in an autonomous way, otherwise the substance would lose its necessary universality and infiniteness. The substance has a full meaning in itself, because it is the supreme good. Finally, the logical sphere reveals itself as the projected shadow of this substance.

Referring to our main theme, it is worth noticing that the characteristics of the substance theorized by Mou are that it has to be self-knowing, self-illuminating, self-understanding, self-willing (*ziyi* 自意). All these words formed with the character "self-" (*zi* 自) are worthy of a deeper analysis, because *zi* 自 has a strict relation with the theme of self-consciousness. *Zi* 自 can express two different modalities referring to the self: the modality of self-representation (*ziwobiaoxian* 自我表現) and the modality of self-determination.

3. Self-representation is based on the epistemological paradigm and indicates that the substance, in order to reach the target of being self-aware, should undertake a dialectical process.

---

35 在經驗統覺中,由緣起事吾人有『變化無常』之概念;在理解中,吾人有『邏輯之理的系統不能得最後圓滿』之概念;在智的直覺中,吾人有『只是一主觀意義之無限』之概念。吾人即由此三概念向後翻,翻至一與此概念相反一絕對真實之本體概念。Ibid., II, 666.

In order to understand itself, the pristine, simple, and unique substance should exteriorize itself in the material world, and through knowledge return progressively to itself. In this reflective way, the substance recognizes that the totality of the universe is just its objective representation, like a reflex in the mirror. In light of this meaning, zi 自 implies a movement that returns from the exterior world to itself, so that the substance finally will recognize itself, and refer to itself. In order to achieve self-knowing, self-illuminating, and self-understanding, the substance should divide itself in two polarities, subject and object, and then merge these polarities in itself. This kind of operation is clearly visible in the idealistic systems of Fichte and Hegel. But Mou rejects the idea that self-knowing entails the dialectical polarization of subject and object: "Self-knowing is thoroughly disclosing the totality of oneself without leaving anything behind, not breaking oneself in subject and object."[36] Mou upholds that the ability to know is a feature of the substance, but this kind of apprehension is totally different from the understanding of the cognitive mind. The self-knowing of the substance is "direct and without curve," i.e., the substance knows itself in an intuitive way.

4. The second modality bears an ontological value. As Mou already stated, we can find the totality of the universe in every piece of reality. In discussing the intuitive mind, Mou claims that in every web knot we can find the entire web, but the ability to manifest this ontological structure is subordinated to the limits of the knowing mind. The mind of the quiet shining fleetingly gets a glimpse of the outline of the universe, but its sharp, penetrating gaze cannot reach the metaphysically endless implications and imbrications of reality. Granting that the substance possesses this ability, the dynamism of self-understanding does not require any dialectical mediation. The substance wholly permeates itself, and so, from an ontological perspective, in every real being there is the totality of the substance; nothing is external and foreclosed, and there is no

---

36   自知者即其自己之徹底無漏之全幅透露, 非其自身可破裂為能所也。Ibid., II, 673.

necessity of self-exteriorization. Since the substance utterly unfolds itself in everything, its self-knowing is one and the same with its infinite being. The necessary condition of this ontological outcome is that everything in the substance possesses dynamicity and actuality. The meaning of *zi* 自 is similar to self-governing. The substance has its own source, light, and principle in itself. The substance is inside everything and therefore, looking at itself, it sees everything.[37] Mou Zongsan, in order to express this meaning, introduces the Buddhist term *ruru* 如如 (suchness). The substance understands itself in its suchness i.e., it does not need any other condition to manifest itself. In fact, the substance is its own manifestation and ontological root. The necessary condition of this is that the substance, like Leibniz's monad, is a pure spiritual entity and is not spatially or temporally determined. If *zi* 自 means that substance is inherent to everything and knows itself through the totality of things, this implies that its most adequate manifestation is moral action. The interiority/internality of this "in itself" is not static or abstract, but means that the substance is endlessly involved in reality, and confers guidance and vitality to everything in the universe: "What sees the universe in a detached and separated way, is the epistemological knowledge. On the contrary, the knowledge of the substance is ontological knowledge. Ontological knowledge represents the sovereignty of the mind, which is inside everything and permeates and rules everything."[38]

---

37 本體在其自身中看自己,同時亦即在其自身中看一切。Ibid., II, 674.
38 其在超然的距離上看一切,是認識論的知。但本體之知亦可以是本體論的知。本體論的知是神智之主宰性。此則內在於一切而潤澤之而主宰之。Ibid., II, 675.

3. The "Diaphanous Subject" in Daoist Thought

3.1 Daoism as the Metaphysics of the State of Mind

In the previous chapter, we analyzed the features of what Mou calls "the mind of quiet shining" or the intuitive mind. This intuitive mind manifests itself in any activity of the mind aimed at transcending and erasing a solidified boundary. It entails a dynamic force that uninterruptedly sprouts from the cracks of those transcendental frames, like space, time, and categories, which emanate from the mind in order to make the flux of inner life intelligible. As objectivations of the mind itself, these frames are the necessary conditions for accomplishing the highest task of human knowledge, i.e., preserving and disclosing meaning. However, they represent at the same time a crystallized and limiting stage of development and are unable to satisfy the unrestrainable dynamism of the mind. The restoration of subjectivity as never-ending movement and spontaneous activity requires that the intuitive mind permeates, liquefies, and dissolves the products of its own objectivation and self-limitation, offering us a glimpse of the intuitive apprehension of the entire interweaving of relations, which constitute the universe. The mind of the quiet shining therefore has three characteristics: 1. it is dynamic and functional, 2. it has a negative nature, relying on the uninterrupted effacement of boundaries, and 3. it is ephemeral and impermanent, since it lacks the foundation that only a transcendent mind, which is at the same time the endless substance of reality, could provide. These characteristics, derived on an epistemological basis, are representative of that "negative intellectual intuition," which Mou sees as perfectly accomplished in the Daoist way of thought. In his works and lessons devoted to Laozi, Zhuangzi, and the Wei-Jin Neo-Daoism

©2025 Gabriella Stanchina, CC BY-NC 4.0   https://doi.org/10.11647/OBP.0442.03

(*Xuanxue*), Mou elaborates further the ontological features of Daoist thought. As we will see, the features we draw from the depiction of the intuitive mind bear a meaningful resemblance to or correspondence with key aspects of Daoist ontology.

The core of Mou's work is a systematic and profound investigation and re-interpretation of Chinese thought, conducted in a comparative way with respect to the Western philosophical tradition, in particular with Kantian thought. This thorough confrontation with Chinese tradition leads Mou Zongsan to strongly affirm the inescapable significance of its contribution to human enterprise. Re-evaluation and cross-cultural comparison are densely interwoven in Mou's works. This warp-and-weft dynamic carries with it the danger of being misinterpreted as a binary confrontation between two paradigms: Mou's moral metaphysics pivoting around Confucian "vertical system," on the one hand, and Western epistemological pursuit, quintessentially embodied by Kant, on the other. In order to avoid this oversimplification, and to recognize the vibrant and nuanced pattern of Mou's work, it is necessary to appreciate the variety of its constitutive threads. In the last decade, several scholars have paved the way by analyzing the influence that Buddhism, and notably the Tiantai school, has exerted on Mou's portrayal of the Chinese mode of thought. The place of Daoist philosophy in Mou Zongsan's work has not yet received equal attention. As Kaspars Eihmanis remarks,[1] Mou Zongsan's study of Daoism "comprises a minute fraction of his voluminous oeuvre." Out of thirty-three volumes in the *Complete Works of Mou Zongsan*, only a single work, *Caixing yu xuanli* (才性與玄理 *Physical Nature and the "Profound Thought"*), is totally devoted to Daoism, and more precisely to Wei-Jin Neo-Daoism, broadly referenced as *Xuanxue* (玄學 *Mysterious Learning*). It entails Mou's reading of Wang Bi's commentary on *Daodejing* and Guo Xiang's commentary on *Zhuangzi*. Aside from the specific chapter devoted to Classical Daoism in *Nineteen Lectures on Chinese Philosophy*, the most important source for an appraisal of Mou's interpretation of Daoism are two series of lectures about Laozi and Zhuangzi delivered at Hong Kong's New Asia

---

1 See Kaspars Eihmanis, *Study of Mou Zongsan's Interpretation of Laozi*, Unpublished paper delivered at Institute of Chinese Literature and Philosophy, Academia Sinica, Taiwan, http://www.litphil.sinica.edu.tw/home/news/2010051</wbr>9/20100519.htm

Institute in 1986 and 1987. However, meaningful references to Daoism are scattered throughout his pivotal works, like *Phenomenon and Thing-in-Itself*,[2] or *Intellectual Intuition and Chinese Philosophy*.[3] These references act as a constant counterpoint, that enriches Mou's Confucian-based reasoning with slightly variant melodic lines, and reveals its polyphonic character. I decided therefore to attempt in this chapter a hermeneutic reconstruction of this textual constellation, adopting as a red thread the concept of self and subjectivity. Whereas the Buddhist idea of self has been widely analyzed and even adopted sometimes as a term of comparison in contemporary Western philosophy of mind, the Daoist model of self still requires deeper consideration. Whilst referring the reader to the seminal studies available about the role played by Buddhist psychology and metaphysics in Mou's thought,[4] in the following pages I aim to cast light upon the peculiarity of the Daoist idea of self in the interpretation of Mou Zongsan.

Western ontology pivots around the concept of "being," intended as a substantial foundation. From a methodological viewpoint, Western mainstream thought analyzes the characteristics of the finite being, trying to reconstruct the conditions of its constitution. The goal of ontological investigation is to respond to the question of "how" or "in what way" something is grounded and constituted. These questions have therefore a distinctive epistemological character. The focus of Chinese ontology, on the contrary, is the transcendental research of "the reason why" (*suoyiran* 所以然), which leads to the identification of a creative principle, which permeates and rules the universe. Mou does not underestimate the variety of the paths undertaken throughout the development of Western philosophy; however, he marvels at the similarity between the achievement of Plato's ontology of pure forms, Leibniz's plural ontology of monads, or Heidegger's formulation of the

---

2   Mou Zongsan (牟宗三), *Xianxiang yu wuzishen*. 現象與物自身 (Phenomenon and Thing-in-Itself). *Mou Zongsan xiansheng quanji* 牟宗三先生全集 (Complete Works of Mou Zongsan), vol. XXI, Taipei: Lianhe baoxi wenhua jijin hui, 2003.

3   Mou Zongsan (牟宗三), *Zhi de zhijue yu zhongguo zhexue*. 智的直覺與中國哲學 (Intellectual Intuition and Chinese Philosophy). *Mou Zongsan xiansheng quanji*. 牟宗三先生全集 (Complete Works of Mou Zongsan), vol. XX, Taipei: Lianhe baoxi wenhua jijin hui, 2003.

4   For a first bibliographic reference, see Jason Clower, *The Unlikely Buddhologist: Tiantai Buddhism in Mou Zongsan's New Confucianism*, Leiden: Brill, 2010; and John Makeham, *The Awakening of Faith and New Confucian Philosophy*, Leiden: Brill, 2021.

ontical-ontological difference in the introduction of his magnus opus *Being and Time*. Their basic principles are epistemologically-oriented and static, i.e., deprived of a creative power. In the Western world, Christian theology takes charge of the problem of creation, assigning this function to God, i.e., an infinite individual being who can be theologically investigated, but not adequately experienced and embodied through moral practice. Chinese ontology, argues Mou, despite revealing the sprout of immanent thought in the onto-cosmology of *qi* 氣, which is responsible for the constitution of the myriad things through its coagulating and rarifying tendencies, is primarily centered on finding a principle of creation or actualization. This principle should be able to transcend the finite universe and to provide it with meaning, value, and generative force. In Confucian thought, this principle manifests itself as a transcendent, universal, and moral substance that vivifies and rules everything between heaven and Earth, and is accessible to the mind of the saint through ethical practice and spiritual elevation. The two other mainstream movements dominating Chinese history of thought, Daoism and Buddhism, while lacking an ultimate foundation in moral substance, nonetheless promote the vertical self-improving of the mind, the embodiment of the transcendental principle in the mind of the saint, and the dynamic creative force radiating from the mind when it is detached from the boundaries of myriad things.

One of the greatest contributions of Daoism to Chinese thought is the synthesis of all these aspects—practical ascension, embodiment, and dynamic creation—in what Mou calls the "metaphysics of the state of mind" as opposed to the metaphysics of being. What does state of mind mean? It is not a mental condition, like mood variations or a specific kind of temperament, which belongs more to the horizontal approach of psychology, but a subjective way of seeing the world achievable through a path of self-cultivation. In order to understand Daoism, we should abandon the Platonic and Aristotelian image of the universe as an objective hierarchy of beings and enter a frame of mind in which everything is moving and changing incessantly in accordance with the inner state reached through my practice. The keyword "Dao" or "mind of Dao" is not something that I can cognitively achieve, grasping it with my mind and expressing through a definable noun. Dao is, first of all, a path, which is made visible through my pursuit of it. Instead of thinking of the world as constituted by enduring and permanent substances, the perspective suggested by Dao is that of a perpetual movement and an inexhaustible being concretely involved in the events of the universe. Mou praises the English philosopher Alfred North Whitehead, who, in his masterful work *Process and Reality*, suggested that the world is constituted by a web of interrelated processes, a perpetual flux of experiential occasions that requires my actual participation in order to exist. In a similar way, Laozi and Zhuangzi, through a lyrical and challenging language, which is more suggestive than definitory, outline a reality where things are events actualized in my subjective practice of embodiment (*tixian* 體現) and experiential illumination (*tihui* 體會). In this metamorphic space, the distinction and opposition between subject and object, inner and outer world, has not yet happened. I should therefore resist my temptation of drawing boundaries, separating things from things and crystallizing them in concepts and definitions, if I aim to restore this original inchoate state. Experiencing and attuning to this state lets reality be open to endless possibilities, and further lets my mind be one and the same with the germinal force that pervades and nurtures it. In what way is this vibrant, spring-like spirit attained? In *Daodejing* 4 we read:

> The Dao is (like) the emptiness of a vessel; and in our employment of it we must be on our guard against all fulness. How deep and unfathomable it is, as if it were the Honoured Ancestor of all things! We should blunt our sharp points, and unravel the complications of things; we should attemper our brightness, and bring ourselves into agreement with the obscurity of others. How pure and still the Dao is, as if it would ever so continue! I do not know whose son it is. It might appear to have been before God.

Pursuing emptiness and withdrawing to unfathomable obscurity is the realization of *Wu* (nothing). Nothingness and being are not abstract ontological domains, but processes I should realize in my spiritual practice, so that they become active and manifest in myriad things. Mou highlights that *Wu* is not to be understood as a noun expressing the logical absence of being, but as a verb, suggesting the activity of self-emptying and self-diminishing. I am entangled in a static web of things and names, which seems to exist from the very beginning, but is actually produced by my inadvertent attachment to the projections of my defining mind. I have no other way to unravel from it than to abdicate from my alleged cognitive sovereignty, detaching myself from the things and letting them go one by one.

This posture is rarely seen in Western thought, and the reason may reside in the difference between the metaphysics of being and the metaphysics of the state of mind formulated by Mou. How could it be interpreted in the frame of Western metaphysics of being, this practice of diminishing the self and detaching ourselves from the ordered reality we have construed through our concepts? In order to clarify the differences between the two metaphysical models and to highlight how the choice between them undergirds our vision of the world and the value we attribute to our subjectivity, we may refer not to a philosophical text, but to a seminal drama about self and nothingness, *Exit the King* by Eugène Ionesco. At the center of the theatrical scene, there is a dying king who desperately struggles to not lose his grip on his world, which is fatally fading away. In the context of Western thought, the king at the center of his kingdom bears resemblance with the Cartesian Cogito in the middle of an unreliable and delusional world. Moving in concentric circles, the subject refuses to trust the different appearance of reality, only to discover in itself, i.e., in the rational core of the ego the steadfast indestructible foundation of being. Radiating from this core, human understanding can extend its ownership over the rest of the world, like Kant's transcendental apperception does, synthesizing in itself every aspect of the sensible and intelligible universe. In this frame of reference, pivoting, as Mou stresses, around substance and the hierarchy of beings, any attempt to diminish the ego or to persuade it to withdraw from its possession, can be experienced with anguish and alarm, since it implies the disappearing of the world or its return to an unthinkable pre-egoic chaos. In Ionesco's piece, while the king is performing a pointless rebellion against his death, the kingdom, progressively shrunk to the confines of his garden wall, is crumbling around him, the network of reality is disintegrating, even space and time dissolve in "a great and mighty nothingness." We may repeat here the words of the Ming dynasty philosopher Wang Yangming 王陽明 (1472–1529): "Consider the dead man. His spirit has drifted away and dispersed. Where are his heaven and earth and myriad things?"[5] Ionesco represents the frailty and arrogance of the modern ego before the event of death, and the *horror vacui* raised by the decay and dilapidation of a world based on the hegemony and ownership of the ego. In the frame of the metaphysics of being, the loss of control and the final surrender of the ego is not a practicable option, because it implies the apocalyptic annihilation of the concrete world. This is the reason why the path of the Daoist saint can be meaningful and exemplary only if it is interpreted through Mou's conception of the metaphysics of the state of mind.

In the state of mind paradigm, I embrace a practical and transformative vision of myself. In Western classical thought, subjectivity is dominantly represented as the statical subsistence of an ego in which only two modalities are possible. Or the subject is present and extends its dominion and control to the totality of things, or it expires, like in death or in deep sleep, and its absence determines the cessation of his universe. In Chinese thought, this binary of presence-absence is transcended in favor of a vertically higher level. Subjectivity is something that can be molded, reconfigured, nurtured, and perfected through a life-long spiritual practice. At any stage of this self-improvement, reality correlatively discloses itself with an increasing clarity, liveliness, and authenticity. In Daoist thought, the only way to ascend in spiritual dominion is to return to the source of all. I cannot recede endlessly in the chain of cause and effect that characterizes the determined being of things. To avoid falling into the paradox of the infinite regress from being to being, I should argue that the primal root of being resides in nothingness (*wu* 無). From a spiritual and performative viewpoint, I should practice *Wu* as a path of abandoning the calculating and restless mind and its attachment to reality. In this way, I remove any obstruction caused by the attachment, letting the things exist and thrive in their spontaneous being-so. We have here a peculiar mode of creation, a "generation without generating." We passively abstain to intervene and artificially mold the things. We detach ourselves from the concepts we use to grasp the world, in order to clear any obstacle to the endlessly rich and multifarious flux of beings. In this way, I attune myself with the mind of Dao, the dynamical and unceasing

---

5   Wing Tsit-Chan (ed.), *Instructions for Practical Living, and Other Neo-Confucian Writings by Wang Yang-Ming*, New York and London: Columbia University Press, 1963, p. 258.

spontaneity of everything. As Mou remarks, this kind of passive creation is totally different from the ontological *creatio ex nihilo* of the Christian God. At the same time, it contrasts with the moral creativity of Confucianism, which actively operates in the world through the mind of benevolence, righteousness, propriety, and wisdom, actualizing the innermost and authentic nature of everything.

The "generating without generating" in Daoist thought is a transposition of the creative generation in the sphere of subjectivity. If I let things go, they will autonomously grow, if I return to the root, everything is nurtured, if I quietly retreat in the silent clarity of the beginning, everything will luxuriantly sprout. If I elevate myself, all the universe is elevated in me. If I plunge into attachment, all the universe is chained and spoiled in me. The mind of Dao does not substantially produce the world, but the mind of Dao and the universe are mutually and concurrently revealed. This kind of concurrent revelation based on state of mind and subjective contemplation (*guanzhao* 關照) implies the horizontality of the practical expression in Daoism, because everything, the free-and-easy wandering of my detached mind and the unbounded self-subsistence of the universe, happens simultaneously and on the same level. *Wu*, as Mou explains, is not substantial nothingness, but the practice of *wu*-ing, which is an abbreviation of *wuwei* 無爲. This expression denotes the art of renouncing any intentional effort of forging and subjugating the world around me on the basis of a subjective, prefixed standard. The Daoist saint, letting go of attachment to specific beings, stops the germination of opposites and discards all partiality and bias. This act of relinquishing and withdrawing is the only possible disclosure of nothingness itself, and it is therefore subjective. The word "subjective" here does not refer to the duality of subject-object, since any kind of separation and mutual limitation in the heart of the being is removed, but rather means subjective on the vertical axis, i.e., the state of mind that can be achieved through spiritual practice. Nothingness is not a substance, but can be maintained only as a constant unceasing movement of detachment and soaring above things, and is therefore a pure and endless function. As the mind progressively withdraws, reality concurrently becomes blurred and unfocused for the subject, returning to the state of primordial chaos (*hundun* 混沌). In the previous chapter, we analyzed the mind of the quiet shining and its punctual appearing and disappearing, jumping over stiff boundaries and limited viewpoints. Here a similar function, expressed on the level of self-cultivation, is embodied by the act of *wu*-ing, which liquefies and dissolves what is fixed. Sitting in meditation and oblivion, emptying oneself, the saint attains oneness with the universe. The goal is to descend from the ramification of beings, in order to embracing the primeval root. This inchoate state of mind, as Mou remarks, is often represented in the post-Han Xuanxue school, as *Taiji*, the great culmen and formless pivot that rules and accomplishes everything in the universe in a non-purposive way.[6] Zhuangzi, in "All Under Heaven," illustrates how the Daoist saints pursued oneness and emptiness as a way of self-perfection:

> To regard the source as pure and the things that emerge from it as coarse, to look on accumulation as insufficiency; dwelling alone, peaceful and placid, in spiritual brightness there were those in ancient times who believed that the "art of the Way" lay in these things. The Barrier Keeper Yin and Lao Dan heard of their views and delighted in them. They expounded them in terms of constant non-being and being and headed their doctrine with the concept of the Great Unity. Gentle weakness and humble self-effacement are its outer marks; emptiness, void, and the noninjury of the ten thousand things are its essence.[7]

3.2 *Jingjie* as Spiritual State and Hodological Space

In an article, Fang Zhaohui remarks that "It is extremely difficult to translate '*jingjie*' (境界 state of mind) in Western languages, to the point that we can consider it untranslatable. For example, some scholars translate it as 'the world' (James Liu and Joer Bonner), others translate

---

6 Regarding the correlation between the culmen and the nothingness, David Pankenier claims on the basis of archeo-astronomical data, that during the Warring States period and the Han, the culmen of the celestial vault in the northern hemisphere was not identifiable with a Polar star and therefore it could appear as a numinous emptiness: "It can hardly be coincidental that during the preceding two millennia while this mystical vision was taking shape there was no distinctive pole star, no physical presence at the pivot of the heavens, so that the marvel of an efficacious nothing at the center of the rotating dome of the heavens was nightly on display, inviting wonder." David W. Pankenier, "A Brief History of *Beiji* 北極 (Northern Culmen), with an Excursus on the Origin of the Character *di* 帝," *Journal of the American Oriental Society*, 124:2 (2004), 211–236 (p. 220).
7 Burton Watson (ed.), *The Complete Works of Zhuangzi*, New York: Columbia University Press, 2013, pp. 294–295.

it as the sphere of reality delineated (Adele Austin Rickett), the spiritual realm (Diane Obeinchain), the world or horizon (Tang Junyi), the state (Derk Bodde), the sphere or realm (E. R. Hughes), and so on. [...]. Strictly speaking, the simple fact that in Western languages we do not find a concept similar to the Chinese *jingjie*, i.e., a word entailing the level of self-improving as given through a specific subjective spiritual experience, isn't in itself proof of the relevant difference between Chinese and Western civilization?"[8] Mou Zongsan, in *Nineteen Lectures on Chinese Philosophy*, recognizes that "it is hard to find a comparable term for *jingjie* in English. We may at best try to define it as the state of mind (spiritual state) reached through specific practices, whether Confucian, Daoist, or Buddhist."[9] Self-cultivation produces a specific vision or insight through which we understand the world. This world, interpreted through such a perspective, arises from our cultivated vision and differs from the empirically observed world of scientific research. This latter world is determined, whereas the world of *jingjie* changes according to our vision, and can be elevated or oriented through the diverse paths of self-cultivation. Mou continues: "The elevated and variously oriented worlds, on the other hand, are worlds in the realms of value, with spiritual values cultivated through practices."[10] There are therefore three aspects that coalesce in the word *jingjie*: an underlying spatial imagery, a spiritual dimension of vertical ascension through practice, and the "world" or "sphere" itself attuned to a specific vision, changeable in accord with subjective experience. A brief review of the origins and development of the word and its components *Jing* and *Jie* is highly meaningful, since it provides us with a map of the semantic cluster condensed in the word *jingjie* and the interlacing threads that undergird and unify its meaning.

Originally, the word *jing* 境 was coined in the Warring States period and was strictly related to the term *bianjing* 邊境 (frontier), conveying the idea of a territorial extension defined by its boundaries. Starting

---

8   Fang Zhaohui (方朝晖), "Zhongguo wenhua wei he chengxing jingjielun?" 中国文化为何盛行境界论? (Why Is the Idea of *Jingjie* Prevailing in Chinese Culture?), *Guoxue xuekan* 1 (2020), 109–114 (pp. 112–113).

9   Mou Zongsan, *Nineteen Lectures on Chinese Philosophy: A Brief Outline of Chinese Philosophy and the Issues It Entails*, Scotts Valley, CA: CreateSpace Independent Publishing Platform, 2015, p. 138.

10 Ibid., p. 139.

from the Western Jin era (265–316), the compound word *jingjie* came to represent the administrative and cultural units and boundaries within the Chinese empire. The art of cartography, bringing together the geopolitical and spatial relevance of the outer and inner frontiers in organizing territory, discloses a horizontal and vertical structuration, which not only divides and encloses, but also hierarchically systematizes the world.[11] The spiritual development of the discourse on *jingjie* can be traced back to the introduction of Buddhist thought and the need to find adequate words for translating the original Sanskrit texts in Chinese, a process that will finally lead to the gradual absorption and accomplished Sinicization of Buddhism in China. Buddhism presents a distinctive spatial imagery, spreading from the geographical depiction of the Pure Lands of the Buddhas to the idea of enlightenment as a journey crossing from the domain of illusion to the domain of emptiness. This justifies the adoption of the territorial concept of *jingjie* in translating the different levels implied in human understanding, from *viṣaya*, i.e., bodily limitedness constraining human knowledge and diverting it from the true vision, to *prajñā*, direct insight into the truth, which is accessible to the saints. Mou, in *Nineteen Lectures in Chinese Philosophy*, writes that the concept of *jing* in Buddhism refers to external objects, but the School of Consciousness-Only (*Yogācāra*) observes the dependence of objects on consciousness, stating that "objects are produced by consciousness only," so that "the doctrine of consciousness-only subjectifies external objects and asserts that all phenomenal changes are changes in consciousness (*shibian*)."[12]

The negation of a dichotomy between reality and mind leads to the idea of *jingjie* as a ladder, comprising vertically-arranged spiritual territories that can be ascended through spiritual effort up to the mental realm of enlightenment. Song-Ming Neo-Confucianism, starting from the Cheng brothers and Zhu Xi 朱熹 (1180–1200), developed the discourse on *jingjie*, criticizing the inactivity and passivity of Buddhist meditation, and substituting Buddhist aspiration to awakening for the "*jingjie* of void and emptiness" with the pursuit of the ideal *jingjie* of the

---

11 For a thorough analysis of the geopolitical Ur-meaning of *jingjie*, see Christina Han, "Territory of the Sages: Neo-Confucian Discourse of Wuyi Nine Bends Jingjie," PhD dissertation, University of Toronto, 2011, pp. 12–33.
12 Mou Zongsan, *Nineteen Lectures on Chinese Philosophy*, p. 137.

saints. The conflict in Chinese Buddhism between sudden or gradual attainment of enlightenment is reformulated in the two main schools of Neo-Confucians, the School of Principle and the School of Mind, as the variable relations between moral effort and the attainment of sageness. Zhu Xi in a letter to Zhang Shi 張栻 (1133–1180) presents the attainment of the *jingjie* of the saints as the fruit of life-long self-cultivation: "How can we in one day see this *iingiie*? Therefore, the saints had to tell us: Rectify your heart-mind. In order to rectifying your heart-mind you must first make your intent sincere. To make your intent sincere, you must first extend your knowledge: this is not one day's work." [13] On the contrary, Lü Zuqian 呂祖謙 (1137–1181) claims that the realm of the saints is already located in my mind in a beclouded way, and I have only to remove the spiritual obstructions to restore it: "In my bosom there originally was a sagely *jingjie*. I can go back and search it, and it must be there. This can be compared to the meaning of all things under heaven returning to humaneness through overcoming oneself and restoring propriety." [14] In parallel with the discussion on moral practice, *jingjie* was widely used in the aesthetic field, conveying the essence of landscape poetry and painting. *Jingjie* can be translated here as "poetic and spiritual landscape," and represents the perfect fusion between the portrayed scenery and the emotion of the artist. One of the most influential scholars and literary critics, Wang Guowei 王國維 (1877–1927), in his *Poetic Remarks in the Human World* analyzes extensively the idea of *jing* or *jingjie* as a visionary realm, in which affective response and natural scene are harmoniously blended. He divides *jing* into two subcategories: *jing* with I (or self) (*youwo zhi jing* 有我之境); and *jing* without I (*wuwo zhi jing* 無我之境). In the former, the insight and spiritual perspective of the observer is paramount, whereas in the latter the observer is capable of sublimating and obliterating his self, so that the landscape seems to be described from the point of view of the landscape itself.

Feng Youlan, in the fourth volume of his *A New Treatise on the Nature of Human Beings*, describes human existence as ontologically constituted

---

13 Translated by Christina Han in "Envisioning the Territory of the Sages: The Neo-Confucian Discourse of *Jingjie*," *Journal of Confucian Philosophy and Culture* 22 (2014), 85–109 (p. 99).

14 Translated in Han, "Territory of the Sages," p. 11.

by a hierarchy of *jingjie*. This term is variously translated as sphere, realm, and horizon.[15] According to Feng Youlan, we have four kinds of *jingjie*: innocent, utilitarian, moral, and transcendent (literally, "the *jingjie* of heaven and earth", *tiandi jingjie* 天地境界). *Jingjie* expresses four different levels of understanding of the meaning of life and the universe, and these levels produce four different categories of individuals. In the "innocent *jingjie*," the individual behaves according to their instinct or the custom of their society without further self-reflection; in the "utilitarian *jingjie*," the individual possesses a materialistic self-centered consciousness and pursues only utilitarian values: together, they represent two forms of inauthentic existence. In the "moral *jingjie*" and the "transcendent *jingjie*," we find respectively, the "worthy person" who is able to follow benevolence and righteousness, as well as to assume social responsibilities; and the saint who has achieved the highest "understanding and self-consciousness" (*juejie*) not only of his role in society but also of his position in the universe, and is therefore able to transcend the inner struggle between "human desires" and the "heavenly principle."

This use of the word *jingjie* to express a horizon of understanding finds its more systematic articulation in Tang Junyi. Tang, in his final monograph, *Human Existence and the Worlds of the Mind*, delineated nine "horizons" (*jingjie*), organized into three categories: objective, subjective, and transcending-subjective-and-objective. Through this work, Tang aimed to propose an ambitious chart of all the possible visions of the world and the correlated modes of existence. Tang highlighted that the meaning of horizon (*jingjie*) goes far beyond the Buddhist term *jing*

---

15 "Sphere" is the English translation adopted in *The Spirit of Chinese Philosophy*, London: Trench Trubner, 1947, and *A Short History of Chinese Philosophy*, New York: Macmillan, 1960. Diane Obenchain's translation is "realm" or "spiritual realm." Lauren F. Pfister in the essay "Three Dialectical Phases in Feng Youlan's Philosophical Journey," (in: David Elstein (ed.), *Dao Companion to Contemporary Confucian Philosophy*, London and Berlin: Springer, 2021) translates "*zuigao jingshen jingjie* 最高精神境界" as "horizon/realm of the highest intellectual and spiritual realization" (p. 146), remarking in this way that the practical aspect of realization is implied in the idea of horizon. Xunwu Chen in "Being and Authenticity" similarly prefers the term "horizon," establishing a terminological and conceptual relationship with Georg Gadamer's key concept of "horizon" as the breadth of spiritual vision and understanding that we may acquire. Our horizon influences and delimits the intelligibility and significance of the world in our understanding. See Xunwu Chen, *Being and Authenticity*, Leiden: Brill, 2004.

(interpreted here as *viṣaya*, a field of cognitive object) and the Yogācāra term of cognitive object (*suoyuan* or *ālambana*). Mind and horizons (*jingjie*) are mutually resonating and they develop themselves not only as epistemological steps, but also as graded and progressive levels acquired by the practicing mind. As Lauren F. Pfister writes: "[...] the structure of the nine horizons is not simply a conceptual representation of mental activity, but also counts as a veritable roadmap to moral and spiritual development."[16]

Summing up, the concept of *jingjie* retains first of all its original value as a spatial metaphor, so that the ideal *jingjie* of saints can be reached, entered, and maintained. These actions are performed through a vertical effort of ascension, and therefore the subject in the metaphysics of *jingjie* is, first of all, in the act of making or becoming oneself through progressive self-cultivation. The subject is an uninterrupted dynamism and, through the idea of *jingjie*, acquires a vertical dimension, that of the practice, characterizing itself as the "performative self."

Through contraposing Western "metaphysics of being" and Chinese "metaphysics of *jingjie*," Mou Zongsan turns the spotlight on the concept of *jingjie*, identifying it as the irreducible distinguishing trait of Chinese philosophy as a whole, whether one focuses on Daoism, Confucianism, or Buddhism. Understanding Mou Zongsan's philosophy of the self is thus of utmost importance, in order to delve into the imagery and the semantic value of this word. We should examine why the plurality of translations provided by scholars (place, realm, sphere, horizon, state of mind etc.) make visible each time only an aspect of its multifaceted meaning.

As Kuan-min Huang remarks in his analysis of Tang Junyi's "nine horizons," horizon (*jingjie*) is not properly a spatial metaphor, but a topological metaphor, involving a "doctrine of place": "place entails an interconnected reality (*mailuo* 脉络) and an affective environment (*qingjing* 情境) fusion of feeling and scene, on the contrary space as an abstract concept is strictly related to the progress of contemporary natural sciences."[17] An example of *jing* as topological metaphor can

---

16 Pfister, "Three Dialectical Phases," p. 240.
17 Kuan-min Huang (黃冠閔), *Gantong yu huidang: Tang Junyi zhexuelun tan*. 感通與迴盪: 唐君毅哲學論探 (Affective Communication and Echo: An Exploration of Tang Junyi's Philosophy), Taipei: Lianjing chuban gongsi, 2011, p. 121, n. 6.

be found in a more advanced stage of Daoist thought, starting from the practices of inner alchemy developed during the Han Dynasty, and epitomized by the idea of the "inner landscape" (*neijing* 內境). The inner landscape is a symbolic representation of the human body, which often takes the form of a complex map, chart, or diagram, for the scope of Daoist meditation and traditional medicine. The most famous modern reproduction is the "inner pathways diagram" (內經圖), an engraved stele dated 1886 in the White Cloud Temple of Beijing, but the first symbolic maps of the human body date back to the tenth century. The earliest anatomical diagrams reporting the expression *neijing* 內境 are attributed to Yanluozi 煙蘿子 (tenth century) and preserved in the 1250 CE "Cultivating Perfection Ten Books" (*Xiuzhenshishu* 修真十書).

In these maps, the interior of the body is imagined as an ordered microcosm with mountains, rivers, paths, forests, stars, and figures derived from Chinese mythology. Those who contemplate them must be able to get rid of the attachment to worldly appearances, and also of the spiritual blinding produced by shapes and colors. The meditating subject is invited to grasp reality as a web of forces that flow, vibrate, and respond. The inner landscape transcends the dualism of mind-body or interior-exterior. Whereas the Western anatomical sections display a purely physiological body that is objectified by the scrutinizing gaze of the expert observer, the various maps of the inner landscape offer a symbolic topology of the indissoluble whole of the human being. In the human being, the spirit is structurally embodied, and the body is imbued with spiritual value. What matters most is that the inner landscape is a living interconnected weft in which the microcosm of human being bears a dynamic correspondence with macrocosmic forces. The self is vertically expanded on the three concurrent and mutually responding levels: heaven, earth, and human being. These diagrams of the "inner landscape" are not conceived to satisfy our desire of knowledge, but to offer a roadmap for the inner ecstatic flight. During the practice of meditation, the spirit penetrates this multifaceted landscape, regulating and refining the *qi*, nurturing the mind-body with life, enhancing its ability to resonate (*ganying* 感應) with the totality of the universe. We are here in Zhuangzi's realm of transformation (*huajing* 化境), in which the boundaries between the mind and the cosmos are dissolved in a subtle web of interpenetration and resonance. The "inner landscape" represents the topological character of *jingjie*, and how it necessarily depends on practices of self-cultivation in order to manifest itself. As a place, it is subjectively constituted, i.e., it is permeated and molded through a subjective qualitative vision and is endowed with meaning and value.

This vision-related world bears a similarity with Edmund Husserl's phenomenological idea of noema, i.e., an "objectivity belonging to consciousness and yet specifically peculiar,"[18] it is the object as it is perceived and imagined and it is always structurally correlated to a noetic act or noesis, the subjective activity of bestowing sense to the world. In the *Fifth Logical Investigation*, Husserl distinguished between "the object which is intended," the factual reality that is grasped through my understanding, and "the object as it is intended," inseparable from my lived experience. The similarity between the inner landscape and Husserl's noema resides in their transcendental character, which overcomes the naïve scientific thinking of the object as something that simply exists on its own, independent of any subjective apprehension. Both terms represent an object as constituted and manifested through my intentional glance and my embodied living experience (*Erlebnis*), and both refer to reality as something disclosed in our inner horizon, a kernel of living significance. However, Husserl articulated his theory as an answer to the question of knowledge, aiming to clarify the way an object is given to a knowing subject, and how it is originally inseparable from its "mode of presentation." Inner landscape as an epitome of *jingjie* is not aimed to provide us with an alternative way of explaining reality. Using Mou's terminology, *neijing* is not collocated on the horizontal, epistemological axis, but is reachable only when ascending on the vertical axis through practical effort. As a practical field of self-realization, it has a constitutive dynamism at its core. It presents itself as a place of possibilities in which my vision is not a static viewpoint but the practice of turning the eyes inside and flying through myself, transforming my embodied mind in the horizon of a spiritual journey.

In this continuous reversal of inside and outside, there is an aspect of complication and compenetration that cannot be reduced to the horizontal correlation between noesis and noema, but can only take

---

18 Edmund Husserl, *Ideas I*, New York: Macmillan, 1913, §128.

place in the verticality of the practical self. Reality changes according to the changes in my vision, not merely because there is an intentional relationship between knower and known, but because I reached through meditation an ideal place or *jingjie* in which self and the world are no longer separated but are caught in a continuous process of transformation and reversal. Flying inside myself with the help of the chart, I can transform and refine my inner landscape, and in doing so I undergo a process of self-transformation, making my inner landscape more viable, fluid, and open to transformation. Instead of positioning themselves at the opposite polarities of the gaze, as in cognitive acts, subject and object are caught here in a process of mutual implication. The self is enclosed in the landscape, but at the same time the landscape is enclosed in the self, blurring the distinction between inside and outside in a dynamism very similar to the mutual compenetration and transformation of yin and yang. This mutual and synchronous concurrence of self and the world is produced through my practice, and is therefore subjectivity-based. What subjective means here is not the subjective polarity of the intentional act, which is on the horizontal plane of knowledge, but the dependence of *jingjie* on the practice of self-cultivation. On the vertical dimension, through our spiritual effort and ascending dynamism we transcend the duality subjective-objective. In the case of the Daoist saint, claims Mou, when returning to the root, the universe is restored in its original potentiality and true nature, "when the subjective mind clearly manifests the state of 'tranquilness through void-ful unity', the world will be peaceful and quiet, and everything will be in its rightful place, follow its nature, grow to its potential, and rectify to its properness." [19]

Summing up the characteristics of the *jingjie* as exemplified through the "inner landscape," we observed the coalescence of the topological meaning, the dependence from the subjective practice, and the vertical axis on which the place of transformation is established and disclosed. Besides the concept of "topology," place, and inner landscape, I think that the concept of "hodological space" may convey the connection between *jingjie* as place of spiritual journey and Dao in its etymological meaning of "way" and "viability." The word "Hodology" derives from the Greek *hodos*, meaning "way," and refers to the study of lived space

---

[19] Mou Zongsan, *Nineteen Lectures on Chinese Philosophy*, p. 127.

as constituted by the possibilities of movement available to the subject. Hodological space is the practicable horizon of our existential projects, and therefore is at the same time subjective and objective. Subjectively, it is determined by our virtual movement; objectively, it is a web of crossing pathways, openings, and obstacles that determine our potentiality of moving.

The philosopher Jean-Paul Sartre develops this concept in his essay *Sketch for a Theory of the Emotions*, wherein he depicts the phenomenological sense or experience of lived-space as being "hodological" in nature. In this experience, all individuals bear a "hodological map," meaning individuals possess a sub-cognitive and non-representational lived-sense of the pathways of action, instrumental availabilities, closures, openings, potentialities, blockages, varying alternative routes, etc., where this lived sense of space is organized around one's projects. The space is interpreted as "lived" in the first person and is distinguished from the objective and measurable Euclidean space, which is considered "represented" in a scientific way, i.e., in the third person. The lived experience of walking, flying, ascending, and descending, both in a physical and in a spiritual way, transforms a space into a vectorial space, impregnated with affective and practical values, and structured by a guiding dynamic principle. Hodology is therefore a knowledge of the path/way (*dao* 道).

A poem by Chao-Ping Wen, a scholar of the Sung period, suggests the imaginary flight in the landscape and the spiritual goal that a painting by Wu Yuan-chih (fl. 1190–1195), "Fisherman and Woodcutter Immersed in a Conversation," has allowed him to achieve:

> These two old men have long forgotten the world,
> and taken trees and rocks as their followers.
> When they happen to meet each other,
> wind and moon must have directed them there.
> Decline and rise of [empires] is not my business;
> why should I be engaged in these petty affairs?
> I only know that my own feelings
> Seem to have been depicted in the painting on paper.
> At one time I am the fisherman,
> traveling in spirit on vast rivers and lakes.
> At another, I am the woodcutter,
> In a dream becoming lean in mountain and marsh.

3. The "Diaphanous Subject" in Daoist Thought

With my self shaped by what I dwell in,
Which one is my true self?
Since I've forgotten whether I am the one or the other,
how much less can I return to the distractions of court and market?
The west wind blows down the setting sun
And at the ford there is smoke from a single chimney.
I neither ask nor answer,
But chant at length: "Let us return."

跋武元直漁樵閒話圖
元代：趙秉文
兩翁久忘世, 木石以為徒。偶然相值遇, 風月應指呼。
廢興非吾事, 胡為此區區。但覺腹中事, 似落紙上圖。
一以我為漁, 神遊渺江湖。一以我為樵, 夢為山澤臞。
形骸隨所寓, 何者為真吾。尚忘彼與此, 況復朝市娛。
西風下落日, 渡口炊煙孤。無問亦無答, 長笑歸來乎。[20]

The poet moves along the landscape evoked in the painting, adopting the viewpoint of the two human figures, workers and craftsmen, who, like in the *Zhuangzi*, are the real masters of Dao. Oblivious of everything, detached from human affairs, the two figures have attained a deep spiritual communion with the landscape that surrounds them: rocks and trees are their disciples, but also, their masters in the understanding of the laws of the cosmos and of the virtue of non-action (*wu wei* 無為). The painting conveys and enables an experience of identification. The journey of the spirit in the vastness of the landscape is at the same time a transformation of the body (the shrinking of the body due to the Daoist hygienic practices), which implies a distillation of vital energy. The painting allows Chao-Ping Wen to forget the narrow dimensions of the human microcosm revolving around the imperial court, and to evaluate the whole course of history. Examining the vicissitudes of the rise and fall of empires, the poet comes to understand human ambition as a trivial matter. The officer can lay down the mask of his bureaucratic role and transpose himself into the fisherman or the woodcutter, who are harmonized with the rhythms of the rivers and mountains to the point of being oblivious of the turmoil of history. What makes this different from an escape into an idealized fantasy world is the irreversible change

---

20 See Susan Bush, *The Chinese Literati on Painting: Su Shih (1037–1101) to Tung Ch'i-ch'ang (1555–1636)*, Hong Kong: Hong Kong University Press, 2012, p. 106.

that it is able to produce. Totally immersed in the painting, the officer does not remember his identity and allows any element of the scroll to mold him. This condition of estrangement makes him unable to act in the mundane world based on the dialectics of useful and useless, of loss and profit. What remains of him is a melody in the landscape, the song of return, tinged with the subtle melancholy of the home where someone is silently preparing the evening meal for those to come, while the smoke of the chimney, trace of the humble domestic activity, fades quietly into the sunset. The officer returns to the pivotal axis of the world, the Dao of the thousand transformations which human language is unable to describe. Like in the *Zhuangzi*'s history of "Intelligence Travelling to the North," the inquietude of the question and the adequacy of the solutions are finally solved in the absolute simplicity of the Dao. In order to ascend to this place of metamorphosis and realization, I should retreat in my uniqueness and solitude, abandoning any political ambition and generally any intentional attempt to perfect the world.

The Daoist vision is here antithetical to the Confucian ideal of "sageness within and kingliness without." Daoist hodological space is not the same as the Confucian one, i.e., a concrete world of human relations that I aim to realize in their authentic value, bringing them to accomplishment through my moral action. On the contrary, it is a hodological space constituted through a spiritual and linguistic withdrawal from any involvement with and commitment to an illusory reality. An example of this place, marked by my retreatment, is Zhuangzi's "Land of Nothingness," where the highest value is recognized in what is useless and unbelonging, or the utopic land described in the legend of the "Peach Blossom Spring," a secluded settlement in a grotto-heaven where one finds respite from the turmoil of hierarchy and power. The poet Su Shi celebrates his meditative space of retirement inspired to this utopia:

> 不如我仇池 It cannot be compared to my Qiuchi,
> 高舉復幾歲 Raised high above for how many years!
> 從來一生死 Where life and death are always treated equal;
> 近又等癡慧 And lately, the foolish and the clever have also become the same.

This *jingjie* is raised high above, on a vertical dimension where the opposites are blurred and equalized. Roaming freely through an oneiric space, his mind bears as reference points the secluded hermitages of two scholars, which, not by chance, are described as *jing* and *jie*:

> 羅浮稚川界 Mount Luofu is the territory of Zhichuan
> 夢往從之遊 In dreams I follow their roaming;
> 神交發吾蔽 The encounter of our spirits shall clear my delusions![21]

The two scholars, Ge Hong 葛洪 (283–343) and Anqi Sheng 安期生, both practiced inner alchemy, liquefying and transforming through meditation their inner landscape, and finally attaining immortality.[22] "In the topography of mental reality, a true land of bliss is accessible only in absolute spiritual spontaneity. Going to this land is seen as "returning"—a return toward the original state of authenticity and spontaneity." In this secluded metamorphic place "one is free from the tyranny of environment, of fate, or of an absolute monarchy—not by removing these obstacles from one's path, but by renouncing even the vaguest desire to go down that path."[23] In another lyric, Su Shi aspires to make a return to a pristine state without distinction between "guest and host" (*hun kezhu yiwei yi* 混客主以為一). The terms *ke* (客 guest) and *zhu* (主 host) may refer in Chinese to the object and the subject. Renouncing the external material goals and the internal subject, a cluster of selfish attachments, the poet reaches back to the source of myriad things, removing any obstruction and maculation, restoring the vivifying flux of the pristine energy and reflecting the macrocosm inside his mirror-like spirit.

To sum up, the concept of hodological space partially restores the structure of *jingjie*. It depicts a condition in which the hierarchical relationship between subject and object, typical of human cognition, is transcended toward a mutual correspondence and determination. The space as an external and objective sphere is qualitatively molded by my living act of dwelling, roaming, and ascending. The directionality of my subjective movement transforms the object into a place of possibilities, and its openness and closures determine in turn my intention to

---

[21] See Zhiyi Yang, "Return to an Inner Utopia: Su Shi's Transformation of Tao Qian in His Exile Poetry," *T'oung Pao* 99 (2013), 329–378 (p. 367).
[22] Calamus Gully is in Mt. Baiyun 白雲山 (in modern Guangzhou, Guangdong). In the local legend, Scholar Anqi found a nine-gnarled calamus root which sprouted purple blossoms, ate it, and became an immortal.
[23] Yang, "Return to an Inner Utopia," p. 370.

create an uninterrupted mutual transformation. To approach the idea of *jingjie*, we should translate this spatial imagery into the horizon of practice and self-cultivation. The spiritual dynamism generated by my practical effort discloses worlds that are graded on a vertical axis, and are therefore infused with values and significance. They are dependent on my subjective ability to ascend and self-improve through a specific practice, which in the case of Daoism is a practice of withdrawal from attachments, renouncing my selfish ego, equalizing all things. Through a meditative absorption and embodiment, the boundaries between my self and the world are blurred and made one and the same in mutual consonance (*ganying*), which is spontaneous and ever changing.[24]

3.3 Withdrawing and Progressing: Western Subject versus Daoist Subject

In what way, according to Mou, should the dynamism of the spiritual state be interpreted? In his "Lessons on the Laozi," Mou remarks that the discourse of the *Daodejing* is organized, just from the beginning, around a bifurcation of two sorts of Dao, the say-able one and the unsay-able one. According to Mou, this is an epitome of *yi xin kai er men* 一心開二門, "a single mind opens two doors," which can be considered "the common paradigm of philosophy, and the common modality through which the wisdom of humanity is inaugurated."[25] The opening of these two

---

24 Behind all the representations and cognitive acts, however, another type of transcendence is to be revealed as a kind of enveloping or enfolding that contains all entities positively and vertically, as Mou explains: "The intellectual act of lively *prajñā* enfolds all the entities, making it possible for them to realize themselves. Yet this enveloping is nothing but the actional and horizontal enfolding (*shuipingde juzu* 水平的具足); it is still not the ontological and vertical one (*shushingde juzu* 豎生的具足)" (Mou Zongsan, *Phenomenon and Thing-in-Itself*, p. 404.) Obviously, such an enfolding is no longer comprehensible as a type of mental action; nor is it the "ground" of subjectivity because it is not a substance. That which enfolds all the entities is describable only with the idea of the non-ground—once again, the emergence of all beings from the non-ground. In addition to the performative perfection of emptiness, the Tiantai school arrives at the ontological perfection (*cunyoulunde yuan* 存有論的圓), which means the horizontal enfolding of all acts. See Asakura Tomomi, "On the Principle of Comparative East Asian Philosophy: Nishida Kitarō and Mou Zongsan," *National Central University Journal of Humanities* 54 (2013), 1–25 (pp. 17–18).

25 Mou Zongsan delivered a series of lectures on Laozi and Zhuangzi Hong Kong's New Asia Institute in 1986 and 1987 respectively. "「一心開二門」是哲學的一個

thresholds leading to opposite routes can be traced back to the auroral phase of thought, both in Western and in Chinese culture. The expression "Two-door's mind" actually derives from the Mahayana Buddhist classic *Treatise on Awakening Mahāyāna Faith* (*Dasheng qi xin lun*《大乘起信论》 *Mahāyānaśraddhotpādaśāstra*).[26] In this context, however, Mou highlights that this bifurcation is visible in different traditions of thought. If in Western philosophy, it extends from Plato's dualism between intelligible world and sensible world to Kant's opposition between phenomenon and noumenon, in Chinese thought it is traced back to a difference that is not only ontological, but refers also to different practical states of mind. Whereas the Buddhist tradition discriminates between a "mind of birth and death," still entrapped in the world of becoming, and a "Buddha-mind," or "mind of the suchness" emancipated from every attachment, Confucianism and Daoism stress the divide between a mind of the Dao and a mind of habit and fixation. In the *Laozi*, the discourse about say-able and unsay-able Dao demarcates two directions, which, albeit lacking the moral hue of Confucianism, hint at different practices of self-realization. "In the pursuit of learning, everyday something is acquired, in the pursue of Dao, every day something is dropped."[27] If we pursue the way of knowledge, we gradually accumulate experiences and increase our ability to deal with the world, which is usually perceived by society as a praiseworthy enrichment and empowerment of the self. Those who follow the path of the unsay-able Dao instead experience a paradoxical diminishing, decrease, and evanescence. We are confronted here with two spiritual modes of being. We can move forward, refining our knowledge to align with the nature of things, becoming more and more analytic and masterful in dealing with the world. At the same time, this penetration and participation in the determinacy of beings produces a growing entanglement in the boundaries of the finite world. A forward-directed model of subjectivity is projected toward the increment of knowledge

---

共同的模型，是人類智慧開發的一個共同的方式。在古希臘柏拉圖就分兩個世界 (intelligible world 與sensible world)，兩個世界就是二分嘛。在佛教就說「一心開二門」,「二門」就是兩方面，兩個界域。到康德就講 noumena 與 phenomena." Mou Zongsan (牟宗三), "Laozi Daodejing yanjianglu." 老子《道德經》講演錄 (Lectures on Laozi's "Daodejing"), *Ehu yuekan* 334–343 (2003/2004).

26　The English translation of the *Treatise*: J. Jorgensen, D. Lusthaus, J. Makeham, and M. Strange (ed.), *Treatise on Awakening Mahāyāna Faith*, Oxford: Oxford University Press, 2019.

27　為學日益, 為道日損. Daodejing 48.

and power, and it is characterized by an unquenchable thirst to possess. Mou epitomizes this constant yearning for an accomplishment, which is concretely unattainable but operates as an ideal catalyst for progress, in the figure of Faust. In his "Lessons on the *Zhuangzi*," Mou, rethinking Faust through the mediation of Hegel, writes: "The Western world loves the 'spirit in tension' and its 'dramaticity'." In *Moral Idealism*, Mou argues that "it can be said that the modern spirit is Faust's spirit of quest in terms of the general feeling of life."[28]

This reference to Faust as representative of the spirit of modernity, and in particular of Western society, horizontally stretched out toward scientific and technological advancement, is widely diffused in the New Confucianism movement. Tu Wei-Ming mentions the "Faustian drive to explore, to know, to conquer, and to subdue,"[29] whereas Keping Wan remarks that in the thought of Thomé Fang 方東美 (1899–1977), "As regards the modern European culture, it is convenience-centred and for this reason it worships power, might and right. Its belief in knowledge as power is reflected in the sense of Faustian dissatisfaction. Hence, Europeans tend to be so engrossed in their endless pursuit of knowledge, seeming to be lost in it and never to return."[30] In this perspective, for Thomé Fang, "'Faust' is usually conceived of as an image of the European mentality that is aligned not only with a persistent investigation into the unknown, but also with non-stop curiosity about creating something novel."[31] Faust is the paradigmatic example of a subject who attempts to construe himself along the horizontal axis. He explores all the areas of living, and the ephemeral satisfaction of any desire, without finding a dwelling place. Lost in the multifariousness of things, exhausting himself in the frustrating pursue of finite things, he cannot return to the origin. The only thinkable vertical movement is an ultimate ascension

---

28 近代的精神，從一般生活情調方面說，可說是浮士德的追求精神。但是還有一面可說，這就是為科學所領導，環繞科學而形成的。所謂就虛幻不實的概念之澄清來說兩極化的形成，就是指的這方面說。Mou Zongsan (牟宗三), *Daode de lixiangzhuyi*. 道德的理想主義 (Moral Idealism), *Mou Zongsan xiansheng quanji*. 牟宗三先生全集 (Complete Works of Mou Zongsan), vol. IX.1, Taipei: Lianhe baoxi wenhua jijin hui, 2003, p. 244.

29 See Tu Wei-Ming, "The 'Moral Universal' from the Perspectives of East Asian Thought," *Philosophy East and West* 31:3 (1981), 259–267 (p. 261).

30 Keping Wang, "Thomé Fang's Pursuit of a Cultural Ideal," *Asian Studies* 8:24 (2020), 183–207 (p. 190).

31 Ibid., p. 201.

to an unsee-able god, or the attainment through logics of an abstract universality. In this frame, Mou denounces the failure of Western ontology to conceive of being without deriving its features from finite beings. In *Critique of the Cognitive Mind*, Mou already acknowledged the impossibility of fulfilling the universal statement (the Russelian paradox of incompleteness) and foresaw the need to transcend the horizontal epistemological axis through an intelligible intuition. According to Mou, Daoism perfectly exemplifies that, in order to attain sanctity, we should stop progressing forward, and start turning back to the origin.

This subject who strives for expansion and progress is ultimately doomed to preside over a reality that remains fragmented and scattered in the plurality of things. It becomes attached to the objects of its longing, but its desire for perfect knowledge and domination is always unsatisfied and postponed, creating the endless "bad infinity" described by Hegel in the *Science of Logic*. Novalis expressed this structural failure of the subject in his famous aphorism "We seek everywhere the unconditioned (*das Unbedingte*), and we always find only things (*nur Dinge*)."[32] The Romantic self, epitomized in the character of Faust, in pursuing limited and transitory things is confronted again and again with their boundaries, and therefore reminded of the deadly finiteness of the self's own nature. Trailing off endlessly into the distance, this infinity reveals only the absence of an end, i.e., of an ultimate foundation in which thought can dwell and be accomplished. How does one abandon this dead universe of scattered debris and restore the life-giving root of being? As Mou repeatedly says in his lectures on the *Laozi* and *Zhuangzi*, true wisdom is not only straightforward, square, and directed toward knowledge (*fangyi zhi* 方以智), like in Western thought, but also curved, like in Chinese tradition. Curve here means "circular and spiritual" (*yuan er shen* 圓而神).[33] The circle symbolizes heavenly power and the spiritual dimension that vertically transcends and encloses the pursuit of knowledge. However, the mention of

---

32   See Novalis, *Novalis Schriften. Teil 2, Hälfte 1*, ed. by Erst Heilborn, Berlin: De Gruyter, p. 1 (*Bluethenstaub*).

33   The image derives from the "Xici shang" (繫辭上) commentary of the *Yijing*: "The milfoil virtue is round and spiritual, and the hexagram's virtue is square and thereby knowing" (蓍之德, 圓而神; 卦之德, 方以智) (translated by Edward L. Shaughnessy (ed.), *I Ching: The Classic of Changes*, New York: Ballantine Books, 1996, p. 199).

circularity here clearly suggests that inverting the direction of our quest is not enough. Plato's philosophy, writes Mou, is the example of a line of thought that privileges the backward direction. Through a dialectical process, Plato traces back the ever-changing sensible things back to their archetypical ideas. This kind of inquiry, however, can be represented as a vertical gaze that intersects with the horizontal axis of empiric knowledge. Albeit ascending from the finite beings to a higher and more perfect level of reality, what dialectical thought ultimately envisions is a hierarchy of static determined forms. Daoism, on the contrary, aims to lead us back to the source from which the multifarious beings draw life and generate power. The Dao as *fons et origo* of the determined being should necessarily be in itself immeasurable and boundless, as well as dynamic and nimble. Turning around and moving back to the root does not simply mean a reversal of direction, but implies the restoration of a spiritual state that allows and promotes the inexhaustible generation of the myriad of things. By moving backward to the origin, we are involved in the bursting forth of life, and spring forward toward the beings. This dynamic ebb and flow is the expression of a "curved wisdom" in which even the forward movement acquires a new meaning.

Contraposed to the progressing subject personified in Johann Wolfgang von Goethe's figure of Doctor Faust, Daoism and Confucianism privilege a "reverting subject" aimed at returning to the heavenly principle of origination. If the movement forward allows the self to increase in knowledge and possessions, and the corresponding reality to multiply along an endless chain of cause and effect, how can we imagine a subject moving upstream—away from being—more and more? As we saw in the first chapter, Daoism strives to reach the *Wu*, the nothingness, assigning to it a role that is "similar to a substance," i.e., identifying the nothingness with the foundational source of reality. However, writes Mou, the more accurate way to represent nothingness is to not take it as a static noun, but as a dynamic verb. Nothingness is a *jingjie* acquirable through the practice of renouncing every attachment, of withdrawing from the deceitful discourses that ossify the world in definitions and opposites, and ultimately even abandoning the masks and the roles provided by society, and the autobiographical narrative through which we construe our ego. As previously noted, we can consider *wu* as the contracted form of *wuwei*, the effortless aligning with the cycle of the Dao, letting the myriad beings burst forth and effloresce without obstacles. The relationship the Daoist saint entertains with "nothingness" is neither cognitive nor volitional, but practical, and is conveyed through the verb *ti* 體 (to experience, to embody). Since we cannot regress ad infinitum in the chain of beings, we should move to the vertical axis of self-cultivation. Only in this way can we "embrace the primordial chaos" (*hundun*), "returning to the root and restore the source of life" (*guigen fuming* 歸根復命), "wandering carefree in nothingness" (*xiaoyaoyou* 逍遙遊), "fasting the mind and sitting in oblivion." In what way is this experience different from the ascent to the world of ideas performed by the Platonic subject, the unshackled prisoner who wakes up from the delusion of the cave? Is the emancipation from the domain of shadows and opinions (doxa) and the return to the supreme source of light not a dialectical vertical journey? In fact, Mou remarks that the constellation of paradoxes we can find in the text of the *Zhuangzi* signals that we are abandoning the everyday, familiar world and entering a dialectical process, turning our sound judgment upside-down. This kind of a dialectical conversion makes us able to reach the origin. However, we may perceive a radical difference of approach in the metaphorical discourse itself.

In Plato's allegory of the cave, there is a climbing upwards from the darkness along the vertical hierarchy of beings, in order to find the supreme being, which is the transcendental archetype of truth, goodness, and beauty. Leaving behind the dark vagueness and shadowy indistinction of the cave, the subject is elevated to a higher dimension where everything is increasingly clear, transparent, and well-defined to the spiritual sight. In the end, the prisoner must look directly into the sun, the supreme source of light and truth. In contrast, the journey of the Daoist saint resembles more a sinking into an unfathomable depth, as suggested by Laozi's imagery of the ravine and the valley, where everything is merged and undifferentiated, like muddy water, and the ideal vision is blurry, out of focus, nebulous. The reverting subject of Laozi and Zhuangzi is not ascending to the light, but on the contrary is submerging itself in the amorphous chaos that precedes birth. This is the reason why pursuing nothingness cannot simply be resolved in the act of cognitively grasping it. Nothingness cannot be known or exhausted, but only embodied (*tiwu* 體悟).

Ti 體 has many nuanced meanings. First of all, it means to experience directly, in first person, like in the word *tihui* 體會; second, it is metaphorically bounded to the corporeal sphere (*shenti* 身體) and means to embody, to make something present through your flesh and blood; third, we can translate it as becoming something through your practice, for example, *tiwu* 體無 does not mean contemplating *wu* 無 as an exterior object, but becoming it through the act of *wu*-ing, so to realize the verbalization of the noun in your practical activity. In this regard, *ti* entails agency and dynamism. As Mou explains, *tiwu* in Daoist texts found its adequate expression in the metaphysic of *jingjie*, since Daoism (but not Confucianism) lacks the dimension of the metaphysics of being. The classic duality between *ti* 體 and *yong* 用 (usually translated as substance and function) is not to be confused with the Western distinction between a static substance and its contingent attributes. *Ti* and *yong* are necessarily concurrent and mutually inseparable. Together they convey the inner life and dynamism of a being in its foundational and functional states. If we state with Wang Bi that the *ti* is nothingness and the *yong* is being, we would paradoxically affirm that being is grounded on nothingness, and it brings nothingness to expression. Translating it in accord with the metaphysics of *jingjie*, nothingness is the spiritual state of inchoateness and incipiency, teeming with possibilities yet to be expressed, and being is the actuality of this abundant energy and its punctual manifestation in the endless stream of beings. There is a further use of *ti*, when it is collocated at the end of a word, as in *Constitutive Mind and Constitutive Nature* 心體與性體. As we will see in the next chapter, Mou expressly develops the significance of this suffix in his interpretation of the Confucian tradition. The suffix *ti* is not meant to crystallize the word in an abstract metaphysical substance, but, on the contrary, is meant to signal the inherent unceasing activity of creation, which is constitutive of the word. In Mou's reconstruction, this disclosure of the beings as the source of creativity, and the intertwined relationship between *ti* and *yong*, will be rediscovered and brought to full accomplishment in the Song-Ming Neo-Confucianism.

Wang Bi says that Confucius embodies nothingness, but does not speak about it. Embodying is contraposed to the faculty of expressing through words. Being able to speak about the nothingness implies making the nothingness an object of my discourse, a meaning that can be analyzed in a logical-predicative way. Since *wu* 無 is a verbal form, denoting an activity of self-emptying, any attempt to objectify the *wu*, and insert it in a logical discourse as a predicative object, leads to paradoxical conclusions. The text of the *Zhuangzi* is studded with antinomies baffling our comprehension, and the only way to overcome this situation is to transcend the level of predicative language and adopt what Mou defines as "curve" or "dialectical" wisdom. According to Mou, the activity of embodying nothingness is structurally dialectical and therefore practical. Daoist dialectics goes far beyond Hegel's methodology, because it cannot ultimately be solved through a synthesis of two antithetical positions. Hegel's dialectic is developed in the domain of the language whereas Zhuangzi's dialectic forces us to "jump over" the horizontal axis of knowing and reasoning and to undertake the vertical effort of self-cultivation. But what is dialectic, if we should abandon the boundaries of language?

Mou in his "Lessons on Zhuangzi"[34] answers in an epigrammatic way, that "dialectics means to digest, in order to transform something in your flesh and blood."[35] Interestingly, the organic process of digestion is one of the favorite tropes to exemplify assimilation, self-reflection, and therefore interiorization.[36] According to Mou, the saint is able to *ti wu* 體無 when spiritually and existentially embodying and enacting nothingness. Sitting in silence and meditating, she assimilates herself to the nothingness, so that her consciousness, movements, and

---

34 Mou Zongsan (牟宗三), "Zhuangzi 'Qiwulun' yanjianglu." 莊子«齊物論» 演講綠 (Lectures on Zhuangzi 's "Qiwulun"), *Ehu yuekan* 318–332 (2002/2003). Mou Zongsan's lectures on Zhuangzi's second chapter were earlier published in Tao Guozhang's arrangement but the text differs from the one published in *Ehu yuekan*. See Mou Zongsan (牟宗三), *Zhuangzi Qiwulun yili yanxi* 莊子齊物論義理演析 (Development and Analyses of Meaning of Zhuangzi's Qiwulun Chapter), Taipei: Taiwan shangwu yinshuaguan, 1998.

35 辯證的是消化成你自己的血肉 (Mou Zongsan, "Zhuangzi 'Qiwulun' yanjianglu", n.p.).

36 This happens, for example, in Hegel's thought: "Indeed Hegel himself parallels self-reflection and digestion. Noting that in chemical interactions each substance 'loses its quality,' whereas the animal always 'preserves' itself by 'sublat[ing]' the 'object and the negative,' Hegel describes reflection as digestion and digestion as the 'organism's reflection into itself': its 'uniting of itself with itself' (PN 395). Hegel himself characterizes his philosophy as assimilation." Tilottama Rajan, "(In)Digestible Material: Illness and Dialectic in Hegel's *The Philosophy of Nature*," in: Timothy Morton (ed.), *Cultures of Taste/Theories of Appetite: Eating Romanticism*, New York: Palgrave Macmillan, 2004, pp. 217–236 (pp. 217–218).

appearance irradiate this perfect equanimity. We are here on a spiritual level, which is related to the language of materialist dialectic only in a metaphorical way.

In the seventh chapter of the *Zhuangzi*, there is a parable that contrasts the mere knowledge of nothingness and the practical embodiment of nothingness. The first character is the shaman Ji Xian, who perfectly exemplifies the one who confronts reality as an external object, trying to decipher his nature from subtle hints: "In the state of Zheng there lived a spirit-like shaman named Ji Xian. He could foretell whether men would live or die, grow old or be cut down young, prosper or perish. He could foretell these things to the year, month, and day, like magic—like a spirit." Liezi, a Daoist philosopher presented here as the pupil of Huzi, is fascinated and intoxicated with his ability to penetrate and grasp reality, to the point that he doubts that the self-cultivation practiced by his master Huzi is the better way to fathom Dao. Huzi tells him to bring the shaman. Ji Xian tries several times to detect Huzi's state of health, looking at him when the master is embodying increasingly rarefied levels of Dao. Ji Xian changes his mind every time, contradicting himself in his foretelling. "The next day the shaman visited again with Huzi. His feet had barely come to a standstill when he lost control of himself and ran away. 'Go after him!' cried Huzi, but Liezi could not catch up with the shaman. When he returned, he told Huzi, 'He's disappeared, I lost him. I just couldn't catch up with him.' Huzi said, 'What I showed him just now came before the first emergence of our ancestor. I took him with me into emptiness, yet twisting and turning; he no longer knew who he was. Now wavering reeds, now tumbling waves—so he fled'."

We see here the confrontation between the one we called the forward subject, whose approach to reality is based on the sight from afar, and the receding subject, who aims to become the manifestation of reality, letting all the subjective involvement fall, being void and unbiased, responding in a docile fashion and corresponding to the universe like an ideal mirror. Ji Xian, trying to unravel the enigma embodied by Huzi through cognitive tools, does not find any fixed and distinguishing feature to anchor his knowledge to. Huzi is like a lake without ripples, unbiased and unperturbed. His lineaments and his posture are inchoate like that of a child, but this pristine pureness does not appear like a smooth opaque wall, but as a continuous transformation between opposites.

Like the primeval chaos, it is twisting and turning, i.e., moving in an unpredictable way. Ji Xian experiences a terrifying loss of the spatio-temporal coordinates: the web of causes and effects that the human mind produces to orient itself is unraveled. In the end he flees, because he is overwhelmed by something that falls outside his cognitive capacity, not because of its complexity, but because it is the vertiginous simplicity that precedes the birth of mind. How did Huzi acquire this ability to be at the same time ceaseless movement and undisturbed quiescence? Huzi, as the epitome of the "receding subject," embodies a dialectical curvature in which the opposites are captivated in a continuous circle of diversion and exchange. The failure of Ji Xian reveals that his "curved" wisdom cannot be a conceptual gain, a synthesis acquired through pure thought. Dialectic, as Mou said, is a process of digestion and embodiment that only practice can obtain. By letting all the subjective involvements and attachments fall, the saint, like Huzi, becomes progressively able to access the *jingjie* of nothingness, making himself one and the same with nothingness. We may wonder which kind of spatial metaphor is evoked by the *jingjie* of the Daoist saint. As an inexhaustible metamorphosis, it is not similar to a place where the soul can metaphorically dwell. It seems, on the contrary, to be reduced to the single point of equilibrium that the practicing subject, like a tightrope walker, should re-gain at every moment, letting the different turning forces be exactly balanced and canceling each another out. It is a dynamically maintained state of mind, which requires an unceasing self-cultivation.

The reason why the *jingjie* of nothingness appears to us as punctiform and unsteady, and the receding subject as a paradoxical position, which should be incessantly regained and performed, can be found in the difference, frequently stressed by Mou, between Daoist and Confucian practice. According to Mou, Daoism is structured only around the metaphysic of *jingjie*, but lacks a foundation in the frame of the metaphysic of being (substance). Otherwise expressed, Daoism cannot refer back to a positive substantial principle of actualization. In the Confucian tradition, this principle of actualization is manifested in the moral domain. The reality of humanness (*renti* 仁體) and authenticity (*chengti* 誠體), moral knowing consciousness (*liangzhi* 良知), and heavenly principle (*tianli* 天理) are some of the manifold names that Confucian tradition attributed, throughout its history, to the supreme moral principle. This principle, Mou affirms, manifests itself in our moral intuition as the metaphysical root of beings and the principle of their universal resonance. This principle discloses itself fully in the human moral mind as spiritual creativity actualized in practice. The intuition of the supreme moral reality can be clarified and perfected through our self-cultivation, and is therefore a metaphysically grounded state of mind. This state of mind is spontaneously able to actualize itself in ethical deeds, providing the universe in which our practical will operates with a stable source of meaning and value. This spiritual territory disclosed inside our moral consciousness is positively grounded in the supreme principle of reality, and is something that can be strengthened and widened through our ethical effort. Metaphorically, we can reach this state of mind and dwell in it, progressively clarifying its intrinsically luminous virtue (*mingmingde* 明明德) without having to produce it from nothing. Daoist *jingjie* does not possess a self-reliant foundation, but should be continuously reenacted by our subjective self through abandoning any attachment, leveling every bias, embodying the inchoate source of being and tracing the spatio-temporal universe back to the dimensionless point where it all started. The vertiginous challenge of the receding subject is to be a self without concretizing in a determined and partial ego.

3.4 The Three-Step Dialectics of Daoism

As Zhuangzi says, "Do not be an embodier for fame; do not be a storehouse of schemes; do not be an undertaker of projects; do not be a proprietor of wisdom. Embody to the fullest what has no end and wander where there is no trail. Hold on to all that you have received from heaven, but do not think you have gotten anything. Be empty, that is all."[37] Zhuangzi warns his lecturer to resonate and respond without accumulating and storing (*ying er bu cang* 應而不藏), remaining infinitely elastic and malleable. This continuous process of self-canceling makes the subject similar to a palimpsest, a page or a wax-coated tablet from which the text is continuously scraped and washed off, so that the blank surface, now re-smoothed, can be reused for another document (*palímpsēstos*, from

---

37 Watson (ed.), *The Complete Works of Zhuangzi*, cap. 7.

παλίν + ψαω = "again" + "scrape"). This process of overwriting leaves behind faint remains and blurred signs, which are the only appearance of the subject that we can grasp for an instant, only in its fading away. This subjectivity is characterized by its "ontological thinness." The thin subject paradoxically appears only in its act of letting go and fading away; however, its constant self-emptying mental disposition (*xinjing* 心境) is the threshold that we should trespass in order to bring back reality to the universal Dao, the root and law of the universe. In *Caixing yu xuanli* (才性與玄理 *Physical Nature and the "Profound Thought"*), Mou writes: "We cannot interpret the Dao as an entity (*shiwu* 實物) whose concept is given in the ontological domain, we should understand it only through the concept of prodigious function of the inexhaustible void. [...]. Furthermore, if we move to the objective aspect and we call Dao as the ancestor of the myriad things, they depend on him in order to be generated and to be accomplished, its ancestor is the root of their generation and accomplishment, we have to pass through the mental disposition of the self-emptying in order to contemplate it as suchness itself."[38] We should perform a curvature in our approach to things, and the thin receding subject is the turning point. Dialectic as curved wisdom is the mental practice that allows the subject to embody nothingness and free herself from any attachment. The triadic movement of Hegelian dialectics, starting from a position, proceeding through negation, and ultimately reaching a higher level of synthesis, is the benchmark of dialectic thought for Mou. If the structure of Daoist dialectics bears a formal resemblance with Hegel's thought, however, Mou declares that the dialectic of Laozi and Zhuangzi is far more perfect in its ability to elicit a practical effort of spiritual cultivation, than the purely logical method of Hegel's work. Mou individuates three steps in the subjective process of self-emptying.

The first step is expressed in the statement "the square is not a square." I pose a logical contradiction in order to detach my mind from the things I isolated and labeled through my defining language. As Mou explains, this is not to be understood as a logical paradox like Russell's Paradox, which problematizes the ways properties apply or do not apply

---

38 Mou Zongsan (牟宗三), *Caixing yu xuanli*. 才性與玄理 (*Physical Nature and the "Profound Thought"*), *Mou Zongsan xiansheng quanji*. 牟宗三先生全集 (Complete Works of Mou Zongsan), vol. II, Taipei: Lianhe baoxi wenhua jijin hui, 2003, p. 136.

to themselves. The logical paradoxes can be solved through refining our comprehension of predicative language, e.g., distinguishing among different levels and meta-levels implied in our use of language. With this kind of paradox, we are still inside what Mou calls the horizontal axis of logical-epistemological discourse. The strategy of studding the text with antinomies is aimed in Laozi and Zhuangzi to radically unhinge our system of thought, putting in doubt the reliability of our linguistic acts and of the phenomenal world, which is generated by language. Shaken to its very foundation, this horizontal discourse in which the things are isolable and univocally definable, should be abandoned moving up in the vertical dimension of practice. When the tissue of phenomenal reality is torn apart, the nothingness, the void at the root of everything, shines through. How do we overcome the temptation of illusorily grasping the void, transforming it in a concept, and using it as a substantial foundation?

The second step is synthesized in the proposition "the square is also a square." This affirmation discloses a mental state in which the un-attachment to things, realized through the renunciation to any intentional effort (*wu wei* 無為), permeates, without obstacles, the totality of being.[39] In the first step, I realize that a thing is not reducible to the name and definition I provided for it. When I stop being focused and attached to the concepts I created, I let them go and this relinquishment makes the contour of the single thing blurred and undefined, and my soul is wide open to the new. The void reveals itself, shining through the spaces among things. However, my mind is naturally prone to grasp the object of every experience—in this case the *wu* 無, the absence of fixed definition—and interpret it as a new concept, reifying my experience and the mental state of freedom I achieved through it. In this way, I can intend *wu* 無 not as a verb, but as a noun, and elect nothingness and void as the grounding substance of the universe. The second step is therefore to "empty the void itself," returning to my mental state and realizing that the void is a dynamic act of freeing the world and myself from their fixed boundaries. Through this practice, my mind becomes infinitely responsive to all things, and the things are a dynamic field of transformation that can freely host its previous meaning, leaving

---

39   Ibid., p. 137: 表示一種圓通無礙, 沖虛無執之無外之心境, 亦即沖虛之玄德。

space for further meanings. The mental state that makes possible this intelligence of reality is called, Zhuangzi tells us, "the space of transformation" (*huajing* 化境).

During the first step, I accomplished the negative movement of receding, going back to the root. Through the second step, I move forward in order to complete the circle. The third step is expressed by Mou as "In the square, I follow the law of the square." The unlimited malleability and opening of my spiritual state make it possible for any single thing to exist conforming to itself, without being subdued to external definitions and determinations. This spontaneous "being-in-itself" is the suchness, the being-so. It means that any single thing now possesses in itself the source of its meaning. This state is achieved because the emptiness at the core of the universe uninterruptedly flows, becoming the force of living and transforming. Following its internal rhythm of life, every single thing is generated, blooms, and wanes, transforming into the other, in the unceasing circulation of nature (*ziran* 自然). It is worth stressing that Mou, in order to indicate the inner law of being and becoming, does not use the term "principle" (*li* 理), as he will do in the major part of his works, but "law" or "model" (*fa* 法). This is very meaningful, since the principle, or the reason why, was defined by Mou as being peculiar to Confucian thought, whereas the Daoists are interested in the practical question of how, in what way, and so on. Confucian thought recognizes the positive existence and creative efficacy of a heavenly principle, which is not hidden or unreachable for the human mind, but manifests itself in innate moral consciousness and finds its full actualization in moral actions that reaffirm and verify the dynamic unity and interconnection of all beings.

The character of "principle," 理 *li* has the radical of jade, and according to the *Shuowen Jiezi* it originally refers to the process of extraction of jade, splitting the jade from the uncut stone, and carving it along its inner texture. The jade contains within itself the reason for its preciousness, with its complex grain distinguishing it from the coarse stone, guiding the hand of the artisan as they carving it. Daoism, in Mou's interpretation, does not recognize a positive rule engraved in both the human mind and the universe, but only the dynamic, omnipervasive flow of Dao. The character 法 *fa* contains the radical of water, and instantiates therefore the fluid and also the measure of horizontality given by the water level. The plainness of the water surface belongs to the aquatic imagery of the Dao, and refers to the natural condition of the undisturbed mind, which reflects without biases reality as it is, like a wave-less water-mirror. Saying that in the square I should conform to the law (*fa*) of the square does not express an active, intentional self-modeling in accordance with a fixed rule, but the passive withdrawing from any interference to let single things emerge in their spontaneous nature (*ziran* 自然). The Chinese word for nature, 自然 *ziran*, perfectly reflects the movement to disclose the blank endlessly malleable space of pure being in which the thing can emerge and flourish following their internal law. As I wrote in the first chapter, *zi* 自 means "self" in the dynamic sense of gushing out in accord with our innermost source. *Ran* 然 expresses the modality, the "how", which is, according to Mou, the paramount question of Daoism. *Ziran* 自然 is contrasted with *suoyiran* 所以然, a phrase composed of the characters *suo-yi* 所以 ("effect-cause"). Daoism, lacking a positive metaphysical principle responsible for the ordered generation of things, does not recognize any other dynamism of actualization than the horizontal phenomenal chain of cause and effect, that has revealed itself as delusional.

The Daoist dialectical line of thought entails that the process of overcoming determined beings and our habitual mindset through the practice of *wu* 無, or self-voiding, cannot proceed ad infinitum, because our mind is always tempted to substantialize the *wu* as metaphysical principle, falling back into attachment and boundedness. The necessity of a movement beyond the illusion of a substantialized *wu* resides in the nature of the *wu* itself. *Wu* is not an abstract concept soaring above the world of life, but is a passive principle of actualization, since it prepares the spiritual *jingjie* in which all the beings are allowed to exist and thrive without interference from any external condition. The act of withdrawing is at the same time an act of opening a mental space where the generation of beings is profuse and unceasing, and any single being can bloom, wane, and transform, conforming only to the flow of Dao. It is worth recalling that in Daoist tradition "Dao" is not a supreme mind intentionally creating the world, nor an abstract ultimate rule to which the things should obey in order to be; Dao is the simple being-so of the multifarious thing, the suchness or *ziran*. If *wu* is the practice of "*wu*-ing," i.e., the dissolution of determinacy, being (*you* 有)

has a verbal significance of "*you*-ing," the process of letting the myriad things be as they are, in their immanent and "seamless" process of fruition and maturation, extinguishment and metamorphosis. Being and not being are not opposite poles in a dualistic worldview. They are ultimately interflowing, reversing one into the other, and this dynamic exchange and intermingling is the circular accomplishment of the Dao as *xuan* 玄. The circular accomplishment and its failure are the same time an account of the two possible spiritual states in human beings. Every time the mind loses its tranquility, its plainness without biases and attachment, things become reified, closing themselves in a fixed physiognomics. In this way, it is impossible for the mind to attune to perpetual transformation, and its rigidity becomes an obstacle to life. The finite thing arising as the object of attention and desire in our perturbed state of mind is not totally unrelated to the plainness of the mind embracing nothingness. In metaphorical terms, the heap and the earth share the same material cause, the earth; however, the heap is not spontaneously produced by the soil as its efficient cause. Instead, it appears to be incongruous and artificially constructed. Similarly, the world of determined things is brought to being by the same mind that in its tranquility and equilibrium allows the circular flow of *xuan* 玄 to unimpededly pervade everything.

What decides the difference is the state or *jingjie* reached by the mind in its practice. In the carefree detached *jingjie* of the saint, the circulation of vital breath (*qi* 氣) is not obstructed, like the wind blowing in the pipes of heaven described in Zhuangzi's parable (chapter 2): "When (the wind) blows, (the sounds from) the myriad apertures are different, and (its cessation) makes them stop of themselves. Both things arise from (the wind and the apertures) themselves—should there be any other agency that excites them?" Everything arises and wanes in its spontaneous suchness, the selfish ego is removed, and there is no grasping subject and, consequently, no grasped object. When the mind loses this ideal state, it starts focusing on the differences, expressing predilection and aversion. Reality is fragmented in a couple of opposites, their contours shimmering in the whimsically movable spotlight of the mind, and constituted as external objects of my attachment. The objective world is born and the subject defines itself as inner space contraposed to external space.

In tracing the circular dynamism of the Dao, we are projected toward the sphere of the being (*you* 有), called the "Mother of all things" in the *Daodejing*. Mou expresses this movement forward as "directionality" and "generation without generating." We may wonder why this directionality, though apparently following the same path forward, does not overlap with the horizontal cognitive process of increasing through accumulation that characterizes the *shunqu zhi lu* 順取之路, the path of conforming to and grasping things. To explain the difference of these two ways of leaning forward upon the myriad beings, Mou emphasizes that the primary meaning of being in Daoism is "exiting the *wu* (nothingness)." Being is therefore dialectically connected with the state of tranquility and the void-ful unity we obtain through detaching ourselves from any attachment to and dependence on things. However, if we define the *wu* on the basis of pure negation of any determined thing (as no-thing), we only have the abstract and logical frame of *wu*, devoid of any content. But *wu* is not primarily a logical or ontological concept, but a *jingjie*, a state of mind of clearness and freedom in which we align with the Dao as an inexhaustible source of life, and every possibility is disclosed. Mou writes: "*Wu* is not a lifeless object. It is a lively and nimble state of mind. It is lively and active with or without this world, and regardless of whether this world is full of things and events. It does not need any object in order to show its directionality."[40] And again: "That the mind activates nimbly from a void-ful state to respond to all possibilities is the wondrous function of the mind."[41] The active nature of *wu* derives from its functional nature. If we analyze *wu* in light of the traditional distinction between substance and function, we may appreciate how the substantial nature is perfectly resolved in the functional nature. *Wu*, as we have seen before, is the practical source of the myriad beings without being in itself a positive substance. The aspect "*ti*" is dynamically resolved in the verbal meaning of *ti* as embodiment. The relationship between *ti* 體 and *yong* 用 is hence a seamless flow in which the state of mind of *wu* is enacted or dialectically digested (*ti*) by the mind through the practice of withdrawing and self-voiding. The unbiased plainness deriving from my subjective becoming "*wu*" is not a nihilistic indifference, but an enfranchisement of the subject and its

---

[40] Mou Zongsan, *Nineteen Lectures on Chinese Philosophy*, p. 98.
[41] Ibid., p. 96.

world from any artificial boundary and obstruction. *Wu* is not merely a blank space, but, on the contrary, the disclosure of an infinite stream of life, nurturing and eliciting the myriad wondrous functions of the mind (*yong*). This organic and living unity of substance and function is fully expressed as directionality.

The term "directionality" indicates a springing out and a streaming forward toward beings. This orientation to things can be misleading if we consider it parallel to the idea of intentionality, which undergirds Western phenomenological thought. As indicated by the Latin etymological root *tendere*, intentionality is the structural attitude of the mind to be directed toward an object. According to the Austrian philosopher Franz Brentano, the hallmark of any mental phenomenon is its capacity to refer to, or be "about" something other than itself. The main idea behind this mental directedness toward (or attending to) objects is the inseparability, in the act of knowledge, affection, or perception, of mind and object. According to Mou, the origin of this condition in which mind and things are contraposed lies in the mind losing its silent tranquility and attaching to the thing, which consequently becomes alienated and a fixed obstacle for the flux of the mind. Directionality, however, is the movement forward of a mind that cannot fall in this externality, since it is the function of the "mind of Dao," which precedes any duality of subject versus object. Directionality is, first of all, the movement of gushing out from the dull and tasteless pre-natal anteriority of *wu*, in order to proceed toward the mother, which represents the process of birth and growth. In doing so, directionality signifies the unconditioned openness to the multiplicity of beings, a disclosure that does not impose any *a priori* mental structure or prefigured meaning. It merely projects forward a mental space of clarity in which the myriad beings are welcomed in their spontaneous unconditioned being-so. When this directionality is focused on a specific thing, it can bring the thing to actualization. At the same time, the mind runs the risk of losing its original unbounded openness and becoming completely absorbed by the thing. If this happens, the mind and the thing are ossified in their role of viewer and viewed, and we fall into the mode of horizontal incremental knowledge. But when the state of tranquility and silence is restored in the mind, directionality reappears in its pristine responsiveness and all-embracing wideness, manifesting itself as the ground of actualization for myriad beings.

In Zhuangzi, we can find the idea of directionality exposed as a movement from the unlimited (the state of *wu*) to the realm of limits (*you* 有). In this movement forward, the saint does not fall among things, and is not limited by things. The realm of being is different from the Platonic "world of ideas." Ideas have a determined shape and can produce only the things that conform to this model. On the contrary, the realm of being (*you*) allows all things to happen according to their rhythm of growth and decline. Its shapelessness welcomes any shape without being constrained by it, and ceaselessly recovers its infinite opening to all possibilities. As Zhuangzi expresses it, "that which treats things as things is not limited by things. Things have their limits—the so-called limits of things. The unlimited moves to the realm of limits; the limited moves to the unlimited realm. We speak of the filling and emptying, the withering and decay of things. [The Way] makes them full and empty without itself filling or emptying; it makes them wither and decay without itself withering or decaying. It establishes root and branch but knows no root and branch itself; it determines when to store up or scatter but knows no storing or scattering itself."[42] Mou synthesizes this coexistence of being and nothingness as infinite wondrous functions (*miaoyong* 妙用): "The Daoists explain the state of mind of 'tranquilness of void-ful unity' with the phrase 'infinite, wondrous functions.' That the mind activates nimbly from a void-ful state to respond to all possibilities is the wondrous function of the mind."[43] This wondrous functional state is different from the definite use (*dingyong* 定用) we make of things in everyday life, because it has no limit and dwells in no place (*miaoyong wufang* 妙用無方). We can wonder what kind of subject may enact this limitless displacement, and what kind of realization it can bring to things, all while avoiding any entanglement with reality.

The Daoist saint, who embodies the perfect model of being human, stands in stark contrast to ordinary people, who are in the word of Zhuangzi, "servants to circumstance and things, they delight in change, and if the moment comes when they can put their talents to use, then they cannot keep from acting. In this way, they all follow along with the turning years, letting themselves be changed by things. Driving their bodies and natures on and on, they drown in the ten thousand

---

42 Watson (ed.), *The Complete Works of Zhuangzi*, p. 348
43 Mou Zongsan, *Nineteen Lectures on Chinese Philosophy*, p. 96.

things and, to the end of their days never turn back."[44] The saint, on the contrary, "discards knowledge and purpose and follows along with the reasonableness of heaven. Therefore, he incurs no disaster from heaven, no entanglement from things, no opposition from man, no blame from the spirits. His life is a floating, his death a rest. He does not ponder or scheme, does not plot for the future. [...] His spirit is pure and clean, his soul never wearied. In emptiness, nonbeing, and limpidity, he joins with the Virtue of Heaven." [45] The first aspect we may highlight is that the Daoist ideal self avoids any entanglement with and participation in events and is therefore able to subtract itself from the force of attrition operating in the world. In a passive and purely negative meaning, the ideal of plainness is realized, allowing the subject to glide on the surface of reality without leaving traces behind.

3.5 The Daoist Subjectivity According to Mou

If the Daoist subject is, first of all, a state of mind, what are the features of the mind, in a nutshell? Mou synthesizes the basic characteristics in this way: "Being a mind means having spiritual ability to perceive the world,[46] having creativity, dealing with the thing as thing without letting the thing reify you, and having sovereignty: in this way you are an absolute subject, which eternally cannot be considered an object." [47] When I turn back to the source of the universe, I cannot transform it to the object of my gaze. This ever-flowing wellspring of life is an absolute *"dynamis,"* i.e., its constitutive nature is activity, inherent movement, force. The core of reality always flows and is impossible to fully capture it in static, abstract forms. Adopting the words of Henri-Louis Bergson, the contemporary philosopher who attempted at the maximum degree to redefine reality as process, creativity, and pure mobility, the root of reality is "unceasing creation, the uninterrupted upsurge of novelty."[48] This living force that is irreducible to any objectivation is defined by Mou as the "absolute subject" or mind. Since this fountainhead, regardless of vitality, cannot

---

44 Ibid., p. 383.
45 Ibid., p. 151.
46 In Buddhist language, *jingjie* is also the spiritual and enlightened nature of all beings.
47 Mou Zongsan, *Physical Nature and the "Profound Thought"*, p. 96.
48 Henri Bergson, *The Creative Mind*, Westport, CT: Greenwood Press, 1968, p. 17.

structurally be the object of a reflexive discourse, the only way to experience it is through assuming a subjective posture and realizing its intuitive immediacy. In what way does the absolute subject realize and manifest itself? First, as the spiritual ability to perceive things without being subjugated and reified; second, as creative action; and finally, as the ability to assume a role of guidance and sovereignty over things and events. The term *zhuzaixing* 主宰性 contains the character *zhu* 主, which bears the meanings of "host," "owner," "primacy," and "taking in charge" and is the semantic backbone of the words "subject" (*zhuti* 主體) and "ancestor" (*zongzhu* 宗主). Whereas the etymology of the English word "subject" traces back to the Latin *"subjectum"* and the Ancient Greek *"Hypokeimenon,"* meaning underlying thing or substratum, *zhuti* 主體 conveys the idea of leading role, mastery, and possession. *Zhudong* 主動 means taking the initiative, acting spontaneously in accord with one own's will.

In several passages of *Caixing yu xuanli*, Mou argues that in Daoist thought one of the characteristics of Dao as the ancestor is to be *wu zhu* 無主 (not-leading), or *buzhu zhi zhu* 不主之主 (master without leading). The Dao occupies therefore the first position, but this primacy does not entail the exercise of an authority or the intention to give an order to the world. The term *zhu* as a noun is preserved, but its verbal form, the action of *zhu*-ing, is refused. More precisely, the master is characterized just by its renunciation of the exercise of the power implied in its function. Exploring the polysemy of the word, we may as well define the Dao as a legitimate holder who relinquishes any right of possession, or a subject who retains its active function without subjugating things. We can observe here the deployment of that dialectical strategy, which according to Mou, is the hallmark of Daoist "curved wisdom." Adopting the previous example of the square, the first affirmation is that a subject is not a (subjugating) subject. In other words, the Daoist subject is unable or unwilling to position itself as the agent in the discourse and in the practice. In a judgment, the subject refuses to be the main theme to which the predicate refers. Going back to Zhuangzi's parable of Huzi and the fortune-teller Ji Xian, Huzi, through the wondrous transformations produced by his meditative state, systematically eludes any attempt by Ji Xian to say predict or define him. Swerving constantly and meandering freely through diverse cosmogonic stages, he employs a diversionary tactic, baffling Ji Xian in his attempt to speak about him, and leaving behind only delusional appearances to be grasped. Finally, his ultimate enacting of the primigenial chaos is so inconceivably close to nothingness that it renders the possibility of discourse itself unthinkable. Ji Xian runs away, shouting, because of this in-articulable *horror vacui*. Huzi is therefore a subject who refuses to be a subject, i.e., the main theme and the "aboutness" of predication. He avoids also the social role of talking subject: he does not aspire to be the creator and divulgator of a new teaching and does not convey a meaningful theory about himself in order to rectify Ji Xian's mistakes. He simply embodies the unutterable and discloses something that is unbearable for the rational speaker.

The second dialectical stage should however be the acknowledgment that "the subject is also a subject." This affirmation leads us to abandon the horizontal axis and ascend along the vertical dimension, the dimension of practice and *jingjie*. What Huzi performs is a metamorphosis, a mutation of the inner landscape (*jingjie*), and of the world he projects around himself. This ability, conquered through a life-long practice of self-cultivation that allows him to embody the Dao in its inchoate state, restores the value of subjectivity as practice. Huzi reenacts in front of Ji Xian the paradoxical development of his own spiritual training of self-voiding. Paradoxical, because its evolution is actually realized through a movement backward and downward, diminishing his ego, uprooting its attachment, sinking into the shapeless deepness of the Dao. Meditating on the silence that is at the core of sound, and on the beginning before any beginning, he reaches the *jingjie* of the luminous vacuity, irradiating his spiritual accomplishment in his bodily appearance. Like a whirlpool, he drags down language to its unspeakable root, making the interpretive tool of human understanding useless and deceptive. The performative domain of spiritual practice is, according to Mou, the epitome of subjective activity, because it envelopes and transforms reality through a first-person vision. The transformation of the inner landscape *jingjie*, however, does not rely on any ontological precondition, because reality is intended here not as objective exteriority, but as the phenomenal world disclosed by the vision.

The subject, intended as fixed ego contraposed to the objective thing, should constantly be overcome, because the dualisms of subject and object, inner and outer space, ultimately ossify the thought, and create obstacles in the stream of life. But, according to Daoism, the only way to do this is through a path of relinquishment and self-voiding, where the object ceases to be seen as something present, stable, and usable for our projects (as in Heidegger's concept of *Vorhandenheit*), and the subject is no longer the self-centered "I think." Actually, the self-voiding subject represents the highest level of subjectivity, intended as a practicing and self-transforming activity. There is a subject structurally tied with the objects, and this bipolar relation is expressed in Chinese with the pair *zhuke* 主客. This subject is a practicing agent who discloses the *jingjie*, in which the dualism of subject and object may appear. This practicing subject is a transcendental subject, if we do not interpret transcendental in the Kantian way. For Kant, "transcendental" means an *a priori* formal condition of the cognitive mind. Instead, the practicing subject exists in advance, but this anteriority is not a metaphysical or epistemological one—it is a practical event that inaugurates the *jingjie* and is coextensive with it, like an all-encompassing atmosphere. We cannot properly define this subject as transcendental, because, as Mou highlights, it does not belong to a metaphysics of being, but rather fits within a vision-type metaphysics of the state of mind. This subject, who opens the world with its practice, is not a substance or a principle. Its relation to subject-object dualism is not an intellectual or moral transcendence, but a dynamic position of soaring aloft, detached from the phenomenal reality. The dualist horizontal subject is produced by the vertical subject through its action of falling and being tethered in the empirical world. There is a higher *jingjie* in which the practicing subject is freely ubiquitous and wandering at ease, and a lower *jingjie* in which it appears ossified and restrained in an inner dimension, cognitively correlated with an external world of things. What we called the horizontal phenomenal dimension is a *jingjie* generated by a fall and a self-limitation. To become aware of this condition of determinedness and captivity is in itself an act of return, a withdrawal from the endless quest forward in which the subject is caught. This return is already an effort of self-elevation along the vertical axis, a restoration of the wide-open and ubiquitous subject that is oblivious to himself and is one and the same with heaven and earth. We will revisit this issue in a subsequent chapter, analyzing the crucial factor of the relationship between the true moral self and the cognitive self in the later works of Mou Zongsan.

Summing up, the Daoist subject is a subject (*zhuti* 主體) that paradoxically renounces the task and privilege of "*zhu*-ing." The saint as the perfect model of subjectivity does not use language in order to dominate. Dominate refers here to the capacity of providing things with their proper name. The power to name things is correlated in several traditions of thought with the capacity of mastering the world through assigning a defined place and role to every single thing. In the Book of Genesis, God manifests his creative will, calling things by their names, and this act of utterance has the power to elicit the world into existence. The Daoist saint does not actively create beings, and renounces any attempt to define and control them. Quoting the twenty-second chapter of the *Daodejing*, "He is free from self-display, and therefore he shines; from self-assertion, and therefore he is distinguished; from self-boasting, and therefore his merit is acknowledged; from self-complacency, and therefore he acquires superiority. Therefore, the saint puts his own person last, and yet it is found in the foremost place; he treats his person as if it were foreign to him, and yet that person is preserved. Is it not because he has no personal and private ends, that therefore such ends are realized?"[49]

3.6 The Diaphanous Subject

How should we describe this "great transcendental subjectivity" that the Daoist saint embodies and that is the core of the Daoist "Metaphysics of Vision," based on practical action? Taking up precisely this metaphor of "vision" that for Mou Zongsan synthesizes in the most effective way the concept of *jingjie*, we could speak of this ideal subject as a "diaphanous subject." I adopt the term "diaphanous" in its etymological meaning of "shining, manifesting itself through," applied to a body or a fabric that allows one to glimpse at least the contours of the object placed behind it. What is placed behind the subject is that nothingness, *wu* 無, to which the subject tends through emptying itself and withdrawing from every predicate attributed to it. Nothingness is not given except as a practical effort of self-elevation, and can only be embodied through an interminable dialectical process. We are on the vertical plane, that of

---

49   *Tao Te Ching*, tr. by James Legge, Oxford: Clarendon Press, 1891, ch. 22.

the tension toward a spiritual state of perfect tranquility and harmony. This practical dimension could also receive the name "evanescence," understood as a continuous tension toward emptying. Nothingness is not given as a determinate substance, but only as a practical process of progressive spiritual attenuation, and, from the point of view of the world opened by my subjective vision, as the tendency of things to become indistinct and unutterable. The diaphanous Daoist subject is therefore not perfectly transparent. If it were, it could inwardly access the Dao through a direct intuition, whereas instead, as Mou writes, the source of light and life that the Dao represents is given only as a "retrospective manifestation" (*fanxian* 反顯), as a "*translucēre*" that is never graspable as a determinate object. Through its own diaphanous nature, the Daoist subject makes things manifest by blurring their contours, removing them from their fate as cognitive objects, and instead making visible their movement back to their undifferentiated origin.

If the subject is affirmed as the cognitive subject in its dominant and defining role of perspective focus, the thing is separated from its life-giving and illuminating root, and is concretized as dead object. We can represent this act of focus and attachment as a thickening of the diaphanous surface into a stain or mottling that blocks the passage of light. When a subject asserts itself as subject, it becomes self-conscious as the center of the perspective that gives order to all things, limiting them with respect to itself and naming them. This is the act of dominating and regulating (*zhu* 主) through which the subject that intervenes to make things be (*wei* 為), has the ability (*neng* 能) and the prerogative to assert itself as I (*wo* 我) and be the constitutive center of the universe. Consequently, an object is delineated, a thing produced by it and dependent on its gaze, and alienated, that is, made other than the I. Using Daoist terminology, Mou emphasizes that in this way the source of the Dao is obstructed, the subject-object duality impedes the transmission of life, and things lose their ability to return to the generative root of their being. We are in the domain of perception (*jue* 覺), of focusing, of relativity and mutual dependence (*xiangdui* 相對) of subject and object.

But there is another way of being subject, what we have called the "diaphanous subject," which is subject as far as it is the practice of self-emptying, of dissolving every concretion that hides the luminous void of the Dao. All the characteristics of subjectivity are taken up here but changed in meaning. The diaphanous subject is first without dominance, because by withdrawing from itself, it moves closer to the origin, to the ancestor (*zongzhu* 宗主), which is the Dao, allowing it to shine and manifest itself. The focus, which arrests things in their boundaries and reifies them, is opposed by the permeation (*tongtou* 通透) of the world by the Dao, which pervades and nourishes everything. So we pass from a solid metaphor (the concretion, the obstacle) to a liquid one, which is characteristic of the Dao understood as perennial flowing. If the subject no longer acts as a barrier but thins out and becomes vague and indistinct, it becomes the very manifestation of the Dao and its unstoppable generative force, through which there is nothing that is not brought to completion (*wuwei er wu buwei* 無為而無不為) without effort. Mou speaks here of a "generating without generating," or "generating without mind," meaning a passive, negative mode of making things appear. Passive, because it requires the subject to keep himself in a state of stillness, abstaining from any intentional action on the world. Negative, because this spiritual stillness removes all obstacles and unlocks the source of being. In this way, it allows things to be in their simple being-so ("suchness"), to blossom and decline in the pure spontaneity (*ziran* 自然) of their being. This is a mode very similar to what Heidegger calls *Gelassenheit*, that is, abandonment: a quieting down and calming of the spirit, maintaining itself in a state of openness, at the point from which everything opens up. In this state, the subject allows the world to simply be, without interference or imposition.

We saw in the first chapter how one of the terms that give us significant access to Mou's conception of the subject is *zi* 自, which in compounds can take on various shades of meaning. In the word *ziji* 自己, *zi* 自 usually indicates the self as the result of inner reflection, while in the term *ziran* 自然, usually translated as "nature," *zi* carries the meaning of autonomy and absolute spontaneity. Here, *zi* 自 is the equivalent of the Greek αὐτός, i.e., "same, proper, in person"—that which happens by itself, independently, without involvement of others. *Ziran* 自然 is the condition of that which in its being does not depend on anything external to itself. Mou in *Caixing yu xuanli* points out how in Western languages the term "nature," understood as the object proper to the natural sciences, indicates in reality that which in its structure is maximally dependent on something else, in that it manifests itself as a concatenation of causes and effects. Nature would therefore be better defined as *taran* 他然, where *ta* 他 is equivalent to the Greek ἕτερος "other, different." True spontaneity (*ziran* 自然), Mou writes, is neither a definite entity nor a concept graspable by thought, but is the highest spiritual state (*jingjie*) that we can embody and actualize in ourselves. When we reach this level of inner elevation all things appear to us as self-subsistent (*ziyou* 自由, *zizai* 自在) and self-determined (*ziding* 自定). They are complete in themselves, in their solitary foundation, they are generated ceaselessly by the impulse of the Dao, which is not an external principle to them but the pure being-ness of all things. The condition for this to happen is for my self to be *ziyi* 自已 and *zizhi* 自止, capable of abstaining, of stopping, of not interfering, of obliviousness to the self and maintaining myself in a condition of equanimity and luminous emptiness,[50] which is the mysterious becoming of the self and the other (*biwo* 彼我). Maintaining myself in this subjective spiritual condition, I do not resist the life-giving flow of the Dao; as a result, ten thousand things arise from themselves spontaneously, freed from mutual causal dependence. In this way, what Zhuangzi calls "the equalization of all things" is realized beyond the division between subject and object.

3.7 Self-Awareness and Trans-consciousness

We might now ask whether this model of subjectivity that the saint embodies, and which is presented as exemplary, still has anything to do with the activity of the mind, which for us contemporaries is the root of subjective identity, and whether in particular it is endowed with self-consciousness. The insistence that letting things subsist in themselves amounts to "mindless generation," or as Zhuangzi puts it, "forgetting the self" (*wang wo* 忘我), seems to suggest a subjectivity that is not self-conscious. A famous debate of the Wei-Jin era centers on the question of whether the saint is devoid of feelings (*qing* 情). Although the subject matter of the debate here is narrower, dealing essentially with whether it is possible to be a saint while maintaining passionate attachments, it is nonetheless a demonstration that the saint appears as distanced from mortals, almost devoid of an inner life. In his lectures on the *Zhuangzi*,

---

50 Mou Zongsan, *Physical Nature and the "Profound Thought"*, p. 174.

Mou presents us with the structure of the mind as articulated in three levels: non-self-conscious, self-conscious, and trans-conscious. The non-self-conscious or preconscious level is called by Mou "original harmony" and is comparable to the "heart of a child," simple, raw, undifferentiated. The authenticity inherent in this condition is that which in the *Daodejing* (*chapter 55*) Laozi expresses by stating, "He who embraces virtue with the highest integrity can be compared to a child," which Mengzi (book 4) reiterates by noting that "The great man has the heart of a child." The child is perfectly equanimous; he has no preferences or attachments. His mind is boundlessly open without prejudice to incoming novelty. Mou does not understand this germinal harmony as a state of absolute unconsciousness, but as a potential readiness to harmonize with everything that enters his horizon, without focusing exclusively on partial realities. The term *jue* 覺 has a twofold meaning: on the one hand, it indicates the state of wakefulness and undivided awareness, and on the other hand, the grasping of a specific reality, almost lifting it from the flow of being, and with it solidifying a disposition of the mind. The term "unconscious" (*bu jue* 不覺) negates the second semantic value, and could therefore be translated as "pre-egoic," since in this incipient state of consciousness an ego has not yet solidified. The state of self-consciousness implies a separation between the subjective and objective poles, between the ego and the world, and, at the heart of the ego, a split between the act of observing ourselves and our ego as observed, and thus the emergence of a reflective consciousness. However, the mind cannot stop at this level. The state of mind of the saint, trans-consciousness, is the highest level of consciousness that can be acquired through self-cultivation. It involves an awakening of the pristine mind in the heart of separation, and the dialectical absorption of opposites into a state of "secondary harmony." Mou emphasizes that this process is not logical-epistemological, like that perfected in the West by the Hegelian dialectic, but is a path of practical-moral elevation.

Analyzing now the development of these three levels in what we have called the "diaphanous subject," we note first of all that they appear as three mental states (*jingjie*). While, as we shall see in the next chapter, Confucian thought is affirmed as a "metaphysics of substance" based on a substantial creator principle, Daoism is realized only in the sphere of subjective "vision." The original stage, that of nothingness (*wu*), or pure undifferentiated simplicity, is not given to us in the form of substance first, but only as subjectively pursued and manifested in the actions of the saint. Although it is presented as origin (*yuan* 元), source, and root, nothingness subsists only as far as it is embodied by the saint, who realizes it in his effort towards self-emptying. Similarly, the original chaos (*hundun* 混沌) as undivided unity that precedes all differentiation, is given to us only as far as the saint is called to "embrace chaos" by dropping all partiality and attachment. To return to it is to rediscover the "heart of a child," the absolute plasticity of water that fluidly assumes and abandons every form without leaving a trace. Mou writes: "The saint is not affirmation, not negation, not intention, not necessity, not solidity, not ego, it cares about nothing and its disposition is that of heaven and earth, how could it adhere to things, have the slightest obstacle, the slightest concern? As Wang Bi says, 'the saint embodies nothingness.' But this in fact is only a subjective disposition of the saint; his having attained the sublime cannot be interpreted as a substance." [51] There is nothing objective about the "nothingness" or "chaos" of this primal simplicity. Nothingness and chaos are not a subsistent pattern like Plato's ideas to which the saint can direct himself or conform. The Dao, the "Way," is totally resolved in the act of walking a path, and nothingness is totally resolved in the self-emptying that the saint pursues in his effort at self-cultivation. In the first chapter, talking about the Dao, I introduced the concept of hodological space, that is, a space that exists only in the experience of walking in it, and therefore cannot become an objective space, isolable and measurable. In the same way, nothingness, chaos, the source, the root, are hodological spaces that the saint traces within himself as he detaches himself and spiritually traverses the world. Although in texts such as the *Daodejing* they appear as names that describe substances, in reality they are expressions that do not have a descriptive function but a performative one: they consist in performing an action or in cultivating and experiencing an inner state. We are here at the extreme limit of what is sayable, where language is subject to violent twisting, or, as in Zhuangzi, paradox after paradox, endlessly inscribed and erased like a palimpsest. In this thought,

---

51 聖人無造無莫, 無意、必、固、我, 無可無不可, 氣象同天地, 何嘗有一毫之沾滯, 此即王弼所謂『聖人體無』。然實則此只是聖人之化境與氣象, 而不可即以此為體。Mou Zongsan, *Physical Nature and the "Profound Thought"*, pp. 319–320.

founded on the "mental state" (*jingjie*), subjectivity cannot be removed, because it is always silently presupposed as the spiritual space in which everything happens.

If the second stage, that of self-consciousness, can be thought of as reflective self-awareness, as we saw in the first chapter, how does it differ from the third dialectical stage, that of trans-consciousness? If we refer to the three-stage dialectic elaborated by Hegel, and to which Mou refers, even if only as a logical-formal device, trans-consciousness should be the product of the "negation of negation," that is, the overcoming of the narrowness into which I fall when I abandon the state of primary harmony and try to become self-conscious. But in the context of Daoist thought, as it emerges from Mou's analysis, can there really be an evolution toward trans-consciousness? Am I not always referred back to the Dao that is the root of everything? Daoism, as we have seen, does not promote a forward progress or an increase in knowledge, but a continuous awakening and going back to the source of everything. Can we speak here of an actual evolution from pre-consciousness to trans-consciousness, if what is required of the diaphanous subject is an uninterrupted thinning, emptying, "embodying nothingness"?

It is worth dwelling on this aspect, because it brings to light a substantial difference between the evanescent Daoist subject and the subject of Confucian moral metaphysics, to the exploration of which Mou will devote the most substantial part of his work. First of all, it is necessary to briefly consider what aspect the element that should act as antithesis and that should be assimilated and overcome in the dialectical movement takes: reflective self-consciousness. We saw above how the Dao has a circular course, in which everything tends to return to the One, and yet this undifferentiated One is not substance but pure function. The tension to return toward nothingness as root is at the same time a propulsion toward the infinite plurality of being. The metaphor of the root must also be thought of as function and pure dynamism. It is not a question here of analyzing the hierarchy of substances by grasping one of them as a static foundation to which everything ontologically refers. Nothingness as root is the function of immersing oneself in the inexhaustible fecundity of the Dao and conveying the lifeblood toward the luxuriant branching of things. The metaphor of the spring with even greater clarity represents this principle that is pure action, pure coming out of oneself and gushing forth. "Coming out of oneself" is not to be understood as implying that the power of the Dao suggests a pre-existing static condition to be left behind, but instead that the "self" is nothing more than this act of endlessly pouring into beings.

One runs the risk of becoming entangled in the inadequacy of language whenever one tries to think of the principle as pure act. We can think of Doctor Faust in chapter 3, who, in translating the incipit of John's Gospel "In the beginning was the Logos," is dissatisfied with the traditional rendering of the "logos" as Word, ponders alternative translations, trying to immerse himself ever more in the vertiginous unspeakability of the beginning, and finally bursts out: "The Spirit helps me! Here I see clearly and, now certain, I write: 'In the beginning was Action'!" Philosophical idealism will explore all the paradoxical consequences of thinking the origin as pure action. Mou notes how in the biblical doctrine of *creatio ex nihilo* itself, in order not to fall into the contradiction of an eternal being who at some point is forced to change his nature in order to make himself the creator of the world, I am forced to admit that God is nothing more than his pure act of creation, without ontological residue. And yet God's is a "creating with mind," it implies a creative will and intention, and an ordering principle that permeates creation, while Dao is pure "mindless generating." There is no subject that dominates and wills the appearance of the world, but there is a diaphanous subject that, precisely by virtue of its self-emptying, causes the wonderful, subtle function (*miaoyong* 妙用) of the Dao to be fulfilled by passing through it. Where this diaphanous subject reaches perfection in its practical and spiritual elevation, the teeming, irrepressible richness of the world shines through in its vision, and all things generate and subsist by themselves in their perfect independence and spontaneity (*ziran* 自然). I and the world manifest together in a concurrent presence, because in my act of attaining the subjective spiritual state of empty stillness, all things appear without interference, in their spontaneous being-ness (suchness).

Using Kantian terminology, Mou explains that in this creating without creating, maintaining oneself in a state of pure passivity, things appear not as phenomena but as things-in-themselves. If they were phenomena, they would be dependent on the knowing subject, as mediated by the *a priori* forms of the intellectual and sensory structure of the mind. The subject here is not a knowing subject, but a practicing subject, aiming at the evanescence and oblivion of self, and this subjective emptiness is the unfolding of the space in which all things appear from themselves in their solitary foundation. In his *Critique of the Cognitive Mind*, Mou attributed to Daoism the merit of having recognized in the human being the capacity for intellectual intuition; however, unlike what Mou finds in Confucianism, this intuition would be purely passive. The diaphanous subject has an innate capacity to intuitively grasp things in a non-objectifying way, letting them be as they are in themselves. In addition to objectifying knowledge, which Mou designates by the term *shi* (識), there is knowledge through wisdom (*zhi* 智), which is attained through spiritual cultivation.[52] Without making use of discursive reasoning, and without transforming things into phenomena, that is, pure objects of epistemological-scientific knowledge, this intuitive wisdom presupposes the practical effort of elevation and manifests things as having value in themselves: "Knowledge stemming from understanding opens toward natural world, manages systems of knowledge, for example, in the realm of physics and so forth. Practical moral knowledge (inside awareness) paves the way for a realm of values, enabling the developing of a moral individual and its ultimate goal is to become a saint."[53]

With respect to Confucian thought, this practical knowledge, which aims to elevate the world to the vision of the saint, does not have a moral scope, that is, it does not presuppose an act of creative realization of value in concrete historical action. Of the Kantian "thing-in-itself," this limitless generation of self-subsistent things retains only the "negative" aspect. Since the diaphanous subject recedes without end, dropping

---

52 Mou's concept of wisdom may be indebted to Xiong Shili: "[...] Xiong believed that our inner moral knowledge is that by which we can realise Reality. For him, since Reality is self-evident—that is to say, what realises Reality is Reality itself—innate moral knowledge is precisely Reality. Based on this understanding, Xiong describes the realization of Reality by innate moral knowledge as an immediate realization without the constructed distinction of subject and object. Xiong also expresses his above view of Reality [...] by means of the concept of 'wisdom' (*zhi* 智) or 'luminous wisdom' (*mingzhi* 明智)." Yu Sang, *Xiong Shili's Understanding of Reality and Function 1920–1937*, Leiden: Brill, 2020, p. 188.
53 Mou Zongsan (牟宗三), *Xinti yu xingti*. 心體與性體 (Constitutive Mind and Constitutive Nature), 3 vols, I, 145, in *Mou Zongsan xiansheng quanji*. 牟宗三先生全集 (Complete Works of Mou Zongsan), vols. V–VII, Taipei: Lianhe baoxi wenhua jijin hui, 2003. Translation by Sébastien Billioud, *Thinking through Confucian Modernity. A Study of Mou Zongsan's Moral Metaphysics*, Leiden: Brill, 2012, p. 80.

every claim to an ordering comprehension, things emerge nakedly in the light of its disappearance, deprived of all those characters that the thing known derives from my intellect or the senses, that is, from the relationship with the I who knows. Between the evanescent subject and the world there is a horizontal relation, which Mou calls, with a term borrowed from Buddhism, "competing presence." On the one hand, there is an absolute, unrelated exteriority between the subject and the teeming of things in their self-sufficient solitude. On the other hand, the background from which all the life of things originates is none other than the luminous emptiness and stillness that the subject embodies in its retreat. This equal distance finds its expression in the language of the "metaphysics of vision," that is, in the metaphor-guide of the gaze.

3.8 Priority of the Sense of Sight

Sight is the sense that does not require contact, but is best realized precisely in distancing itself. It does not meet things and does not mix with them, but grasps everything from a position of static distance. According to Mou, Daoism values contemplation (*guanzhao* 觀照), deep vision (*xuanlan* 玄覽),[54] the vision of return (*guanfu* 觀复). All these modes of spiritual vision and contemplation are, for Mou, inherently "artistic,"[55] that is, based on a permeating but static and passive vision that does not intervene in reality by transforming things through moral action. Two parallel terms summarize for Mou the difference between this active contemplation and Confucian moral action: silent radiating (*jizhao* 寂照) and silent corresponding (*jigan* 寂感). *Ji* 寂, which I have translated as "silent," represents the latent and potential state of the world. Wang Yangming, the greatest Neo-Confucian thinker of the Ming era, a proponent of the thesis that "there is no reality that is external to the mind," uses this term in a highly significant passage. Asked by one of his disciples what is the fate of a branch of red flowers that has blossomed in a remote mountain area when no observer is there to look at it, and thus "make it be" with his mind, he replies, "When you did not look at these flowers, the flowers and your mind were both

---

54 Mou Zongsan, *Nineteen Lectures on Chinese Philosophy*, p. 131.
55 Ibid., p. 126.

3. The "Diaphanous Subject" in Daoist Thought   167

gathered in silence. When you looked at the flowers, their color became manifest. From this you can know that these flowers are not external to your mind."[56] *Tong guiyu ji* 同歸於寂, which I translated "they were both gathered in silence," could be rendered as "they had both returned to their solitary stillness." *Ji* is here the latent state of things, as opposed to their manifest being.[57] This latent state in Daoism belongs to the realm of annihilation (*wu* 無), of primal chaos gathered in its silent sphericity and without openings to the other and to the outside. Since, according to Mou's analysis, we are not here in the realm of substance where being is opposed to non-being, but in the practical realm based on one's mental state, this tranquility and calm silence is the spiritual condition of the saint. He is imperturbable, that is, similar to the flat surface of a body of water untroubled by wind and waves. In both *jizhao* and *jigan* we have an apparent contrast, a movement of systole and diastole that in the heart of the calm silence finds propulsion toward things. In Daoism this going out of self toward things is given in the form of *zhao* 照, of illuminating or radiating so as to make visible. By gathering myself into stillness, the whole world appears in its empty silence, that is, in its primal state, untainted by my attachments or thoughts. In the Confucian tradition, on the other hand, the term *gan* 感 expresses the idea of affecting reality, of reaching out and responding to its stimuli, as in the passage from the *Yijing*: "The principle of change does not think, does not act, in its quiet and silent being (*ji*) responds to and connects with all things under heaven".[58] Mou writes: "This should be contrasted with the Daoist advocating 'calm reflection' (*jizhao*) and the Buddhist practicing ceasing [illusion] and meditating [on reality] (*zhiguan* 止観,

---

56 Wing-Tsit Chan, *Instructions for Practical Living*, p. 222.
57 "It is obvious that what he means by "*ji*" (寂 silent vacancy or tranquil) is a "sleeping" or "non-awaking" state of something potentially able to realize the spirituality, or life, of the universe. But why does the spirituality, or life, have to be revealed, activated or awakened by humans' mental acts and actions? Generally speaking, it is because humans are the *xin* of heaven, earth and the myriad things of the universe." Fung Yiu-ming, "Wang Yang-ming's Theory of Liang-zhi—A New Interpretation of Wang Yang-ming's Philosophy," *Tsing Hua Journal of Chinese Studies* 42:2 (2012), 277–278.
58 *Yi wu si ye, wu wei ye, ji er budong, gan er sui tong tianxia zhi gu* (易無思也, 無為也, 寂而不動, 感而遂通天下之故).

śamatha, and *vipaśyāna*). The different emphases show the differences in their teaching. 'Creative feeling' is the spirit of Confucianism."[59]

Although Confucianism and Daoism are both "vertical" systems, in which through spiritual elevation one understands the hierarchical relationship between things and their foundation (e.g., the Dao), the vertical system of Daoism has only a horizontal expression. The quieting of the mind and the appearance of things occur on the same plane. If I am subjectively in a state of luminous emptiness, the whole universe is illuminated and subsists in itself without my having to act, thanks to that "concurrent presence" that is static and passive. In the case of Confucianism, as we shall see, when the supreme spiritual state is achieved, I do not merely radiate things but actively respond to them with my moral mind. The moral mind is creative in that it is involved in all things, acts upon them by conferring value and meaning, and thus possesses vertical expression. "If the mind is collected in silence, everything is enlightened" is contrasted with the active exercise of moral intention. For in this second case, "If the mind is collected in silence, it responds to everything and is a participant in every event." In the first case we are on a purely subjective and contemplative plane, while in the second case the mind is realized in objective reality, which receives its own objectivity and concreteness precisely from the concentration and action of the moral mind on it. The goal of the Confucian saint, as we shall see, is thus to achieve a state of self-cultivation that allows the synthesis of subject and object in the metaphysical mind. Through moral judgment, this mind or innate moral consciousness (*liangzhi* 良知) is revealed as the absolute foundation of the mutual connection between all things.

The ideal goal of the Daoist saint is to be neither subject nor object (*wu zhu wu ke* 無主無客), equidistant from all things, immersed in an endless and ever-renewing effort to relinquish all attachment to self and the world. Mou quotes in his lessons this passage from the second chapter of *Zhuangzi*: "The saint leans on the sun and moon, tucks the universe under his arm, merges himself with things, leaves the confusion and muddle as it is, and looks on slaves as exalted. Ordinary men strain and struggle; the saint is stupid and blockish. He takes part

---

59 Mou Zongsan, *Nineteen Lectures on Chinese Philosophy*, p. 132.

in ten thousand ages and achieves simplicity in oneness. For him, all the ten thousand things are what they are, and thus they enfold each other".[60] This passage is significant for Mou, because it reminds us that "The highest spiritual state (*jingjie*) of all ethics and religion is to descend to the bottom, not to rise to the top. What is high they already possess; they are imbued with it." [61] This downward movement, which follows the act of detaching oneself from the world and flying above things, is that immersion in finite things that represents the antithetical aspect of every dialectic. Only through this act of exteriorization and realization can I verify the validity of the principle, removing it from its abstract dimension and then returning to it.

Mou states that every spiritual tradition is modeled around this movement of descent and return. He adduces the example of Christianity, in which God descends in the son, self-limiting himself in the son, so that all finite things may be proof that God the Father is pure spirit, that is, able to permeate and embrace everything beyond distinctions. In Confucianism, the Dao of heaven, the supreme principle, finds the verification of its spiritual creativity, realizing itself concretely in moral action. We can ask ourselves, however, what are the characteristics of this descending movement in Daoism, which in the dialectical process corresponds to antithesis. Antithesis establishes the realm of distinction, in which the divarication between subject and object can be realized. In this divarication the subject sees its objective manifestation as placed outside itself and can begin to recover and assimilate it anew through self-consciousness. In reflexive self-consciousness, the self as subject mirrors itself in the self as object and recognizes itself, and this recognition is the beginning of the recomposition of what is divided through cognitive assimilation or moral practice. Finding in all things the trace of its own action, the subject loses its abstractness and realizes itself in the concreteness of the objective world, while the object is no longer pure exteriority but finds in itself the trace of the acting subject in the form of meaning. The next step is the elevation to the mental state of trans-consciousness, which represents the perfect fulfilment of this

---

60 Watson (ed.), *The Complete Works of Zhuangzi*, pp. 47–48.
61 凡是宗教都有這個精神, 道德、宗教的最高境界都是這個精神, 它往下不往上。它已經往上, 已經通透了嘛。Mou Zongsan, "Zhuangzi 'Qiwulun' yanjianglu", p. 189.

assimilation of the objective world, and the overcoming of that fracture between subjective and objective on which self-consciousness is based.

How can the diaphanous Daoist subject encounter the objective other than itself? This cannot happen in what Mou calls the "directionality" of being. Although it is a movement of the spirit opposite to that of self-emptying and returning to the indistinct origin, and represents a directing of the mind toward the inexhaustible plurality of being, there is nothing in it that can stand in dialectical opposition to the subject. As we saw earlier, "directionality" is not Husserlian "intentionality;" it does not express a necessary relationship of the subject with the objective world, but is just another mode of manifestation of the original Dao. That "nothingness" that is at the root of all beings is not static but dynamic, it is not substance but pure function. There is a movement of systole and diastole: to return to drink from the one source of all being means to participate in its infinite vital power, in its uninterrupted gushing out, in its manifestation in the inexhaustible plurality of things. These things, however, are not "objects" that the mind can grasp and possess, but their pure being-so, spontaneous and independent. Taking the example of the jug, the room, and the wheel, whose functions are fulfilled thanks to the emptiness that these things hold, the heart of "nothingness" that beings possess is the autonomy and the overflowing richness of life of that which has its root in itself and does not have to lean on anything else, neither on an external cause nor on the gaze of a subject. We are here in that endless circulation that Mou calls *xuan* 玄, the vast and profound mystery of the Dao.

So when is the split between subject and object produced that makes reflective self-consciousness possible? It is when we focus on a single thing, separating it from its root, and attach ourselves to it in the desire to possess it. Then the subject coagulates and conceals its origin, and the things separated from the infinite, life-giving flow of the Dao are alienated and become obstacles to the development of the mind. This is what we have described as a spot or wrinkle in the diaphanous nature of the mind. Because of it, the world is no longer "nature" in the sense of the Dao, i.e., *ziran*, being-in-itself of everything, but "nature" as scientific knowledge represents it, a succession of causes and effects between external and determinate objects that rest on each other and on the subject that knows them. This descent into a mechanistic world is not only subordinate to the act of knowing, but also has a spiritual value, in that the subject loses its transparency by also attaching itself to preferences and habits and becoming a "mind of habit." The conditions for reflective self-consciousness are therefore produced only now, when the mind can cling to its inner flow and know itself as the object of psychology. We are here confronted with what Mou in his later writings will call the "psychological ego," understood as a "false ego" that represents a descent and self-limitation from the higher level of the moral ego. Already in *Critique of the Cognitive Mind*, Mou had spoken of this level of mind as "psychological states," or in Kantian terms as "object of inner sensibility." With respect to them, perception (*jue* 覺), which is the nonobjectifiable activity of the mind, must continually free itself by "jumping out" (*tiaoqi* 跳起) and reasserting itself as the "absolute subject." Also, in *Caixing yu xuanli*, Mou speaks of the need to "leap out of the mind of habit," or, with Zhuangzi, of "detachment from the calculating and anxious self-consciousness," a detachment and elevation that do not imply, however, a "falling into unconsciousness," but the proceeding toward the "trans-consciousness" of the saint who knows how to forget his own egoistic self (*wang wo* 忘我).

Does this descent into the determinate objectivity of things and into the mind of habit represent a dialectical progress, just as in the Hegelian dialectic the antithesis allows its own negation and overcoming to a higher level than the original one? In Mou's formulation, this fall into particularity is defined in a purely negative and incidental way. To better illustrate this claim, we can compare this model with the Confucian model, centered on the moral mind, which will be the focus of Mou's major works. In Mou's interpretation, Confucian thought is not a metaphysics of the subjective mental state, but a true metaphysics of substance. That is, the original principle is not a pure spiritual practice of self-emptying, but a positive and creative substance. As we shall see, Confucianism in the course of its evolution has called this principle by many names, as Dao Mind (*daoxin* 道心), Heavenly Principle (*tianli* 天理), Great Culmination (*taiji* 太極), or innate moral consciousness (*liangzhi* 良知). It is in each case the same dynamic substance that gives rise to heaven and earth and manifests itself in the moral mind as a living interconnection between all things. The relationship that this substance or first principle establishes with things is generative and creative, that is, it is their principle of realization and actualization. In Daoism, nothingness (*wu*), the original chaos, is embodied in the absolute equanimity of the saint, who lets the world generate itself, withdrawing from any claim of control over things and opening the space in which they can spontaneously occur. The Confucian subject does not limit himself to "letting being be," but incarnates himself in things by ordering them and giving them a unitary meaning. This "embodiment" (*ti*) is not that of the Daoist subject who aspires to "embody nothingness" (*ti wu* 體無), that is, to achieve a certain detached subjective posture, but is an authentic realization in all things.

The original principle is here a dynamic moral mind that contains in itself its own law, that is, in it the supreme law of things and the moral will to realize it are merged. Therefore, this original principle cannot remain closed within itself, but is a force that tends to realize itself in all beings and all particular events. Here too, therefore, there is a movement of descent and particularization, but it is not a form of alienation or attachment, but rather the positive actualization of the moral law in every event, without any aspect being forgotten or left behind. In this lies the moral and not purely aesthetic nature of the principle, which cannot contemplate things motionless from above while preserving its own detachment. On the contrary, it responds to the call of things, implies itself in them, participates in their smallness, neglects none of them. The descent is therefore not, as in Daoism, a "fall" or an "obscuration" that must always be overcome again by those who aspire to holiness. The Daoist saint affirms the truth of himself by "jumping out" of every exclusive predilection, every clinging to habit, dropping even his own limited ego, in order to return to the undifferentiated root of the Dao, that is, to his own spiritual state of absolute freedom. The Confucian moral mind, too, must avoid clinging to a single perspective, from solidifying itself in a partial view, for in doing so it would deny itself, it would lose the universality of its own creative force. The Confucian subject must have an ever-active inner vigilance that prevents it from turning into the selfish "little I." But particularity here has not only the negative value of limitation and partiality, but above all the positive value of being the living realization of the principle. By actualizing itself in all things and in all historical events, it fills them with meaning and rescues them from neglect and oblivion. At the same time this descent into the particular is not simply inevitable because of the imperfection of the subject, but necessary, and an integral part of the development of the principle. In it the subject becomes self-conscious, discovering itself one with heaven and earth, and finds itself again in its relation to all things, elevating itself to an authentic moral subject. The passive-contemplative character of the diaphanous Daoist subject and the negative character of the particular that becomes an obstacle and obscuration prevent the recovery of the movement of descent and self-limitation in that movement of the dialectic that Hegel calls *Aufhebung*. *Aufhebung* is removal and negation, but at the same time lifting (sublation) to a higher degree and thus reversal. In Daoist thought as reconstructed by Mou the objective particular is only taken away and denied to reinstate the circular movement between nothingness and being, between the return to the undifferentiated and the infinite wonderful subtle function (*miaoyong* 妙用) of the self-generation of everything. This circularity in which nothingness is found in the heart of being and beingness in the heart of nothingness is the *xuan* 玄, the vast and profound mystery of the Dao in which the saint spiritually immerses himself. The dialectical movement is also circular, but in actualizing itself it progresses and grows on the vertical plane, like an upward spiral. The Confucian saint gathers and sublimates every event, reaching the unity of subject and object, while the Daoist saint is realized in a state of mind that is "neither subject nor object," therefore not synthesis but detachment from both. If therefore we reach the third and highest moment indicated by Mou, that is trans-consciousness, we see that in the case of Daoism there is no real evolution, neither gain nor loss, so that the beginning (before reflective self-consciousness) and the end (above reflective self-consciousness) are identical.

But what is this "trans-consciousness" of the mind? Like the other two phases, it designates only a *jingjie*, a spiritual state to be reached through practice. It is not a metaphysical mind, creative in its substance, that generates things, as in Confucianism, but only a subjective state of mind, where "subjective" means only "attained in practice." If there is in it, however, nothing subjective nor objective (*wuzhuwuke* 無主無客), are we to understand this mental state to be devoid of self-consciousness? It is certainly devoid of reflective self-consciousness, of that "self-recognition in the mirror" which presumed, precisely, a mirror, that is, an objectivity outside the self. This reflexive self-consciousness, as we have seen, is not a cognitive act, but first and foremost a way of standing in relation to the world that implies a value judgment. It is clinging to oneself, to one's partialities, to the habitual mechanism of one's inner flow, solidifying into an ego (which Mou designates here by the terms *wo* 我, *ji* 己, or *siji* 私己, ego or private self). The diaphanous subject then is devoid of this ego and yet is subjectivity to the highest degree, and indeed, as Mou writes, "absolute transcendental subject." This subjective nature manifests itself precisely by letting go of the ego, eroding and liquefying it at the moment when the ego stops, becomes hard and refractory. Behind the "calculating and anxious" self-consciousness, preoccupied with itself, gathered about itself reflexively, as if it wanted to attest its presence with a continuous act of self-recognition, in such a way as not to forget or lose itself, there is therefore a background subjectivity. This background subjectivity reveals itself only indirectly in the act of erasing the ego, of withdrawing from the ego. However, it is not an unconscious level, like a deaf impulsive activity that precedes consciousness. Thinking of the mind as a hierarchically layered reality is still an illusory way of grasping oneself by representing oneself as a spatial image. As we have seen, the Daoist saint is realized in the circular identity of the non-conscious (*bu zijue* 不自覺) and trans-conscious (*chao zijue* 超自覺). That which precedes the ego as its origin also eternally transcends it, making it disappear. The kind of consciousness the saint has of himself is not that of looking ahead of himself at his own image, but rather what Mou calls retrospective intuition (*fanjuewu* 反覺悟). Mou in his work often speaks of *fantizheng* 反體證, retrospective verification, but it implies that the moral mind creatively realizes itself in things and, rebounding, intuits its own authenticity and creative efficacy. An example is given by Mengzi's famous sentence: "The myriad things are all within me. To turn inward and discover the authenticity: There is no greater joy than this!"[62] In Daoism, as we have seen, operating in things is a dulling of the self that imposes a negation and a return to the self. Retrospective

---

62 *Wanwu jie bei yu wo ye. Fanshen er cheng, le mo da yan* (萬物皆備於我也。反身而誠, 樂莫大焉).

intuition is thus a grasping of oneself moment by moment, in the very act of erasing all stiffening of the self.

3.9 Subject, Ancestor, Host

But what are the characteristics of this subject that is given to us as a sort of luminous vastness of background, perceptible only in the evanescence of our ego? How can we understand a subject that is only the abandonment of every egoistic concretion and return to the origin, that intuitively does not manifest any semblance or content, and appears only as the practical action of returning? A possible way to find an answer to this question is indicated by Mou affirming, as we have seen, that the "nothingness" (*wu*) of the origin is not to be understood as a noun but as a verb. There is no substantial nothingness to embrace, but there is the act of *wu*-ing, of self-emptying as spiritual practice. Applying this dialectic of the contrast between verb, which expresses fluidity and action, and noun, which indicates stiffening, we can now reconsider those linguistic clues involved in our discussion of the subject. It is worth noting that in Daoist texts we find, according to Mou's interpretation, a metaphysics of vision or spiritual state, while a metaphysics of substance is missing. This implies that when we use a noun, there is no real and positive substance behind it, such as "the Good, the Beautiful and the True" might represent for Mou. Instead, these are merely the outcomes of our subjective act of focusing, a halting and clinging of the mind that does not presuppose a pre-existing objective reality to which we grasp. It is the very act of clinging to one's illusions that produces in the subject that arrest, that wrinkle that obscures the light that comes from the original Dao, which the mind interprets as a thing, an objective obstacle. Dialectically, Mou describes it as alienation, the illusory becoming-other of the self.

First of all, let us consider the term *zhu* (主), which in the expression *zhuti* 主體 or *zhuguan* 主觀 indicates respectively the grammatical subject and the subjective point of view. In its original meaning it represents the one who guides and governs or the ancestor, the one who performs a guiding function precisely because he came first. Mou asserts that the one embodied by the Daoist saint is the "*zhu* of non-*zhu*," the practical action indicated by the verb that manifests itself only in removing and transcending *zhu* as a noun. The saint who conforms to the Dao guides and rules things but never constitutes himself as reigning. The Dao has an internal rhythm, the alternation of yin and yang, which regulates things in its flow. Like a piece of music, it exists only in its performance, its temporal flow, and the auditory experience we have of it. But, as Laozi reminds us in chapter 12, "The five colors blind the eyes. The five sounds deafen the ear." If I want to grasp the music, to hold it and define it in my mind, I detach myself from the flow of sound, I stop perceiving the piece of music as it flows and appears ever new. I have to free my mind from this obstruction so as to become sensitive and responsive to the flow of sound again. In the same way the Daoist saint is one with the Dao in removing all objectification or partial embodiment from himself. The saint, or as we have called it the diaphanous subject, is the act of regulating and guiding everything from within as the Dao does, without yielding to the temptation to constitute itself as a guiding principle or abstract rule. The subject is the subtle inner or immanent regulation of the flow of things, which is only possible if I eliminate my mind's claim to be sovereign or an ordering principle.

Developing the shades of meaning in the term *zhu*, we also find "the ancestor." The diaphanous subject comes first, in that the self-cultivation required to be perfectly attuned to the Dao and unveil the entire spiritual landscape (*jingjie*) in which things come into being is the practical premise without which no being is given. This premise, however, is not placed on the same plane as being. The term "spiritual state" (*jingjie*) implies, as we have seen, a horizontal relationship, in which, having reached a certain level of elevation, the subject unveils a world that is the one corresponding to that stage of vision. In other words, my elevation or decay in spiritual practice involves an elevation or decay of the world given in my vision. If the subject has achieved holiness, things are manifested to him as generated and crossed by the nothingness, *wu*, that is their source. As Mou points out, in the Daoist texts, and especially in the *Laozi*, nothingness appears as similar to a prime substance from which everything springs. In reality, if I return to the origin and the root, I do not find a substantial nothingness, but only my act of emptying and withdrawing myself so that the world can be in its autonomy. That is, I must move to the vertical plane of practice. The diaphanous subject is therefore prior to everything in its retreat and elevation, but it is not an ancestor understood as a first cause on the horizontal plane. It can precede things by opening the space of their manifestation, but to do this it must renounce being a first cause, identifying itself as an ancestor on the horizontal plane. My being first is the originating principle that Mou calls "value." Adopting the language of the *Yijing*, it is the *kun* (坤) or the *yuan* (元), the ushering in and unveiling of the world that is not itself a mere "first among equals," a pre-eminent and dominant thing among other things. All things return to that which is not a thing but a dynamic event, my embodying the equanimity of the Dao so that everything can spontaneously manifest without interference. The diaphanous subject is thus the coming first and the giving origin, which withdraws itself, refraining from being an ancestor or first cause.

There is a third meaning of *zhu*, which manifests itself in the word *zhuke* 主客 with which I express the duality of subject and object, but which in its original meaning indicates the host and the guest. The Dao of the saint, Mou writes, is *wuzhuwuke* 無主無客, neither subject nor object, neither guest nor host. What is at issue here is the separation and juxtaposition of these two terms, which refers us back to the horizontal cognitive model, in which the subject is an inner entity seeking to apprehend the extraneous exteriority of the world. In rising, the saint, like the Dao, hosts everything, welcomes everything without hindrance or predilection. But he is not for this reason a guest who chooses whom to admit into his house, who has a partial will and judgment, who is exclusive and limited in the face of an outer world that presses to be recognized. By depriving himself of his own prerogative of being the guest, the subject realizes himself as a pure act of hosting and giving space, being flat 平平, that is, without preference. With this he frees things from their outward being, embodies the place without inside and without outside in which everything is born and consists. Taken together, these three modes—first, subtly regulating everything without imposing myself as an authority or regulating principle; second, being what comes first, inaugurating the world by renouncing the role of first cause and ancestor; and third, keeping open the space in which everything happens, without asserting myself as the central host subject—refer to what Mou calls "generating without mind," or "creation without creating."

Another way, of Buddhist derivation, to express the subject-object duality is *nengsuo* 能所. Already in *Critique of the Cognitive Mind*, Mou emphasized the difference between "perception 覺" and psychological states by stating that perception is an absolute subject (*neng* 能), as it can never be grasped by internal sensibility as the passive flow of psychological states, but plays only an active role and escapes any objectification. By stating that the Daoist saint is ultimately the "absolute transcendental subject," Mou refers us back to the idea of *neng* as agency, dynamism, and pure action, setting aside the second meaning of *neng* as power, having a capacity. In this case, the accomplished Daoist subject is a pure act of elevation of the self and the world, an unlimited outpouring, without a *neng* (能), understood in the sense of function, capacity, being identified in it. The diaphanous subject does not claim possession of inner faculties, as is the case, for example, with the Kantian cognitive subject. I cannot look at it as a transcendental structure endowed with sensible and intellectual capacities, because these internal partition lines would be wrinkles and obscurations in its infinite striving toward evanescence. Otherwise stated, the subject would have an objectifiable nature, able to be studied as a cognitive structure. This epistemological approach is what must be eliminated if I want the subject to give itself to me as pure agency, a practical dynamism that precedes any division between the exterior world and the interior world. The diaphanous subject is an interminable process of return to the Dao, that is to that original state of non-attachment to anything, of "free and easy wandering" (*xiaoyaoyou* 逍遙遊), whereby the soul can penetrate everything without being limited and reduced to utensils.

Like the blade of the cook of Ding, which slips between the gaps of emptiness of the ox's body and never wears out, so the ideal subject has no ego, that is, it has no partiality or desires, it does not allow itself to be seduced by things and concepts, and it does not allow its attachment to things to reduce its ego to a thing, that is, to the immutable perspective of a subject that is opposed to the objective exteriority of the world. If I drop this little substantive "I," I can reach the verbal "I," that is, the evanescent subject that is pure dynamism, process, and act. The Dao that I want to embody is not something superior to other things, it is not the Dao as a noun "the Way, the doctrine," but the Dao in its verbal aspect, the act of walking that has no predetermined path, but creates its own path at every moment. This processuality is what the diaphanous subject tends toward in its continuous self-emptying, in its thinning out. If the ego is a limited focus of perspective on reality, the diaphanous subject is a continuous blurring, an oblivion of the finite self in order to be one with the Dao, with the luminous vastness always flowing and overflowing beyond the edge of the limited ego. This subject as pure verb, as "going beyond and higher," is what the term *neng* expresses. It is the pure interminable and ever-vigilant practice of the saint, a letting go of hold on things, that never reaches a final perfection. It is not directed, like the Confucian moral self, toward the substance of the good, the beautiful, and the true. It is a pure wandering and free movement, without direction. When it finds that it has assumed a direction or is aiming at an end, it forgets them and lets them go. This aspiration to self-perfection is always threatened by selfishness and desire. I must ceaselessly go beyond all definition, and in this act perceive myself as one with the vastness and life force that runs through all things. This alone is the "absolute subjectivity" that can never be captured in a name or concept, and can only be experienced as the practical negation of all boundaries. The subject is one that continually practices, goes beyond, and renews itself, and only in this infinite practice does it consist.

3.10 Diaphanous Subject and Thin Subject

It may be clarifying at this point to compare Mou's vision of the "great transcendental subject" with some contemporary outcomes of the philosophy of the self. In the different theories of consciousness outlined in the introduction, we can find some key terms that seem to suggest a similarity with our definition of "diaphanous subject." I refer in particular to the so-called "thin subject" or "minimal subject," theorized for instance by Dan Zahavi and Galen Strawson in the framework of the phenomenology of mind. Remember that the idea of a "thin subject" is proposed in order to overcome the aporias generated by the "thick subject" model. By thick subject we mean the traditional conception of the subject as a persistent substance, be it an immortal soul or a complex brain structure, that continues to exist as such even when the self is not experiencing the world. This ontological persistence of a self detached from its experiential experience poses, as we have seen in the introduction, several problems, which have led many scholars to define as illusory the existence of the self understood as an "actually existing ontological independent self-entity who is the owner of experience and the thinker of the thoughts."[63] A possible response to this rejection is the redefinition of the self as inseparable from the "living moment experience" in which it is immersed. As Zahavi writes: "Self-experience is the self-experience of a world-immersed self, or, to put it differently, our experiential life is world-related, and there is a presence of self when we are worldly engaged."[64] In this reformulation, therefore, the ontological claim of independence of the self is dropped, and it is emphasized that the self appears to us solely in the experiential flow, not as an object of reflection but as a necessary orientation of experience in the direction of the self, as being-for-the-consciousness of everything that enters my experiential field. This thin subject through which the world can be given in the first person, is not placed outside or above the changing experience as its principle of synthesis and organization. Its "thin" and "minimal" character thus lies in its renunciation of a "strong" metaphysical foundation: the self is neither substance nor transcendental principle, but a ubiquitous and permeating modality of lived experience.

Are there similarities between this subtlety and the evanescence of what we have called the diaphanous subject? First of all, it should be noted that the question at the basis of this phenomenological approach is strictly epistemological, i.e., aimed at exploring how I come to know myself and what the conditions and limits are of such knowledge. To use Mou's terminology, we are on a horizontal logical-constructive level, while Chinese thought, be it Daoist or Confucian, privileges a vertical type of research, that is, based on the cultivation of oneself through practice.

---

63 This refusal can be translated into affirming that our "elusive sense of a subjective presence" does not need to be underpinned by a pre-existing unbroken consciousness that observes the changes without itself changing (see Miri, *Analytical Buddhism: The Two-Tiered Illusion of the Self*, New York: Palgrave Macmillan, 2006, p. 155), or into the proposal of a "no-self alternative" that puts outright the fictitious idea of "being or possessing a self" (Thomas Metzinger, "The No-Self Alternative," in: S. Gallagher (ed.), *The Oxford Handbook of the Self*, Oxford: Oxford University Press, 2011, pp. 279–296).

64 Dan Zahavi, "Unity of Consciousness and the Problem of Self," in: Shaun Gallagher (ed.), *The Oxford Handbook of the Self*, Oxford: Oxford University Press, 2011, pp. 316–335 (p. 328).

The latter contains within itself a hierarchy of values that exalts self-improvement and self-elevation, while in Western phenomenological research every value judgement is excluded, or, as Husserl would say, "put in brackets," in order not to invalidate with subjective prejudices the methodological correctness of the research. Mou, however, identifies two horizontal dimensions that are embedded in Daoist thought and can therefore be the object of comparison: the duality of subject and object, which is produced when the ego, out of selfish desire, clings to itself and to things, and that which characterizes the "concurrent presence" of the ego and the world, that is, their simultaneous unfolding in the "vision" or "mental state" (*jingjie*).

The first case occurs when the diaphanous subject falls back into the mind of habit, limiting itself and becoming an obstacle to the flow of the Dao. At this level the subject becomes a limited ego opposed to external things. This "small ego" that obscures the "big ego" of the diaphanous subject is related to things because of its attachment to the world. The dimension investigated by the Western "philosophy of mind" is, in Mou's view, the microcosm of the mind of habit oblivious to its practical origin. In this embedded dimension, subject and object are mutually opposed but indissoluble, comparable to the two poles, subjective and objective, of the intentional act. In this case the ego is considered as a subject immersed in experience, and, as the thin subject, is unthinkable outside its cognitive relation to the world. Autonomy and self-subsistence are precluded because the dimension of *autonomy* (*zi* 自), of existing in itself and for itself, is attainable only in the directionality of being, that is, in that spontaneous germination and growth of everything that is the multiple actualizations of the Dao. The vitalizing force of the Dao can flow only if every temptation to appropriate oneself and the world is dropped, and therefore if the hindering ego has been removed. Daoism's critique of grasping and accumulating knowledge and of the path of knowledge in which, for Laozi, the subject grows illusorily, forgetting its own root, does not allow Daoism to attribute an autonomous value to the cognitive subject. As we shall see, for Mou the cognitive dimension is fully justified and validated only in its being voluntarily produced by the moral mind. Only by reaching into the moral sphere, as Confucianism does, is the descent into the finite dimension of the cognitive self not merely the result of egoic attachment, but possesses an intrinsic positivity because it allows the moral mind to actualize itself in the plurality of events without neglecting anything. As we have seen, one of the limits of the Daoist dialectic consists precisely in the impossibility of giving positive value to what is conditioned, partial, and the result of attachment. The "little I," which is constituted only in its opposition to the object, and is therefore on the same level as things, can only vanish into the "big I" of the Dao mind when the diaphanous subject awakens to the truth of itself.

The butterfly-ego with which Zhuangzi in his famous dream identifies himself, immersing himself totally in the immemorial and blissful subjective experience of flight, has many similarities with the thin subject of contemporary philosophy of mind. As a pure lived present, which knows itself only in the intoxicating flow of its experience, it is destined to dissolve when Zhuangzi wakes up and discovers that he has only dreamed. In the dream, the dreamer is limited in a subjective point of view, and sometimes his perspectival position transitions from one person to another (*person* is here taken in the Latin meaning of "mask, role"). What he does not know, because his condition is obscured and precluded, is that he is the source of his entire dream. As Michel Foucault writes: "The subject of the dream, the first person of the dream, is the dream itself, the whole dream. In the dream, everything says, "I," even the things and the animals, even the empty space, even objects distant and strange which populate the phantasmagoria."[65] Awakening is the unexpected act by which the "little I" of the cognitive mind awakens to the truth of self, to the "big I" of the Dao mind, which is ubiquitously present in everything. The small self is a temporary obscuration, in which I self-limit myself into a "calculating and anxious" consciousness, a wrinkle that must be ironed out and returned to the flat, equanimous being of the saint.

The diaphanous subject,[66] which is the evanescence of every limited ego, has a second horizontal modality, which is precisely the concurrent

---

[65] Michel Foucault, "Dream, Imagination and Existence," in: Ludwig Binswanger and Michel Foucault, "Dream and Existence," *Review of Existential Psychology and Psychiatry* 19:1 (1985), 29–78 (p. 59).

[66] According to Aristotle, "Il diafano è visibile nella sua attualità illuminata, solo attraverso un colore altro" (οὐ καθ' αὑτὸ δὲ ὁρατὸν ὡς ἁπλῶς εἰπεῖν, ἀλλὰ δι' ἀλλότριον χρῶμα) [the diaphanous is not visible in itself, but because of the colour of something else which is seen through it] (see Berenice Cavarra,

presence of self and the universe. Horizontality in this case, Mou warns, is not due to the logical-cognitive setting, but to the fact that the diaphanous ego has no superior creative function. It is a "mindless generating, generating without generating." It does not act factually so that things are accomplished, but limits itself to withdrawing from every "little I," dropping every ego and every intention, and contemplating in silence the happening of the universe. We may ask whether this horizontality could be approached from those hypotheses of explanation of consciousness that prescind from the ego. As we have seen, there are scholars who deny the need for an active ego to unify the flow of experience. The various declinations of this "egoless hypothesis" converge in affirming the fictive and retrospective nature of the ego. The world that I experience and this experience itself have no creative center; they develop and structure themselves by virtue of their specific internal nature. The illusion of an ego that governs and supervises this anonymous happening arises when I turn back and try to give meaning to what happens by going over it in memory. Making meaning is equivalent to finding a coherent narrative thread, and it implies the uninterrupted existence of a narrating and omnipresent I in every moment of experience, or its retrospective reconstruction. The objection that is most commonly made to these theories is phenomenological in character and is based on the idea that experience as such cannot be anonymous or impersonal, like a machine that has within itself the instructions for its own self-completion. However much reflexive self-consciousness may be absent in most of my everyday mental operations, what happens in the sphere of my acting is nevertheless an experience that is given to me. We return, then, to that minimal "selfhood" that underlies what Zahavi and Shaun Gallagher call the "thin subject." This being given to me, this selfgiveness, is nonetheless a passive "datitude," a condition in which I am immersed and from which I intermittently emerge as self-consciousness grasping itself.

Is the "mindless generation" that Mou ascribes to the diaphanous Daoist subject, its passive-contemplative disposition, comparable to this minimal datitude, this "mineness" that runs beneath my experience

---

"*Parousia*: colori, diafano e luce in Aristotele e nella tradizione aristotelica," *Medicina nei secoli. Journal of History of Medicine and Medical Humanities* 32:2 (2020), 543–558 (p. 550).

of the world, without requiring my active presence? There is also here a radical difference that allows us to characterize the specificity of Chinese thought in the vertical interpretation that Mou elaborates. The diaphanous subject does not creatively intervene in the happening of the world, because it is not, as in Confucian thought, a subject who is the embodiment of a moral mind, that is, of a constitutive principle capable of actively transforming reality. However, the absence of this "creativity," as Mou understands it, does not detract from the fact that the diaphanous subject is maximally active in its endless retraction. Without its becoming evanescent, without the continuous effort to remove egoic ego, or as we have written above, without its relinquishment of being a noun to instead become a verb, nothing could spontaneously arise or give itself. The giving itself as it is (*ziran*) of the ten thousand things requires that the subject strives to open up the space of spontaneity and suchness, making itself the realm of absolute spontaneity. The concept of mental state (*jingjie*) in which Mou recognizes the specificity of Chinese thought, whether it is declined as Daoist, Buddhist, or Confucian, expresses this inseparability of the self and the world. The self or diaphanous subject that is the unveiling of the horizon in which everything happens, is not simply a phenomenological subject in whose horizon the world obtains awareness and manifestation. It is a practicing subject that realizes the opening of the world by working on itself, shaping itself in daily effort, and striving for self-elevation. It is not a "self-defining subject," such as that which is the subject of contemporary philosophy of mind, but first of all it is a "self-refining subject." Its relation to any property or predicate is not to possess that characteristic, but to become it by progressing in exercise. It is not nothingness, but becomes it in self-refining. It is not the Dao, or rather it is in the only way a Way (Dao) can be embodied, that is, by walking it. The practicing, elevating subject has received peripheral attention in Western thought, gathered in self-understanding.

Some contemporary Western philosophers have actually challenged the traditional interpretation of philosophy as theoretical and purely rational activity, claiming its practical-oriented and life-changing significance. Among them the arguably most influential are Pierre Hadot, who in *Philosophy as a Way of Life*[67] reexamines the history of

---

67 Pierre Hadot, *Philosophy as a Way of Life. Spiritual Exercises from Socrates to Foucault*, Malden, MA, and Oxford: Blackwell Publishing, 1995.

ancient Greek-Roman thought as "spiritual exercise" that requires effort, training, and existential engagement, and Peter Sloterdijk, who in his works *You Must Change Your Life*[68] and *The Art of Philosophy*[69] develops a general theory of "practicing life," "askesis," and "vertical ascent." Sloterdijk, in particular, defines the uniqueness of human being as a constant striving for self-perfection through a regulated physical or spiritual training. For Sloterdijk the inward movement that establishes the realm of inner life is not an intellectual-cognitive act, as in Descartes' "I think," but the exercise of uprooting ourselves from our mechanical habits. If the goal of every spiritual, religious, or philosophical practice of self-cultivation is to de-objectify and de-automatize ourselves, the specificity of subject, which distinguishes it from the objective things, is to be a never-ending effort of autopoietic subjectification.

This approach, which in Western thought is in the minority, is instead for Mou defining of Chinese thought. If the diaphanous subject, as we have seen, is given to me only through a "retrospective intuition," it is not because I focus on it and reconstruct it *a posteriori*, as it happens in the "subject without ego," or in the "narrative subject," but because what I grasp is not a substantial subject, but a dynamic process, an incessant exercise of self-elevation. We have spoken of "hodological space" to indicate the practical nature of *jingjie* and to complement its classical translation as "mental state." The practicing subject is not a state but a spiritual field of action. It is his exercise of incessant self-transformation that simultaneously generates himself and the world. In his making himself equal all things "equalize," in his emptying himself all things rediscover the original silence from which they arose, in his free wandering the boundaries of things blur. While the phenomenological experience is marked by the suspension of prejudice, in order to focus on my self, with a learning vision, the dynamism of the practicing subject is never reduced to a psychological and cognitive attention. As Romain Graziani writes about this Daoist "art of the spirit": "The luminous perception of things, the intelligence of change, the spontaneous adaptation to the course of things, the ease of being in harmony with

---

68 Peter Sloterdijk, *You Must Change Your Life. On Anthropotechnics*, Malden, MA, and Cambridge, UK: Polity Press, 2013.
69 Peter Sloterdijk, *The Art of Philosophy: Wisdom as a Practice*, New York: Columbia University Press, 2012.

others, all these phenomena are never described in psychological or analytical terms: it is never a matter of analyzing, judging, dividing, distinguishing. The realizations of the spirit are most often described in terms of centering, penetration, circulation, journeying, unfolding, attainment, completion." [70] The dynamism of the practicing subject is the self-transformative and self-elevating dynamism of becoming spirit (*shen* 神), or as Zhuangzi writes, of "listening with the spirit," after having transcended the limited and hindering faculties of the ears and mind.

"Spirit" indicates the highest possible dynamization and fluidization, the realm of the power of becoming, of that transformation into pure "verbal" form that occurs when I renounce focus, grasp, and the possession of things. "Don't let things turn you into a thing," Zhuangzi admonishes, tracing the path to an active dispossession and renunciation of all that reifies, apprehends itself in "substantive" form. Even the "subtle subject" of phenomenology, emptied of any substantial content, still implies a being "for me," an orientation of the experienced universe "toward me," i.e., toward my being as a central point of perspective. The "diaphanous subject," the "great transcendental subject" that Mou sees at work in Daoism is not only a paradoxical dematerialized subject, devoid of any faculty, centrality, and possession. It is an active willingness to become all things and to dissolve things in the practice of becoming. *Ti wu* 體無, embodying emptiness, awakening and ceaselessly returning to that universal dynamism from which my subjective faculties and experienced things emanate simultaneously. This pure act, this ceaseless dynamizing is what Mou refers to as "spirit" (*shen* 神), warning, however, about the risk that spirit, in the absence of a moral dimension, is reduced to an "ethereal soul" (*xuling* 虛靈). The vertical practical dimension is, in Daoism, the reaching upward by refining oneself until one reaches the indeterminate origin of things, and then contemplates the spontaneous sprouting of the plurality of beings. This practice in which self-forgetfulness and the effortless flow

---

70 Romain Graziani, "Le Roi et le Soi; ou de quell Soi parle-t-on dans la Culture de soi? Contribution à une anthropologie philosophique en Chine ancienne," in: *Cahiers du centre Marcel Granet—Cahier 2: Sujet, Moi, Personne*. Paris: Presses Universitaires de France, 2004, p. 168 (translated by the author).

of being merge on the horizontal plane of "mindless generation" risks being reduced to a purely ecstatic and artistic experience.

An example can come from hypoegoic mental states, such as the experience of "flow" analyzed by Mihaly Csikszentmihalyi as he reports the testimony of a musician, who in terms very similar to those of Daoism describes the state of "flow": "You yourself are in an ecstatic state to such a point that you feel as though you almost don't exist. I have experienced this time and time again. My hand seems devoid of myself, and I have nothing to do with what is happening. I just sit there watching it in a state of awe and wonderment. And it flows out by itself."[71] This experience, which can occur without will or intention once a certain degree of mastery has been reached through artistic exercise, exemplifies well the art of "generating without mind." However, it lacks stability and continuity, that is, an objective foundation that roots it in the concreteness of life. The practical subject that is actualized in the exercise, having reached the acme of perfection, seems to dissolve and be permeated passively by the pure event of flowing, in a state of almost oneiric immersion. In order for the verticality of self-perfection to be maintained, it is necessary to bring it to completion with the descent into things, so that the incarnation (*tiwu*) involves the whole of objective reality without anything being neglected, and so that everything is given meaning and value. But in order to achieve this it is necessary that the subject be not only pure dynamism but the unfolding and realization of an objective principle. It is therefore necessary to generate it with the mind, that is, with intention and moral will. This process, according to Mou, is brought to completion by Confucian thought in its historical development, and it is to the study and systematic reinterpretation of it that Mou devotes his most significant works, such as *Constitutive Mind and Constitutive Nature*, *Phenomenon and Thing-in-Itself*, and *Intellectual Intuition and Chinese Philosophy*.

---

71 Mihaly Csikszentmihalyi (1975), cited in: Kirk Warren Brown and Mark R. Leary (ed.), *The Oxford Handbook of Hypo-egoic Phenomena*, Oxford: Oxford University Press, 2016, p. 53.

4. *Constitutive Mind and Constitutive Nature*: The Moral Subject in Confucianism

4.1 Confucianism and "Authentic Subjectivity"

According to Mou Zongsan, only Confucianism is able to embody and to accomplish the "Perfect Teaching". With Lee Ming-hui's words, "Functional perfection is shared by all the three Chinese traditions including Confucianism, Daoism, and Buddhism, and is not sufficient to display the characteristics of Confucian 'perfect teaching'. It is only in ontological perfection that the characteristics of the Confucian 'perfect teaching' lie."[1] In order to preserve the existence of things on the ontological level, we need an infinite creative moral mind, and therefore a radical rethinking of the idea of 'mind' and 'subject' based on Confucian tradition.

One of the most relevant theoretical findings of *Constitutive Mind and Constitutive Nature*[2] is that Mou identifies the distinctive feature of

---

[1] Lee Ming-huei, "Mou Zongsan: Between Confucianism and Kantianism," in: David Elstein (ed.), *Dao Companion to Contemporary Confucian Philosophy*, London and Berlin: Springer, 2021, pp. 255–275 (p. 266).

[2] Mou Zongsan (牟宗三), *Xinti yu xingti*. 心體與性體 (Constitutive Mind and Constitutive Nature), 3 vols, in *Mou Zongsan xiansheng quanji*. 牟宗三先生全集 (Complete Works of Mou Zongsan), vols. V–VII, Taipei: Lianhe baoxi wenhua jijin hui, 2003. The title can be alternatively translated, as "Inherent Mind and Inherent Nature," or, as suggested by N. Serina Chan, "Moral Creative Reality: Mind and Nature." The word *ti* 體, placed after a term, indicates its substantial and inherent aspect. In the dyad *ti-yong* 體用, the first represents the essential constitution of a thing, whereas the second conveys the meaning of function, realization. I agree with Sébastien Billioud in translating the title as *Constitutive Mind and Constitutive Nature*, highlighting that putting *ti* after words like *xing* (nature), *xin* (mind), or *cheng* (authenticity), enables Mou to emphasize "the reality of each of these elements (their ontological dimension), while at the same time paving the way for their concrete manifestation, since *ti* and *yong* cannot be separated". Sébastien Billioud, *Thinking through Confucian Modernity. A Study of Mou Zongsan's Moral*

Confucianism in the emergence of authentic subjectivity.[3] According to Mou, Immanuel Kant's attempt to arrive at a rethinking of Western philosophy by placing the subject at the center is doomed to fail. The greatest contribution that Confucianism therefore offers to the history of thought is to lay a solid foundation for affirming the subject in its fullness. According to Mou, the decisive intuition of Confucius would have been to indicate the moral practice of *ren* (仁, translated as "benevolence" or "sense of humanity") as the way to heaven, that is to say to the first principles: "His great contribution was to temporarily put aside the objective ideas of God, heaven and celestial decree, without talking about them (but at the same time without denying them), and to disclose the source of moral value, to open the door of moral life starting from the subject, through the concept of *ren*. [...] This temporary setting aside in his discourse the objectivity of God, of heaven and destiny, does not mean denying or devaluing heaven, but reaffirming what is the

---

Metaphysics, Leiden: Brill, 2012, p. 30. Mou relates this use of *ti* to the idea of metaphysical creativity. In any case, the term *ti* derives its meaning from moral metaphysics and active moral engagement. The term "constitutive," having the double meaning of "essential" and "having the power to enact or establish," is, in my opinion, the most suitable way for expressing the dynamic and performative character of Mou's metaphysical reality.

3 Chen Li Kuo inserts Mou Zongsan's ultimate coalescence between supreme truth and subjectivity in the wider mainframe of the twentieth-century's debate between China Institute of Inner Learning and New Confucians. The core of the debate is the seminal Buddhist work *Treatise on Awakening Mahāyāna Faith*. Whereas the former criticizes the *Treatise* on the basis of Yogācāra Buddhism, claiming that the supreme truth, or suchness, has an objective nature, and can therefore be obtained through a gradual practice of cognitive absorption and transformation, the latter embraced the idea of the truth as pure, innate, and pristine subjective mind: "[...] the New Confucians identified themselves with the Treatise; and because they adopted the position of transcendental subjectivity, they believed that suchness cannot merely be the principle of emptiness, and neither can it simply be 'what is mentally appropriated as a cognitive object' (*suoyuan* 所緣). Rather, suchness must at the same time be the mind. Principle is the mind; the mind and principle are one. Therefore, suchness is 'dynamic' [...]". Mou in *Xinti yu Xingti* retraces a similar bifurcation in the difference between Cheng-Zhu School of Principle (*lixue* 理學) and Lu-Wang School of the Mind (*xinxue* 心學). What is a stake is the possibility of thinking the supreme reality in itself as authentic subjectivity, i.e., as the spiritual dynamism of self-awakening which is innate in me. See Lin Chen-kuo (林鎮國), "The Treatise on Awakening Mahāyāna Faith and Philosophy of Subjectivity in Modern East Asia: An Investigation Centered on the Debate between the China Institute of Inner Learning and the New Confucians," in: J. Makeham (ed.), *The Awakening of Faith and New Confucian Philosophy*, Leiden: Brill, 2021, pp. 455–496.

subjective-practical foundation that allows the human being to enter into contact with heaven, reaffirming authentic subjectivity. [...] Confucius by saying 'practicing the *ren* to know heaven' reawakened this authentic subjectivity; on the other hand, he emancipated God, heaven and destiny from the merits and demerits of kings and governmental structures."[4] Mou points out that this subjectification does not reduce the objectivity of heaven's transcendent consciousness, but rather inherits and reinforces the traditional Chinese view that heaven possesses a transcendent consciousness. But it is precisely through this development that the human acquires a conscious respect for transcendent consciousness.

Although Confucius' teaching represents the beginning of this discovery of authentic subjectivity, in the *Lunyu* this process of subjectification has not yet reached full unfolding. The reason for this lies in the fact that Confucius does not yet use the word mind (*xin*), and does not expressly say that the *ren* is the self-manifesting trace of my fundamental moral consciousness. "Mind" and "subjectivity" are two concepts implicit in Confucius, and although according to Mou it cannot be denied that there is in his teaching a link between *ren* and mind, this latent intuition has not yet developed into a clear and manifest theory of subjectivity. It is only from Mengzi, who defines the *ren* as "the mind of not being able to tolerate," that it can exercise its full function in inner morality, ultimately projecting into the domain of onto-cosmology. Not only does Mengzi bring the *ren* back to the realm of mind, but he establishes a full unity between *ren*, mind, and nature, so that "authentic human subjectivity" for the first time is firmly grounded and enlightened. Teaching that "All things are already complete in us. There is no greater delight than to be conscious of sincerity on self-examination,"[5] Mengzi endows the finite human mind with an infinite capacity for moral extension and elevation, which can serve as the foundation for an absolute universality of moral law. Building on the Confucian teaching of *ren* and Mengzi's theory of mind and nature (心性學), Song-Ming era Neo-Confucianism gradually brings to fruition

---

4   Mou Zongsan, *Constitutive Mind and Constitutive Nature*, I, 23–24.
5   萬物皆備於我矣。反身而誠, 樂莫大焉。(Mengzi 4.1) See James Legge (trans.), *The Chinese Classics: Translated into English with Preliminary Essays and Explanatory Notes by James Legge. Volume 2. The Life and Teachings of Mencius*, London: N. Trübner, 1875, p. 326.

the unification on the metaphysical plane of moral practice and the creative energy of the universe. Mou Zongsan calls this theoretical progress "internalization and indwelling." Both of these terms, as well as "authentic subjectivity," deserve attention because they refer to the inner realm of the mind, and thus pose a challenge to those who want to understand what Mou thinks about the self and self-consciousness.

On the surface, Mou seems to be describing a progressive trajectory that leads from the objective transcendent substance of heaven to the absolute mind deployed in moral consciousness. By means of the doctrine of the unity of mind and nature, the terms "heaven" and "heavenly destiny" descend into the inner world of the self, and the generative capacity proper to the substance of the universe is internalized in the human moral domain. Finally, heaven and mind find their perfect expression and verification through the creativity of moral effort. If, however, we interpret this process of internalization, which Mou sees at work in the Neo-Confucian tradition, as a shift of the center of gravity from transcendent objective substance to the self, so that self-consciousness replaces celestial destiny as the axial pivot of the world, there would seem to be much affinity with the shift in the focus of Western metaphysics from Aristotelian substance to Kantian pure reason. In reality, this would be a misunderstanding of Mou's thought, which sees in Confucian schools an ever more perfect fusion between the subjective and objective perspectives: "Hu Wufeng and Liu Jishan, as well as Lu Xiangshan and Wang Yangming, represent the two directions of Perfect Teaching. The former proceeds from the objective to the subjective, becoming evident and authentically realized by means of subjectivity; the latter proceeds from the subjective to the objective, becoming grounded and objective by means of objectivity. The fusion of both directions is the essence of the orthodox tradition of Song-Ming Neo-Confucianism."[6] According to Mou, the crucial feature that allows the foundation of a metaphysical morality is precisely making the subjective and objective elements one and indissoluble. On the basis of this, Mou criticizes Kantian transcendentalism, as it would not allow the full unfolding of subjectivity. Only since the Hegelian

---

6 五峰、蕺山與象山、陽明是一圓圈兩來往：前者是從客觀面到主觀面，而以主觀面形著而真實化之；後者是從主觀面到客觀面，而以客觀面挺立而客觀化之。兩者合而為宋、明儒之大宗。Mou Zongsan, *Constitutive Mind and Constitutive Nature*, I, 51–52.

4. Constitutive Mind and Constitutive Nature 193

philosophy of spirit does one begin to transcend the structural limit that Kant imposed on the constitution of the subject. Certainly, in the sphere of Western philosophy, the greatest merit recognized to Kant is that of having initiated from the *Critique of Pure Reason* onwards the internalization of the conditions of the constitution of reality, that is, the *a priori*. Mou, on the contrary, affirms that not having gained the concept of creative moral nature, Western idealistic thought "cannot descend into reality, but only explicate itself in the form of a great Logic."[7] In fact, Mou adopts precisely from Hegelian philosophy the concept of "authentic subjectivity." Hegel believes that the structural weakness of Kant's thought should be sought precisely in the idea of "transcendental apperception" or "I think," which remains abstract, separating the self-conscious subject from concrete reality. Through dialectical movement, Hegel aspires to realize this formal and contentless subjectivity, elevating it to authentic reality through the dialectical flow of history. Mou holds that, although Hegel understood the source of Kantian contradictions, he was nevertheless unable to transcend the boundaries of a "grand logic," that is, he remained within the horizontal cognitive model that is characteristic of Western philosophy. If the limits of empirical knowledge are projected into the moral realm, they lead to the practical ineffectiveness of the moral law, making it a postulate that has no autonomous force of manifestation and implementation in itself: "This is not a limitation of moral philosophy or practical reason, it is a limitation only of pure reason and empirical knowledge, but since such knowledge imposes itself as the standard that pervades everything, it proves impossible to arrive at a practical manifestation of moral truth (the law) and the moral subject (the will), mistaking this for a failure of practical philosophy itself."[8]

Through the interpretation of the Confucian "Perfect Teaching" in its historical development, Mou lays the foundations of his "moral metaphysics." With this term Mou designates the subversion of traditional metaphysics, which in the West finds its admirable synthesis in the Kantian critiques, but also in China is manifested in the Zhu-Yi

---

7 [...] 總不能落實, 只展現為一大邏輯學。Ibid., I, 42.
8 這其實不是實踐哲學實踐理性的極限, 乃只是經驗知識思辨理性底極限, 而因以知識為貫通一切的標準, 又因不能正視道德真理(法則)與道德主體(意志)之實踐地呈現, 遂錯覺地誤以為實踐哲學之極限。Ibid., I, 166.

school, as an offshoot from the trunk of Confucian thought. In traditional metaphysics, a horizontal-epistemological approach prevails, whereby the rational analysis of the ontological structure of the universe constitutes the first and most important movement of thought, from which the meaning and the very possibility of moral action are deduced. The result of our cognitive penetration of the world, be it Platonic dualism between the world of ideas and phenomenal reality, Baruch Spinoza's (1632–1637) pantheism, or Christian creationism, determines what we recognize as supreme value. The analysis of human nature and man's place in the hierarchy of beings also allows us to establish the limits of our freedom and the origin of the moral law in us. What Mou proposes is to overthrow this way of thinking, starting from the primary evidence of value, which manifests itself to our consciousness as a directional force toward the good embodied in moral praxis, and arriving through it to reveal the nature of things. Moral philosophy should not be the subsidiary development of a metaphysical representation of things gained through axioms and definitions, but the very key that opens us to the mystery of things.

The advantage that derives from this reversal in the study of the self and subjectivity is particularly worthy of attention. We have seen that selecting self-consciousness as the object of our knowledge constantly reproduces a gap that seems insuperable, and that paradoxically removes from our sight the peculiarity of the subject just as the exploration of the foundation of self-consciousness seems to have reached a depth hitherto unparalleled. The increase in our knowledge of the neural bases of the mind and the increasingly refined mapping of the faculties of attention, perception, learning, memory, and thought offered to us by the cognitive sciences seem to lack grip when it comes to explaining the *qualia*, that is, the inner and subjective experience with which we primarily identify. A similar difficulty is found when metaphysical thought, having established the primary substance and therefore the supreme principle to which we must conform, nevertheless does not know how to awaken the dynamism of the will and the inner tension that ultimately motivate our moral action. In both cases we have an objectifying knowledge that cannot structurally account for that pure and free act that characterizes the subject as an inexhaustible ability to transcend given conditions. Must we resign ourselves to considering the inner life of the self as the irreducible and ultimately ineffable horizon of our knowledge, and insuperable the gap that opens between what we know of ourselves and what we ultimately are? Mou's proposal, in which he intends to distill the essence of Confucian thought, is precisely that of starting from the moral dimension and the lived experience of value that manifests itself in the practicing subject, and then reformulating through it the nature of the reality in which we are immersed. It is not simply a matter of substituting one interpretative and terminological apparatus for another that has proved inadequate, but of bringing to fruition in a radically different way that "Copernican revolution" with which Kant promised to place the subject at the center of the world. A change of paradigm that requires shifting attention from the horizontal axis of knowledge to the vertical one of praxis with which the subject spiritually forges itself, at the same time elevating reality and revealing its creative force.

In order to appreciate the originality of the contribution that Mou's moral metaphysics offers, we can reconstruct what for Mou is the main limit of Western metaphysics, namely the fracture between being and value, between being and dynamism. What follows from this fracture is the impossibility of thinking freedom as a vital expression of the subject. Mou Zongsan in *Constitutive Mind and Constitutive Nature* follows the evolution of the Confucian "Perfect Teaching." What becomes more and more clear in it is, for Mou, the fact that the mind must be a law unto itself. However, it can only be so when, exercising itself in the spiritual practice of self-perfection, it transcends the boundaries of its limited self to become one with the universe. In opposition to this, Mou proposes the paradox of the Kantian moral subject, torn by the divorce between the abstract and formal imperative of "you must," which in order to be universal law must banish all content, and the multiform dynamism of the mind, in whose vital richness every principle is relative, determined, and changeable. Before following Mou's impassioned reconstruction of the mind of the saint, i.e., the ideal Confucian subject, who in moral effort can say "The ten thousand things are in my self," it may be useful to sketch the consequences that the gap between being and value produces in the horizontal-conceptual model that dominates Western thought. This quick mapping has the advantage of making the need for the paradigm shift that Mou Zongsan so urges in the more mature phase of his work stand out in contrast and justification.

If we examine the pivotal problem of moral philosophy, that is, free will, we can see how in the Western tradition it finds its best illustration in the image of the fork in the road, that is, in a plurality of possible choices that unfolds before the will. The ethical dilemma, like the famous problem of the railway carriage formulated in 1967 by Philippa Ruth Foot (1920–2010), presents itself in the form of a mental experiment in which at least two equally viable but ethically conflicting alternatives are submitted to the decision of the subject. The guarantee of being free consists here in an objective factor, that is, in the concrete accessibility of several options and therefore in the condition of indeterminateness that allows the subject to "have play," that is, to be able to oscillate with thought in a homogeneous but ambiguous space. The subject must also be able to gather within himself, in an immobile pause of time, to reflect and deliberate. The concrete occurrence of empirical conditions must not steer my thought in a predetermined direction. This ideal space-time in which the drama of freedom can take place is reminiscent of the smooth, nomadic, absolute space that Gilles Deleuze (1925–1995) in *A Thousand Plateaus* contrasts with the striated space, that is, an enclosed space, defined by boundaries and walls (*limes*), that guides the body according to a pre-established cartography. The expanse—empty and, as far as the eye can see, comprising the desert or sea—in which at every instant a deviation and a rethinking of direction is possible, not only translates into spatial form the doubting arrest of free will, but reveals its ultimately objective and not subjective character. Even the inner condition of free will in fact manifests itself to us in levelling out every concrete existential singularity, every undue affective attachment, eliminating everything that could unconsciously determine the direction of my action. The objective is that reason, placed in front of an ideal chessboard, can extend its vision to all factors, weighing up between opposing solutions, deciding only on the basis of its understanding of the values at stake. The origin of this idea of freedom from the horizontal-cognitive paradigm becomes evident here.

It is not surprising, therefore, that one of the key debates in Western thought about the actual freedom of choice that human beings can enjoy is that concerning the apparent irreconcilability between divine foreknowledge and free will. If God by virtue of his omniscience knows in advance the path of every human being in life, must this vision of the outcome of every human choice in the eternal instant of the divine mind imply a predetermination of my destiny? If from the beginning God knew of Adam's fall, as St. Augustine expounds it, "since God foreknew that he was going to sin, his sin necessarily had to happen. How, then, is the will free when such inescapable necessity is found in it?"[9] The possible equation between foreknowledge and predetermination effectively illustrates the difficulty of defining freedom in a system of thought based on knowledge and not moral praxis. If my mind is cognitively absorbed in a higher mind, my freedom is likely to prove illusory, because the empty space of indeterminacy that made it possible is already forever determined by a gaze from above. In divine omniscience, destiny is traced at every bifurcation and the moral dilemma resolved in the map of a labyrinth. When Mou Zongsan calls for the centrality of the mind and entrusts Confucianism with the task of opening the door to subjectivity, he has in the background the outcome of this objectifying knowledge. Contrasting it, Mou argues that freedom can only be internal and intrinsic, that is, an expression of total autonomy of a mind that is its own law. It is not the ontological landscape in which it is embedded that conditions its possibility of existence, but only its internal dynamism, its drive to expand the boundaries of the self and become universally responsive. The keyword of freedom is *zi* 自, the *autonomy* of the Greeks, the moral center of gravity to which to return, not the "Know thyself" (*gnōthi seauton*), but rather, the "awaken to your authentic nature and become what you are." Without falling back into voluntaristic subjectivism, Mou believes that consciousness is an infinite capacity to awaken in everything and actively recognize oneself in everything, a fusion of being and movement.

4.2 Freedom and Indeterminacy

In Western thought, freedom has, as its antagonist necessity, that which must be and cannot not be. Moral philosophy must be formulated in

---

9 Augustine of Hippo, *On Free Choice (De Libero Arbitrio)*, Book III, Indianapolis, IN, and Cambridge, UK: Hackett Publishing Company, 1993. For a reconstruction of Augustine's argumentation against this "theological fatalism," see Ann A. Pang, "Augustine on Divine Foreknowledge and Human Free Will," *Revue des Études Augustiniennes*, 40 (1994), 417–431.

such a way as to preserve the indeterminacy of duty and the compulsion it operates, at the risk, however, of depriving it of its force of injunction and motivating effect. In the model that Mou designates as horizontal-cognitive, and which is preeminent in Western thought, ought-to-be takes the dual form of ethical duty on the plane of value and ought-to-be, understood as the principle of identity, the "that for which" I am what I am, that is, what constitutes my nature, my proper and permanent substance. These two domains, that of value and that of being, are not identical, as in the moral metaphysics that Mou seeks to elaborate. On the plane of value, moral duty is an interior injunction, a law to which I am called to conform. This law appeals to me and I am somehow subject to it. Even if it manifests itself only in my interiority, as is the case with the Kantian categorical imperative, it reveals itself to me as something objective. This exteriority and objectivity of the law can take different forms. It can present itself as the expression of the will of a creator God, or as a call to conform to my social role, or to what I myself would decide if I were in an ideal state, unpolluted by empirical conditions and passions that can lead me to error.

In Kant's thought, the law must therefore be compatible with my free will, and distinct from the natural causality that is necessary and infallible in its fulfillment. The plurality of concrete duties endowed with a specific content does not exhaust the plane of moral injunction, but refers back to a supreme duty, the pure universal form of the imperative "you must." A classic theme of Western moral philosophy is precisely moral failure, that is, the inability to adhere to a precept or value whose goodness I have rationally recognized. The problem here is one already mentioned, of the abstractness and immobility proper to a truth achieved through knowledge. Using Mou's terminology, the problem is that the truth known remains only on the plane of being, lacking life and intrinsic movement. Even though I have thus had access with the rational mind to the plane of the supreme good, or of the value which I ultimately acknowledge I must obey, there remains the difficulty of making effective that which in itself is not dynamic, but only a fixed and abstract principle. What I would need is a driving principle endowed with a constricting capacity that determines me to take action. At the same time, however, this element of necessity and compulsion must be denied if I wish to preserve my free will and to differentiate moral law from natural causality, which produces only necessary and determinate effects.

The being to whom duty and moral law are directed, the being who can recognize value and follow it, but also evade it, is a free being. Freedom does indeed imply the evaluative capacity of reason, but it is transformed into moral judgement only when it belongs to a subject who is not subjugated to it, just as animals and non-sentient things are subjugated to the necessary concatenation of causes and effects. What distinguishes the human from animal nature, in which it is also partially rooted, is this capacity to withdraw and transcend. Freedom of will, on the level of being, therefore requires a certain degree of ontological indeterminacy. The animal unconsciously obeys its own determination, God overrides all determination and, in his perfection, his will and his being are one and the same thing. The human being, in that quiddity that is proper to him and defines him, is in the liminal zone between the two. It is a stratified being, constituted, according to traditional metaphysics, of body and psyche; it participates in both domains of being without resolving itself in one of them.

Let us therefore return to the theme of indeterminacy on the level of being as a condition of my being that is immune from all inner and outer constraints. The foundation of the freedom of the will is the inability to settle down and find definitive dwelling in one of the levels of being. The difference between the necessity with which the animal is subject to a heteronomous law that determines it and the necessity that God possesses in his perfect coincidence with himself lies here also in this emptiness, in this "interval of play" that always pushes me out of every momentary center of being. Freedom is therefore above all a negative freedom, the always open possibility of deviation, the non-coincidence with anything determined. This makes man a stranger in being, a wayfarer capable of wandering. This uninterrupted displacement comes close to the negative freedom of the Daoist saint, who drops all belonging and attachment to the concreteness of things, and owes his free and easy wandering, his frictionless gliding in all directions, to this continuous nullification. In the divarication between being and movement, human freedom is constituted as movement without being, a pure act of transcending every identity achieved, a decentralized being that in every action is always already outside and beyond itself.

Since the dawn of Western thought, the problem of this free act has arisen: that is, it is without cause and unpredictable. Already Epicurus, wishing to distance himself from the iron necessity at the base of Democritean atomism, introduces the idea of a clinamen, a random deviation without ontological foundation in the structure of things, and Lucretius in *De Rerum Natura* emphasizes how the idea of the clinamen has at its base not physical but ethical reasons, as human freedom is guaranteed precisely by this act of pure spontaneity: "But that the very mind feels not some necessity within in doing all things, and is not constrained like a conquered thing to bear and suffer, this is brought about by the tiny swerve of the first-beginnings in no determined direction of place and at no determined time."[10] The necessity that in the human there should be this indeterminacy, this "parenthesis of nothingness," this being constantly outside of any barycenter, that is, of a fixed and predetermined ontological location that would limit the freedom of its making, appears in multiple forms and formulations in the history of Western thought. In all cases the dominant model is the cognitive one, and therefore freedom is thought of as a shunning of every possible definition, of every determination that can be thought and learned. Freedom has to be a dynamism that precedes and transcends all conceptual understanding, the unknowable and unpredictable deviation from any essence, because to possess an essence is to be assimilated by a mind, be it the divine mind or that of other human beings. To understand something is to possess and control the boundaries of that thing to the point of being able to anticipate its future evolution. In a cognitive-horizontal paradigm, the freedom of the subject must therefore be declined as elusiveness, and therefore as absolute unavailability to become the object of knowledge.

Among the many and diverse attempts to decline this flight from being, one can point, by way of example, to those of Jean-Paul Sartre and Emmanuel Lévinas in contemporary philosophy. Sartre coined the famous formula "Existence precedes essence," to indicate the condition of the human being who, like other beings, does not have an essential nature that makes him catalogable, but is projected beyond any present and graspable identity, because it is projected toward a future always

---

10 Lucretius, *On the Nature of Things*, tr. by Cyril Bailey, Oxford: Clarendon Press, 1910, p. 75.

open.[11] Freedom is realized on the practical, performative, not cognitive level: Man will be what he has freely planned to be, and therefore can only be grasped in his becoming. The human being does not "be" at any moment, but only "will be" what his freedom has planned. This evasion from the regime of being finds in Lévinas an approach that is apparently reversed with respect to existentialism, because the subject here is not a pure act that experiences the vertigo of its own unpredictable creation, but a *sub-jectum*, a subject with no way out. Here it is the encounter with the other, the ethical obligation that comes to me from the face of the other, that attracts the center of gravity of my being outside of me. This decentralization that I undergo uproots me from myself and pushes me toward a totally foreign place, the face of the other human being, preventing me from appeasing myself and dwelling in my coincidence with myself (the Cartesian "I think, therefore I am"). Although this condition of detachment and nomadism seems imposed, or in any case preceding and prevailing over my free will, Lévinas emphasizes how it is precisely this being drawn outside the domain of essence, that is, of fixed and immutable determinations, that makes possible for me "the subjectivity that breaks, as in extreme youth, with essence. My being boundlessly open to the other is the condition of all transcendence and the horizon of my being free insofar as I am called to assume infinite responsibility."[12] While for Sartre the time of freedom is the unpredictable future, for Lévinas it is the immemorial past, my finding myself already always involved in the relationship with the

---

11   "What do we mean by saying that existence precedes essence? We mean that man first of all exists, encounters himself, surges up in the world—and defines himself afterwards. If man as the existentialist sees him is not definable, it is because to begin with he is nothing. He will not be anything until later, and then he will be what he makes of himself. Thus, there is no human nature, because there is no God to have a conception of it. Man simply is. Not that he is simply what he conceives himself to be, but he is what he wills, and as he conceives himself after already existing—as he wills to be after that leap towards existence. Man is nothing else but that which he makes of himself." Jean-Paul Sartre, "Existentialism is a Humanism," in: Walter Kaufman (ed.), *Existentialism from Dostoevsky to Sartre*, Cleveland, OH and New York: World Publishing Company, 1969, pp. 287–311.

12   "But the relationship with a past that is on the hither side of every present and every re-presentable, for not belonging to the order of presence, is included in the extraordinary and everyday event of my responsibility for the faults or the misfortune of others, in my responsibility that answers for the freedom of another [...]." Emmanuel Lévinas, *Otherwise than Being, or, Beyond Essence*, Pittsburgh, PA: Duquesne University Press, 2011, p. 10.

other. An interesting aspect that we can point out here—and which we will take up again in the analysis of Confucian thought—is precisely the impossibility of constituting subjectivity as freedom in the present. This depends on the fact that in a horizontal-conceptual model the present is the place of presence as representation, that is, as graspability by the intellect. The present is what is in the cone of light of my consciousness and is therefore present to me, as sensible data or concept. If I want to rethink the present as the locus of realization of my freedom, I must move to the plane of practice and moral action. But in it, Mou argues, freedom is no longer a pure act, a momentum without a determinate nature, but the perfect fusion of being and movement, of immanence and transcendence.

With regard to the dependence of Mou's moral metaphysics from Western ethical tradition, a challenging and thought-provoking criticism to Mou's moral metaphysic is proposed by Tang Wenming in his *Secret Subversion. Mou Zongsan, Kant, and Early Confucianism*. The core of its criticism can be found in his interpretation of Mou Zongsan as representative of "Confucian moralism." According to Tang, Mou Zongsan fails to provide a correct interpretation of Confucian ethics in its historical context, replacing the original classical Confucian virtue ethics with a law ethics centered on autonomy and compassion. This moralistic misreading bears a distinctive Kantian flavor, and it pivots on a pure and voluntary altruistic tendency which reveals the internal awakening of a noumenal moral ego. The moralistic interpretation of the original Confucian concern-consciousness based on benevolence is particularly misleading because "it considers the moral sense of compassion as an essential connotation of the concern-consciousness idea, and it considers the concern-consciousness as a moral, noble emotion, an 'empathetic feeling for others' sufferings and a sympathetic concern for all creatures.'"[13] This spontaneous, altruistically-oriented tendency of the moral mind represents the substantial standard of moral value, whereas the internal autonomy of the rational subject represents the formal standard. Tang Wenming's critical examination follows two complementary paths. First of all, adopting Friedrich Nietzsche's

---

13 Tang Wenming, *Secret Subversion I. Mou Zongsan, Kant, and Early Confucianism*, London and New York: Routledge, 2021, section 2, "Do the Zhou people's concern-consciousness and respect for virtue constitute a moral breakthrough?".

(1844–1900) critical tools, he traces back the origin of autonomous subject to the internalization of Judeo-Christian theonomy, i.e., to the subjection to divine command, remarking the dependency of Mou's moralism to the Western metaphysical tradition. Secondly, he argues that Confucian moralism fails to understand that the key-concept advocated by Confucius and Mengzi is "learning for the sake of one's self" (*wei ji zhi xue* 為己之學), and the constant effort to realize the inherent ability and virtue bestowed by heaven. In Chinese classical tradition "the self is not an empty, disembodied and altruistic moral subject deprived of all particular traits but is a person who seeks vividly and actively puts into practice his moral conduct in a context of individual personality."[14]

In the present chapter, I will try to adumbrate an alternative interpretation of Mou's moral metaphysics. My aim is to demonstrate how a performative-creative paradigm can provide a more suitable framework for understanding the originality of Mou's theorical proposal. Tang Wenming correctly highlights that the effort of self-realization and of spiritual self-amelioration is a distinguishing tenet of Chinese Confucianism. I aim to prove that Mou's modern reappraisal of Confucian ethics represents a full actualization of this practical concern for self-cultivation. At the same time, in my opinion, the harmonization with the nature appointed by heaven finds in Mou a peculiar dynamization, in which nature bestowed by heaven is a creative force that requires to be actualized through an expansion of the subjective sphere. Finally, in the present chapter, I contend, through a comparative analysis with Lévinas, that Mou's moral metaphysics does not require to be altruistically-oriented in order to justify the structural connection and responsiveness to the others and to the universe. The peculiar Chinese concept of *ganying* 感應 provides Mou's moral subject with a creative synthesis of responsiveness and responsibility, aimed not only to extend and elevate the self, but also to creatively overcome the divide between internal and external realm.

---

14 Ibid., section 3, "Is the Confucian doctrine of benevolence a moralistic doctrine?".

4.3 The Performative Subject

In *Constitutive Mind and Constitutive Nature*, Mou outlines a new conception of the subject, completely redefining the horizon within which to understand it and the instruments of such an understanding. What Mou proposes with his moral metaphysics, which he considers the most faithful expression of perfect Confucian teaching, is to radically rethink reality as something that is given first of all to moral consciousness, and that is fully realized only in moral effort. Reconstructing the world along the vertical axis means no longer thinking of it as a cognitive field, but as a performative field, hinged in action and transformation. Vertical is the effort of self-perfection through which the human being raises the whole world to the fullness of its meaning, but vertical is also the descent, the manifestation of the absolute mind that descends to intersect everyday reality. What is the difference with the horizontal cognitive model within which Western thought develops from its Greek origins to culminate in Kant? The performative field is traversed by forces, waves, and lines of change. Being and dynamism are one, being is dynamic, a source of uninterrupted creation and a flow that vitally permeates everything. Dynamism is being, not pure effort of will without ontological foundation, but an incessant becoming of what one already is, and in becoming this content also authenticates it, brings it to manifestation. Mou finds the first model of dynamic thought at the roots of Chinese thought, in the *Yijing*. The reality that must be interpreted through the hexagrams is characterized by incessant transformation, and consequently the instrument that allows its reading, the hexagrams and trigrams, are a continuous cycle in which one flows into the other.

But movement alone is not enough to define the vertical tension that things possess in this performative field. Mou continually urges us to liquefy our concepts of substance, subject, object, and nature, abandoning the immobile rigidity that necessarily characterizes them if they are to be grasped and catalogued by defining thought. Yet there are horizontal representations of change, such as Heraclitus' eternal flux, or the scientific doctrine of natural evolution. What dominates in them is the material (i.e., *qi*-based) character of change, which is a pure uninterrupted succession of causes and effects, actions and reactions that develop through the passage of time. It is not enough to say that the nature of things is the process itself and reality is its very proceeding, changing, tending toward the future. This is the dimension of biological life, of uninterrupted generation that follows the directional arrow of time, representable on the basis of what Mou calls the principle of material and quantitative constitution. What Mou tends toward is not the infinite generation but the creativity inherent in it, not the flow but the mystery of the source and origin, "that which moves but is not itself moved" (*dong er wu dong* 動而無動),[15] that which changes having in itself the force of its own change. That which, for Mou, is being and movement draws on the creative inexhaustibility of the beginning.

Moving from change as a simple character defining being to the perfect fusion of being and dynamism in transformative moral action requires, according to Mou, a self-conscious will. Creativity is accomplished only on the plane of the spirit. The spirit is not to be understood as a defined entity, for example a transcendent and individuated God as in Christianity. In Christianity, Mou affirms, we arrive at the awareness that God cannot be a static entity to which the creative act is added as its supplement. The infinitude of God requires that God be all in all, and therefore his creation cannot be occasional but must express and manifest the totality of what God is. God is an infinite mind, a will that has its own principle in itself, and is therefore both perfectly free and perfectly necessary. If, however, the spirit remains an entity ontologically separate from creation, as in the case of God, it does not meet the requirement of being all in all, of being realized in every single thing without anything

---

15   Iso Kern analyzes the expression activity (*dong* 動) in Wang Yangming, and differentiates between activities which are at the same time calm and stable, because in them the authentic essence of the innate moral knowing can freely manifest itself, and the activity is attuned to the ordering principle of the moral mind, and activities triggered by the desire of external things, which are passively being moved. What he writes about Song-Ming Confucians applies to Mou as well: "The relationship between rest and movement plays an important role in the thought of Song-Ming Confucians. What is at play is the contraposition to Buddhists and Daoists, who withdraw from acting in society and conduct a life based on the calm or the 'void' of mind. Wang Yangming and the other Confucians recognize the high value of a calm and concentrated spirit, but at the same time they believe that being tirelessly active in society is essential." See Iso Kern, *Das Wichtigste im Leben. Wang Yangming (1472–1529) und seine Nachfolger über die «Verwirklichung des ursprünglichen Wissens»*, Basel: Schwabe, 2010, p. 222 (translated by the author).

being excluded. I cannot make myself God, nor can I raise the whole of creation with me to the divine.

Alternatively, Mou finds in the Chinese philosophical tradition a different interpretation of spirit. It should not be thought of as a noun that indicates an individuated entity, but rather as a verb, a mode of being in which the human can also participate, a *jingjie* 境界 or spiritual state to which the human can rise through subjective practice. At the same time, this state of mind has within it concrete universality, that is, the guarantee, verifiable at every moment, that it can be realized objectively.[16] By declaring that "the human is a finite that can make itself infinite," Mou tells us that transformative action is moral action, an inner tension to realize in me all things in their autonomous value and meaning. That for which man is man must be that for which heaven is heaven, Mou writes, I must be able to embody everything by making it the center of my being, fusing subjective and objective. To know is to reawaken, to act, to embody, to interpenetrate, to be responsive and to participate morally in every event. At the same time, this moral drive of mine to be one with all things must be the manifestation of a mind that objectively is this interpenetration of everything into everything, this infinite relationship in which everything is in everything. But all this, according to Mou, finds its proper place in moral practice. Gottfried Wilhelm Leibniz, too, with his monads, tried to imagine sentient entities that contain within themselves the whole universe. However, he did so on the basis of the cognitive paradigm. The monad is a subject insofar as, endowed with sensitive cognition, it represents everything in itself from its perspective point of view. This perspective is, by definition,

---

16 Romain Graziani, analyzing various Chinese classical poems, similarly remarks the peculiarity of the dynamical and performative language adopted to represent the spiritual domain: "[...] the luminous perception of the things, the intelligence of the change, the spontaneous conforming to the course of things, the ease of the mutual comprehension, all these phenomena are never described in psychological or analytical terms. It is not about analyzing, judging, deciding, distinguish. The achievements of the spirit are usually described in terms of centering, penetration, circulation, walking, displacement, attention, obtainment, accomplishment.
This ensemble of gestures based on the categories of movement and prehension defines better this paradigmatic experience of the spirit." Romain Graziani, "Le Roi et le Soi; ou de quell Soi parle-t-on dans la Culture de soi? Contribution à une anthropologie philosophique en Chine ancienne," in: *Cahiers du centre Marcel Granet—Cahier 2: Sujet, Moi, Personne*. Paris: Presses Universitaires de France, 2004, p. 168 (translated by the author).

incommunicable and unimpartable, which determines the closure of the monad, sealed to the point that all contact and relation between monads can only be apparent. The truth of being in relation with the world, that Confucianism expresses in the thirdness of the human being as mediator between heaven and earth, cannot therefore be manifested through a static plural ontology like that proposed by Leibniz. What is necessary is a paradigm shift that rethinks all concepts as traversed and actualized by moral practice.

First, in the performative domain in which Mou develops his thought, everything is dynamic and marked by moral action. Action to have moral value must involve self-awareness. This self-awareness is not reflection, but the manifestation of my *autonomy*, of absolute spontaneity and freedom. The principle of my action is not outside me but comes from the heart of my being, it is the root-mind. This mind has a metaphysical value because of its necessity and absoluteness, but it does not overpower me or create the finite mind. The root-mind is what I can be on every occasion in which I abandon the selfishness of my isolation and by acting morally experience the expansion of my self that is concerned with the needs of the world. The root-mind is therefore what I already am in a latent form in my daily somnambulism, and which in the act of my awakening to the world is actualized. The mind of habit, my "little self," is not a separate entity from the primordial mind, but, like ice and water, it is just a different spiritual state, characterized by attachment, distraction, anchoring myself to the finitude of things. Awakening is my jumping out of the suffocating boundaries that I have imposed on myself by treating the world as other than me. This act of liberation is like the mighty flow of a torrent at the moment of thaw; it dissolves the psychological and material concretions restoring the free flow of the mind. It is a transcendence different from that of a supreme and unattainable divine mind, which I cannot become and embody in my insuperable creaturality. But it is also different from the Kantian transcendental, from the abstract pure *a priori* forms that precede my experience. Transcending, according to Mou, is the ever-active possibility of emancipating myself from my attachments and awakening to the infinitude of my being one with all things.[17] This awakening is

---

17 In the same text, R. Graziani highlights that in the spiritual practice of the Chinese saint "the dynamism of interiorization, which, starting with the emancipation

not accidental, but requires my moral will to self-perfect, lifting the world with me. For in this vertical dynamism, other human beings, nature, and things cease to be material obstacles to my action, objects of my knowing, or means to be used, but rise through me to absolute ends, revealing themselves as a vital and inexhaustible sprouting and correspondence without end.

Although this requires for Mou an act of transcendence, i.e., the effort of moral cultivation against the inertia of habit, the root-mind, i.e., the spiritual state that subtly penetrates everything and is not extraneous or indifferent to anything, is not something that comes as an unguaranteed fruit of my effort. It is above all the manifestation of what I have always been. And what I am is the source of that flow of life and meaning that has never disappeared, but has only been concealed from view. The only way to manifest the root-mind is not to enunciate it or strive to know it, but to actualize it by my actions. By taking care of every single event and every human being I concretely realize the universality of the mind that has nothing outside itself and nothing leaves, I transform every occasion into the point of fall and realization of that vertical dimension that intersects the horizontal succession of things. This is what Mou calls the effort of *ti* 體, of making myself a body with everything in my moral commitment. The metaphysical mind then is "always already happened" and at the same time "not yet happened." In my daily practice of refinement, allowing its actualization in everything I encounter, I can retrospectively verify that its spiritual flow has always been uninterrupted in me, even in silence and latency, and at the same time that I never definitively possess it. The metaphysical mind-substance can never be a concept conquered and possessed by my knowledge, but every practical occasion refers me back to my responsibility, always active and never concluded, to become the place where it becomes real.

---

from the desires of external things, leads the spirit to the return to oneself, is actually not the movement of self-constitution of a subject, the self-awareness of an individual. (Interiorization) enables the self-elevation to a superior regimen of mental activity, in which all the relations with the exterior domain are restored, or better, another way to dwell in the world emerges, in which the individual is one and the self with the cosmic power of Dao." Ibid., p. 179 (translated by the author).

4.4 The Subject as Incipience and Origin

The performative subject is what Mou calls "The Authentic Subjectivity" (*zhenzheng de zhutixing* 真正的主體性) or the "Great Subject" (*da zhu* 大主). The "little self" as a mind of habit is a pure succession of psychological states that exist because they grasp at the external stimuli from which they arise. Even the cognitive mind, which attempts to conceptually grasp the real with which it sensitively comes into contact, stagnates in its indissolubility from the objective world. Even when it turns to itself in order to know and define itself as a self-conscious subject, the mind of habit is forced to go back to its own identity through the flow of memories. It is not by chance that Hegel, in the final chapter of the *Phenomenology of Spirit*, dwells on the German term *Er-innerung* and its double meaning of "memory" and "interiorization": "As spirit's fulfillment consists in perfectly knowing what it is, in knowing its substance, this knowing is its withdrawal into itself in which it abandons its outer existence and gives its existential shape over to recollection."[18] Withdrawing from the present instant, from the here and now in which experience is produced, the spirit must retrace its entire historical development in order to arrive, for the first time, at full and absolute self-consciousness. The self-consciousness of the "little I" of the psychological and cognitive mind is necessarily mediated by the experience of time. I know that I am there and understand myself by reabsorbing my past, that is, all the phases in which I acted in the world unaware of me. In gathering myself from this dispersion of experience I affirm myself as subject, but I still depend on the memories I have preserved to ultimately find myself again. In reflection, I require an objective world that I place outside me like a mirror, and this dependence on what is external to me is the predetermined fate (*mingding* 命定) of my inauthentic subjectivity.

Rather, the authentic subject for Mou is defined by its capacity to free itself and jump out of every static and determined form in which it can actualize itself. We could say that the true subject of moral practice is nothing other than this continuous and unstoppable transcending, this original impulse that comes out splitting what is solidified and immutable, like the bud that in its pure vital energy, in its always new

---

18 Ibid., p. 433 (translated by the author).

being, splits the bark in spring. Mou often uses metaphors related to the awakening of nature at the beginning of spring, such as the "awakening of the insects" (*jingzhe* 驚蟄), or the "spring rain" (*chunshui* 春水), two solar terms of the Chinese calendar that indicate the coming out of hibernation and hibernation of animals and the first fertile rains. These imaginative terms both refer us to the thaw, to the liquefaction of what had stiffened, and at the same time they bring us back to the qualitative unfolding of time. The authentic subject, thought of as pure creative dynamism, does not refer to memory, but rather to an ever-renewed beginning. How to think about this beginning? A relevant clue comes from the term coined by Mou Zongsan to evoke and define moral creativity: *jigan zhenji* 寂感真機, often translated by Mou as "creative feeling." Mou derives the constituent elements of this expression from the *Xici*, the most famous commentary on the "Classic of Changes" (*Yijing* 易經), traditionally attributed to Confucius. The term *jigan* 寂感, which could be translated as "silent perceiving," indicates the latent and indeterminate phase that precedes the performance of the action:

易無思也，無為也，寂然不動，感而遂通天下之故。非天下之至神，其孰能與於此。

In (all these operations forming) the Yi, there is no thought and no action. It is still and without movement; but, when acted on, it penetrates forthwith to all phenomena and events under the sky. If it were not the most spirit-like thing under the sky, how could it be found doing this?[19]

That which is maximally spiritual, that is, life-giving and pervasive, is quiet and silent, but as soon as it responds affectively to reality, it penetrates all things. *Jigan*, silent resonance, appears as an oxymoron, as the fusion of latent being and manifest being, of that which is incipient and that which is brought to completion. Mou distinguishes this mode of feeling and corresponding spiritually to *kegan* 客感, to the perception that has an external object, such as that which he analyzed in the *Critique of the Cognitive Mind*, and which for Kant corresponds to the Transcendental Aesthetic. The "silent perceiving and responding" of the *jigan* 寂感 reminds us that, for Mou, perception is not merely horizontal and cognitive but, shifted to the vertical plane of moral practice,

---

19 *The I Ching: The Book of Changes*, tr. by James Legge, New York: Dover Publication, 1963, p. 170.

possesses an intrinsic activity. The percipient mind is listening and responding, weaving the web that interconnects all beings in mutual moral attention. The term *ji* 寂, which I translated as "silent," represents the latent state of things. Wang Yangming, in a famous passage from the *Chuanxilu*, responds to a disciple who challenges him about his thesis that "nothing is outside the mind." The disciple asks what relationship there is between the mind and red flowers that grow and bloom on a mountain far from human sight. Wang replies that when I am not looking at the flowers, the flowers and the mind have returned together to the stage of *ji* 寂, of silent latency, while only when I see the flower does it shine in the fullness of its color. This example shows that latency expresses a precise original ontological quality to which one can return.

The relation between latent and manifest, here and in Mou's thought, is partially different from the relation between potency and act in Aristotle. Aristotle adopts these two complementary terms to explain the becoming of things according to their "internal reason" (*entelechy*). "Power" (*dynamis*) is the latency that precedes actualization and contains within itself the evolutionary possibility of a thing. However, Aristotle asserts the superiority of being in act over mere being in potency, which he identifies with the superiority of form over matter. The dynamism intrinsic to the term *dynamis* is recovered and enhanced with the advent of Neoplatonism, where *dynamis* will come to represent the spiritual creative energy of the One. This reinterpretation, carried out mainly by Plotinus, comes closest to Mou's use of the concept of potency or latency. If the manifest stage of being is presented as totally developed and determined by its characteristics, the latent stage is not a simple abstract potentiality of becoming, but is the indeterminate origin that contains within itself still intact its creative drive. The mind and the flowers, in Wang Yangming's example, return together, because their empirical contact will only be the manifestation of a deeper co-partnership. That origin, which for Daoism was nothingness (*wu* 無), from which every change flowed and to which it was necessary to return, for Mou and Wang Yangming is the transcendent and infinite moral mind. It ceaselessly creates the visible from the almost invisible, the manifest from the potential. As Mou often points out, the creativity of the moral mind is not a creation of being from nothing. That which is latent or potential has within it the germ of what will be unfolded through action, but this germ, like the "sprout of good" that Mengzi discerns in human nature, already has its own intrinsic dynamism, a subtle force that emerges spontaneously, carrying within itself a totality not yet limited by the circumstances of its realization in the empirical world.

This meaning of emerging force is reiterated in the last two characters of the expression *Jigan zhenji* 寂感真機. The character *ji* 機, which can also be rendered as 幾, indicates that which has just begun to arise, the almost imperceptible temporal instant in which the new begins. In the *Yijing* we find *ji* (幾), the incipient, juxtaposed with the profound and the spiritual. The wise man is the one who penetrates everything because he intuits and explores the vertical dimension that intersects the course of things. This depth, hidden to most men, is at the same time the imperceptible gushing forth of things, the nascent state of the universe. Only by examining the universe in its beginning does one become capable of carrying out moral practice, realizing its promise and realizing it in all things. Embodying within oneself the profound and imperceptible beginning enables one to rise to the spiritual state, which has no limits of time and space, and can permeate and fertilize everything.

> 夫易,聖人之所以極深而研幾也。唯深也,故能通天下之志。唯幾也,故能成天下之務。唯神也,故不疾而速,不行而至。子曰:"易有聖人之道四焉"者,此之謂也。

> The (operations forming the) Yi are the method by which the saints searched out exhaustively what was deep, and investigated the minutest springs (of things). "Those operations searched out what was deep"—therefore they could penetrate to the views of all under the sky. "They made apparent the minutest springs of (things)"—therefore they could bring to a completion all undertakings under the sky. "Their action was spirit-like"—therefore they could make speed without hurry, and reached their destination without travelling. This is the import of what the Master said, that "In the Yi there are four things indicating the way of the saints."[20]

In the divinatory logic of the *Yijing*, knowing the first clue means foreseeing the entire course of the event, since everything that will be

---

20 Ibid., p. 370.

manifested is but the unfolding of what already exists in the initial stage. Here, it is not only a question of legibility of signs and advance knowledge of the future. Divinatory knowledge is at the service of human action, the initiation of things is a stimulus to practical initiative. What the continuous generation of the universe and moral creativity have in common is this dynamism whose aim is to incarnate and implement all things without neglecting any of them. François Jullien writes: "By opening itself to the inciting virtue of the real (which never ceases, that is, to develop reality) and remaining 'on the alert' (*jue* 覺), it [the consciousness] always manages to place itself ahead of the development of the course of things. From here, coinciding with the emergence of phenomena, it evolves freely with respect to them, rather than passively suffering their heaviness downstream. Its 'creativity' thus pertains to this: that its inner dispositions [...] do not cease, like the phenomena of the world, to 'transform' and renew themselves rather than fix themselves."[21] If the incipient is the point at which onto-cosmological generation and moral creativity intersect, it is because it refers back to a qualitative appreciation of time. Using Greek terminology, the incipient does not belong to the *chronos* (χρόνος), the temporal succession that can be measured, but to the *kairos* (καιρός), which designates the opportune moment, the opportunity that must be seized. In the horizontal line that goes from the past toward the future, the *kairos* is a fleeting instant, a point that is barely visible, but full of potentiality. It refers to a vertical and qualitative time, which possesses infinite depth and density. The whole of the past and the future thickens in this propitious occasion that only the wise man knows how to recognize and make use of. For Mou, in this instant is contained the bud of the future, it is the point in which time is alive, it gushes out like water from a spring. While in Greek thought it is a very brief temporal parenthesis, a specific occasion that once passed is irretrievable, in Mou's moral metaphysics every instant of time can and must contain the vitality and creativity of the beginning. The effort of moral perfection that culminates in the mind of the saint coincides precisely with the ability to find meaning and inexhaustible

---

21 François Jullien, *Figure dell'immanenza. Una lettura filosofica del I Ching* [Original: *Figures de l'immanence: Pour une lecture philosophique du Yi King, Le classique du changement*], Milan: Laterza, 2019, pp. 45–46.

value in every occasion, to be always in contact with this gushing and dynamic source, to embody this infinite capacity for renewal.

The *ji* 幾 is the minimum of movement, but it is also the *jixi* 幾希, the small detail that distinguishes man from animal: Mengzi said, "That wherein human beings differ from the birds and beasts is but slight. The majority of people relinquish this, while the noble person retains it. Shun was clear about the multitude of things and observant of human relationships. Humaneness and rightness were the source of his actions; he did not just perform acts of humaneness and rightness."[22] This detail, Mou writes in *Cong Lu Xiangshan dao Liu Jishan*,[23] is the mind of benevolence and righteousness, that is, the innate moral conscience, our moral self. What Mou is concerned with is not defining the distinctive capacity or faculty of the human, according to debate from Aristotle to modern neuroscience. This tradition asks: What is the human specificity, the irreducible protrusion that separates us from animality? To be bearers of Logos, that is of reason and speech, as Aristotle wants; the capacity for symbolic language, as Hobbes writes; the being a world-former who has access to the meaning of things, as Heidegger argues; or the possessing of a "theory of mind," as hypothesized by some neuroscientists? For Mou the difference is dynamic and appears in moral practice. The mind of benevolence is a sprout that can be neglected or cultivated to holiness, it is the ability to internalize the source of our being by making it our authentic nature. Mengzi stated that Shun, an example of holiness, was indistinguishable from the rough inhabitants of the mountains except for almost nothing (*jixi* 幾希), "But when he heard a single good word or observed a single good action, it was like a river in flood or a spring flowing forth—nothing could contain it."[24] The mind in its generative force is this endless gushing out, this principle of movement that never ceases to renew itself, that total and residue-free activation that Mou

---

22 孟子曰:「人之所以異於禽獸者幾希, 庶民去之, 君子存之。舜明於庶物, 察於人倫, 由仁義行, 非行仁義也」。See Irene Bloom and Philip Ivanhoe (ed.), *Mencius*, New York: Columbia University Press, 2009, Section 4B19.
23 Mou Zongsan (牟宗三), *Cong Lu Xiangshan dao Liu Jishan.* 從陸象山到劉蕺山 (From Lu Xiangshan to Liu Jishan), *Mou Zongsan xiansheng quanji.* 牟宗三先生全集 (Complete Works of Mou Zongsan), vol. VIII, Taipei: Lianhe baoxi wenhua jijin hui, 2003, pp. 31–32.
24 孟子曰:「舜之居深山之中, 與木石居, 與鹿豕遊, 其所以異於深山之野人者幾希。及其聞一善言, 見一善行, 若決江河, 沛然莫之能禦也。」. Bloom and Ivanhoe (ed.), *Mencius*, Section 7A16.

designates by the term "subjectivity." Mou, analyzing the thought of Lu Xiangshan, points out that the original intuition of the unity of the universe and the mind is mediated by the awareness that both are inexhaustible (*wu qiong* 無窮). The minimal space that is mind is this overflowing, florid inexhaustibility whereby the universe and mind contain and overflow into each other: As Lu Xiangshan poetically summarizes: "The myriad things luxuriate in the space of a square inch; the mind manifested in full fills the universe."[25]

We can see here the development of a founding intuition that can already be found in the *Critique of the Cognitive Mind*. In this founding text of the first phase, centered on logic and knowledge, of Mou's thought, we already find the need for a leaping out, for a springing forth without premises, in order to speak of the freedom of the subject that becomes self-conscious. Although Mou's analysis begins with the observation that the mind and the world arise simultaneously—determining each other in the sensitive contact between things and our sense organs—this, strictly speaking, is not yet the principle of everything. At this stage the mind is still confused with the flow of sensory experience, by which it seems to be unconsciously and passively dragged along. The subject, and with it the possibility of absolute beginning, appears only in the next stage as perception (*jue* 覺). Perception, which is, in one and the same act, also apperception or self-discovery, dissolves from the tangle of psychological and empirical conditions, jumping out and asserting itself as that which can in no way be reduced to an object. Perception is this absolute subject, this activity of leaping out, which is the irreducible vitality of the mind. From it, in fact, the mental faculties such as imagination and intellect, become capable of autonomously emanating (*yongxian* 湧現) their own principles. Remaining on the horizontal cognitive plane that is characteristic of the *Critique of the Cognitive Mind*, Mou reaffirms at every step the limit of this absolute subjectivity that cannot find its own settlement and its own objective justification.

Like other terms in the book, this *jue* 覺 reappears in the next phase of Mou's thought, radically rethought on the vertical moral plane. *Jue* 覺 is no longer cognitive perception but the vigilance of the mind that

---

25 萬物森然於方寸之間, 滿心而發, 充塞宇宙. In: Lu Xiangshan (陸象山), *Xiangshan quanji* 象山全集 (Complete Works of Lu Xiangshan), Taipei: Zhonghua, 1965, 35/10a.

is the possibility of practical effort, of forging oneself and continually surpassing oneself. As wakefulness, vigilance, and awakening, it requires the highest capacity to respond to the other, to be always in the imminence of a call, and to pay attention so that nothing is left behind. It is then connected to that *jigan* 寂感, to that "silent resounding," or, according to Mou's translation, to that "ontological feeling" in which even feeling (*gan* 感) no longer has the epistemological meaning of sensory experience, of which it retains only the contact, but translated in its moral aspect as *ganying* 感應, being responsive to all things. This awakening, this kindling of vigilance in me is that tremor that I feel when I grasp the child about to fall into the well, and this tremor (*zhendong* 震動) is not simply consciousness of my present being, as happens in the Cartesian Cogito, but is a reawakening of what is higher, that ever-active moral mind that I already am but must also become, expanding myself to the other and making myself one body with all that exists. In the words of Sébastien Billioud and Peng Guoxiang: "The idea of a subject making itself one body with everything, has the immediate consequence that this subject cannot be regarded as an individuum. The subject is a stimulated being (the idea of *gan* 感 that may be found in the words *ganying* 感應 and *gantong* 感通), who is inscribed in a relation I-You. One becomes an authentic subjectivity only when one is capable of resonating and fecundating (*runze* 潤澤, *ying* 應, *tong* 通) the myriad things, or, in other words, when one shows moral creativity".[26]

Placing the moral mind as an authentic subjectivity ensures that it is a creative beginning, as well as the inexhaustible source of renewal to which, through the effort of practical action and self-cultivation, I can realign myself at any moment. This process of returning to the origin and realigning with the beginning allows me to awaken to myself, that is, to make myself one with the creative moral mind. As Mou writes in analyzing the thought of Cheng Mingdao: "The self that fully possesses the heavenly principle and substantial nature is concretely the true beginning of creation. [...] all moral actions, concrete moral realizations, are generated by this true creative beginning, are subsumed in this

---

[26] Sébastien Billioud and Peng Guoxiang, "Le sujet moral dans la philosophie de Mou Zongsan (1909-1995)," in: *Cahiers du centre Marcel Granet—Cahier 2: Sujet, Moi, Personne*. Paris: Presses Universitaires de France, 2004, p. 255 (translated by the author).

4. Constitutive Mind and Constitutive Nature

true beginning. On the basis of Confucian moral metaphysics, the generating and changing of the universe in the cosmological order, and moral creation in the moral order, are one and the same in their concrete meaning."[27] While in Christianity, although everything comes from divine creation, it is not possible to say that every individual possesses this absolute "true creative beginning," in Confucianism this is possible. Absorbing in oneself, introjecting this true creative beginning, this source understood as origin in its value sense,[28] is what is proper to the human in its tension toward the good, and what is realized in the mind of the saint.

Returning to the initial discussion, we can contrast this vertical, performative view of the moral self as an ever-new beginning with the Hegelian conception of the self as principle. The question of principle runs throughout the history of Western thought. It bifurcates into two questions, one theoretical and the other methodological: What is the ultimate principle on which to ground things, and what is the principle, that is, the beginning, from which thought must start as from its own origin? Starting from the Cartesian intuition of "I think, therefore I am," the two questions intersect and merge increasingly in the consciousness that the subject has of itself. Through Kant and Idealist thought, particularly Fichtian thought, the self-consciousness from which thought originates increasingly becomes the foundational act of all things. Hegel, in the introduction to the *Science of Logic*, seals this identity between thought and being, between the "thought of the beginning" that explores the source of being, and the "beginning of thought," the original and immediate truth from which my thought must spring. Hegel writes: "Accordingly, logic is to be understood as the system of pure reason, as the realm of pure thought. This realm is truth unveiled, truth as it is in and for itself. It can therefore be said that this content is the exposition of God as he is in his eternal essence before the creation of nature and of a finite spirit." This vertiginous *a priori* that precedes the unfolding of the creative act is attainable by the human

---

27 蓋我『從那裡來』所完具之天理性體實即是一創造之真幾。[…] 一切道德行為、道德實事, 些為此創造真幾之所創生, 亦即些為此創造真幾之所涵攝。依儒家道德的形上學言之, 宇宙生化底宇宙秩序, 與道德創造底道德秩序, 其內容的意義完全同一。Quoted in Mou Zongsan, *Constitutive Mind and Constitutive Nature*, II, 63.

28 "The origin is the beginning, the first, a concept of value" (元是始, 是首, 是一價值概念), ibid., II, 53–54.

being because it is at the same time the inauguration of thought itself: "Hence it is that even the act of the subject is grasped as an essential moment of objective truth, whence arises the need for method to be united with content, form with principle. Thus the principle also has to be the beginning, and that which is the Prius for thought, also has to be the First in the course of thought."[29] But if I backtrack in my reasoning, dropping all accidental content, what I find as the original principle is the absolutely simple, which in its being stripped of all determination is also what is supremely abstract, that is, pure being. It, however, insofar as it cannot presuppose anything, nor be mediated by anything, is an absolute void. Pure being is overthrown into pure nothingness, and what can arise from this is only the elusive paradox of becoming, that is, the fact that being is never given except as already having passed into nothingness, and vice versa.

I have dwelt on this reasoning because, at a superficial glance, it seems to evoke the Daoist thought of the origin, which is the fusion of being (*you* 有) and nothingness (*wu* 無). However, while in Daoism this conclusion is reached as the result of the practical effort to purify myself, to drop all pretensions to possession, to strip myself of all limits, here we are on the horizontal plane of logic and knowledge. What we have gained is only the impossibility for thought to grasp and define the beginning, except as what is never present, never sayable, always already past in the other. The beginning then is already memory, or as we wrote at the beginning of the chapter, *Er-innerung*, remembering and re-entering itself. According to Jacques Derrida (1930–2004), this is the only way in which the self can be thought of as an absolute beginning. The subject is like a fountain of water, something that has always already given itself, has always already gushed out of itself. The subject has no sense of its own, because it is a continuous giving of sense to the world. But the origin of sense is never given as present, it is similar to the blind spot of the eye that allows the vision of everything at the price of never being itself graspable and visible.

According to Derrida, my ego—that is, "the point of source from which everything makes sense, appears, looms and is measured"—is not present in the world that it unveils. To be the source and spring of

---

29 Georg Wilhelm Friedrich Hegel, *The Science of Logic*, Cambridge, UK, and New York: Cambridge University Press, 2010, p. 29.

4. Constitutive Mind and Constitutive Nature

everything is to be thrown out of oneself. "If consciousness and the pure self are like the source, it is because they cannot return to themselves," therefore "the pure self, the source of all presence, is reduced to an abstract point, to a pure form, devoid of all thickness, of all depth;" it is an absolute passivity because it is already always outside itself, "very close to being a non-ego." Not the God who precedes creation but the God of a negative theology that seeks to grasp itself, "an absolute gaze that, always out of its sockets and cast toward the visible, cannot see itself from itself and never leaves its night."[30]

This brief excursus is exemplary of the difficulties that thought faces if it wants to know the beginning (from an epistemological point of view) or to be the beginning as absolute divine consciousness (from an ontological point of view). The impossibility of seeing oneself, of turning to oneself, of grasping the generative force and making it one's own, of which Derrida speaks, reproduces a difficulty that is also characteristic of Daoism. "Daoism's greatest defect," Mou writes, "is that it lacks the effort of what is anterior to heaven (*xiantian* 先天)." What is anterior to heaven is the condition of the Dao that precedes its unfolding in the real world, the mystery of the origin from which everything springs forth without its power (in the sense of *dynamis*, generating force) being exhausted. This origin, writes Hegel, is the ultimate in simplification and abstraction, a continuous reversal of being and nothingness on which my gaze cannot focus. I can only know that it has already passed, grasp it by recoil, but in itself and to itself it can never be present, Derrida concludes. With respect to the mystery of the indeterminate origin, the only possible effort is that of the then, of "what is after heaven," states Daoism in Mou's interpretation. Embodying the original nothingness (*tiwu* 體無) is not the effort of being present in my acting as infinite creative consciousness. What I can do is only to start from what is after the sky, that is, from my being already immersed in the world, and let fall every quality, every determination, stripping myself of everything, renouncing to possess it, ideally rarefying myself like the Daoist saint who withdraws from everything. Staying in the obscurity of this origin, discovering it already operating in my mind, and bringing it to act in the

---

30 Jacques Derrida, "Qual Quelle: Valery's Sources" in: *Margins of Philosophy*, Brighton: Harvester, 1982, pp. 273–305.

concrete happening of things, is not possible for Mou, unless we move to the moral plane.

The Confucian "Perfect Teaching" gives this origin a name, the mind of benevolence (*renxin* 仁心) or original moral consciousness (*liangzhi* 良知). To give a name here is not to define and limit but to set a practical and ethical task, to feel the need to rise to the vertical plane resonate in me. Like someone who climbs a tower, and at each step sees the horizon around him become vaster and vaster, the effort I make is to expand (*tui* 推) the radius of my benevolence and responsiveness until my ego and the supreme consciousness coincide and realize all things in me. *Jigan zhenji* 寂感真機, to inhabit this authentic beginning in my silent resonance with all things, is the imperceptible instant of birth (*ji* 機) and what is always before, the origin (*yuan* 元) in the value sense. It should be noted that the time upon which Mou builds his metaphors of incipient and origin is not chronological time, but, as we have said, the time of *kairos*, of aligning myself with the perfect occasion and bringing my destiny to fruition. Time is what makes possible the relationships, events, and history that are to be brought to fruition. And following the *Zhongyong*, destiny (*tianming* 天命) is not an inscrutable fate towering over me and imposing itself on me, but what gives me my *xing* 性, my essential nature. *Xing* 性 and *xin* 心, nature and mind, are the objective and subjective sides of moral consciousness. Nature is the co-belonging to everything, mind is the jolt in which it presents itself to me in moral action as what is in me, what is proper to me, the destiny that my free will brings to fulfillment. As Spanish philosopher Maria Zambrano (1904–1991) writes about being born, "The animal is born once and for all, the human, on the other hand, is never completely born, he must face the effort of generating himself anew or hoping to be generated. Hope is hunger to be born completely, to bring to completion what we carry within us only in a sketchy way [...]; his birth is incomplete and so is the world that awaits him. It must therefore finish being born entirely [...], it must ceaselessly give birth to itself and the reality that hosts it."[31] For Mou as well, accomplishing myself and accomplishing things (*cheng ji* 成己; *cheng wu* 成物) is not an abstract fantasy, but is the

---

31 Maria Zambrano, *Verso un sapere dell'anima* [*Hacia un saber sobre el alma* (Towards a Knowledge of the Soul)], Milan: Cortina Editore, 1996, pp. 90–91 (translated by the author).

bringing to completion of myself and the world in their moral value. The human is not already given in me, but I must ceaselessly become human in action, bring to concrete actualization the mind of benevolence from which, by the decision of my free moral will, all things spring.[32] This "ceaseless becoming" is the ever new and inexhaustible beginning that I can embody, the generating source that runs through my conscious action, that sum of beginning and presence that for Hegel and Derrida, on the horizontal plane, was impossible to think of.

4.5 Constitutive Mind and Constitutive Nature

The title of Mou's major work, *Xinti yu Xingti* 心體與性體, can be translated as "Constitutive Mind and Constitutive Nature," or rather, "Inherent Mind and Inherent Nature." Mou writes that mind is the manifestation, inherent nature is the content of the manifestation. If we understood this in a purely horizontal cognitive sense, we might come to the conclusion that mind and nature relate as the sign to the thing symbolized. Are not words and language the typically human way of bringing things to expression, removing them from their empirical opacity and revealing their hidden meaning, thanks to the penetrative activity of the mind? Between words and things, however, there remains an insuperable gap. As Zhuangzi reiterates, language is structurally incapable of manifesting the true nature of things. There is an unfathomable remainder of reality that eludes all our attempts to define and express it through words, and the verbal signs we create can proliferate into word games that have no objective referent. Between these two orders of reality there is an incongruence, such a disconnect,

---

32   Tu Wei-Ming claims that to be a human being means to be in the process of becoming human: "The reality of the human is such that an eagerness to learn in order to give full realization to one's heart, to know one's own nature and to appreciate the meaning of humanity is the surest way to apprehend heaven. [...] We are not circumscribed to be merely human. Rather, our proper destiny is an invitation, a charge to take care of ourselves and all the beings in the world that is our abode. We must learn to transcend what we existentially are so that we can become what we ontologically are destined to be. We need not depart from our selfhood and our humanity to become fully realized. Indeed, it is through a deepening and broadening awareness of ourselves as humans that we serve heaven." Tu Wei-Ming, *Confucian Thought. Selfhood as Creative Transformation*, Albany, NY: SUNY, 1985, p. 63.

that I can imagine turning words into pure tools. As Zhuangzi writes: "The fish trap exists because of the fish; once you've gotten the fish, you can forget the trap. The rabbit snare exists because of the rabbit; once you've gotten the rabbit, you can forget the snare. Words exist because of meaning; once you've gotten the meaning, you can forget the words."[33] Is this perhaps the relationship between mind and nature? Can content and its manifestation be mutually foreign? Critiquing Zhu Xi's perspective, Mou argues that if nature is understood only as an abstract defining principle—such as the class and species we ascribe to a living organism—without incorporating the concreteness of the plant or animal, and if the mind in turn is only the product of an extreme rarefaction of qi energy, with the thing at the other extreme as its maximum condensation, mind and nature can never overcome their mutual externality. In this case, the prospect of making all things one body will remain nothing more than an unattainable ideal—a perpetually illusive goal that I may approach but can never fully achieve. But what Zhu Xi and the school of the principle represents is for Mou no more than a side-branch of the orthodox Neo-Confucian tradition, and it is at the same time an ever-open temptation of horizontal relapse of thought.

If we can maintain the vertical dimension that is proper to moral metaphysics, mind and nature, manifestation and content, are inseparable but irreducible. The manifestation that is proper to mind is not mere symbolic expression, but is concrete realization. In "bringing things to realization without any of them being lost" (*ti wu er bu ke yi* 體物而不可遺), the "mind of benevolence" concretizes the moral principle by penetrating into the infinite particularity of situations, "like mercury" that fills every empty space by flowing, and erases every separation. To manifest is to practically enact in reality, and at the same time to be a participating witness of the expansion of my self-consciousness, to experience myself by recoil as the capacity to incarnate myself in all things. This concrete dilatation and caring for everything, because everything is part of me, is also a liberation, a jumping out of the empirical mind, caught up in the flow of memories and feelings that make me limited and folded in on myself. The inherent nature is the being-in-itself of everything and of myself, the objectivity of the

---

33 Burton Watson (ed.), *The Complete Works of Zhuangzi*. New York: Columbia University Press, 2013, p. 233.

principle that is not an inert content, but has in itself the force of its own actualization. There would be no liberation possible if I, acting morally, could not recognize that there is a perfect correspondence between the direction of my action and what I and the universe intimately are, between what is necessary because it is conferred by heaven (*tianming* 天命), according to the dictate of *Zhongyong*, and the absolute freedom and autonomy of my spirit.

How does the "authentic subjectivity" that Mou finds in Confucian thought fit into this conceptual framework? First of all, it is not reducible to the mind, as we contemporaries would be inclined to think on the basis of twentieth-century "philosophy of mind." For Mou, both mind and nature belong to the dimension of the subject. Commenting on Hu Wufeng's sentence: "Nature guides the flow of energy, mind guides the flow of nature," Mou points out how the term "guide" (*zhu* 主), which can be interpreted either as "guiding principle" or as "subject acting as guide," plays a different role in the two parts of the sentence. The flow of energy represents the uninterrupted mutation of things, and with respect to them nature is law and guide in an objective sense, while the flow of nature is not an empirical mutability but a moral and metaphysical dynamism, just as we speak of a "flow of the celestial principle," and the guiding function is subjective, coinciding with the self-conscious subjectivity that brings nature to fulfilment: "The authentic, concrete, brought into relief [i.e., manifested] of this flowing can only be seen in the inherent mind. If I speak of 'flowing' in relation to nature, it is an empty, objective but formal name. Its point of falling into reality is the highlighting function of the self-conscious subject. If this function is lacking, the flow of nature is only a latent and unmanifested self-perpetuating."[34]

The term "guide," referring to the function that inherent nature performs with respect to the mutability of empirical things, has an ontological meaning, similar to a red thread that runs through the weft of a fabric. The guiding function of the mind, on the other hand, is a bringing into relief, a making manifest of a principle by concretizing

---

34　但其『流行』之所以為『流行』之真實義、具體義、形著義，則在心體處見。於性說流行，是客觀地虛說，亦是形式地說，其落實出是心之自覺之『形著之用』。無心之形著之用，則性體流行亦只潛隱自存而已耳。Mou Zongsan, *Constitutive Mind and Constitutive Nature*, II, 455.

it in moral action. "When the inherent mind illuminates and is illuminated in its totality, and the inherent nature is illuminated and brought into manifestation, nothing is outside the mind and nothing is outside nature, and mind and nature are fused into one [...]."[35] To define this dynamic unity of mind and nature in moral action, Mou uses the term *yuandun* 圓頓, which in the Tiantai school of Buddhism means "instantaneous and perfect enlightenment." In thinking about this teaching, Mou in a later text refers to the dialectic of spiritual effort, writing that the three great Chinese traditions, Confucianism, Daoism, and Buddhism, on the one hand affirm that spiritual effort must never cease, and on the other that it is at all times accomplished and perfect: "Of course, the practical philosophies of Confucianism, Buddhism, and Daoism can also teach a 'dialectical synthesis' in Hegel's sense in the course of spiritual effort, in which 'spiritual effort must never cease.' But at any moment they can also teach a perfect and sudden teaching, immediately abolishing a dialectic, realizing the being-in-itself, and manifesting a spiritual state in which 'suchness is self-so' (*ruruzizai* 如如自在), one 'roams carefree, wanting for nothing' and 'the heavenly principle flows along' (*tianli liuxing* 天理流行). At one and the same time, 'spiritual effort never ceases' and yet without contradiction you are also 'complete here and now.'"[36]

To sum up, the character of subjectivity as autonomy and agency does not belong exclusively to mind, but to the fusion and inseparability of mind and nature. What nature brings is the principle that gathers and gives meaning to the changing fabric of reality. This principle penetrates reality as the "nature of itself" or the "being-in-itself" of things. Through nature, the being-in-itself of things, their structural unity as principle and meaning, are preserved and perpetuated. In the absence of the self-conscious function of mind, however, this organic order of things, which is their principle and value, remains only a latent ontological property. We are not only on the plane of being, but also on that of dynamism, for this latency, as we have seen in reference to incipience, is a nascent state that is already integrally being and movement together. What the mind brings is practical actualization in the concreteness of circumstances, and

---

35   至乎心體全幅朗現, 性體全部形著, 性無外, 心無外, 心性融一, [...]。Ibid.
36   Jason Clower (ed.), *Late Works of Mou Zongsan. Selected Essays on Chinese Philosophy*, Leiden: Brill, 2014, pp. 120–121.

this from a moral point of view is equivalent to bringing to completion what is intrinsic to nature, while from the metaphysical point of view it is illumination and emphasis, in which empirical reality is manifested in its value. The transcendent moral mind manifests itself through the retrospective gaze of our self-consciousness. Interpreting its function as a focusing, entering into a cone of light, we could say that the thing illuminated in the circle of attentive action and moral care, refers simultaneously to the apex of the cone of light, that is, to the source of light and moral care that is the moral mind.

The interaction between mind and nature in moral practice is circular, as the character *yuan* 圓 (circular, perfect) in the term *yuandun* 圓頓 suggests. In self-conscious moral action I descend into the concreteness and plurality of the real and manifest nature by actualizing it. This realization of the value of all things as things-in-itself, and at the same time of the moral mind as autonomous, would be impossible if the nature-in-itself of things were not what stimulates the moral mind. My autonomy and self-consciousness are nothing other than the making recognizable of the principle that asserts itself as internal to me, that is, as my own nature. To have the principle as internal to me and as my own nature is a practical knowledge, that is, necessarily a moral action that unfolds and becomes concrete in reality. What we have called the *autonomous* (自), that is, being-in- and for-itself, manifests in in the mind as auto(self)-nomy and self-consciousness (*zijue* 自覺). This represents the practical affirmation, in every single circumstance of acting, that the principle that constitutes and defines me is not external to me, but pervades me from within, because it coincides with my own nature (*zixing* 自性). By acting morally I free myself from the fetters of all that is external to me and makes me passive: the empirical randomness of worldly circumstances and the inertia of my psychological attachments and habits. This rising up as a free being is made possible by my autonomy, that is, by the fact that my law and my destiny act in me as my own nature. This circular relationship between mind and nature is reminiscent by analogy of the relationship between substance and function, which we encountered earlier. Mou uses this conceptual model to express a dynamic duality: a tension at the heart of the two concepts that simultaneously reveals their inseparability and their becoming one without reducing them to abstract equivalence.

The subject is to be thought of not only as mind, but as this making itself one of mind and nature. It implies an unceasing effort, Mou writes. There are two levels of this moral effort. Nature can possess in itself roughness and curvature, coagulate into empirical things and remain attached to them, losing its own being as principle and guide, its own being as subject (zhu 主). In turn, mind, too, can lose its subjective function, fading into the repetitiveness of the habits and propensities of the psychological and empirical mind. At this fallen level, mind and nature mutually constitute themselves as an opposition between an inner and an outer domain, between perception and thing. They no longer belong to each other, they are strangers to each other, they statically confront each other as cognitive and horizontal opposites, and the mechanism of authentic moral subjectivity comes to a halt. There is thus a first necessary effort, which is to emancipate oneself from the stagnant dependence on the senses and wear and tear that is proper to empirical things. Mou calls this effort "the effort posterior to heaven," that is, the effort of self-perfection and abandonment of attachments after empirical reality and psychological mind have coagulated as static empirical entities. This effort is incessant in the sense that it must be started again and again.

The "spiritual effort" of which Mou speaks can, however, also be understood as "the effort before heaven," that is, the effort that is made when in moral action we return to the original mind, and restore and manifest through it our inherent nature. This effort is ceaseless insofar as it is grounded in the human capacity to awaken and extend to all beings our mind of benevolence. It coincides with the continuous renewal, through our free will, of the circular relationship between mind and nature. In this case "incessant" has the positive value of inexhaustible, of infinite movement that knows no stopping. According to Mou, Mengzi shows us these two levels of effort. In the effort anterior to heaven, in Mengzi's words, "I exercise the mind, I know nature and heaven"; in the effort posterior to heaven, "I preserve the mind, nourish nature, and realize heaven." In the first level, knowledge is clearly not a theoretical endeavor but is intuitive penetration of my essence, which I achieve by deploying the power of my mind. I dilate my capacity to resonate with and embody the other from me, until nothing is foreign to me anymore, there is nothing that is not comprehended within my self, and in the quiver of this moral vastness I discover, with astonishment, myself. After heaven, that is, after the world and my self become actual, I preserve, nurture, and realize. These are the actions of wisely cultivating the finiteness of my individual self and the finiteness of the circumstances of my action, constantly freeing myself from all dross and all thickening.

Overall, "the mind can exhaust nature" (*xin neng jin xing* 心能盡性). To exhaust (*jin* 盡) is to put into practice but also to bring to completion. By exercising my mind of compassion, by being deeply concerned (*guanqie* 關切) for every being, by abandoning every part of me that is insensitive to the other, I make my nature evident in the eyes of the world. This circular revelation of mind and nature is the source of the human, that which makes the human being human, and that justifies the position of intermediary between heaven and earth that Chinese philosophy ascribes to man from the very beginning. As Zhang Zai writes: "To make the mind great is to make it capable of embodying everything under heaven. If one thing is not embodied, the mind has something external. The mind of the common man stops at the narrow field of what can be seen and heard. The saint exercises his nature, and does not chain his heart to the visible and the audible. Looking beneath the sky, there is nothing that is not his own self. That is why Mengzi speaks of exercising the mind, so as to know heaven and nature. The vastness of the sky has nothing external, because a mind that would leave anything outside itself could not coincide with the heavenly mind."[37] Mou comments, "That the mind of benevolence has nothing outside itself is not just a formal expression, but can concretely be seen in the term *ti* 體 (embody) of 'embodying things under heaven.' This term 'embody' (*ti*) expresses the fact that 'nothing can be external to benevolence,' it is something concrete, concerning being, and that in practice authentically manifests the moral mind in its pure transcendence, truly experiencing sorrow and caring for all things under heaven. Only at this point is it the heavenly mind that leaves nothing outside itself."[38]

---

37 大其心，則能體天下之物。物有未體，則心為有外。世人之心止於聞見之狹。聖人盡性，不以見聞梏其心。其視天下，無一物非我。孟子謂盡心則知性知天，以此。天大無外，故有外之心，不足以合天心。Cited in Mou Zongsan, *Constitutive Mind and Constitutive Nature*, I, 560.
38 仁心之無外亦不只是形式地說，而實由『體天下之物』之『體』字而見。此『體』字是表示『仁必無外』是具體的、存在的，這要在實踐中純粹的超越的道德本心真實呈現，對于天

In *Constitutive Mind and Constitutive Nature* we see the progressive affirmation of harmony, or organic unity, between mind and nature. According to Mou, the orthodox teaching develops on the one hand by emancipating itself from excessively material and naturalistic conceptions of *qi* and of the perpetual transformation of entities, and on the other hand by overcoming the danger, represented by the School of Principle of Zhu Xi and Yi Chuan, of a relapse into a horizontal and knowledge-centered vision. The result is precisely that of matching the transformative dynamism of the universe and the creativity of the moral mind by synthesizing them in the discourse on mind and nature (*xinxinglun* 心性論). We might ask why Mou still maintains a distinction between mind and nature. Right from the title, we see that the inherent mind and inherent nature are separated by the proposition "and" *yu* (與), which does not indicate a simple listing of elements of equal degree and potentially overlapping, as the proposition *he* (和), also translatable as "and," would, but rather an inseparability between elements that are at odds with each other. Why does Mou not ultimately resolve the relation between mind and nature into a kind of monism centered around the perfect equivalence and interchangeability between the two concepts? Mou does not deal directly with this theoretical problem, but limits himself to showing the progressive affirmation of a conception that sees the inseparability between the two concepts, and the function that both concepts play, infinitely referring one to the other. One possible explanation lies perhaps precisely in this mutual referral of mind and nature, and in the tension between them that maintains and generates again and again the circular and perfect movement of self-conscious moral practice. Mou is, in general, always sensitive to the risk that a system based on a single principle ends up concealing a part of reality. The hermeneutical strategy adopted by Mou in order to dialectically preserve the dual character of reality is one derived from the *Awakening of Faith in the Mahāyāna* (*Dasheng qi xin lun* 大乘起信論), and summarized in the principle by which "one mind opens two doors" (*yi xin kai er men* 一心開二門). If the Buddhist doctrine intends in this way to articulate the relationship between two states of mind and domains of

---

下之物真感到痛癢, 始有此天心之無外。Ibid., I, 561.

being, namely the "mind of true thusness" (*zhenruxin* 真如心) and the "mind of arising and ceasing" (*shengmiexin* 生滅心), Mou expands the field of action of this principle in the direction of a two-tiered ontology that, in affirming the creative force of the most spiritual level, implies its necessary actualization in the sensible domain of concrete reality. The aim is to guarantee the legitimacy and intrinsic value of historical and empirical reality, and to ground, as we will see in the next chapter, the full legitimacy of logical-scientific knowledge within the Chinese tradition.

In the case of mind and nature, we are not in the presence of an ontological system vertically stratified into two levels, one spiritual and the other empirical. Rather, we are dealing, as in the case of yin and yang, or substance and function, with a duality of aspects or directions of thought. By implying each other and referring back to each other, they establish the continuous renewal and return to the origin that is proper to moral practice. To use Cheng Mingdao's expression, there is only one root, which in the saint becomes visible as the perfectly accomplished unity between life energy and the heavenly guiding principle. This unity "before heaven" must be concretized and actualized "after heaven," amid the roughness and manifold conditions of historical reality. The root is unique, Mingdao writes, but I must manifest it both in its being substance and in its being function, as "penetrating substance and realizing function" (*tong ti da yong* 通體達用).[39] Its penetrating everything and thus the absolute universality of the moral principle must manifest itself in the concreteness of life as that which "leaves no thing behind," however small. The mind that neglects nothing is in empathic resonance (*ganying*) with everything, has nothing dead or insensible in it, and thus has no external realities that it cannot subsume and embody. Where my engagement with the world is not perfect and total, and there are, so to speak, dead zones or blind spots in me, corresponding to them are concrete beings and situations that appeal to me without receiving a response. Such things or situations therefore remain irrevocably foreign to me and opposed to me, they are an "outside of me" that is opposition and a stumbling block for my action.

---

39   Ibid., II, 102.

Perfect circularity demands two directions. Mou speaks of a "great going toward" (大往) and a "great returning" (大來),[40] of moving away toward what is vast and remote, and returning to the light that is my moral consciousness. By going toward the other, by embodying myself in the minute complexity of life, I realize the authenticity (cheng 誠) of the moral law that moves me. At the same time, I run the risk of estrangement, of losing myself in the infinite casuistry of concrete facts, of alienating myself from my consciousness and losing myself in an objective reality that is no longer in an original relationship with me. However, within this going toward things, there is a flow that goes against the current and returns toward the moral mind. This stream is that of spirit (shen 神). By descending into the concreteness of things I realize myself in what is plural and limited, but I have within me the spiritual force to rise up, transcend all limits, and return to my original creativity. In doing so, I listen to the other, I grasp him in his concrete fullness, and I bring him back to the original unity and sharing that is the moral mind. In this circular motion of coming and going, I experience the tremor (zhendong 震動) of finding myself in the other, of recognizing in the other the manifestation of my true face. The truth of the moral law that is my nature (xing 性) lies not in its abstract purity, but in its manifestation as mind, as spiritual vigilance, that is, as a being sensitive and responsive to all things. Fulfilling myself in reality, I discover in retrospect the infinite power of dilating myself and participating in the life of the world that is my spiritual consciousness. I bring what is fragmented and extraneous back to its full value as an absolute end, that is, to its being thing-in-itself, only when I discover that everything is for-me, endowed with meaning, one with my active and creative being. This circularity is the truth of moral action and of my inner tension toward fulfilment. In every moment of action this going and returning, leaning toward the other and returning to stillness, is visible and perfectly accomplished on the plane of meaning, even if I must still remain active and vigilant.

In the dynamic between these two directions, it is possible to perceive a similarity with the analysis of Daoist thought, and in particular with what we have called the "diaphanous subject." In that case the return

---

[40] Ibid., I, 470.

movement led to an ineffable origin, thought of as "non-being" (*wu* 無). Conversely, the outward movement toward things, being termed "being" (*you* 有), represented the eruption of the finite universe from the primordial chaos of the Dao. The only possibility for the subject to adhere to the origin was a progressive spoliation, a letting go of all attachment to a defined reality, renouncing what, being distinct, can be named. This becoming diaphanous of the subject was a negative path of refinement and elevation. The merit of orthodox Confucian teaching, according to Mou, is to have instead placed as its origin something maximally positive and attainable through human freedom. Mou writes: "By saying 'reality,' what is meant is the supreme reality, what in the orthodox Song-Ming teaching is called the substance of the Dao, nature, mind, spirit, benevolence, authenticity, etc. By saying 'spirit,' what is meant is the most actual and inner spiritual essence. In this way, the freedom of the will and the existence of God are not two opposing postulates, as in Kant, but something that manifests itself in the process of unfolding and becoming one. 'Man is a god in potency; he must become an accomplished god.' This is the most pertinent expression, the essence of Eastern religions and of the Confucian teaching that the human is divine (Confucians say 'every man can become holy,' Buddhists 'all the manifold can become Buddha'), and it is different from the Christian 'becoming man of the God.' Here we are dealing with something that practical reason can achieve and bring to full fruition, which with the actualization of 'moral metaphysics' must necessarily be achieved." [41]

In returning to the origin, the practicing subject must not only transcend the dross of empirical reality, purify and refine himself to one with the unspeakable mystery, but rise to a more authentic subjectivity. To reach it is to discover that the original moral mind is my innermost nature, and the self-cultivation that is required of me is a nurturing of the spirit and expanding the space of my benevolence and moral care

---

41 說『實有』，這就是最高的實有，宋、明儒之大宗所謂道體、性體、心體、神體、仁體、誠體等；說精神，這就是最真實最內在的精神。這樣，意志自由與上帝存在不再是並列的兩個設準，像在康德本人那樣，而是打成一片而在『展現』中呈現。『人本身便是一潛勢的上帝，現下應當成就的上帝』，這話尤其中肯，這是東方宗教因而亦是儒教『人而神』的精神，(儒家所謂『人人皆可以為聖人』，佛家說『一切眾生皆可成佛』)，這是與基督教『神而人』底教義不同的。但這卻是實踐理性充其極，『道德的形上學』實現後所必然要至的。Ibid., I, 190–191.

to the whole universe. The direction of "going toward" is a concrete actualization in all situations, a lowering and embodiment of the moral law in reality, an inexhaustible fruitfulness. At the heart of this self-realization is already the movement of return, the "retrospective verification" with which I intuitively grasp and affirm in myself the concrete actualization of moral consciousness. No longer a diaphanous subject that refines itself and erases its own traces, but an authentic subject, that is to say, real and effective, that in every moral action rediscovers and restores its own inexhaustible nature.

4.6 Subjectivity and Interiority

The expression "internalization" used by Mou Zongsan can give rise to misunderstandings. In fact, if we interpret Mengzi's phrase "The ten thousand things are in my self" as "The principles of things are inside my mind," the spatial metaphor of interiority may lead our thinking to adopt a horizontal hermeneutic model. The horizontal "path of progressive absorption" of Zhu Xi and Yi Chuan can be translated as a gradual appropriation of an external principle by the human mind. The purpose of such absorption is not simply to expand our empirical knowledge, but has an ontological value, in which being is devoid of dynamism. Mou writes: "If I consider the *ren* of Confucius only as a principle, and I transform Mengzi's root-mind into a factual mind made up of vital energy (*qi*), an immanent effort is required, that is, the horizontal-cognitive effort that aims to investigate beings and extend one's knowledge (*gewu zhizhi* 格物致知). If I aim at 'quieting the mind and illuminating the principle,' the point of fall and implementation of that effort is the investigation of things and the extension of knowledge, which is what sums up the 'path of progressive absorption.'" [42]

The thought of Zhu Xi and Yi Chuan represents for Mou a collateral deviation from the perfect Neo-Confucian teaching precisely because it corresponds to a specific horizontal ontological model. It is no coincidence that Mou makes a comparison between Heidegger's ethics of essence and Kant's ethical heteronomy. Although the ethics of essence, introduced by Heidegger in the 1947 *Letter on Humanism*, has

---

[42] Ibid., I, 53.

as its aim to overcome Kantian formalism, Mou believes that this aim is not achieved precisely at its crucial point, leaving being external to man. Kant wants to harmonize theology with morality, but fails to bridge the gap between divine transcendence and the immanence of the human mind. After the so-called "turning point" (*Kehre*), Heidegger will try to replace the idea of God with the idea of Being, without succeeding, however, from Mou's point of view, in solving the problem of dualism and the exteriority between mind and being. A similar problem arises for Mou in the thought of the School of Principle of Zhu Xi and Yi Chuan, in that, because of the knowledge-centered paradigm, there remains a division and foreignness between mind and principle. We can describe this cognitive paradigm using the metaphor of the mirror. The mind that through the exercise of the investigation of things and the expansion of knowledge succeeds in penetrating everything is comparable to a smooth, unblemished mirror. Since the principle I seek to attain here is, according to Mou, the mere principle of existence, therefore simple, universal, and eternal, our mind does not have to add any content to it, but simply refine and purify its own essence in order to reflect the principle with the utmost fidelity and conform passively to the purity of the heavenly principle. This process of "polishing" resembles the progressive simplification by which Descartes arrives beyond doubt at the elementary evidence of "I think, therefore I am," which Kant would translate as transcendental apperception. The Cogito and transcendental apperception both represent the summit of thought because their content is reduced to the pure law of self-reflection. We have seen above what theoretical contradictions are implicit in the idea of reflective self-consciousness, but here we can also point out its ineffectiveness on the level of moral action. Kant ultimately fails to merge the empty self of transcendental apperception and the morally acting subject, so that any law based on this idea of the self lacks necessity and practical effectiveness.

There are, I believe, two fundamental similarities between the conception of mind in Kant and in the School of Principle. The first is the unsurpassed gulf between mind and principle. In Zhu Xi, although the mind tends to become a pure mirror reflecting the principle, the immanent nature of this mind made of *qi* 氣 (vital energy) is diametrically opposed to the heavenly principle. In Kantian thought the mind of transcendental apperception seems to coincide with its principle, that of being pure reflexivity. However, this reflexivity of the self is purely logical, abstract, and formal, whereas Zhu Xi's reflexivity has a value of moral law. The starting point of post-Kantian idealism lies precisely in the attempt to restore to this reflexive nature of the self a creative capacity, so that reflection is no longer only the principle of existence but also the principle of actualization. The second element of similarity lies in the irreconcilability between the subject of morality and the subject of knowledge. The cognitive mind analyzed by Kant in the *Critique of Pure Reason* does not meet the requirements of the moral self as described by the *Critique of Practical Reason*, since the pure Cogito does not necessarily imply the free will necessary for moral action. Considering Zhu Xi and Yi Chuan, Mou points out how the principle of existence, the "that for which something exists," having no specific content, cannot guide the mind in the concrete circumstances of life. If we wanted a principle that admits in itself multiplicity and differences, we would have to adopt the "principle of constitution," the "that for which the thing is structured in a certain way," giving the mind an inductive function limited to empirical knowledge. The aim of Zhu Xi and Yi Chuan's thought, however, is to pursue not empirical knowledge but moral knowledge. According to Mou, such a goal would require that the principle of existence and the principle of constitution be interwoven like warp and weft into a single fabric, but this can be achieved only by rising to the "principle of actualization," which can operate and materialize in reality, being based on the fusion of being and movement, of actual being (*shiran* 實然) and ought-to-be (*dangran* 當然).

What form and meaning does inwardness or "internalization" take when rethought on the basis of the principle of actualization? What, then, is the meaning of interiority in *Constitutive Mind and Constitutive Nature*? The textual starting point is the sentence of Cheng Mingdao, a Neo-Confucian scholar of the Northern Song era: "The 10,000 things belong (inherent) to the self (*wo*): This refers not only to the human being, but also to things. Everything derives from this. It's just that things can't extend (*tui* 推), while the human is able to extend."[43] The human mind and the myriads of things in the universe participate in

---

43 萬物皆備於我, 不獨人爾, 物皆然。都自這裡出去。只是物不能推, 人則能退之。Ibid., I, 74–75.

4. Constitutive Mind and Constitutive Nature

a common ontological nature. "All things form one body" (*wanwu yiti* 萬物一體). However, this must be understood from two distinct points of view. From an ontological point of view, the human and things have one nature; from a moral-performative point of view, only the human mind has the capacity to actively realize the principle of this nature through empathic correspondence and moral participation. Of course, common nature from the ontological point of view does not refer to a static and unchanging material substance, nor even to an abstract metaphysical principle, but is rather an uninterrupted generative flow that constitutively permeates the entire universe. The nature common to man and things indicates here an onto-cosmological creative force.

To describe it, Mou adopts and enlarges the meaning of several expressions from the *Zhongyong* and the *Yijing*, such as *tianming shiti* 天命實體, which encapsulate being and movement. Their universality is not logic-defining, but implies possessing the performative capacity to fill and bring to completion each individual. This substance having universal efficacy not only "generates the myriads of things," but "inheres in things as their own nature." It should be emphasized that the term "inhering" in things has the meaning of "full ontological possession" (*bentilun de yuanju* 本體論的圓具), that is, cherishing in oneself and participating in the universal efficacy of one heavenly principle. Inherence, being "in," is here equivalent to possessing: things possess a substance and a principle, and human beings equally enjoy this possession. According to Mou, Cheng Mingdao's statement—"The 10,000 things belong (inherent) to the self (*wo*): This refers not only to the human being, but also to things,"—can be interpreted as saying that not only the human mind, but also every single thing in the universe possesses a self, not in the sense of a self-conscious subjectivity, but in the sense of an active generating fulcrum (*chuangzao zhi zhongxin* 創造之中心).[44] Reality is not a static reality, endowed with being but not dynamism, but an uninterruptedly generating force that traverses and unifies the entire universe. However, the thing does not have spontaneity in itself, it is not capable of autonomously arousing this restless generation that constitutes it, and therefore its possession is purely virtual. The thing receives its meaning from the human mind: if the human were not

---

44 Ibid., I, 65.

there to awaken the moral creative force of the universe, things could not come into manifestation, nor reveal their intrinsic value.[45] Therefore, Mou can say that the principle of actualization is not inherent in things, but transcendent to them. "Being in things as their own nature: This inhering is a 'being within,' a purely passive and latent interiority." The asymmetrical relationship between the human being and things consists in what Cheng Mingdao calls the capacity for extension. In *Constitutive Mind and Constitutive Nature*, Mou writes, "Only if there is this capacity for extension can moral creation be produced, can the heavenly principle be brought into relief." Mou uses this diagram to explain this crucial difference between man and things:[46]

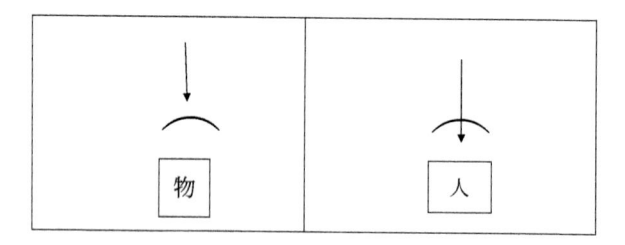

Fig. 1 Diagram explaining the crucial difference between man and things. Created by author, adapted from Mou Zongsan, *Constitutive Mind and Constitutive Nature*, I, 105.

The arrow represents the moral creative nature (which can exercise and bring to fruition the actualization principle), while the curved bracket represents the difference between different types of nature. In the human being, the arrow penetrates the curve, and moral creativity is thus internalized as its own nature. In the thing, on the other hand, the arrow is not able to penetrate, thus remaining transcendent, that is,

---

45 As Wang Yangming already stated: "My clear intelligence is the master of heaven and earth and spiritual beings. If heaven is deprived of my clear intelligence, who is going to look into its height? If earth is deprived of my clear intelligence, who is going to look into its height? If earth is deprived of my clear intelligence, who is going to look into its depth? If spiritual beings are deprived of my clear intelligence, who is going to distinguish their good and evil fortune or the calamities and blessings that they will bring? Separated from my clear intelligence, there will be no heaven, earth, spiritual beings, or myriad things, and separated from these, there will not be my clear intelligence." Wing Tsit-Chan (ed.), *Instructions for Practical Living, and Other Neo-Confucian Writings by Wang Yang-Ming*, New York and London: Columbia University Press, 1963, p. 257.

46 See Mou Zongsan, *Constitutive Mind and Constitutive Nature*, I, 105.

not inherent in the thing's own nature. Grass, trees, and stones do not have moral creativity, and therefore cannot absorb it within themselves as their own nature. What things ontologically possess is only the nature of the principle of existence, and this nature does not possess spontaneity, autonomy, the capacity to self-determine its own direction and autonomously exercise its own function-guidance (sovereignty, in the dynamic and spiritual sense). The thing does not have the character of subjectivity, and therefore does not have as its own nature the capacity to actualize, realize, and concretize.

The interiority of the human mind therefore expresses the capacity to embody the principle of actualization, that is, the law of moral creativity, to the point of making it its own distinctive nature. This interiority manifests itself as a force of universal extension, that is, as the capacity to confer meaning and value on all things without letting any of them fade into indifference. With respect to the mind, this force is both centripetal and centrifugal. In the Western tradition, of which the Cartesian Cogito is here the highest expression, the "I think" is constituted by a centripetal movement, that is, of leaving the world and returning to the center of the self. In the *Discourse on Method*, René Descartes, by means of absolute doubt, withdraws from everything that is not based on evidence, starting from the things of the world and involving the structures of the mind called upon to represent them. The movement of doubt is here a downward spiral, which subtracts cognitive confidence from ever larger areas of reality and of the mind, until it narrows down to the "I think," which in this process reveals itself to be the only point-like truth endowed with indisputable self-evidence.

Instead, as per Mou, as I proceed in my effort of spiritual self-cultivation, I can correspondingly extend more and more my interiority, that is, the area of my participation and moral responsibility. Contrary to Plato and the thought he influenced, inwardness is not a closed spiritual realm that excludes the body, but rather it is a bodily and spiritual totality, that is, it involves the whole human, including sensitivity and emotional life. Cheng Mingdao argues that the lack of empathy and moral responsivity (*bu ren* 不仁) is similar to the paralysis of a limb that the body no longer sensitively recognizes as its own, and is therefore physiologically unresponsive (*mamu bu ren* 麻木不仁). The thought that "the whole universe is a single body" (*wanwu yiti* 萬物一體) is therefore fully realized if the human extends his or her self to all things, not in an intellectual or voluntaristic sense, but by perceiving the universe as a part of his or her own vital and sensitive extension. Mou takes the terms "resonance" (*ganying* 感應) or all-embracing responsivity (*gantong* 感通) from the Confucian tradition to describe this moral sensibility. In *Cong Lu Xiangshan dao Liu Jishan*, Mou, analyzing the teaching of Wang Yangming, summarizes his own thought as follows: "[Wang] Yangming interprets the principle 'the universe is one body' by means of the resonance of innate moral consciousness (*liangzhi* 良知), just as Mingdao interprets it as the all-embracing responsiveness (*gantong* 感通) of the mind of benevolence (*renxin* 仁心). This teaching is proper to Confucianism, and there can be no distinction about it."[47]

It is worth recalling that the term *ti* (體), expressed here as "one body," has a double level of meaning. Placed after a term, as in *xinti* 心體 or *xingti* 性體, it indicates its substantial and inherent nature, which is not static, but is a creative and generating force that imbues everything with itself. When *ti* precedes a verb, as in *tiren* (體認) or *tiyan* (體驗), it indicates a direct participation in the experience or a specific spiritual state (*jingjie* 境界) in which I am involved in interest in all that lives, taking care of it as if it were a part of my body. In any case, the term *ti* (體) derives its meaning from moral metaphysics and active moral engagement, condensing into itself the mutual correspondence of self and world.

The idea of "interiority," as in the case of the Cartesian "I think," also implies a form of self-awareness acquired through self-reflection. In Descartes, the interiority of the Cogito can be understood as an instantaneous self-reflection and the intuition of the self-evidence of the self that follows from it. The Chinese term for "cognitive reflection" is *fansi* (反思): the movement of returning (*fan* 反) to the self in order to recognize oneself. Mengzi's expression "The myriad things are in the self, turning to myself I achieve authenticity," or "The ten thousand things are all brought to completion in me. The individual has to look back into himself (*fanshen* 反身) and he will find his authenticity" (萬物皆備於我, 反身而誠) contains this same returning or turning back (*fan* 反), but here it indicates neither the self-reflection of reason nor

---

47 Mou Zongsan, *Cong Lu Xiangshan dao Liu Jishan*, p. 158.

psychological introspection (*fanxing* 反省). Both, in fact, presuppose a temporary detachment from the world (or, to use a term dear to Husserl, "putting the world in brackets") in order to get back into the privacy of one's own interiority and make oneself one's own object. In the Confucian tradition exemplarily represented by Mengzi's sentence, the returning, turning back (*fan* 反) of the term *fanshen* (反身) more properly expresses the idea of "trace back to the root." The extension of the moral mind to embrace all things is what enables the revelation of their meaning. In this process, the activity of the mind and the value in itself of the thing come simultaneously to manifestation. *Fanshen* (反身), to return to the self, to return to that which is one's own, is equivalent to returning to the original manifestation and correspondence of the self and the universe. "The self," "what is proper," is not here an unchanging universal substance, but the concrete fulfillment in moral action of the principle whereby "the whole universe is in me" (萬物備於我).

Mengzi tells us that this returning to the origin is authenticity (*cheng* 誠). Mou takes this term from the *Zhongyong* to indicate the perfect correspondence of the inside and the outside: "According to the *Zhongyong* 'authenticity' means that there is no separation between the inner and the outer, the unity of the subjective and the objective point of view. The *Zhongyong* also says: 'the way of heaven and earth may be completely declared in one sentence. They are without any doubleness, and so they produce things in a manner that is unfathomable' (天地之道, 可壹言而盡也。其為物不貳, 則其生物不測). The way of heaven and earth is the reality of perpetual generation, and the unity of the inner and outer I call 'authenticity.'"[48] Not being dually separate from things implies "not being opposed to things." The moral and performative endeavor is not a cognitive process, and therefore the self and the things involved in it are not opposites, and the universe cannot simply be the object (*ob-jectum*, 對象) of knowledge, but the realization of the absolutely universal. From the point of view of ontological properties, "the proper nature (*xing* 性) is the realization of the metaphysical principle that descends to penetrate all things and dwell in each of them (flowing into each individual thing)."[49] But from the moral-performance

---

48 Mou Zongsan, *Constitutive Mind and Constitutive Nature*, I, 33.
49 Ibid., I, 34.

point of view, only man can consciously exercise the moral creative function, and therefore only man can have the metaphysical principle as his own inner nature. Lu Xiangshan says, "The myriad things luxuriate in the space of a square inch [in the self],"[50] all things are assumed in the human mind. Mind and nature both belong to the human as inherent realities, because only man possesses them inwardly by virtue of his ability to be self-conscious.

The idea of interiority is also connected to active perception or to the state of vigilance (*jue* 覺), which, if turned back to the subject itself, become self-consciousness (*zijue* 自覺). We saw in the chapter on the *Critique of the Cognitive Mind* that for Mou the term *jue* or "perception" can have, on the epistemological level, four characteristics: 1. The act of perception cannot be reduced to the rank of object, it has the pure nature of subject; 2. Every act of perception involves pre-reflective self-awareness; 3. The act of perception cannot be reduced to the status of an object; it has the pure nature of a subject; 4. The function of perception is to manifest the meaning of things, but for this to happen, the subject must be an active participant in the world. Since perception already plays a dynamic and performative role, it can act as a bridge between the horizontal-conceptual level and the vertical-moral level. In *Constitutive Mind and Constitutive Nature*, the semantic field of this concept is enriched, becoming an integral part of the moral metaphysics advocated by Mou. Mou writes: "Perception (*jue* 覺) in the sense of fecund and vigilant inter-affectation (*gantong juerun* 感通覺潤) arises from a feeling of disquiet, of concern, of compassion, it is a brimming with life, a concentration of warmth, its effect is similar to the seasonal rain that fertilizes everything, and therefore we call it 'fecund awareness'. Where my spiritual awareness is able to fecundate, we have life force and potential of growth, it is through my spiritual awareness that everything is fecundated and full of vigour. Horizontally spoken, it is fecund awareness, vertically spoken, it is creativity. [...] If I synthesize both meanings, I have the principle of benevolence and the mind of benevolence."[51] In this further phase of Mou's thought, *jue*

---

50 In: Lu Xiangshan, *Xiangshan quanji* (Complete Works of Lu Xiangshan), Taipei: Zhonghua, 1965, 35/10a.
51 覺即就感通覺潤而說, 此覺是由不安、不忍、悱惻之感來說, 是生命之洋溢, 是溫暖之貫注, 如時雨之潤, 固曰『覺潤』。『覺』潤至何處, 即使何處有生意, 能生長, 是由吾之覺之

覺 as vigilance and spiritual awareness transcends its cognitive aspect and does not require empirical assumptions. The feeling of alarm, concern, not being able to bear the suffering of others is part of the same process of active manifestation of the moral mind that precedes the subject-object distinction. The principle by which all perception is apperception, that is, self-consciousness (see Point 2) finds its ultimate foundation in the moral and active realm. In my reawakening myself as structurally involved in the universal resonance (*ganying* 感應) of all things, my moral mind manifests and certifies itself in what Mou calls "retrospective verification (*nijue tizheng* 逆覺體證)." It should be noted here that the term *retro-* (逆), like the turning back (*fan* 反) mentioned above, does not imply a reflexive turning back on oneself to observe and objectify one's inner world, but is inextricably linked to the prefix auto- (自) of self-consciousness. The moral mind is autonomous, that is, it has its own standard and active reason in itself. Wanting to express this autonomy, we could say that in this case the principle or law is "in" the mind, and as such it is "intrinsic" to it, without this referring back to a closed inner space.

The meaning of "interiority" and the metaphors related to "being inside" or intrinsic being on the moral-metaphysical level is the inseparable union of objective law and the subjective urge to act. Or, to put it another way, authentic inwardness is "having nothing outside" (*wuwai* 無外), both because the mind has no external precepts to guide it, and because it realizes itself by embodying and realizing itself in all things without leaving any out, that is, by being one with all other human beings and their universe, living them as a constitutive part of itself. This capacity to extend itself to infinity is, as we have seen, the creativity proper to the mind. We are not speaking here of artistic creativity or evolutionary development, but of the creativity of authentic spiritual life, which unfolds through the retrospective intuition of its own unlimited potential. Moral creativity not only unfolds its interiority, but also has the responsibility to value things, not to treat them as mere instruments, but to make each of them a "thing-in-itself," that is, an

---

『潤之』而誘發其生機也。[…]。綜此覺潤與創生兩義, 仁固是『仁道』, 亦是『仁心』。
Ibid., II, 237. Mou specifies that the horizontal meaning implies the all-embracing idea of being one body with everything, whereas the vertical meaning implies the moral creativity that makes this absolute universality possible.

absolute end. This "inseity" that goes far beyond the Kantian noumenon is the ultimate manifestation of interiority on the performative level, that is, the "making thing as thing-in-itself." This is the last step that Kant rejected because of the insuperable gap that the Western tradition establishes between the finite mind and the infinite mind of God. What Kant lacks is the concrete possibility of becoming holy, or, as Mou writes, "the concrete wisdom permeated by the origin. [...] I see the spiritual realm of the saint in its authenticity and compassion as the most accomplished and final realization of his [Kant's] system."[52] The Confucian principle that by the effort of self-cultivation "every human being can become a saint" is what would make Kantian morality no longer a mere postulate, but a concrete manifestation that is renewed in every action.

4.7 Conclusion: The Child in the Well

In these concluding paragraphs, I will try to illustrate and summarize the concepts discussed so far through a concrete example. It is the famous example, formulated by Mengzi, of the child who is about to fall into a well. Mengzi explains that when I see a child about to fall into a well, my feeling of compassion is immediately awakened. What I perceive in my emotional intelligence is a sense of urgency and concern that results in my spontaneous act of grabbing the child. We could analyze what happens in this way: in the instant that I see the child, that is, that I passively receive a visual stimulus from the outside world, I immediately experience a sense of urgency to act, and we could say that urgency and a sense of alarm are simultaneous to my immediate action, which is simply its bodily expression, so that urgency and agency are two sides of the same coin. Recalling the way of reasoning of Western moral philosophy, we could also say that the condition of this urgent experience is the presence in me of a moral conscience, capable of recognizing the absolute value of the child's life. It allows me to evaluate the contradiction between my moral system and the condition of danger that the outside world poses to the child's life, and it gives rise to an inner conflict in me that manifests itself as a reawakening of the sense

---

52   Mou Zongsan, *Constitutive Mind and Constitutive Nature*, I, 144.

of responsibility. My action represents my practical reaction aimed at resolving this inner apprehension, restoring an order to the world that conforms to my moral standards.

This description, consistent with Kantian moral philosophy, represents in Mou Zongsan's eyes a distortion based on a horizontal-conceptual model, which implies that I possess a knowledge of good and evil, and that there is a cause-effect relationship, or rather an action and counteraction relationship, that dominates my relations with the external world. In fact, this explanation, according to Mou, is not faithfully reflected in our experience. In the given concrete situation, this intolerable sense of urgency and inner pressure has nothing to do with the principle of reaction to the stimulus, but means on the contrary that I do not consider the child a phenomenon of the common external world. The way the child at the edge of the well manifests itself to us is similar to the way an injured limb manifests itself to us. It is not necessary for me to seek in myself a stimulus to action, for this manifestation of urgency and pain possesses in itself an active force. The appearance of the child does not require that it be mediated by any concept, nor that my moral consciousness give it meaning, because absolute value possesses a force of self-manifestation. We might ask: But does this absolute value belong to the child itself, or rather is it a characteristic that is conferred by my moral consciousness? Having absolute value is something that Kant acknowledges to the thing-in-itself. In *Constitutive Mind and Constitutive Nature*, Mou uses the term *zixing* 自性 to illustrate this moral reality, writing that moral creativity can be defined as making the thing a thing-in-itself (自性). The term autonomous (*zi* 自), as we have seen, does not mean having the nature of reflective self-consciousness, but having in and from itself its own nature. On the one hand, the appearance of the child is not subordinate to my subjectivity, that is, it does not require the *a priori* schemes of pure reason or practical reason to constitute itself as a phenomenon. That the child manifests itself as a part of myself, a limb of my body, means that between me and the child there is no separation.

On the other hand, however, although the value of the child is ontologically "in itself," the illuminating manifestation of this absolute reality occurs in and through me. If I, selfishly, blinded by my private self (*zayi jisi* 雜以己私), regard the child as a mere accidental element of the external world, I cannot broaden the field of my responsiveness,

I cannot "embody" (in the verbal sense of *ti* 體) the child. This means that I cannot personally experience and verify the absolute unity of my substantial nature and that of the child, and therefore I fall back into the horizon of the "little self" whereby interior and exterior are opposed. Conversely, the senses of compassion and urgency are not mere feelings, but possess an unlimited power of creation and actualization: "That the mind of benevolence has nothing external to itself, is not only said in a formal sense, but can be experienced in a concrete way starting from the term 'embody' of 'embodying all things under heaven.' This term, 'embody,' tells us that the being of nothing external to the mind of benevolence is something concrete and actual. For it is the actual and real manifestation, through practice, of the pure and transcendent moral mind-root. Only when I actually experience sorrow and concern for all things under heaven can the non-exteriority of the heavenly mind originate."[53]

If I consider subjectivity as this space of experience and manifestation, how does this meaning differ from the idea of subjectivity elaborated in Western phenomenology? As mentioned in the first chapter, one of the most important difficulties that has arisen in phenomenological thinking is that of thinking the other without turning it into an object constituted by my subjective consciousness. In order to preserve the uniqueness and transcendence of the other, the French philosopher Lévinas emphasizes how the other human being does not belong to the phenomenal world produced by the intentional act of my self and subordinated to it. The way in which the other manifests itself to me is that of an uninterrupted transcendence and rupture of the concept that I make of it. This mode of manifestation is, for Lévinas, characteristic of the appearance of the face of the other. While the object-thing appears in the world as a product of my intentional gaze, the face presents itself directly from itself, entering my world but without belonging to it. The other human being bursts into my world, destroying the boundaries and desire of the self, awakening my sense of infinite responsibility and establishing itself as the authentic transcendence. Lévinas does not emphasize here the common human nature, and the sense of responsibility with which I feel invested is therefore in danger of being limited to a subjective

---

53 仁心之無外亦不只是形式地說, 而實由『體天下之物』之『體』字而見。此『體』字是表示『仁必無外』是具體的、存在的, 這要在實踐中純粹的超越的道德本心真實呈現, 對于天下之物真感到痛癢, 始有此天心之無外。Ibid., I, 561.

condition, which does not offer an adequate objective foundation for the interaction between human beings.

Contrariwise, following Mou's thought, if in my mind I consciously highlight the common substantial nature between my own and the other, then I can verify in practice the absolute universality of the root mind. The fact that I personally experience and recognize the absolute value of the "nature in itself" of the other implies that I am actively participating in its manifestation. If I am unable, through moral commitment, to refine my inner capacity to be responsive, I will never discover that there is a capacity within me to expand infinitely, make my self great, and actualize the harmony between my self and the universe. My subjectivity is the principle of actualization and authentication because absolute universality is not simply a conceptual value or a psychological state. My feeling of urgency and caring has an ontological foundation, allowing me to participate personally in the creation of a world with moral value and meaning. Mou Zongsan points out that for me to attain knowledge of this all-embracing moral reality is not the result of a cognitive act of universalization, but a "retrospective verification." What does "retrospective" mean here? For what reason do I turn backwards? There is no echo here of the reflexive movement by which I return to self-consciousness, but rather to what Mengzi says: "There is no greater joy than turning to oneself in self-examination and finding authenticity there." By turning to myself in the effort of self-perfection, I free myself from the shackles and limitations of the private, selfish self, and return to my authentic subjectivity, experience for myself that nothing is external to heaven, nothing is external to nature, nothing is external to mind. I can then verify the concrete actuality of Mengzi's saying, "All things are in me," and Zhang Zai's saying, "Under heaven, there is nothing that I am not." My responsibility is to embody the limitlessness of the "mind of benevolence" and at the same time "feel delight" (i.e., realize my most authentic nature in me). As Lee Ming-huei efficaciously synthesizes: "In the all-penetrating and all-pervasive moral creation of the infinite intellectual moral mind, happiness appears wherever virtue goes, and vice versa, that is to say, virtue and happiness collapse into one paradoxically, and the highest good is thus theoretically justified."[54]

---

54 Lee Ming-huei, "Mou Zongsan: Between Confucianism and Kantianism," in: David Elstein (ed.), *Dao Companion to Contemporary Confucian Philosophy*, London and Berlin: Springer, 2021, pp. 255–275 (p. 266).

5. Self-Limitation of the Moral Self as *Kenosis*

5.1 *Kenosis*: History of a Concept

In this chapter I aim to focus on Mou Zongsan's concept of self-limitation or self-entanglement (*ziwo kanxian* 自我坎陷) of the moral mind. The dynamism of self-limitation constitutes the dialectical transition from the vertical dimension of the moral self to the horizontal dimension of the knowing self. This transition is required in order to overcome dangers and obstacles through cognition, and to fully accomplish the moral duties of the authentic self. As Mou writes, "Moral knowing and moral ability is supremely simple and unlabored but it could never fail to know that there exist dangers and obstacles. Knowing that and wishing to overcome them, it must necessarily transform into understanding. Thus, in knowing dangers and obstacles, there is implied a dialectical unfolding. And so its self-negation takes the formation of the epistemic subject (the understanding) as the self-conscious demand of its moral aspirations."[1] This self-negation of the moral mind takes the form of a conscious falling and becoming entangled in the world of objects. More precisely, this dialectical self-limitation produces an ontological bifurcation between the moral world of the things-in-itself and the phenomenal world. Going through a deliberate stopping up, grasping, and holding into itself, the moral mind congeals in an epistemic subject, i.e., in a logical and formal framework aimed to mold and penetrate a spatio-temporal objective universe. The plurality of translations proposed for the expression *ziwo kanxian* (self-negation,

---

[1] Mou Zongsan (牟宗三), *Xianxiang yu wuzishen*. 現象與物自身 (Phenomenon and Thing-in-Itself). *Mou Zongsan xiansheng quanji* 牟宗三先生全集 (Complete Works of Mou Zongsan), vol. XXI, Taipei: Lianhe baoxi wenhua jijin hui, 2003. Translated by Jason Clower (ed.), *Late Works of Mou Zongsan. Selected Essays on Chinese Philosophy*, Leiden: Brill, 2014, p. 221.

self-limitation, self-entanglement)[2] mirrors a hermeneutical difficulty in representing this descension from the enlightened realm of moral action to the bounded and determined realm of discursive understanding. In this chapter, I would suggest that we interpret *kanxian* as *kenosis*, and that we analyze them in a comparative way. I aim to demonstrate that inserting the idea of *kanxian* in the wider frame of the "kenotic models" in Western thought may lead to a deeper comprehension of this crucial and challenging concept.

When we speak of *kenosis,* we are referring to a concept formulated and discussed initially in the theological sphere, then extended to the philosophical one. The original locus is in the Epistle to the Philippians 2:6–8,[3] in which Paul of Tarsus describes the process of self-spoliation by which Jesus Christ, though having a divine nature, voluntarily renounces the prerogatives that derive from this infinite nature in order to assume human form. The Greek term used to express this voluntary spoliation is *heauton ekenosen*, hence the noun *kenosis*, literally "emptying." The relevance of this concept in the philosophical sphere

---

[2] For a comprehensive analysis of the different translations of *ziwo kanxian* proposed by scholars, see the preface to the appendix in Clower (ed.), *Late Works of Mou Zongsan*, pp. 213–217. I adopted the translation "self-limitation" because it is consistent with the spatial-dimensional interpretation of *ziwo kanxian* I suggest. In the ancient world, the concept of limit (in Latin *limes/limen*, in Classical Greek *peras/horos*) occupies a position of absolute importance. In Hesiodi *Theogonia*, the act of limitation represents the pristine divarication between heaven and earth, through which the world emerges from the indistinct primordial chaos. In similar fashion, Mou's self-limitation of the pristine mind inaugurates the cognitive world of division and finitude, epitomized by the separation between subject and object. "Self-entanglement" could evocatively express the idea of constraint and attachment implied in *kanxian*. However, I prefer "self-limitation," in order to avoid a baffling parallelism with the concept of "entanglement" in quantum physics. A further reason for adopting "self-limitation" is the relevance of this concept in the context of the discussion about noumenon in Kant's *Critique of Pure Reason*. See, for reference, Addison Ellis, "Kant on Self-Consciousness as Self-Limitation," *Contemporary Studies in Kantian Philosophy* 5 (2020), 15–36 (p. 34): "To put it another way, we are always at once the 'I' of pure self-consciousness (the 'I' that itself is limitless) and the 'I' of empirical self-consciousness (the I that is inside the limits of space and time)."

[3] "[Jesus Christ], though he was in the form of God, did not regard the equality with God as something to be exploited, but emptied himself, taking the form of a slave, being born in human likeness. And being found in human form, he humbled himself and became obedient to the point of death—even death on a cross." Michael Coogan (ed.), *The New Oxford Annotated Bible: New Revised Standard Version with the Apocrypha*, New York and Oxford: Oxford University Press, 2010, p. 2063.

lies in the fact that it can be used to indicate any process in which a higher metaphysical substance voluntarily renounces the fullness of its character and power in order to manifest itself and act on a lower plane. The key to this descent down the ontological hierarchy lies precisely in the emptying, whereby the higher principle cannot acquire perceptible limits and forms except by passing through emptiness, absence, the negative. There are numerous possible types of *kenosis*, which I shall call in this chapter "kenotic models." The difference between them consists first of all in the nature of the two polarities that this self-emptying connects, e.g., Transcendence/Immanence, Infinite/Finite, Eternal/Historical-Temporal. Secondly, the difference is determined by the way in which we think of this emptiness (*kenós*): Is it an absolute non-being, an absence, a negation or the mere reduction to latency of what was previously manifested?

A bird's-eye view of the development of Western thought allows us to identify various kenotic models. We can, for example, consider the *Enneads* of Plotinus, and how from the perfect light of the One derive in concentric circles the Intellect and the Soul, down to the extreme dark ramifications of matter. Using the metaphors of the fountain of water and the spring of light, Plotinus explains that the One does not shape things as Plato's Demiurge does, nor is it involved in the progressive limitation of the entities that derive from it. The inexhaustibility of its generative force is such that it overflows, like a cascading fountain that leaps down into ever more limited pools, bringing the lower levels into being. The levels proceed from one another, having in themselves an ever-increasing multiplicity, and as they distance themselves more and more from the source, their being becomes increasingly rarefied and opaque.[4] In this processional-emanative model, progressive self-limitation is necessary because of the nature of the world, but it is not directly willed by the One. The One nevertheless wills itself and its infinite begetting, so indirectly it is the origin of the ontological descent that emanates from it.

---

4 "[...] the powers that derive from the primary item differ from it in being lesser and dim, like a dimmer light that comes from a brighter light [...]." Eyjólfur K. Emilsson and Steven K. Strange (ed.), *Plotinus Ennead VI.4 and VI.5. On the Presence of Being, One and the Same, Everywhere as a Whole*, Zurich and Athens: Parmenides Publishing, 2015, p. 76.

The age of German idealism produced a series of kenotic models whose fundamental characteristic is instead the exit from itself of the first principle, here thought of as mind and subjectivity, in order to know itself as object, and thus reintegrate into a fully actualized self-conscious absolute. Friedrich Wilhelm Joseph Schelling (1775–1854) writes, for example: "Primordial being [*das Urwesen*] as the absolute identity of the real and the ideal is itself only subjectively posed; however we must grasp it objectively: It must not remain merely in itself but must also be the absolute identity of the real and the ideal outside itself, that is, it must reveal itself as such, actualize itself [...]."[5] The supreme principle empties itself of itself in the form of an alienation or exit from itself. Its end is to bifurcate into a subject and an object in order to know itself or fully manifest itself in historical reality. In this kenotic model, there is a strong emphasis on the subjective nature of the first principle and its structural dynamism. *Kenosis* here is voluntary, and even where it appears as self-negation, self-loss, or sacrifice, the ultimate goal is that of a circular return to a higher degree of self-consciousness. Sometimes, as happens in Hegel, the absolute abandons its abstract perfection to become concrete and ultimately encompass all of reality in itself. Finally, in the contemporary age, philosophies are affirmed, such as those of Gilles Deleuze, Emmanuel Lévinas, and Jacques Derrida, which interpret the self-emptying of the first principle as dispossession, self-withdrawal, decentralization, so that the finite can exist and acquire its autonomy. The horizon in which these thinkers place themselves is the one opened up by a *kenosis* that has already taken place and is irreversible. At the base there is a renunciation of the first principle to the dominion of presence, fullness, and totality, in order to offer the finite world the gift of life. This kenotic model is the only one that does not foresee a final reintegration. In Christian theology, *kenosis* in fact precedes *theosis*, or theurgy, that is, the ascent of the finite toward its own likeness to God. The Plotinian procession preserves within itself the devouring nostalgia for the origin, which manifests itself in a continuous movement of fusion return to the One, and the idealistic models of Johann Gottlieb Fichte, Schelling, and Georg Wilhelm Friedrich Hegel

---

5   F. W. J. Schelling, "Stuttgart Seminars," in: *Idealism and the Endgame of Theory: Three Essays by F.W.J. Schelling*, trans. by Thomas Pfau, Albany, NY: State University of New York Press, 1944, p. 200.

demand *kenosis* as a temporary sacrifice in virtue of which the real and the ideal interpenetrate, rising toward final completion. Can we think of the self-limitation of the moral ego (*ziwo kanxian*) theorized by Mou as a kenotic movement, and above all, is it referable to one of these models? In the following pages I intend to carry out a comparison between Mou's *ziwo kanxian* and two models of self-emptying. The first is the Hegelian one, which is of crucial importance because many scholars have seen in it a linguistic and theoretical parallelism with the *kanxian* one; the second is Lévinas' model, which aims, like Mou's, at the foundation of an "immanent transcendence," and represents an exceptional attempt in Western thought to rethink metaphysics starting from the primacy of ethics.

According to Mou, *kanxian* is a dialectical movement. This means, first of all, that it cannot be deduced analytically from the concept of moral mind, but it also means that I have to think following a curve, that is, I have to pass from one ontological plane to cross another, as if I were moving between two universes in which different geometrical laws apply. In this case, the plane universe is that of the pure ideal, while the curved universe is that of the concrete, limited, and plural. Only by tuning into the curvatures of the real world can thought achieve its purpose (*quda* 曲達). The self-limiting movement of the moral self implies, in Hegelian fashion, a subsumption (*Aufhebung*) of the concrete and the negative that allows the transcendent moral mind to fully actualize itself in real circumstances, and then resolve them in the circular return to the transcendent dimension. The Hegelian term "subsumption" (*Aufhebung*) possesses precisely this dual meaning of "removing, eliminating" and "preserving by lifting up." Everything that is grasped loses its vital dynamism to become a passive object, and therefore the moral mind, clinging to itself, accepts to temporarily lose itself. In losing itself, paradoxically, it penetrates the limited and phenomenal world and makes it the place of its own realization, ending up finding itself in everything as in its own reflection. The Hegelian metaphor of reality that, like a shattered mirror, reflects the one Spirit from a thousand different perspectives has a strong visual-cognitive connotation. Wanting instead to approach the performative model, we can remember what Mou said in his *Lessons on Zhuangzi*, namely that dialectics "means to digest, in order to transform something in your flesh and blood" (see Chapter 3). It implies a metaphorical embodiment, an assimilation of what is other as part of me (the verbal sense of *ti* 體), dissolving what is negative and limited in it, and making it organically part of my living being. It is not a pure cognitive passage but an active engagement, an implication, which is also an entrapment.

The word *kanxian* 坎陷 has a wide semantic spectrum, in which is included the meaning of falling into a trap, entrapment. From the kenotic point of view, entrapment expresses the risk of loss and non-return contained in the dialectic of self-limitation. How should we understand here being trapped, which in other passages is rendered as voluntary swamping and stagnating? The idea of the finite world as a trap reminds us of Plato's *Timaeus* and his definition of the body as the "prison of the soul." Wanting to develop this suggestion in the sense of *kenosis*/incarnation, Gnosticism is the paradigmatic point of reference. In the Gnostic texts found at Nag Hammadi, the coming into existence of the world is caused by an error or a fault. The spiritual spark that has fallen into the mixture of matter is a prisoner of a world of deception governed by an evil and lying Demiurge. In this extreme interpretation of the Platonic idea according to which the corporal world is the prison of the soul, the spark of the spirit remains irretrievably extraneous to the envelope that encloses it. The dialectical movement of incarnation is impossible here, because the spirit cannot evolve by assimilating the "travail of the negative" and actualizing itself, but can only escape the trapping grasp of matter, keeping itself immaculate while waiting to be able to ascend back to its divine abode. It is necessary for a savior, or a series of savior figures, to descend into the world to awaken spiritual beings and lead them back upward. In the Gnostic models of the Christian matrix, this savior coincides with the figure of Christ. His descent is not a true incarnation, because the dualism that governs these models prevents the divine from mixing with the human. Christ remains intact in his divine prerogatives, and merely assumes an illusory human guise, like a mask that he will later leave behind, without having experienced pain and death. The orthodox interpretation of the incarnation, elaborated in the Councils of Nicaea and Constantinople, is defined precisely in the contrast with this dualism. The divine nature must divest itself of its fullness and descend to dwell in a human mind and body, impregnating them with itself but also voluntarily allowing itself to be limited by

5. Self-Limitation of the Moral Self as Kenosis

their finiteness to the point of death. The premise of this is that human nature is not structurally evil, and its negativity must be traversed and assimilated. The overcoming of this self-limitation takes place through *theosis*, a movement of ascent and reconstitution of the divine, in which, however, finiteness is embraced and saved, and eternally received into divine perfection. It is not surprising, therefore, that Hegel looks to the incarnation of Christ as a paradigm of the dialectic in its ternary rhythm: God in his glory, self-denial of God (*kenosis*), overcoming toward an even more fulfilled and inclusive divine (*theosis*). For Hegel, the dialectic is realized in sacrifice, understood as "sojourning in the negative."

Mou himself perhaps echoes this not strictly religious reading of the concept when he indicates *kanxian* as a voluntary sacrifice: "The *zhiti mingjue* must consciously limit itself, it is a sacrifice to make itself other than itself."[6] The "making oneself other" here expresses the ontological leap that occurs between the moral mind and the cognitive mind. This twisting, introflexion—this impaling, grasping, stagnating—is necessary for the moral mind to assimilate and penetrate every single fact, every single thing (*Guanche yu shishiwuwu* 貫徹於事事物物).[7] This is not a Gnostic fall into a trap because it does not occur by chance, error, or ignorance (*avidya*), but is consciously and spontaneously willed by the moral mind in order to be able to come to fruition, dissolving the obstacles and dangers that naturally arise in the human condition. This implies a positive view of the human, which is finite but can become infinite: "[Human beings] are originally finite entities, yet they can attain an unlimited nature, and it is because of this that they are valuable. There is nothing praiseworthy in finitude which is merely finite or in unlimitedness that is merely unlimited. To be finite while struggling to obtain an unlimited nature; only that is of value."[8]

---

6 其[知體明覺]自覺地要自我坎陷, 是自己捨身而轉為他 [...]. Mou Zongsan, *Phenomenon and Thing-in-Itself*, p. 172. *Zhiti mingjue* refers to the moral self.

7 See Mou Zongsan (牟宗三), *Cong Lu Xiangshan dao Liu Jishan*. 從陸象山到劉蕺山 (From Lu Xiangshan to Liu Jishan), *Mou Zongsan xiansheng quanji*. 牟宗三先生全集 (Complete Works of Mou Zongsan), vol. VIII, Taipei: Lianhe baoxi wenhua jijin hui, 2003, p. 212.

8 本是一有限的存在, 而卻能取得無限性, 這就是他的可貴。有限只是有限不可貴, 無限只是無限亦無所謂可貴。有限而奮鬥以獲得一無限性, 這便可貴 [...]。 Mou Zongsan (牟宗三), *Zhi de zhijue yu zhongguo zhexue*. 智的直覺與中國哲學 (Intellectual Intuition and Chinese Philosophy). *Mou Zongsan xiansheng quanji*. 牟宗三先生全集 (Complete Works of Mou Zongsan), vol. XX, Taipei: Lianhe baoxi

This capacity for self-cultivation and upliftment is, using Mengzi's language, the budding mind of benevolence that guarantees the essentially positive nature of the human. The dialectic of incarnation (embodiment) is here more radical than the Christian dialectic, in that the highest dimension of the spirit is not located in a God originally separate from the finite world, but is a condition of holiness that is ever watchful and proactive in the human mind.[9] The circularity of descending and ascending, of *kenosis* and *theosis* are not the saving initiative of a divine being, but the ongoing fulfillment of a human mind that is a fusion of being and movement, and holds within itself, in the awakening vibration of the moral self, the drive and momentum toward holiness. Mou describes this inner rhythm as an advance and retreat, the movement of a wheel that is the "potter's wheel of heaven" (*tianjun* 天鈞) mentioned in the *Zhuangzi*.[10] According to this metaphor, the saint knows how to place himself in the center of the cosmic wheel, fluidly guiding his becoming without obstacles.[11]

In the *Shuowen Jiezi* and in the *Yijing Tuan Zhuan*, the hexagram 坎 is repeatedly associated with the idea of danger (*xian* 險), with the possibility of falling into a well, of sinking into an underground ravine and therefore being prevented from flowing: "Kan 坎 repeated shows us

---

wenhua jijin hui, 2003, p. 448. Translated by Ady Van den Stock, *The Horizon of Modernity: Subjectivity and Social Structure in New Confucian Philosophy*, Leiden and Boston, MA: Brill, 2016, p. 319.

9 Antje Ehrhardt Pioletti highlights that the dimension of the "divine" cannot be objectified, but only creatively generated: "It is not 'something divine' that stands in front of the agent. Moral action is, according to Mou, an expression of the fact, that the single agent should behave as if she wants to comply with an actual highest divine order, even though this order is produced precisely through this action." Antje Ehrhardt Pioletti, *Die Realität des moralischen Handelns. Mou Zongsans Darstellung des Neokonfuzianismus als Vollendung der praktischen Philosophie Kants*), Frankfurt am Main: Peter Lang GmbH, 1997, p. 93 (translated by the author).

10 See Mou Zongsan, *Phenomenon and Thing-in-Itself*, p. 183.

11 "'So the sage harmonizes the right and wrong of things and rests at the centre of the potter's wheel of heaven. This is called walking two roads.' (See Watson [1968] 2013, p. 11; Mair 1994, p. 17). Accordingly, the sage, resting in the centre of the 'potter's wheel of heaven' (*tian jun* 天鈞)—yet another metaphor for the exemplary being's detachment from common value judgments (for more, see De Reu 2010)—is able to 'harmonize' (he 和) with others' 'right' and 'wrong' by adapting his actions to a concrete situation. [...]. The harmony that the sage thus achieves concerns his everyday interactions and is ultimately based on his understanding of the complex interrelation between the different perspectives (Ziporyn 2003, p. 53)." Andrej Fech, "Seeing and Hearing in the Laozi and Zhuangzi and the Question of Authority and Authenticity," *Religions* 10:3 (2019), 155.

one defile succeeding another. This is the nature of water;—it flows on, without accumulating its volume (so as to overflow); it pursues its way through a dangerous defile, without losing its true (nature)."[12] As the water zigzags through the gorges, it is in danger of coming to a halt in an inlet, becoming a whirlpool that swirls endlessly around its own empty center, no longer flowing or fecund. Entrapment, then, is also and, above all, a getting stuck, frozen, in a situation of closure from which there is the risk of no way out.[13] In any case, the negativity of entrapment is not to be traced back to a structural defect of things. If we want to merge the "curved" and bumpy nature of the phenomenal world with the imaginative power of the *Yijing*, we can say that for Mou that the zigzag nature of the world of things is not equivalent to falling into a trap. Taking into account that the phenomenal world is interpreted by Mou mainly as a *jingjie*, a state of mind, we can recover the previous analysis of the *jingjie* as landscape and hodological space. Navigating in this complex landscape made of gorges and meanders, the saint must know how to steer the boat of his thought in a "dialectical" way, that is, adapting himself to this curvilinear geography. The danger lies in the possibility that the flow will come to a halt, and the stream, clinging too tightly to the concretions of the landscape, will dig deep creeks and become bogged down in them. The attachment to the finite, or rather, the attachment of desire that produces finiteness itself, the space of being born and dying, must therefore be overcome. In this overcoming or *Aufhebung*, the curvatures of the landscape, symbol of the finitude of the human mind, are not flattened but restored to the centrality of that

---

12 習坎, 重險也。水流而不盈, 行險而不失其信。維心亨, 乃以剛中也。行有尚, 往有功也。天險不可升也, 地險山川丘陵也, 王公設險以守其國, 坎之時用大矣哉! Translation by James Legge: "1. Khan repeated shows us one defile succeeding another. 2. This is the nature of water;—it flows on, without accumulating its volume (so as to overflow); it pursues its way through a dangerous defile, without losing its true (nature). 3. That 'the mind is penetrating' is indicated by the strong (line) in the centre. That 'action (in accordance with this) will be of high value' tells us that advance will be followed by achievement. 4. The dangerous (height) of heaven cannot be ascended; the difficult places of the earth are mountains, rivers, hills, and mounds. Kings and princes arrange, by means of such strengths, to maintain their territories. Great indeed is the use of (what is here) taught about seasons of peril." James Legge (ed.), *The I Ching*, New York: Dover Publishing, 1963, pp. 236–237.

13 The translation of *ziwo kanxian* as "self-restriction" proposed by David Elstein (2011) and Stephen Angle (2013) highlights this aspect of "entrapment".

uninterrupted flow that produced them. The dialectic of incarnation, the circularity of descending into the phenomenal and ascending back to the transcendent plane, must therefore be reinterpreted on the basis of the positivity of the finite world. The peculiarity of Confucian teaching lies precisely in this trust in the human. With its effort at self-cultivation, the human can be the third mediator, embodying the dynamic continuity of the finite and the infinite. The image of the trap signals the danger of abdicating this role of mediation, losing oneself in the bad infinity of a cognitive tension that forgets its vertical dimension, of a scientific thought that considers itself detached and indifferent to moral action.

5.2 Paradoxes of Self-Limitation

An interesting aspect of *ziwo kanxian* lies in the paradoxical nature of the act itself, which is reflected in the question of language and the correct translation of this term. *Kanxian*, Mou says, is an act of self-grasping or self-attachment. In fact, what it produces is the logical self, which in content is empty, since it has no nature other than attachment itself. This act of attachment is also a splitting, in that it brings us into the domain of relationality as opposition, and a mutual dependence of opposites. The logical self is an empty frame, but not totally inert in that it has an insoluble bond with the reality it is supposed to frame. Using one of the key terms of phenomenology, the logical self is produced as an intentional subject, that is, directed out of itself, pointed in the direction of the object. Not only subject and object emerge simultaneously as an indissoluble dyad, but at the same time also the conditions of the thinkability of reality, understood as the categories, and in general the *a priori* conditions that in Kantian thought represent the domain of the transcendental. In accordance with Immanuel Kant's dictate, then, it is with one and the same act that the knowing subject, the known object, and the *a priori* categories that constitute the phenomenal world appear, that is, being insofar as it is "for me" and is given in my cognitive act. This unveiling of the cognitive world in the totality of its factors is the product of attachment itself. Being attached or unattached is not only a subjective spiritual condition subject to my choice, but designates two different ontological levels, the noumenal level of moral action and the limited and relative phenomenal level of my knowing.

Mou warns us, however, against the temptation to believe that attachment is something that happens, albeit by conscious and voluntary choice, to the moral self itself. In no way, Mou writes, can attachment be predicated of the moral self, which remains in its ontological condition as a living, inexhaustible creative act. We cannot think of self-limitation as an act that addresses itself by bringing about a change in what performs that act, namely the moral self. If the moral self does not cling to itself, does not limit itself, what is the meaning of that *ziwo* that we translate with the prefix "self"? If attachment does not happen to the moral self, does not concern the moral self, but always only that other which is the logical self, what does that *auton* (αυτόν) refer to? The term *ziwo* or *auton* can be misleading, leading us to imagine a reflexivity within the moral self, a referring of self to self that as in the case of a mirror implies a subject-object duality that can in no way give itself on a vertical-metaphysical level, because its emergence is the primary feature that signals to us that we are within an attached ontology, and we are operating on a horizontal-cognitive level. This autonomous *ziwo* 自我 is not to be understood as a reflexive self, but rather, as Mou reminds us, it is first and foremost the opposite of an instrumental acting (*wei* 為), as in the case of the expression self-knowledge (*zizhi* 自知), which only occurs if I "stop trying to produce it by means of the subject-object opposition," since if I "use the cognitive apparatus in order to know [...] I fall back into the pursuit of a knowing turned outside myself,"[14] and I lose that omnipenetrating inner intuition (*neitong* 內通) that is intellectual intuition, the instantaneous knowing that has in itself its own law and gives itself its own object. The *autonomy* of self-limiting does not mean that the moral self somehow reflexively turns to itself and imposes a limit on itself, distinguishing a limiting self and a limited self. In the moral self a difference between subjective and objective, between acting and suffering would be an illusory and evanescent act, which would be erased in the act of its occurrence (Mou uses the image of the perfectly calm body of water, in which every ripple would be immediately absorbed and smoothed out). Self-limitation means that the moral self is absolutely free and autonomous, and that the initiative, that is, any impulse to act, can only start from it. The beginning, not the

---

14 Mou Zongsan, *Intellectual Intuition and Chinese Philosophy*, p. 266.

principle as origin and substance, but the beginning in the performative sense, the very act of beginning is the prerogative of the moral self. Being pure subjectivity, the decision to self-limit cannot be induced by an external stimulus, and it cannot occur unconsciously, because the moral self is uninterrupted vigilance and transparency to itself. However, the consequence of this action, namely limitation and attachment cannot be predicated of the moral self.

Mou's insistence that the moral "I" and the logical "I" are not two modes of manifestation of the same "I" has its origin in the awareness of this ontological gap that makes the two levels, vertical and horizontal, irreducible to each other. As Brigita Gelžinytė writes, referring to Schelling and his analogous problem of how to justify the entry into thought, "the very idea of *entering* (as one can enter only that which is already there, literally *taking place*), *of stepping and coming in*, is put in contrast to the abstract beginning of *creatio ex nihilo*. It suggests that rather a shift in the *state* is what becomes crucial for the beginning, a shift in the particular *mode of* self-relatedness, a certain mode of being inside and within."[15] Moral ego and logical ego are two states of mind (*jingjie*) that cannot simply flow into each other, because they usher in two different ontological landscapes, endowed with irreducible internal laws. Attachment, that is, the leap from the noumenal world of moral action to the phenomenal world, is produced by voluntary and conscious impulse of the moral self, but it is not something that happens to it, it is not an event of the moral self. On the other hand, if space and time, as *a priori* conditions of the phenomenal world, are produced by attachment, how could a temporal event occur in what is above time as a flow without beginning or end? And how could there be in the moral self a before and an after self-limitation? We are faced with a paradox analogous to that which the concept of the Big Bang poses to physicists: If the Big Bang is the very squaring of space-time, is it fair to ask whether there could have been anything (e.g., an antecedent universe) *before* the Big Bang? If instead we turn our attention to the field of philosophy and theology, we see that every process of *kenosis* raises the same paradox. Medieval European philosophy labored for a long time trying to

---

15 Brigita Gelžinytė, "Performing Reason in Schelling and Hegel," PhD dissertation, Vilnius University, 2020, p. 124, https://epublications.vu.lt/object/elaba:74308027/MAIN

understand whether the historical event of the Incarnation represented a change in God, and thus surreptitiously introduced becoming into the heart of the eternal. The difference between the God before creation and after creation, on the other hand, poses a similar problem, mitigated by the fact that creation from nothing is a cosmogonic process, rather than a specific historical event with precise temporal coordinates. In Daoist thought there is an important distinction between that which is "before heaven" (*xiantian* 先天) and that which is "after heaven" (*houtian* 後天), but the absence of the doctrine of *creatio ex nihilo* and the nature of the Dao as a perpetual flux of transformations reduces change to a simple cyclical transition between the chaotic and the ordered state, or between the latent and the manifest.

One way to overcome this paradox is to analyze the kenotic movement from both points of view, the superior or absolute one and the inferior and spatio-temporally limited one. This method, adopted by some authors to solve the apparent contradiction of an event that seems to occur in the heart of eternity, finds a more rigorous application in the philosophy of Mou. In it, in fact, the obstacle posed to human thought by the impossibility of positioning oneself in the point of view of eternity or of God is overcome, and with it the logical contradiction between the concept of "point of view" and that of the absolute ubiquity of God. In Mou's metaphysics, the moral self is not an unattainable transcendent entity, but a state of mind and being that human beings acquire through moral effort and embody in the figure of the saint. Looking at the world from the perspective of the moral self is possible and not contradictory insofar as it expresses not a mere cognitive perspective, but a self-conscious spiritual state that can be embodied and acted upon (performed) by my self. It is easy to see how the *kanxian* understood as the act in which the moral self grasps itself, limits itself, descends in space and time, is the *kanxian* as it is perceived and interpreted by the cognitive self, which separates acting and suffering, cause and effect, and sees the event as a term that can be located in space-time, a point-like event from which the course of things unfolds. If the logical self wants to portray the moral mind in the only way available to it, that is, by grasping it as a cognitive object, it will end up producing the idea of ethics or moral philosophy as specific and subsidiary branches of knowledge. Or, within Confucianism, it will look at the moral ascent of the soul by separating mind and principle, as happens in Mou's interpretation in Zhu Xi's thought. From the point of view of the moral mind that is above time, insofar as, as a creative source, it is the perpetuity of an infinite beginning, the *kanxian* is reabsorbed in the very instant in which it appears, in a dynamic that is that of uninterrupted action.

Mou represents the relationship between the dimension of the phenomenon and the dimension of the thing itself, that is, the moral self, as a series of vertical descending and ascending lines that cross the cognitive horizontality of space-time. The points of intersection are, for the cognitive self, the continuous repetition in time of the *kanxian* point event, but from the point of view of vertical action it is not a serial repetition of single determinate events, but an uninterrupted circular motion of descent and ascent. The moral mind does not enter into relation with the finite only when an opposition is produced that "forces" it to self-limit itself and generate the logical self to cognitively reabsorb. The moral mind is actually in continuous uninterrupted and structural relation with the finite, since the fulfillment of moral action occurs in its actualization and concretization. The Confucian saint who embodies the moral self is never detached from the world or hovering above finite reality. On the contrary, it is continually participating and responsive, engaged in the real in a beneficial spiritual resonance with it (what Mou calls *ganying*).[16] "Descent" as a drive for realization is an uninterrupted expression of the moral mind, a continuous "rain" that nourishes finite reality and keeps it awake (as one might tentatively translate the expression *juerun* 覺潤, much beloved by Mou). From the point of view of the logical self, it is necessarily grasped as a succession of single points, pierces of reality, and sudden awakenings, which added

---

16 Tu Wei-Ming expresses efficaciously this transcendent immanence of the mind: "*Hsin* (i.e., the mind) manifests itself through a ceaseless process of internal illumination. It constantly transcends itself by fundamentally transforming the particular forms that crystallize its existence." Though no finite expression can exhaust its unlimited creativity, the mind is nevertheless always operating in our living concreteness: "For its own realization, it must work through the subjectivity of a person in time and space. [...] It (the mind) cannot detach itself from the arena in which its creativity resides. Its true nature lies not in radical transcendence but in immanence with a transcendent dimension." Tu Wei-Ming, *Centrality and Commonality. An Essay on Confucian Religiousness. A Revised and Enlarged Edition of Centrality and Commonality: An Essay on Chung-yung*, Albany, NY: State University of New York Press, 1989, pp. 120–121.

one after the other form the timeline. As Mou writes, the *ziwo kanxian* is produced *yixiazi* 一下子, all at once and once forever.

It should be remembered that the vertical structure of the moral self does not merely point to a higher metaphysical plane, perhaps eternally personified in a God, as is the case, for example, with the Kantian idea of God and the archetypal intellect, which not only knows, but has the power to create ex nihilo the object of its knowledge. The moral self is a performative experience to which I can rise through spiritual exercise and refinement. In addition to a transcendent ontological level, it is also a state of mind, a spiritual landscape that is shaped in accordance with my actions. In writing that the moral mind is not without oppositions and obstacles that challenge it, or that it needs knowledge in order not to wither away, Mou reminds us that we are at the dynamic level of action and aspiration for perfection. The obstacles and challenges it faces cannot be found in the phenomenal universe that is generated with the emergence of the logical self. On the plane of space-time phenomena, we have what Mou calls the existent things (*cunzai wu* 存在物), the things on the pure plane of being that are determined by the principle of existence and the principle of formation. Acting meets things to the extent that they become performative things (*xingwei wu* 行为物), or as Mou often calls them, facts (*shi* 事). Facts presuppose the inextricable union between the object of action and the acting subject; they are what the will or volitional intention is aimed at. What determines them is the principle of actualization, that is, that law which is one and the same with the moral mind. Facts represent the point of fall and fulfillment of that vertical tension that drives the mind to actualize itself in reality and to transform it until it has the whole universe as a part of itself.

In this performative dimension, it is possible to act but also to fail, to lose the spontaneous creative flow of the happily realized moral mind, and to decay to a mind of habit (*chengxin* 成心). It is at this level that those habitual and unchanging concretions are produced that are obstacles to moral action and cause its effectiveness to wither and shrink. According to Mou's thought, existing things are implicated in performative things, just as knowing my parents, their demands and needs, and what means I need to correspond to them are implicated in my acting according to filial piety. If I act in perfect accord with the moral self, the concrete and objective data are fluidly and organically implied in the dynamism of my holiness, but if the uncultivated mind becomes arrested in desires of possession and attached to the things of the world, these concretions within and without the soul are obstacles to free flow and the inner moral appeal will urge me to dissolve them. In both cases the voluntary self-limitation of the moral self is necessary. In the first case, however, this mechanics of focusing on objective things serves the moral purpose of leaving nothing behind and neglecting nothing, but being responsive and responsible to all that exists. On the basis of this search for the "concrete universal" in action, obstacles (which are blind, inert, and irresponsible points in the mind) must simply be fluidized and reabsorbed into the holistic dynamism of the moral self. In the second case, the mind must analyze situations of stasis and obfuscation, and it has no other way of doing so than through cognitive attachment.

The kenotic dynamism of self-limitation cannot be thought of in isolation from the opposite dynamism, which, starting from moral shuddering and awakening, goes back toward the origin, emancipating itself from its limitations. Mou refers to this movement, contrary to *kanxian*, as *yongxian* 湧現, thus recovering a term that had already appeared in the first part of his philosophical path, which was mainly oriented toward epistemology. In the *Critique of the Cognitive Mind*, Mou distinguished the passivity of the sensible from the active mental faculties such as imagination and intellect, which are capable of autonomously emanating (*yongxian* 湧現) their own principles. The radical of water contained in the character *yong* 湧 reminds us that the original meaning of the term is to "gush out" in a way that is rich and manifold. *Yongxian* represents the return to the fluidity and creativity of the origin, while *kan* 坎, the first character of the word *kanxian*, significantly has the root of earth, which expresses solidification (or, as we have called it, concretion). Already in its original *locus*, the theological one, *kenosis* is counterbalanced by *theosis*; the descent toward the finite world must produce the ascent of the whole world toward the divine. In general, the kenotic models have a circular character: in Plotinus everything cascades from the One like a light that fades away from the source, but at the same time the whole universe is gathered in the tension of the *epistrophé* (ἐπιστροφή), that is, in the attempt to reunite and dissolve its own finite multiplicity in the rising One. In Hegel, as we shall see, the subjective Spirit comes out of itself in order to objectify itself and thereby know itself. His dialectical movement is an upward spiral in which the Spirit goes through "the travail of the negative" in order to reappropriate itself to a more perfect degree of self-consciousness. Another kenotic model that we will examine in relation to Lévinas, that proposed by the kabbalist philosopher Isaac Luria (1534–1572), sees God withdrawing to let the world be in its independence, but human existence is only completed in *tikkun*, in the recovery and reintegration of the sparks of light exiled in the finite world. Mou finds this circularity at the very heart of Chinese thought, from Daoism to Neo-Confucianism. The intellectual insight by which the moral mind creates and knows its universe together is grounded in the retrospective verification *nijue tizheng* 逆覺體證, in which the term "backwardness" (*ni* 逆) expresses this movement back to the origin. For Mou, the priority of returning to primal harmony distinguishes Chinese thought from classical Western thought, in which the "Faustian man" is stretched forward in desire and pursuit of an often contradictory and unattainable ultimate goal.

5.3 Abyss and Sinkhole: Self-Limitation as Sinking

A final aspect worth addressing is that of Mou's use of spatial metaphors or terms involving spatiality in his attempt to define the nature of the *ziwo kanxian*. First of all, it must be said that Mou's language is often peppered with these terms and metaphors, yet it is easy to notice their thickening in the very texts, such as *Phenomenon and Thing-in-Itself* and *Intellectual Intuition and Chinese Philosophy*, in which the theory of the self-limitation of the moral ego finds its most mature expression. The very term *kanxian*, for example, can indicate a sinkhole[17] and self-conscious cratering. It is thus a kind of impluvium, or a point where, by the exercise of erosion or underground aquifers, the ground has sunk, creating a pit in which it

---

17 "The contemporary scholar Richard Lynn gives 'sink hole' as its basic meaning, and it is clear from a number of early commentaries that it has the connotation of water flowing through it. One such commentary also associates *kan* with the 'rain, by which things are moistened (*run*).' Flowing water and moistening are both positive-sounding, despite the negative connotations of sink hole. In addition, two of the earliest commentaries define *kan* as '*xian*,' or 'pit.' With all this in mind, we should think of *kanxian* primarily as a lowering and limitation, like sinking into a pit." Stephen Angle, *Contemporary Confucian Political Philosophy: Toward a Progressive Confucianism*, Malden, MA: Polity, 2012, p. 25.

is possible to become trapped. This is connected to other terms, such as inflection, which translate this element of the landscape into the terms of geometric space. Mou defines the level of the moral self in terms of flat ground or plain, so this sinking or inflection consistently describes the transition to the phenomenal dimension, which is characterized by the uneasy and potentially hindering curvatures of the multiplicity of beings. This passage occurs through what Mou sees as the cognitive tool par excellence, dialectical curvature, which allows us to embody or encompass the concreteness of beings. Remaining faithful to the metaphor and developing it in all its characteristics, we can deduce that the *kanxian* is a movement of descent and sinking, but it is not a sinking. The abyss (*Ungrund*) is produced where the bottom is missing, where the secret of being seems to be hidden in an infinite, obscure depth, in which the soul can only indefinitely precipitate without ever touching a bottom that makes the return possible.

The *abyssos*—in Greek ἄβυσσος, in German *Ungrund* or *Abgrund*—reappears like a karst river at nodal moments in the development of Western thought, indicating a transcendent and unattainable dimension. In the Greek translation of the Septuagint, *abyssos* is the inchoate watery whirlwind over which the Spirit of God rises at the beginning of Genesis. Already in medieval philosophy, Augustine sees in the expression of Psalm 42:7, "deep calls to deep" or in Latin *abyssus abyssum invocat*, a reference to the unattainable depth of the human soul: "What then is the "abyss" that calls, and to what other "abyss" does it call? If by "abyss" we understand a great depth, is not man's heart, do you not suppose, "an abyss"? For what is there more profound than that "abyss"?"[18] As medieval thought progressed, the expression "Deep calls to deep" increasingly refers to the self-annihilation of the soul in union with God, as in Johannes Tauler (c. 1300–1361): "*Abyssus abyssum invocat*, the abyss draw the abyss into itself. The abyss that is the created [thing] draws the Uncreated Abyss into itself and the two abysses become a Single One, a pure divine being, so that the spirit is lost in God's Spirit. It is drowned in the bottomless sea."[19] God and the soul are two abysses reflected like

---

18 St. Augustine of Hippo, *The Expositions on the Psalms*, trans. by Alexander Cleveland Coxe, Altenmünster: Jazzybee Verlag, 2012, n.p.

19 Ferdinand Vetter (ed.), *Die Predigten Täuler*, Zürich: Weidman, 1968, p. 174. I adopt the translation by Bernard McGynn, "Lost in the Abyss. The Function of Abyss

two mirrors in a literal *mise-en-abyme*, which for Jakob Böhme (1575–1624) is the manifestation of the One superessential to itself. German idealism will be particularly influenced by this suggestion. For Schelling it is in this abyss that the transcendence of the world and the interiority of the spirit coincide perfectly, as on a geometric point where nothing can be distinguished or differentiated. Hegel, taking up Böhme's intuition, affirms that the abyss is the point of origin of the process by which the Spirit becomes self-manifestation, so that, just as the Spirit of God cannot manifest itself without leaving its original source, the spirit of man must also come out of the abyss of its "unconscious source" in order to appear as soul and consciousness. In the twentieth century, the best-known rethinking of the abyss in an ontological sense is done by Martin Heidegger. In *Der Satz vom Grund*, he takes the medieval view of God elaborated by Meister Eckhart (c. 1260–1328) and Böhme, that is, his paradoxical being a foundation without a foundation, and applies it to Being. Whenever Being is used as a foundation or foundation, it ends up lowering itself to the level of being. I must therefore think of being in the groove of truth (*a-letheia*), that is, as something that hides itself in the unveiling of the world: "Each founding and already every appearance of foundability must degrade being to some being. Being as being remains ground-less. Ground remains apart and away from being, namely as its first founding ground. Being: the a-byss".[20] Finally, it is worth mentioning how the fascination with the unspeakable and mystical annihilation that seems to pervade many twentieth-century philosophers finds a salacious critic in György Lukács (1885–1971). Reflecting on the intellectuals of his time, particularly those of the so-called Frankfurt School, he accuses them of having replaced analytical rigor with endless and sterile arguments, intellectual drunkenness, and revolutionary voluntarism. To do so he creates the ultimate imaginative representation of the abyss, accusing the intelligentsia of his time of having taken up comfortable residence in the "Grand Hotel Abyss," a melancholic building whose balconies face a gaping abyss. To limit

---

Language in Medieval Mysticism," *Franciscan Studies* 72 (2014), 433–452 (p. 444).
20 Martin Heidegger, *Der Satz vom Grund (1955–1956)*, Frankfurt: Vittorio Klostermann, 1997, p. 166. Translation by Adam. C. Arola in "The Movement of Philosophy: Freedom as Ecstatic Thinking in Schelling and Heidegger," PhD Dissertation, University of Oregon, 2008, pp. 104–105.

oneself to standing on the brink and contemplating the paralyzing abyss of the ineffable and the insoluble is for Lukács the riskiest blind alley of thought.

Unspeakable, unmentionable, unconscious, mystical: the abyss, so frequently evoked in Western thought, is the absolute limit of knowledge, an endless perpendicular cut, which does not cross any horizontal plane. For those who pursue precisely the progressive horizontal of logic and knowledge, it is both frightening and paradoxical. It upsets at the root every foundational system. Whether it sinks into the darkness of the mind or rises up to break through the limit of the divine, it is always a step beyond any conceivable foundation. It requires a leap beyond rational logic, and with no guarantee of return. Somehow, it is simply the empty, limitless space in which all extreme thought experiments become possible. In Mou's philosophy, the one generated by the wedging of the *kanxian* is not an abyss, but precisely an inflection, a well, a hollow. Being a spontaneous and voluntary act of the moral mind, it cannot present itself as a catastrophic sinking that cuts the plane of spiritual being in two. It must necessarily contain a force of recollection in itself which is the signal of the self-consciousness of the moral self. If Mou sometimes speaks of trans-consciousness,[21] it is certainly not to indicate a loss of consciousness or a state of ecstasy. He only wants to reaffirm that on the moral-metaphysical level self-consciousness is not a reflex play between a subject-ego and an object-ego. The moral self knows itself retrospectively in the act of intellectual intuition with which it knows by acting what is the fruit of its creative activity. This retrospective intuition (*nijue* 逆覺) is not a secondary, temporally successive act, but is given in the very act of intellectual intuition. It is precisely this immediate backlash—that is, the fact that in manifesting its creative energy the moral self is present to itself—that shows us that the moral act is circular, involving a retroactive motion that leads back to the origin. This best explains the metaphor of wedging or inflecting.

---

21 For example, in Mou Zongsan (牟宗三), *Xinti yu xingti*. 心體與性體 (Constitutive Mind and Constitutive Nature), 3 vols, II, 550–554, in *Mou Zongsan xiansheng quanji*. 牟宗三先生全集 (Complete Works of Mou Zongsan), vols. V–VII, Taipei: Lianhe baoxi wenhua jijin hui, 2003. Mou speaks of trans-consciousness (*chao zijue* 超自覺) in order to indicate the synthesis between the subjective realm of moral practice and the objective realm of onto-cosmology.

If the moral mind accepts, in order to realize itself more fully and to overcome obstacles, to sink toward the cognitive dimension, characterized by the division between subject and object, it necessarily encounters and immerses itself in the empirical and phenomenal plane, that is, it actualizes and concretizes itself in it, without, however, going astray. This engagement in reality tends to collect what is dispersed and separated in the horizontal vastness of space-time in order to raise its value by bringing it back to that moral mind that is the source of all meaning and value. The descent of the *ziwo kanxian* 自我坎陷 is not an irrevocable fall and loss of self, it is not a bottomlessness. The phenomenal dimension, and the logical self that constitutes it through its *a priori* categories, forms the bottom. It is not a matter here, however, of a foundation or a plane external to the moral mind that it accidentally encounters, forcing it to stop. The foundation, the logical self and its empirical sphere, is constituted by the moral mind's wedging itself in. It accepts self-limiting itself to give itself a horizontal-noncognitive dimension that represents a background and a boundary, or rather, a self-confinement. It suspends itself, it clings to itself, it discloses an ontological plane characterized by attachment, it temporarily accepts stopping and stagnating. If we remained in the imaginary of the abyss, we would proceed infinitely without accepting a term. The term and the bottom produced by the *kanxian* in the very heart of the moral mind are the condition of possibility of an ascent, of a return to the moral level, of a smoothing out like that which is produced on the surface of a lake when the wind stops blowing.

The idea of the trap, of falling into a trap, contained in the range of meanings of the word *kanxian* refers us to the idea of a pit possessing a bottom and walls that never separate from the flat ground from which they originated. The relation between the finite self and the moral self is inscribed in the broader circular nature of creative moral action, and the attainment of an empirical bottom that can be analyzed with the categories of cognitive reason implies the tendency of the infinite self to transcend this bottom and return to the flat ground of detached ontology. The descending curve is therefore necessarily and seamlessly prolonged by an ascending curve. Adopting again the twofold phenomenal and noumenal viewpoint on the *kanxian* event, we can see that what is perceived as a sinking on the part of the moral self manifests itself in the cognitive self in exactly the reverse way, that is, as a protuberance. The logical mind protrudes like a mound, rigid in its nature as an almost "mineral" frame, so by the influence of external things it raises mental states, similar to small waves or ripples, and then, turning back, absorbs them as phenomena of internal sensibility. The image of the logical ego protruding like a mound from the flat earth, or that of the psychological ego rising like a series of fleeting waves generated in the inner sensibility, are the appearance seen in reverse of the sinkhole that the moral ego produces in its voluntary sinking.

The objection that could be raised to this focus on the spatial character of Mou's preferred metaphors is that they are incongruous and inadequate in describing the dialectical dynamism of the moral self. Space and time, in fact, are not predicable of the moral self, since for Mou, in continuity here with Kantian dictate, they are the *a priori* structures in which phenomena take shape and unfold. Space and time are figuratively represented by Mou himself in *Phenomenon and Thing-in-Itself* as a horizontal grid in which the phenomenal universe manifests itself. The questions that arise in this regard are twofold: 1. Why does Mou's language seem to privilege spatial imagery over temporal imagery? 2. Do the spatial metaphors that dot Mou's discourse contradict the supra-empirical nature of the moral mind?

Given the complexity of Mou's language, a complete answer to the first question transcends the limits of this discussion, and would require a separate study. However, staying within the framework of the *ziwo kanxian* analysis, it is worth mentioning that Hegel himself faces this difficulty, and precisely because of that "self-negation" (*Aufhebung*) that Mou points to as an appropriate translation of *ziwo kanxian*. In the final chapter of the *Phenomenology of Spirit*, Hegel has to deal with that "Absolute Spirit" to which the path of the human soul, through its many stages and dialectical negations, ultimately tends. We should have arrived here at the full harmonious unity of subject and object, of knower and known, without forgetting the process which led to this unity (oneness).[22] Here the Spirit can turn and see unfolded before him the

---

22 Christopher Lauer already identifies here a priority of space over time: "The Phenomenology of Spirit's final sacrifice moves in exactly the opposite direction, releasing the determinacy of the concept into both space and time, thus transforming the predominantly temporal way in which science conceives the

totality of his moments. It is that *Er-innung* or inwardizing recollection of which we spoke in the section on Hegel, through which the Spirit takes possession of all the passages that have generated it, recognizing their necessity and internalizing them in a self-conscious way. In seeing these passages unfold, what the Spirit first of all recognizes is that its self-denial, its sacrifice, its continual coming out of itself and tending beyond have been necessary movements for its development. The aspect that cannot be preserved and that must be overcome in the last negation, is their being given in temporal succession. Time, Hegel writes, is the very incompleteness of finite being, and the continual vanishing of instants and their replacement by new and equally fleeting instants is the very expression of self-denial and its restless projecting beyond. For the Absolute Spirit, becoming conscious of this presupposes a form of spatialization of time in the form of a gallery of self-images that must be ideally traversed and internalized. Even in the conclusion of the book, Hegel cannot help but retain spatial images such as extension, self-externalization, and especially depth: "this externalization is in its own self externalized (*daß diese Entäusserung sich an ihr selbst entäussert*), and just as it is in its extension (*Ausdehnung*), so it is equally in its depth, in the Self."[23] Although the indifferent and abstract spatiality of the empirical world is overcome here, we can say that space, understood as the interconnected structure of the Absolute, still plays a role.[24]

The mind that runs through the frames of its own history and searches for its nexus, or that is ultimately realized as depth, that is, universal interconnection, speaks to us of a qualitative space, a space of directions, structures, paths, which is very similar to that of the explanatory diagrams that Mou inserts in his texts as evidence of the "spatiality" of his own thought. But turning to Mou, we can see

---

necessity of its development into a form of thinking that can also conceive this development with the openness of space." Christopher Lauer, "Space, Time, and the Openness of Hegel's Absolute Knowing," *Idealistic Studies* 36:3 (2006), 169–181 (p. 175).

23 *Hegel's Phenomenology of Spirit*, trans. by A. V. Miller with an analysis of the text and foreword by J. N. Findlay, Oxford: Oxford University Press, 1977, p. 493.

24 "The depth of the world—its inner organization as conceptually mediated, rationally structured, and ethically binding—is revealed as the structure of ourselves as well." Jacob Blumenfeld, "Hegel's Absolute Knowledge and its Many Interpretations," Unpublished Article, 2012, p. 49, https://www.academia.edu/3755446/Hegels_Absolute_Knowledge_and_its_Many_Interpretations

that the spatial metaphors of the Absolute have an even more cogent justification than the Hegelian one. By analyzing the concept of *jingjie*, state of mind or landscape of the soul, we have seen how the moral mind can be described for the one who travels through it in his effort of elevation to sanctity, as a hodological space, that is, a space traveled, experienced, explored. The verticality of moral action and the horizontality of knowing are not mere linguistic devices, but give us back an idea of mind and world transfigured into a field of spiritual action. The Confucian moral metaphysics elaborated by Mou absorbs and brings to a more coherent completion the Daoist metaphysics of *jingjie*. It is no longer merely a spiritual wandering but a realization that is as subjective as it is objective. Wedging and descending, protruding and wrinkling, rising and returning are the dynamic structure of a landscape of the spirit imbued with moral meaning. It is no longer just a structure of logical relationships, according to Mou's critique of Hegel, but a vital, co-responsive, creative interconnection, that of the Holy One that encloses the universe, and that is the task and the truth of our action.

5.4 *Kenosis* as Alienation: Hegel and Mou

Hegel represents an important point of reference for Mou. The English translation of *kanxian* proposed by Mou himself is the term *self-negation*. Other authors, however, believe that the technical term "negation" in Hegel has connotations that risk obscuring the meaning of the neologism *kanxian*, forged on the basis of the rich imaginative language of the *Yijing* (易經 *Classic of Changes*). Personally, I share the hesitations in this regard, as well as the problematic nature of other possible translations, such as *self-restriction*, that are semantically closer to Mou's intentions but lack direct correlation with Hegelian language. Putting aside these linguistic considerations, and staying in the strictly philosophical sphere, it can be said that there are in the Hegelian dialectic other related concepts that can be juxtaposed to the idea of *kanxian*, which provide a basis for a comparison between the two kenotic models of Hegel and Mou. Chief among such concepts is that of alienation (*Entäusserung*), present throughout Hegel's work but, with particular prominence, in the *Phenomenology of Spirit*. The main element of affinity between Mou's moral metaphysics and the Hegelian dialectical system lies in the dynamic and processual nature of their supreme principle. For both, the True and the Absolute are something that is accomplished through a dynamism that is the self-realization of Spirit itself. Initially, the Spirit aspires to find a principle to guide its actions, and it seeks it in the objective world outside itself, making itself a slave to earthly goods or even to the most sublime ideals, such as a God who is transcendent and unattainable. Only when the Spirit progresses dialectically, denying every division and finding in itself the principle and source of its action, does it recognize itself for the first time and reach self-realization. The Absolute, then, is nothing static and objective that can be grasped from the outside. The Absolute is the very process of becoming absolute, and this can only come about by accepting what Hegel calls "the travail of the negative." The Spirit must at every step alienate itself from itself, forget its identity with the original principle, and go through all its contradictions. It must lose and find itself again, extending itself in ever-widening concentric circles, until it restores the identity between itself and things, not in the original form of indistinction but in that of the final and conscious reunification of the whole in the movement of Spirit itself. The True is therefore not a mere result that leaves behind all its own evolutionary stages, qualifying them as errors, but it is the whole that is accomplished only by passing through each of these stages in order to be able finally to consciously sum them all up in itself, not in their empirical randomness but as conceptual figures.

The point of maximum similarity between the Hegelian approach and that of Mou lies in the fact that both conceive the Absolute as subjective, that is, as an organic unfolding of life that returns to itself reflexively: "In my view, which must be justified by the exposition of the system itself, everything hangs on grasping and expressing the true not just as substance but just as much as subject."[25] The terms "subject" and "subjective," here as in Mou, do not indicate the partiality of the logical-cognitive subject, which is indissolubly connected to the object of its knowledge, but the characteristics proper to the authentic spiritual subject, that is, dynamism, creativity, inexhaustible generation of self-conscious life. Both are opposed to the absolutization of the finite I, as it is presented in Kant, i.e., as a purely abstract synthetic function

---

25   Georg Wilhelm Friedrich Hegel, *The Phenomenology of Spirit*, Cambridge, UK, and New York: Cambridge University Press, 2018, p. 12.

that fails to grasp the thing-in-itself, because as a human subject, finite and non-creator, it does not possess the capacity to penetrate reality through intellectual intuition. Hegel also wants to distance himself from the idealistic Fichtian ego, which in its attempt to generate reality is condemned to eternally oppose a non-ego, which is an ever-resurgent obstacle. From Mou's point of view, it is a matter of keeping open that door of authentic subjectivity that Confucianism has opened by placing the "mind of benevolence" (renxin 仁心) as the origin of the moral universe. Speaking of substance, Hegel is thinking of Baruch Spinoza's unique, divine, uncreated substance, which is the ontological foundation of everything but lacks self-conscious reflection and is therefore incapable of becoming actively concrete: "This Idea of Spinoza's we must allow to be in the main true and well-grounded; absolute substance is the truth, but it is not the whole truth; in order to be this it must also be thought of as in itself active and living, and by that very means it must determine itself as mind. But substance with Spinoza is only the universal and consequently the abstract determination of mind."[26]

To think of the Absolute as a living subject is not to deny the objective regulative foundation that substance represents, but to unify both aspects into a self-conscious totality. The doctrine of mind and substantial nature (xinxinglun 心性論) that Mou elaborated in *Constitutive Mind and Constitutive Nature* represents in this respect a considerable theoretical advance in understanding this living and processual unity of mind and substance. The critical target for him is not the Spinozian *Deus sive Natura*, that is, the absolute thought of as a unique, perfect, ubiquitous, and immutable substance. However Mou, in criticizing Zhu Xi, particularly his idea of the transcendent regulating principle to which a mind—always limited and obscured by the qi (氣) energy that constitutes it—yearns, develops the idea of a living interconnection between mind and the foundation of being that has many points in common with the Hegelian Absolute Spirit. For Mou, too, the True can only be the spiritual and its subtle and inexhaustible creative function. It is not by chance that Mou sees in post-Kantian idealism an overcoming of the limits that Kant imposed on reason, an overcoming that goes in

---

[26] Georg Wilhelm Friedrich Hegel, *Hegel's Lectures on the History of Philosophy*, Volume 3, translated by E. S. Haldane and Frances H. Simpson, London: Routledge and Kegan Paul Ltd, 1955, p. 257.

the direction of that fusion of being and dynamism, that is, of substance and spirit that his moral metaphysics pursues. On the basis of this explicit indication by Mou, it is all the more interesting to compare the idea of the Subjective Absolute that Hegel and Mou develop, and to mark the differences between them, beginning with the key theme of the self-limitation (or alienation) of the Absolute in the finite self.

The term "alienation" translates two different terms of Hegelian language: *Entfremdung*, that is, the condition of one who is or becomes alienated from oneself, and *Entäusserung*, that is, self-externalization. As Gavin Rae summarizes: "'*Entfremdung*' describes a process or state where consciousness is separated from, at least, one of the aspects that are required for consciousness to fully understand itself. In contrast, '*Entäusserung*' describes the process whereby consciousness externalizes itself in object form and, through this objectification, develops a better understanding of itself."[27] In both cases, this is a necessary and inevitable dynamic for Spirit to come to self-knowledge. In the *Phenomenology of Spirit*, Hegel writes: "Spirit is the knowledge of itself through its own emptying." This emptying out or alienation is the necessary passage through the "travail of the negative" that the Spirit must go through in order for all that is concrete, empirical, partial to free itself from its own determinacy and partiality and to draw on the truth of itself as self-conscious substance. The experience of the negative or of self-alienation, therefore, is a structural moment in the generative process of the Spirit: it must experience its own boundaries, understand that it has generated them and absorb them into itself by going beyond them.

The self-limitation of the moral ego in Mou is also a structural and inevitable step in its own coming to completion, since the self-limiting "descent" into the logical ego serves to acquire that knowledge of reality without which moral action could not fully materialize. Can we compare this to the self-alienation of the Spirit in the Hegelian sense? As we have seen, this work of the negative has two possible meanings, one predominantly passive and the other active and freely chosen. Estrangement is a condition in which consciousness comes to find itself and which it undergoes, since it does not yet know that it generated it.

---

27   Gavin Rae, "Hegel, Alienation, and the Phenomenological Development of Consciousness," *International Journal of Philosophical Studies* 20:1 (2012), 23–42 (p. 30).

A significant example also for the purpose of comparison with Mou is that of the "unhappy consciousness." At this stage of development, consciousness, which does not yet know that it is a living unity of subjective and objective, builds up an ideal image of itself as pure and perfect freedom unmixed with earthly affairs. This ideal is projected outside itself as God, or the unattainable limit of perfection. It is in fact a pure "limit" without content, since consciousness has created it by abstracting it from the contradictions and imperfection of concrete life. In setting this model outside itself, consciousness deludes itself into thinking that it has thereby found an ideal that drives it to continually perfect itself in an attempt to identify with it. But here arises the contradiction: the perfect ideal cut off from life must be moved ever higher, because in its ascetic movement of self-purification, consciousness finds itself again and again mired in evidence of its own imperfection. Falling back into its own ascetic momentum and engaged in purifying itself of all contamination with the real, consciousness turns into a continual self-scrutiny. In doing so, it forces itself into its own interiority, expelling from itself every trace of its contaminating relationship with the world. On the one hand, therefore, it becomes more and more interiorized, sinking into itself and enclosing itself in an inner sphere that refuses all mixing with the world. On the other hand, it tries to mirror itself in a model of perfection that it has unconsciously projected into its own "sky" as absolute and therefore unattainable perfection. The "Unhappy Consciousness" is characterized by *Sehnsucht*, by nostalgia and an ever-unfulfilled aspiration toward a perfect version of itself, a transcendent divine that is eternally enfranchised by what in its everyday life appears as inessential, transient, and therefore worthless. An ever-widening abyss divides between being and ought-to-be, between the mutable and the immutable, and existential unhappiness is nourished precisely by this dualism, insofar as the subject is defined by the relation to a transcendence to which he can only aspire without reaching it. Mou Zongsan had identified this "Faustian" restlessness at the very heart of Western thought, in a tension toward a transcendent God that the finite subject cannot embody. The predetermined impossibility of becoming God condemns, in his opinion, spiritual and ascetic practice to the "infinite evil" of a restless search that feeds on the desperation of never being, by definition, equal to one's ideal.

This condition of self-inflicted checkmate can only be overcome if the subject becomes aware that he is at the origin of the contradiction, and that the divine perfection already dwells in him who generated it. In this case, then, we have a self-extraction that the consciousness experiences as frustration and unfulfilled tension, and it is precisely this restlessness that drives the consciousness to go further. In most of the stages described by the *Phenomenology of Spirit*, being foreign to oneself is a passive condition that the subject merely endures. If we return to the *Critique of the Cognitive Mind*, we see that Mou had prefigured this unfulfillment as one of the possible engines that drives the subject to hypothesize a metaphysical mind that precedes and exceeds it. Remaining on the cognitive-horizontal plane, this leap toward the beyond remained purely voluntaristic. Only on the transcendent vertical plane of moral action, in fact, does the infinite mind cease to be a postulate and manifest itself in us as the authentic reality of our deepest being. Alienation understood as self-extraction does not, therefore, correspond to that self-limitation of the moral ego that we seek, since the moral mind voluntarily and consciously accepts stripping itself of its own infinitude and self-trap itself in the finite ego. The purpose that moves it, moreover, is wholly positive, that is, the accomplished realization of self in every thing and event in the world, not the aching dissatisfaction with the finiteness of the real. We can recover this idea of estrangement only in a second moment, as a potential motivation that prevents the ego from totally forgetting itself in the dispersion of concrete situations, and impels it to restore the fullness of the moral ego that is its authentic reality.

The second mode of self-limitation, namely *Entäusserung* or externalization, possesses a greater resemblance to the self-limitation of the moral ego. For this mode is active and voluntary, and is constitutive of the life of the Spirit. As Hegel writes, "[...] spirit is knowledge of itself in its self-externalization." This movement of externalization, that is, of exit from one's limited self in the direction of what is other, is the motor of the dialectical process, and implies a kenotic emptying that is not unilateral but reciprocal, because it requires the pairs of opposites that always reappear in the evolution of consciousness to abandon all attachment and overcome themselves in their own infinite reunification. "Spirit has two aspects in it, which are represented above as two converse propositions. One is this, that *substance* relinquishes itself of its own self and becomes self-consciousness; the other, conversely, is that *self-consciousness* empties itself of itself and makes itself into thinghood, or into the universal self."[28] Therefore, it is not only self-consciousness, i.e., the "for itself" that is called upon to divest itself of its partial content, but also the polarity of the substance, i.e., that the being "in itself" must come out of its *enclosure* and abstract identity with itself in order to become self-conscious. The spirit is this living and never totally completed synthesis in which subject and object, self and world, self-conscious mind and substance renounce their own partiality and refer back to each other. The externalization of self-consciousness in particular requires a self-objectification that gives substance to the subjective, but at the same time requires that consciousness lose itself in order to find itself in the objectivity of its own actions and manifestations. Hegel does not exclude the possibility of a loss of the subject in the being of things. A significant example is that developed in the critique of phrenology and physiognomy with which *Observing Reason* culminates. Through these two pseudo-sciences the observational reason underlying the Scientific Revolution seeks to find a perfect correspondence between the multiple cranial regions and specific spiritual activities. In this case, self-objectification reaches an extreme point where, as Hegel summarizes, "The being of Spirit is a bone"[29] and the human subject cannot be reflected in the opaque and inert mirror of matter: "In the presence of a skull, one can surely think of many things, just like Hamlet does with Yorick's, but the skull-bone for itself is such an indifferent, unencumbered thing that there is nothing else immediately to be seen in it nor to think about; there is just it itself."[30] The element of interest here is the prophetic dismantling of any possibility of establishing a correspondence between subjective states and the objective reality of the brain, a position that, as we saw in the introduction, sometimes reappears today in cognitive science as a search for the "neural correlates of consciousness." In the *Phenomenology of Spirit* this risk of self-externalizing and losing oneself without return is overcome only by leaving observational reason behind and proceeding toward active reason. It is a matter of taking a leap

---

28 Hegel, *The Phenomenology of Spirit*, p. 433.
29 Ibid., p. 201.
30 Ibid., p. 194.

forward and recognizing that subject-object unity is not given but must be created through the subject's engagement with the world.

What, then, can we conclude about the relationship between Hegelian alienation, in its double aspect of *Entäusserung* and *Entfremdung*, of going out of oneself in order to find oneself and of always discovering oneself as a stranger to one's own being, and the movement of the self-limitation of the moral self theorized by Mou? A common element resides, as we have seen, in defining themselves with respect to a turn, the Kantian and the Confucian, in the direction of the subject. The subjective, understood as the self-conscious process of the making of the Spirit, becomes the foundation of the real, the fusion of mind and nature. A second aspect is the valorization of the "travail of the negative," whereby this supreme mind cannot be transcendent and abstractly detached from reality, but in the process of its constitution requires immersion, commitment, and continuous mediation with concreteness. The third aspect is the necessity of the continuous overcoming of all finite embodiment and of all determinacy in the direction of a unification between opposites. The Absolute is for both the Whole, the synthesis that crosses, recomposes, and brings to truth the roughness of reality.

Equally and perhaps more pregnant still are the radical differences between Hegelian alienation and the *kanxian* of the moral mind according to Mou. It may first be objected that the self-limitation of the moral mind in Mou represents a contracting and descending into the horizontal domain of attachment by a higher principle. As such, it presents the structural features of a "kenotic" event in the traditional and etymological sense. Hegelian alienation, on the other hand, is an exit from the self and a leaping beyond by a subject who is still incapable of grasping itself as a unity of mind and things. Apparently it seems to move in the opposite direction, from bottom to top, from the illusorily self-forgetful self toward the Absolute Spirit. This different direction, from the contingent to the Absolute, must not, however, make us forget that the Spirit is not only a goal to be reached, but is a process in the act of its fulfillment. Alienation, too, is therefore kenotic, because it is the very movement of the Spirit, it belongs to its constitutive structure. It is improper to speak here of a teleological dynamism, in which everything tends toward a *télos*, a higher goal, and every stage of the approach is purely instrumental and must be abandoned in the ascent. Nevertheless, it is indisputable that Hegel posits Spirit as the end of the process. The ontological time of the Spirit is that of the "not yet accomplished," of the becoming that "is being accomplished" in each imperfect step of the ascent, without ever coinciding perfectly with itself, and therefore always called upon to deny itself, to sink. In Mou, the absolute ego is one with the origin. Its dimension is not that of "not yet," but of "already since ever," even if this "being already since ever" should not be thought of as a perennial and static divine substance. As we have seen, it is in the principle from the point of view of value, and unity of being and movement. To go toward the Absolute is to return to something that has been flowing always, to place oneself in the beginning, to have in oneself the capacity to begin "always anew." It is a generating power, vivifying and germinating, for which Mou uses expressions related to spring, such as the "awakening of insects." This beginning is also such from the practical-moral point of view: It guarantees that the motion of the will of the agent is free and always active and reborn, and therefore that free will is not a Kantian postulate, but a full and uninterrupted manifestation.

The Hegelian Spirit and Mou's absolute ego are two different ways of being beyond chronological time but necessarily having to pass through time in order to be realized, preceding and exceeding it. However, this necessity is different in the two authors. In the *Phenomenology of Spirit*, the necessity of the process is objective, in the sense that all pairs of opposites inevitably end up denying themselves, contradicting themselves, and going beyond. This alienation, which Hegel calls "the travail of the negative," must take place in order for the process to continue and not stop. The process is the making of Spirit, of the absolute, of the whole, and it alone is real. Finite consciousness and its determinate world collapse at every stage of development, because in their limitedness and opposition they are partial, and therefore not real and illusory. Although the absolute is a self-conscious subject who must absorb and recover all reality, the engine of the process is the inevitable dissolution of the negative, like a dream from which the Spirit must awaken again and again. We are here in the sphere, to use Mou's terms, of the horizontal-conscious. The will of the Spirit is the will to know itself reflexively, and this mirroring and recognition in the fleeting reflection of things and of finite consciousness is not the result of freedom, but is determined by what the spirit necessarily is, that is, infinite self-knowledge. Although Hegel reiterates that Spirit is the perfect fusion of the subjective and the objective, there seems to be here a prevalence of the "objective" and "necessitated" aspect. The reason lies in the negativity of the finite, which contradicts itself, does not stand in itself, and has no necessity of being. The only non-illusory reality is the advance of Spirit from awakening to awakening. All the finite must be traversed and recomposed by Spirit, but this does not give it any autonomous positivity. The finite must annihilate itself in order to become infinite, that is, Spirit.

If we take a closer look at Mou's absolute ego, we also see here a synthesis of voluntariness and necessity. The ego must self-limit itself in order to fully realize itself in the finite, but since we have moved here to a vertical-moral plane, what is most highlighted is the free will of the moral ego to self-limit itself in order to realize itself, that is, its subjective aspect. Freedom is perfect autonomy, that is, being to oneself one's own principle and law. This is what is gained in both authors by going beyond the insuperable gap between being and ought-to-be, which is the legacy of Kantian thought, but the prevalence of the cognitive and reflective model causes Spirit in Hegel to pass from illusion to illusion, to be foreign to itself (in the sense of *Entfremdung*) until it is perfectly reflected and owned in this reflection. The finite, that is, every partial stage left behind, is not totally forgotten, but remembered (*er-innert*) as part of itself. What is saved, however, is not the living concreteness of each moment but its logical truth. It is conquered precisely in the annihilation of the finite, which survives as a conceptual skeleton, deprived of its carnal solidity. Its truth, that is, its contribution to the whole, is the particular logical mode of its own overcoming.

In Mou's case, the finite as such is already included in the moral ego understood as an active and creative process. The finite is the place of manifestation and realization, and thus possesses its specific ontological and metaphysical value. The finite is therefore not an abstraction that removes itself from itself, but possesses a positive content. In a totality that is not cognitive-reflexive like that of the Hegelian Spirit, but performative and moral, the finite fact (*shi* 事) is the event of the fulfillment and concretization of moral action. What Hegel calls *Er-innerung*, that is, recapitulating in oneself all the stages of one's formation through a mnemonic-abstractive process, aims at recovering the traces of one's passage and purifying them by retaining their truth, that is, their conceptual skeleton. The finite is left behind; what is saved is its negative imprint, the memory of its own erasure. We cannot say the same about the place of the finite in moral dynamism. The moral mind goes through it and saves it in its "being-in-itself," in its absolute value. Such value comes to it from not being external and opposed to the ego as the object of knowledge is, but from being a constitutive part of the moral ego, that which cannot be forgotten or left behind. As long as the finite world is included in the totality of action, it is in the moral ego as its concrete becoming and as the expression of its capacity for infinite generation. Only if the moral thought-action in which every thing and every ego is interconnected and vibrates in resonance with the specificity of every other being, is interrupted and decays to pure desire for knowledge, does the thing become *ob-jectum*, that which is outside and opposed. In this case, that which is finite loses its value in itself and becomes an instrument, negativity to be traversed and transcended in view of a supreme end, it becomes foreign to the self. *Entfremdung* represents precisely this loss of self, a place where the ego perceives itself as outside itself, estranged, and yearns to return to a dwelling that is always beyond.

In Mou's thought, however, it is not the finite-infinite dualism that counts, but that between attachment and autonomy. Self-limitation is not a finite becoming but the descent into that state of being that Mou calls attached ontology. With attachment, the realm of the "outside" is inaugurated. The logical self projects the world as outside of itself, as an object opposed to itself and as an instrument in view of knowledge. It can no longer find moral principles within itself and make itself its own principle and law; it must conform and tend to an external law. This descent, this impaneling into finitude cannot be merely a decay with no return. If the moral self is law unto itself, this self-limitation must be voluntary, which is why in the way Mou describes it, it is the subjective of freedom, the engaging in the world so that nothing remains behind that prevails. In the preface to the *Phenomenology of Spirit*, Hegel states that "The true is the whole. However, the whole is only the essence completing itself through its own development. This much must be said of the absolute: It is essentially a *result*, and only at the *end* is it what it is in truth. Its nature consists just in this: to be actual, to be subject, or, to be the becoming-of-itself."[31] Paraphrasing him, we can say that for Mou, too, the true is the becoming of itself (i.e., its own being synthesis of being and movement), it is real in each of its events of fulfillment and manifestation. When moral action is accomplished, when one's own infinite nature becomes evident in the concern for all things, the vertical of action intersects the horizontal of reality. This point of intersection is not only "at the end," but is a fulfillment that can take place at any instant.

To conclude, both Hegel and Mou can claim that the true is the whole, and that the true is a process. Both accept the unity of being and movement and the circular nature of that movement, but for Hegel the circularity is that of Spirit, which only in the end recomposes the finite as negated and surpassed, and by reflecting finally arrives at full self-knowledge. The unity of subject and object that was in the beginning, but abstract, undifferentiated and not self-conscious, is finally accomplished as a real, complex, and conscious unification at the terminal point. The circularity of Mou's moral mind, on the other hand, is manifested and made true and verifiable at every instant, because the true is at the origin. The origin, as Mou often reiterates, does not have a chronological value, but a "value value." That is to say, it has the creative power of being always inexhaustibly gushing out, on condition that the human being knows how to incarnate it (*ti* 體) and make it the substance of himself and of his actions. The human is not, as Novalis wrote in summing up Romantic-Idealist thought, "the stranger with eyes full of meaning," and *Entfremdung* or estrangement is not a necessary condition of his being. The human is the third between earth and heaven, and this original dwelling in the center is realized whenever, in moral action, it fulfills its mediating nature. The circularity of the process in Mou is expressed as a fourfold direction. On the metaphysical level, the moral ego proceeds forward as an endless generation, and in order not to lose itself in plurality and attachment, it must simultaneously return back to the truth of its own being. On the moral level, the human is called to move upward on a path of self-cultivation, which is also a momentum of liberation from attachment and from thinking the world and self as

---

31   Ibid., p. 12.

external and opposed. Moving downward, moral action is an effort at concretization that restores the unity and interrelatedness of things. Stating that the supreme principle is the moral self shows that for Mou the metaphysical and moral planes are not distinct. To actively maintain the circularity of these four directions is to restore the absolute value of the universe, to affirm the unity of transcendence and immanence. For the human being who engages morally in the world, it is not an endless desire to return home from alienation, but to discover that he has always been home, and that he has his place in the creative center of the universe.

5.5 *Kenosis* as "Making Space for the Other": *Tzimtzum* and Lévinas

Lévinas' thought echoes another kenotic model that exerted a great influence on nineteenth- and twentieth-century Western philosophy: that of divine self-retraction. It finds its paradigmatic formulation in the work of Luria. One of the crucial questions that Jewish kabbalistic philosophy had to face was that of the relationship between the Creator God and the created world. Beginning with the commentary on Genesis 1:1: "In the beginning God created the heavens and the earth," earlier kabbalists had focused on the first part of the sentence, attempting to decode what happened "in the beginning" and "within the beginning," that is, what dynamic prompted God to abandon the unspeakable and obscure mystery of his perfection in order to emanate something from himself, revealing himself in his creation. Luria is credited with introducing into this debate the revolutionary concept of *tzimtzum*, from the Hebrew "concentration" or "contraction."[32] According to Luria, originally God (also referred to as *Ein Sof*, Infinite One) filled the totality of being in the stillness of His unlimited presence. If no event had occurred in the heart of the divine, the world and its creatures could never have come into existence, since any hypothetical difference or determination would have been immediately absorbed into the ubiquitous fullness of the One. In order for a being distinct from God to exist, it was necessary for a radical transformation to take place in God's

---

32 See Gerschom Scholem, *Major Trends in Jewish Mysticism*, Stuttgart: Schocken, 1995.

own ontological nature. Such a transformation is what Luria designates as *tzimtzum*, i.e., a voluntary self-recruitment of God to leave an empty space in which the world can emerge in its independence. More specifically, in the Lurianic scheme, God concentrates his infinite light almost by sinking into himself, leaving, in his retreat and condensation, an empty space at the center of himself. God therefore performs a voluntary self-limitation, surrounding the empty space like a circular horizon. From it, Luria continues, a subtle ray of God's diminished light feeds like a fountain the finite reality that can now appear and be preserved in its finitude. The traditional doctrine of "Creation from Nothing" is thus reinterpreted by Luria as a two-stage process: in the first stage, there is the creation of nothingness itself by virtue of God's withdrawal and absenting himself; in the second stage, there is the generation of the world, which is accomplished, as in Neoplatonism, by means of a concentric-circle emanation of the various realms of the world (called Sephirot).

We are here in the presence of a further kenotic model that seeks to account for the relationship between the infinite and finite things. The hypothesis of *tzimtzum*, among those considered, is the one closest to the original meaning of the Greek term *kenosis*—that is, emptying. *Ein Sof* is perfect fullness and without limit, but it is precisely this fullness, this saturation of being that prevents the other-from-God from emerging and asserting himself. By withdrawing into himself, God frees the possibility of the finite, of difference, of distance and temporality, and guarantees their autonomous positivity. The two stages, God's absenting Himself from a point at the center of His own being, and the emanation of the finite ray of light that will give substance to the created world, reflect a widespread view in the Kabbalah, namely the idea that there is in God a dual rhythm, of systole and diastole, revelation and concealment. *Tzimtzum*, however, places the fulcrum of creation in the negative moment of God's withdrawal, of his paradoxical absence that allows finite beings to enjoy full autonomy, to the point of confronting God or even disowning him. Lévinas writes provocatively that "it is certainly a great glory for the Creator to have set up a being capable of atheism."[33] The generative gift that God gives to the human is to

---

33 Emmanuel Lévinas, *Totality and Infinity. An Essay on Exteriority*, Pittsburgh, PA: Duquesne University Press, 1969, p. 58.

emancipate him from his ubiquitous presence, allowing him to inhabit a universe that obeys finite laws accessible to the human mind, and to unfold his own freedom without being crushed by divine intervention, even to the point of doubting that anything exists beyond the horizon of his own existence.

Emmanuel Lévinas starts from Edmund Husserl's phenomenology and from the Heideggerian understanding of philosophy as ontology. The self understood as an unceasing work of self-identification, by which we are driven to find ourselves in everything that happens to us, emerges against the background of an anonymous being. This being, which Lévinas refers to as the "il y a," is what Heidegger has the merit of having discovered as the weave of the real from which every existent tries to emerge in its singularity. This being that precedes all, even the subject and its capacity for signification, is an unrepresentable and undifferentiated totality. Lévinas dramatically perceives this motionless presence of being, which is pure verb without noun, that is to say, it is an omnipresent act that continues in the eternity of its being, and reabsorbs every attempt of the existing to emerge and assert itself within its own boundaries. This totality that invades everything calls to mind the dizzying intuition of the real that thunders the protagonist of Jean-Paul Sartre's *Nausea*: "And then all at once, there it was, clear as day: existence had suddenly unveiled itself. It had lost harmless look of an abstract category: it was the dough out of which things were made, this root was kneaded into existence. Or rather the root, the park gates, the bench, the patches of grass, all that had vanished: the diversity of things, their individuality, were only an appearance, a veneer. This veneer had melted, leaving soft, monstrous lumps, in disorder—naked, with a frightful and obscene nakedness."[34] This vertiginous discovery of the anonymous depths of being to which everything is destined to return, reveals the illusory nature of the appearances I perceive, of the names I have imposed on things, and of myself, who presumptuously believed I was a unique and irreplaceable individual. If we are fleeting ripples of an ocean that ignores us and that irretrievably closes in on us, how can we escape from this anonymous and endless expanse?

---

34 Jean-Paul Sartre, *Nausea*, trans. by Lloyd Alexander, New York: New Directions, 1964, pp. 127–128.

Lévinas evokes Husserl and his phenomenology. What it promises is the possibility of "bracketing" everything by which I am passively enveloped in everyday life, and witnessing the constitutive instant in which the subject and things are simultaneously born into the intentionality of consciousness. If Husserl posits the cognitive act as primary, Lévinas believes that we can go deeper into the elementarity of existence. The subject is first and foremost need and enjoyment that arises from the satisfaction of need. Such satisfaction arises from my ability to situate myself at home in the world, affirming my centrality and assimilating the other into the same. As the pulsating center of life, I project around me the horizon that will allow me to make sense of the world. Through work and economy, I will forge a way in which all things are usable. Through knowledge, I will bring everything back to me and to the fulcrum of my self-awareness, giving it a name and a meaning, that is, a relationship to my existing and to the horizon of totality that is given to my thinking. But have I really founded an autonomous and permanent subject through this horizon of meaning? Isn't the continuous grasping onto life and bringing everything that is other than me back into the Same that I am, a reproduction of that nameless and faceless totality of being to which I inevitably end up returning? Am I really constituted in my uniqueness and individuality if what moves me is the logic of the Same that assimilates the other, projecting a horizon that appropriates everything and sends it back to me, and from which I cannot escape?

According to Lévinas, there is only one thing that escapes this logic, and that is the appearance of the face of the other. The other bursts into my life as what is subtracted from my control, what is irrevocably foreign. If I try to grasp it and bring it back to my horizon, it pulls back, recedes, escapes me. At the same time it returns, never defeated, to shatter the horizon of my egoism, to question me from a place that is beyond any space that I can elect as my dwelling. In this questioning he calls me back to my responsibility, to my unique and irreplaceable being, to a freedom that does not come from me and is not reducible to my enjoyment. The appearance of the face of the other is not a possible experience, but an absolute moral call that draws me outside of myself and my horizon, undoes my world, disturbs me and awakens me. This other and the call "do not kill," which is one with the exposed nakedness of his face, is an excess that I cannot recompress, it is the manifestation of something absolutely external to me, of a transcendence that is such because it eludes my grasp, it continues to recede toward an unspeakable outside. This retreat that disrupts every totality of meaning is the image of *tzimtzum*. In it and for it I experience the face to face, the unbridgeable distance that opens up the empty space of my freedom, the infinite difference that reveals itself beyond the anonymity of being. "Infinity is produced by withstanding the invasion of a totality, in a contraction that leaves a place for the separated being. Thus, relationships that open up a way outside of being take form. An infinity that does not close in upon itself in a circle but withdraws from the ontological extension so as to leave a place for a separated being exists divinely. Over and beyond the totality it inaugurates a society. The relations that are established between the separated being and Infinity redeem what diminution there was in the contraction creative of Infinity."[35] The apparition of the face of the other occurs through the human other who approaches me with his corporeity and with the recognizable features of a concrete face—Lévinas recalls the language of the Bible, citing those who in it represent poverty and dereliction par excellence, that is, the orphan, the widow, and the stranger—but he does not reduce the face to the somatic features that would make it identifiable to my knowledge. In the shocking experience of the face, I do not look, but for the first time I am looked at. On the one hand, the face of another unexpectedly bursts into my vital horizon, it comes close to me in questioning me; on the other hand, what makes the face such is its mode of being, that of an infinite retraction.

If the phenomenon is what we see and constitute by relating it to the totality of meaning that has its center in us, in our enjoyment and in our will to know, the face is the noumenon par excellence. It is the thing-in-itself, which escapes the grasp of our thinking, it is uniqueness and absolute novelty, for which there are no common names or categories to which it can be referred. The face puts an end to the domain of interpretation, because in the passivity of my being seen, I am no longer the meaning-giving subject. I am forcibly pulled out of myself, and bound to a relationship with others that precedes my birth

---

35   Emmanuel Lévinas, *Totality and Infinity*, p. 104.

as a self-conscious subject. The moral imperative "Thou shalt not kill" that imposes itself on me in the elusive nakedness of the face, calls me out of the unthinkable "being outside myself," empowers me, by its attraction makes me a subject of desire. In the domain of what I use and understand there is no distance, everything is referred to me. The distance, the empty space of *tzimtzum*, is opened for the first time by the irruption of others, and maintained by their continuous receding and offering me no hold. In this distance I am an I that comes out of itself and responds, and in this responsivity my subject being is grounded and freed from the anonymous totality of being. For this reason Lévinas believes that metaphysics cannot be constructed on the basis of knowledge but only on the basis of ethics, of this leaning out of myself toward the transcendent other who calls me and awakens me: "We call ethics a relation between two terms where one and the other are united neither by a synthesis of the intellect, nor by the relation of subject to object, and where nevertheless one benefits or matters or is signifier to the other, where they are bound by an intrigue that knowledge could neither exhaust nor untangle." The only possible infinity is that which cannot be a projection of the finite. It makes itself present, it is an impelling presence, but it does not give itself to thought, because it is always already absent and portrayed, attracting me beyond. The infinite cannot be thought but only enacted face to face (facing), in being in front, in welcoming, and in fraternal action. "To think the infinite, the transcendent, the Stranger, is hence not to think an object. But to think what does not have the lineaments of an object is in reality to do more or better than think."[36]

5.6 Tremor and Awakening: Mou and Lévinas

The comparison between the kenotic models of Mou and Lévinas must therefore focus on the way in which transcendence becomes experiential in the domain of what is empirical. Indeed, a fascinating correspondence between Mou and Lévinas lies in the way in which the ethical encounter with others is produced. For both authors we are outside of intentional knowledge, that by which I assimilate the other as a particular object of

---

[36] Ibid., p. 49.

my reflection. The encounter with the other and the establishment of an ethical relationship is something that unsettles my being in the depths, awakens me from the inertia of my mind of habit, announces to me the giving of something that is infinite and I cannot appropriate. This original experience of transcendence draws me out of my finite self in a sudden and unpredictable way, like a beast that attacks me leaping from the thicket. Mou designates it with the term tremor (*zhendong* 震動), which can also be translated as *earthquake*. The shaking (*Zhen* 震) is also the 51st hexagram of the *Yijing*, composed of the character of rain, and therefore associated with the thunder that shakes the sky, and 辰 *chen*, the fifth terrestrial branch of the Chinese sexagesimal cycle, corresponding to the period between 7 and 9 am, thus the time of awakening. We are therefore in the presence of something that breaks into the human soul, shaking it and awakening it from its torpor. Mou associates the tremor with awakening (*jingxing* 警醒), as in this passage: "How can I know what my 'constitutive moral knowledge' is in itself? When it is unveiled in the course of specific circumstances (for example, through a feeling of alertness and compassion that anyone can experience when seeing a child about to fall in a well), its own vibrations (*zhendong*) may awaken me (*jingxing*) suddenly and thus enable me to retrospectively know it."[37]

I have spoken of "breaking into the human soul," but more accurately it is a breaking out from one's inner core, from the constitutive moral mind, passing through the finite human soul like a jolt that alerts. Mou speaks of "a sun rising from the depths of the sea." The red disc of the sun erupts from the dark depths of the sea, but it is not this liquid darkness that has generated it. It has always been present, though hidden by the dark mass of the waters. Its bursting forth demonstrates that it can exist in the heart of darkness without being overwhelmed by it, and that it holds within itself the autonomous power to burst forth, to reveal itself. In *Caixing yu xuanli* (才性與玄理 *Physical Nature and the "Profound Thought"*),[38] Mou had used the same image of the sun rising

---

[37] Mou Zongsan, *Phenomenon and Thing-in-Itself*, p. 100. Translated by Sébastien Billioud, *Thinking through Confucian Modernity. A Study of Mou Zongsan's Moral Metaphysics*, Leiden: Brill, 2012, p. 208.

[38] See Mou Zongsan (牟宗三), *Caixing yu xuanli*. 才性與玄理 (Physical Nature and the "Profound Thought"), *Mou Zongsan xiansheng quanji*. 牟宗三先生全集 (Complete Works of Mou Zongsan), vol. II, Taipei: Lianhe baoxi wenhua jijin hui, 2003, pp. 126–127.

from the deep sea to indicate the meaning of the hexagram "Return" (*fu* 復), noting how it contains in a lower position the character of "sun" (*ri* 日). In the hexagram there is the intact and creative force of the origin (understood in a value sense), which can be intuited retrospectively: "The hexagram 'Return' calls 'mind of heaven and earth' this primordial creativity. The word 'mind' indicates the spiritual intuition that also has creative force, 'treats things as things but does not allow itself to be reduced to a thing by things,' has a guiding role, and therefore is an absolute subject that can never be reduced to an object, and is revealed by virtue of retrospective intuition (*nijue*)."[39] As Yang Lihua notes,[40] the metaphor of the sun rising from the deep waters has a crucial value here, because it refers to our awakening into a broader and brighter state of mind, that is, to our rising from the finite mind to the cosmic moral mind. To sum up, this inner shaking announces the awakening in me of the moral mind. My natural state is immersion in reality, being submerged in a somnambulist's stupor (the ocean depths). The moral mind erupts into my finite state of being, and its luminous radiance awakens me, revealing that the creative power of a wider mental horizon is held within me. If before I was sunk in my self-centeredness, now the vibration of this unexpected light allows me to intuit that the creative source of all things, the metaphysical mind that embraces everything and relates everything, has always been the truth of myself. This "retrospective insight" does not require that my sensitive mind be impressed by anything external or that I must discursively reflect on my condition. Shuddering at the child about to fall into the well does not make me conscious of an object outside of me, it simply awakens me to my authentic subjectivity. It is an autonomous quivering of the moral mind (a self-quivering *ziwo zhendong* 自我震動) that is perpetually active and responsive. The vision of the child in distress is not the cause, but only the *jiyuan* 機緣 "occasion" that allows the moral mind to manifest itself, dilating my vision, that is, my thoughtfulness, my ethical interest in all things. As is always the case in retrospective intuition, what I

---

39 此復卦即名此『坤元的創造性』為『天地之心』。心者靈覺義, 而有創造性, 物物而不物於物, 而有主宰性: 此為絕對之主體, 而永不能被置定而為客體者, 故須『逆覺』以露之。Ibid., p. 127.

40 See Yang Lihua (杨立华), *Guo Xiang "Zhuangzi zhu" yanjiu*. 郭象《庄子注》研究 (Research on Guo Xiang's "Zhuangzi"), Beijing: Beijing daxue chubanshe, 2010 (天地之心, 作為敞開).

grasp is a subject, and as such cannot be known by objectifying it, but only acted upon (enacted).

Let us now see how the image of awakening is declined in Lévinas' thought. In *Of God Who Comes to Mind*, Lévinas takes up the model of the *tzimtzum*, that is, of withdrawing myself from the univocity of being by accepting a barycenter outside of myself, in order to think of consciousness as an "unceasing awakening." What, if not an awakening, is the Husserlian project of "bracketed" natural evidence, in which the self is instrumentally immersed in reality, in order to rediscover our truest consciousness? The Cartesian Cogito was already a leaving behind of the different stages of dogmatic numbness, breaking them up with doubt: the sensible data, my certainty of being awake, the logic that can be deceived by the evil demon. What is finally produced is a shaking, a hyperbolic intuition, a recovering from sleep thanks to the undeniable evidence of "I think, therefore I am." Husserl extends and redefines this method of disenchantment. By placing in parentheses what is passively given to me, the background of immanence in which I exist daily, Husserl generates a detachment, a space of emptiness between me and things, which makes possible the appearance of an I that distances itself from the world, a "transcendence in immanence." Referring implicitly to the Lurian model of a God who renounces occupying the totality of being and withdraws, Lévinas sees this detachment of the self as a retroceding and reawakening from the torpor of everyday existence and from my being continually entangled in my psychological states: "that which is identified with immanence and recovered there, detaches itself from itself or comes to its senses, like the instant at which sleep gives way and where, in awakening, the lived experience before us discolores as a dream that is past and can only be remembered."[41] To be self-conscious, to return continually to one's own presence of self to self is to be called back by our somnambulism. In this awakening that always begins again, however, consciousness must cast its center of gravity outside of itself. For it reveals itself as intentionality, as a being always stretched in the direction of the world, dependent on the constitution of this object. This relation to the other remains on a purely cognitive level, because

---

41 Emmanuel Lévinas, *Of God Who Comes to Mind*, Stanford, CA: Stanford University Press, 1986, p. 24.

it is always a matter of an exteriority and otherness that the ego must incessantly assimilate.

Yet, Lévinas asks, before being awakened to self in the collision of things, was there not already a capacity for awakening, a kind of sleepless wakefulness in the heart of the ego? "Even in the passivity of consciousness, where one cannot yet speak of knowledge proper, the I keeps watch. [...] the possibility of awakening already makes the heart of the I beat, from the disturbed and living interior, 'transcendence in immanence.'"[42] Being an I already implies a kind of permanent insomnia, a deep vigilance, an uninterrupted possibility of going beyond everything it encounters. This is why, says Lévinas, the cognitive dimension is not justified by itself, but requires a "being drawn out of itself" that is even more original. I am always and in the first place a response to the call of the other, a being already exposed to the ethical call of the other that shakes me, that makes me irreplaceable and unique in my responsibility. Ethical shaking is an enucleation, an inability to escape the action and the call of the other, an otherness that cannot be assimilated. In *Otherwise than Being or Beyond Essence*, Lévinas dramatically describes this violent shaking that the obsessive recall of the suffering face of my neighbor produces in my self: "Obsession is irreducible to consciousness, even if it overwhelms it. [...]. Obsession traverses consciousness countercurrentwise, is inscribed in consciousness as something foreign, a disequilibrium, a delirium. It undoes thematization, and escapes any *principle*, origin, will, or αρχή, which are put forth in every ray of consciousness."[43] It is only at the ethical level, at the level of being-for-others, that is, of being infinitely responsible for others before I have even acted, that this sleepless vigilance is produced from which I cannot escape, and which condemns me to an eternal exile. It reveals to me that I cannot close myself up and seal myself within the sphere of my I, of the coincidence of me with me that is produced every time I can assimilate an external object. This upheaval reveals to me that I am intertwined with the other, be it my neighbor or God, and that it must evade all representation and disturb me from the depths of myself.

---

42   Ibid., p. 25.
43   Emmanuel Lévinas, *Otherwise than Being or Beyond the Essence*, Pittsburgh, PA: Duquesne University Press, 2011, p. 101.

It is not difficult to see the crucial difference between Mou and Lévinas in the description of this shaking that generates awakening. There is probably underlying a common vital experience, that of a shaking of the ego, which is produced by seeing the suffering of one's neighbor and which serves to break the circle of an interiority that has closed in on itself. However, for Lévinas the ego is a centripetal structure, a fulcrum of needs, enjoyment, assimilation. Nothing can come from within to disturb this enjoyment of self and the world that is one with its emergence out of the anonymity of being. Consequently, this violent call to awakening has its origin in something external, indeed in the most extreme and irretrievable form of exteriority which is the Face of the other. What the ego experiences is the shock and surprise at the appearance of an "outside" that is both unforeseen and unthinkable. In Mou, however much the human being may be immersed in the mind of habit, and traverse his everyday world with the distraction of a somnambulist, the moral mind that is his constitutive nature is always alert and always on the move. One may recall here Wang Yangming's assertion that the innate moral consciousness (*liangzhi* 良知) is perpetually bright and vigilant, even during the state of deep sleep, otherwise one could not explain why a sleeping man wakes up when he hears his name called.[44] There is therefore always a subtle and uninterrupted activity of the mind, vigilant and ready to respond to the call of the external world. I have taken up this statement, perfectly in line with the ceaseless dynamism of the moral self in Mou, because it shows us vividly the contrast with Lévinas.

The French author also uses the metaphor of the call, of the appeal that comes from others and redeems me from immersion in myself, but this call to my irreplaceable responsibility for Lévinas is an irruption that forcibly awakens me. An additional effort of reflection can make me

---

[44] A student once told Wang Yangming he believes that when a person is in a state of deep sleep, "even innate knowledge is unconscious." Wang replied by stating, "If it is unconscious, how is it that, as soon as he is called he answers?". This vividly indicates that *liangzhi*'s awareness and conscious activity in human beings is uninterrupted. See Wing Tsit-Chan (ed.), *Instructions for Practical Living, and Other Neo-Confucian Writings by Wang Yang-Ming*, New York and London: Columbia University Press, 1963, p. 218. Wang specifies that in the state of sleep the mind adequately corresponds to the extinguishing of things and colors as darkness falls, it is therefore, we could say, in a shadowy and withdrawn "yin" function, different from the radiating condition of daytime experience.

5. Self-Limitation of the Moral Self as Kenosis 293

discover that my I, in its jumping out of being, is already presupposed to be intertwined with the other. The "immanent transcendence" of the "I" only demonstrates here that the call of the other somehow preceded my leaping to consciousness and constituting myself as I. As Lévinas writes, the face of other is at the origin of me as an "immemorial past." For Mou, on the other hand, the moral tremor arises from within, it is the true self that vibrates in a permanent vigilance and awakens me from attachment to my finitude. There are two manifestations of my tendency to attachment, Mou writes: the "making myself what" and the "making myself me." In the latter we read the imprint of the finite ego that impresses (affects) itself, becomes the psychological ego, and gets lost in the labyrinth of mirrors of its inner narrative. The authentic moral ego, which is the absolute and perpetually active subject, cannot become the object of itself. The quiver (zhendong 震動) is a confirmation, an authentication of itself:

> It is an empty expression to say that I am awakened, rather it is the root mind that at once awakens itself and, retrospectively illuminated by its own shining, confirms itself. This is called the self-shaking of the essential mind. Shaking itself and waking up in a flash, it grasps itself in its own luminous vastness, and confirms itself [...]. In this situation I come to recognize it as my own essential mind, which spiritually corresponds to everything and resonates with everything, and is autonomous and law to itself, and in this recognition consists what I call "retrospective verification." [...] by virtue of this, I, despite being a finite being, know that I possess the capacity for intellectual intuition.[45]

There is in this jolt, Mou continues, something that awakens and something that is awakened, a being subjectively conscious and an object of which I am conscious. And equally in discovering myself as a law unto myself, there is no moral norm acting on me by forcing me, but rather penetrating me intuitively, being my own luminous presence (langxian 朗現).[46]

---

45 所謂驚醒吾人者, 這乃是虛說。其實是那『本心』一動而驚醒起自己, 故即以其自身之光而逆覺其自己也。此謂本心之『自我震動』。震動而驚醒其自己者即自豁然而自肯認其自己, 此謂本心之自肯; 而吾人遂即隨之當體即肯認此心以為吾人之本心, 即神感神應自由自律之本心, 此種肯認即吾所謂『逆覺體證』。即在此逆覺體證中, 即含有智的直覺, 如是, 遂得謂吾人雖是一有限的存在, 而亦可有『智的直覺』也。Mou Zongsan, *Phenomenon and Thing-in-Itself*, pp. 105–106.
46 Ibid., pp. 81–82.

The quaking of the moral self, in addition to manifesting (*chengxian* 呈現) and illuminating (*langxian* 朗現), also possesses the power of gushing out or erupting (*yongxian* 湧現; see the *Critique of the Cognitive Mind*). The "intellectual intuition" indeed has the capacity to raise itself from itself (*ziqizixian* 自起自現),[47] whereas the psychological self is a corrugation that is raised by sensibility, it is a wave that is moved by the wind. Compared to this autonomous and self-emergent activity, the awakening imagined by Lévinas is a being extracted out of oneself, attracted by the dynamic of desire that has its center of gravitation in the absolutely other. Desire aspires in a disinterested way to the infinite, which reveals itself to me through the face of the other, of the stranger, of that which will never be integrable or assimilable in the economy of my ego. The metaphysical dimension can reveal itself to me in the ethical relationship with the other, but only insofar as it produces a continuous pull toward what is and must be respected in its irreducible difference.

To conclude, Mou's awakening is a jolt from the heart of the moral self, revealing to me my universal participation in things, by virtue of which my finite self can actively and positively be infinite in self-cultivation and moral action. Infinity and transcendence are something I can decline in the first person, because what is beyond the difference between inner and outer, between I and others, is the essence of my moral mind, which expands from the heart of my being. It demands fulfillment and actualization, and concretely reveals its possibility in the figure of the saint, of the human being who is foreign to nothing: "Since I possess intellectual intuition, it manifests itself at the opportune moment and radiates in a single instant. [...] This manifesting in its full totality in a single instant is what is called the 'flowing of the heavenly principle,' and 'the saint.'" This sanctity is not to be interpreted exclusively, for "the myriad of the living is a potential saint. The saint is the myriad of the living when it comes in an instant to enlightenment. And this happens by virtue of what? By their having in common the same substantial mind."[48]

---

47 Ibid., p. 132.
48 但因有智的直覺故, 它亦可以隨時圓頓地呈現即朗現。[…]。及其圓頓地全幅被呈現, 所謂『天理流行』, 亦即聖人, […]。眾生是一潛伏的聖人。聖人是一覺悟了的眾生。何以故?本心同故。Ibid., p. 82.

The "full wholeness in a single instant" *yuandun* (圓頓) echoes the terminology of Tiantai Buddhism, and in particular the meditative practice of "Complete and sudden cessation and contemplation" *yuandun zhiguan* (圓頓止觀).[49] This instantaneous bringing to completion reflects in Mou the positivity of the present in which human beings act. Speaking of the moral mind, we are here at a level that is superior to space and time, understood as structures that are produced only by attachment and descent into the cognitive mind. The term "present"[50] is therefore to be understood in a valorizing sense, as actuality and realization of the moral mind in every single act. It is no coincidence that Lévinas, still closely tied to the Husserlian phenomenological-cognitive model, which indicates the present as the point from which the world is constituted, thinks of the infinite revealing itself in the face of others as the unhinging of the present, because "superiority does not reside in a presence in the world, but in an irreversible transcendence."[51] The infinite manifests itself, or rather recedes and subtracts itself as the immemorial, pre-original past, which has never been present, or as unforeseeable and unimaginable future. The Infinite is that which I discover as grafted forever into my self, without my being able to comprehend and realize it, because the positing in us of this unembeddable idea overturns this presence to self that is consciousness. The awakening to the infinite can be described as "the surprise or susception of the unassimilable, more open than any opening—awakening [*éveil*], but suggesting the passivity of the created one."[52]

Lévinas' point of view is of extreme importance, since it probably represents the most extreme attempt in the history of Western thought to affirm the superiority and anteriority of the ethical relation with respect to any cognitive dynamism. If, however, we compare his thought to that of Mou, we see that the need to question a philosophical inheritance centered on knowledge pushes Lévinas to accentuate the destructive, scalping, ultimately unspeakable element of my relationship with the

---

49 Jason Clower, *The Unlikely Buddhologist. Tiantai Buddhism in Mou Zongsan's New Confucianism*, Leiden: Brill, 2010, p. 196.
50 This corresponds to the meaning of the word *xian* 現 in *chengxian* 呈現, *langxian* 朗現, and *yongxian* 湧現.
51 Emmanuel Lévinas, *En Decouvrant L'Existence avec Husserl et Heidegger*, Paris: Vrin, 1949, p. 201.
52 Lévinas, *Of God Who Comes to Mind*, p. 64.

other. Whenever something is posited or constituted by the subject, the ethical dimension must reassert itself as infinitely anterior, as an origin that precedes every origin, and unmask the false claim of any possible principle or foundation. We are here in the presence of what Mou would call a vertical dimension, that is, transcendent and metaphysical, and yet lacking that element of practical self-cultivation that is the very backbone of the Confucian tradition. First of all, if we return briefly to the kenotic model of the *tzimtzum*, which is a source of inspiration for Lévinas, and compare it with Mou's model of the self-limitation of the moral mind, we see at least one relevant similarity emerge. What Mou proposes with the theory of self-limitation is to recognize the value of those forms of scientific knowledge that are hegemonic in Western horizontal thought. Mou believes that his moral metaphysics, which, in his opinion, synthesizes the authentic spirit of Confucian thought, does not lead to the rejection of logical-scientific knowledge, but assures it a specific value. It is developed at a different ontological level than that of the moral self, specifically what is referred to as the "ontology of attachment." As such, it is not directly opposed to moral metaphysics, but constitutes a state of mind (*jingjie* 境界) that has peculiar attributes, and contains within itself the possibility of an epistemological advancement that has positive repercussions for civilization, and in particular for the sensible and finite level in which human life takes place. The doctrine of the self-limitation of the moral self represents for Mou the dialectical hinge that dynamically unites the two levels of being. Human being is an organic totality that can be realized at different levels without implying a Platonic dualism between spirit and matter. In the formulation that Mou takes up again and again, "man is a finite being who can become infinite." This infinitude is not an unattainable telos, but something that the human being can embody and enact, not by denying finitude and becoming estranged in ascetic practices, but rather by fully and consciously realizing his own constitutive nature. The moral mind, having to unfold itself in its action in a phenomenal world, accepts limiting itself and attaching itself to itself, in order to penetrate cognitively the phenomenal details of the world and to subsume and reverse them in its action. In this way it brings to fulfilment its nature, which is that of not allowing even the smallest thing to be forgotten, but to be brought back into that dynamic flux that it is, and to which nothing can be external.

The retraction of God in the *tzimtzum* and the self-limitation of the moral self represent two attempts to allow the finite world to subsist and unfold without it being thought of as pure negation and continual reabsorption into the infinite mind. The finite (or, in Kantian terms, phenomenal) world is accorded reality and legitimacy. However, in the case of the Lurian Kabbalah, this implies that the divine mind, in withdrawing itself, produces an empty space within which the world, even if nourished by the divine being, can claim its own autonomy. In contrast, the logical (and psychological) self, which is generated by the self-limitation of the moral self, cannot claim an independent status but is a subsidiary part of the dynamism of manifestation of the moral mind. The difference emerges clearly to the eye if we think of the sentence with which Lévinas announces the paradoxical autonomy of the finite, writing that the best proof of God's omnipotence is to have created a being capable of disavowing it in atheism. When Mou's logical self forgets its original function, and goes astray in its attachment to the phenomenal world, what ensues is a loss and arrest in moral action. By precluding the manifestation of the moral mind, the human being does not reveal its glory by contrast but dissipates its existence in negativity and restlessness. Rather, the model of the *tzimtzum* comes closest to the Daoist diaphanous self, which retracts and becomes slender to become a kind of "theophany of original nothingness." This "original nothingness," however, is not the emptiness-of-being produced by the *tzimtzum*, but the inexhaustible inchoate power of the Dao that precedes all determination. Instead Lévinas translates this chaotic state as "totality," and thinks of its infinity and indeterminacy as an expanse of motionless water that sucks up and erases every sign that we want to inscribe in it, an absolute saturation of being that is sufficient to itself, has no void or breath, and admits no generation.[53] The rupture of this

---

53 What distinguishes Lévinas' infinity from the fullness of Plotinus's One is that the former does not tend to effortlessly overflow and give of itself in an unbounded manner. About the overflowing and superabundance in Plotinus's One see John Bussanich, "Plotinus's Metaphysics of the One," in: Lloyd Gerson (ed.), *The Cambridge Companion to Plotinus*, New York and Cambridge, UK: Cambridge University Press, pp. 38–65 (pp. 48–50).

totality is the only way for the finite to awaken to itself and acquire autonomy.

In conclusion, the ultimate justification of the logical self does not lie in being something that detaches itself from the moral self and confronts it. Knowledge must be pursued to the end and with rigor, following the structure and laws of human reason, and having enucleated and described them is the inescapable merit of Kant's transcendental critique. However, the relationship between the logical self and the moral self is not one of mutual externality. The self-limitation that results from attachment in Mou is not identical with the retraction and detachment in *tzimtzum*. In both cases the product is a finite state of being, but the logical self derives the determination of its horizon and its laws from its being an inescapable moment of the self-realization of the moral self. It contributes organically to a broader dynamism, that of the moral mind that tends toward its own fulfillment, concretizing itself down to the minutest dimension of the universe. It is not a space of emptiness and detachment that justifies its existence. On the contrary, the attachment to and emergence of the phenomenal world is the expression of the moral self's desire for absolute engagement and involvement in reality.

If we want the finite to be subsumed and justified in its ethical dimension, and we move in the direction of the thought of Lévinas and his peculiar and creative reinterpretation of the myth of the *tzimtzum*, we notice a substantial difference, which hinges precisely on the theme of subjectivity. In the *tzimtzum* the metaphysical substance is a divine mind that freely and consciously withdraws itself so that the other than itself can be born. Also, in Mou's thought it has a crucial value that the original and originating metaphysical substance is a mind, capable therefore of intention and will, and conscious of itself as that which is for itself its own law. Its absolute subjectivity manifests itself concretely as an irreducible activity that has no trace of passivity in itself, understood as heteronomy, that is, as being subject to a law foreign to the mind, and as reducibility to an object of knowledge. But this character of absolute subjectivity is also the guarantee of my possibility as a finite mind of enacting this moral self. The infinitude of the moral mind manifests itself as identity with my self insofar as, through ethical and spiritual cultivation, it is disclosed in the heart of my being. Like the red sun evoked by Mou, it expands and radiates infinitely, illuminating me and revealing me to myself as light. Man is a finite being who holds within himself the possibility of becoming infinite. The moral mind is infinite in a practical-performative sense: I can become it and embody it, it is in me as the very core of my subjectivity, but it is not solipsistic, because it manifests itself in my acting as interconnectedness and responsiveness to all things. In Lévinas, subjectivity is thought of as egocentrism, it is the act by which we emerge from the indifferent neutrality of the "il y a," settle into the world as our dwelling place, establish the regime of separation, experience it as jouissance. This jouissance is the opposite of the joy of which Mengzi speaks: "I turn to myself and rejoice." Joy is what Mou calls an ontological feeling, it is the recognition of oneself as infinite mind that extends to everything and lives in everything. It is already in itself the outcome of moral cultivation, while jouissance is self-identification as an individual who has separated himself from bare being and rejoices in the instrumental availability of the world, in its assimilability (also cognitive). Enjoyment is the condition of possibility of constituting myself as a subject, a throbbing center of needs: "In enjoyment I am absolutely for myself. Egoist without reference to the Other, I am alone without solitude, innocently egoist and alone."[54]

---

54 Lévinas, *Totality and Infinity*, p. 134.

Conclusions: Facets of Self across Cultures

The Contemplative Subject in Western Culture: Interiority, Reflection, Solitude

One of *Constitutive Mind and Constitutive Nature*'s most important theoretical achievements is to have highlighted how Confucianism ushers in the dimension of authentic subjectivity. According to Mou Zongsan, even the most paradigmatic representative of Western philosophy, Immanuel Kant, failed in his attempt to ground the moral subject, and therefore, the Confucian enterprise represents China's highest contribution to world thought:

> [...] His [Of Confucius] greatest contribution to human civilization has been to temporarily set aside (without denying) the objective aspect of concepts such as the Sovereign, Heaven, and Mandate of Heaven, and starting from subjectivity, point to benevolence as the source of moral value and open the way to moral life. [...]. This is not to deny or take away value from Heaven, but to emphasize the subjective [i.e. practical-performing] foundation of the connection between man and Heaven and to emphasize "authentic subjectivity." [...]. The contribution made by Confucius, that is, to "practice benevolence in order to know Heaven" awakens authentic subjectivity and at the same time emancipates the concepts of Sovereign, Heaven and Mandate of Heaven from the historical ups and downs of the political institutions.
>
> [⋯] 其對于人類之絕大的貢獻是暫時撇開客觀面的帝、天、天命而不言（但不是否定），而自主觀面開啟道德價值之源、德性生命之門以言『仁』。[⋯]。故其暫時撇開客觀面的帝、天、天命而不言，並不是否定『天』或輕忽『天』，只是重在人之所以能契接『天』之主觀根據（實踐根據），重人之『真正的主

體性』也。[...]。孔子此步『踐仁知天』之提供，一方豁醒人之真實主體性，一方解放了王者政權得失意識中之帝、天或天命。[1]

Although Confucius' teachings represent the beginning of the discovery of "true subjectivity," Mou points out that in *Lunyu* this process of subjectification has not yet fully unfolded. The reason for this is that, while Confucius clearly affirms the subjective foundation of morality, he does not yet use the term "mind" (*xin* 心), nor does he see benevolence as a sign of the moral mind. Only Mengzi clarifies the link between benevolence and the inner motion of the mind that does not tolerate the suffering of others, further providing such moral mind with an onto-cosmological extension. Stating that "there is no greater joy for me than to find, on self-examination, that I am authentic" (萬物皆備於我矣，反身而誠，樂莫大焉),[2] Mengzi delineates the all-embracing character of the human mind, which, in benevolence, reveals itself capable of infinite extension and absolute universality. Beginning with Confucius' doctrine of benevolence (*ren* 仁) and Mengzi's theory of mind-nature, Song-Ming Confucianism gradually realized the metaphysical unity of moral practice and cosmological creativity. In *Nineteen Lessons on Chinese Philosophy*, Mou argues that Confucianism "does not start from the objective aspect. For example, Confucius starts from 'benevolence.' We often say that Chinese culture and Western culture develop in different directions. Chinese culture does not deny the objective aspect, but sets aside the objective aspect for the moment and opens the door of the subject from the perspective of the subject, this is true not only for Confucianism, but also for Daoism and Buddhism."[3]

The argument raised by Mou Zongsan, by which it is Confucianism that opens the door to the subjective universe, may seem controversial. Indeed, since its foundation, Western thought seems to have revolved

---

1   Mou Zongsan (牟宗三), *Xinti yu xingti*. 心體與性體 (Constitutive Mind and Constitutive Nature), 3 vols, I, 23–24, in *Mou Zongsan xiansheng quanji*. 牟宗三先生全集 (Complete Works of Mou Zongsan), vols. V–VII, Taipei: Lianhe baoxi wenhua jijin hui, 2003.

2   *Mencius*, Section 7A4, in Bryan Van Norden, *Mengzi. With Selections from Traditional Commentaries*, Indianapolis, IN, Cambridge, UK: Hackett Publishing Company, 2018, p. 172.

3   Mou Zongsan, *Nineteen Lectures on Chinese Philosophy: A Brief Outline of Chinese Philosophy and the Issues It Entails*, Scotts Valley, CA: CreateSpace Independent Publishing Platform, 2015, p. 454.

precisely around the subjective dimension of the spirit. Plato states that, according to the laws of nature, the soul is before the body. The soul is the ruler, and the object is ruled. This is the truest and most perfect truth. The true abode of the soul is the hyperuranic world of ideas, which is transcendent and eternal. Although the soul has fallen into the body, it is consumed by nostalgia for its lost perfection: "When the soul sees beauty in the world, it remembers true beauty, and feels its wings grow and desires to fly high, ignoring and disregarding all that lies beneath."[4] The affirmation of the ontological superiority of the soul over the objective, determinate universe has a decisive impact on Western thought, reverberating in Kantian transcendental philosophy, idealism, and phenomenology. How, then, is it possible to argue that Western thought does not hinge on subjectivity?

To properly understand Mou Zongsan's views, we must think about when, in the history of Western philosophy, the foundations for understanding subjectivity as an inner domain were laid. Peter Sloterdijk, in his book *The Art of Philosophy*, suggests that it was Plato who handed down to us the moment when interiority was established as the world of thought.[5] In the *Symposium*, Plato describes the surprising behavior of his teacher Socrates. At times, Socrates was so absorbed in his thoughts that he would freeze and stand motionless in a room or town square. Staring into the distance into the void, he seemed to see or hear nothing more, immersed in an expressionless stillness. Not only did he lose all sensory contact with the world, but he was also completely detached from the reality around him and did not interact with other people. This trance state could last even for many consecutive hours, and when Socrates awakened, he would tell his students that he was captivated by the flow of his thoughts, to the point of allowing himself to drift in that inner current. Reporting these episodes, Plato wondered where Socrates' essence, that is, his spirit, dwelled. When Socrates was immersed in his thoughts, his body (what Plato called the "little self") was in the room or shared space, but where was his authentic self, the abode of his rational faculty? Contemporary philosopher Hannah Arendt wrote an

---

4   Plato, *Phaedrus*, 249D
5   See Peter Sloterdijk, *The Art of Philosophy: Wisdom as a Practice*, New York: Columbia University Press, 2012, chapter 1.

essay entitled, "Where Are We When We Think?"[6] This simple question has a profound meaning. The place of thinking is the inner realm of the self, but in Socrates' time, this inner space was not yet defined in its separateness, so much so that his disciples had devised a mythological explanation, thinking that during these states of deep contemplation, Socrates was conversing with his *daimon*—a private, inner guiding deity. We can say that the question raised by Plato, namely where Socrates was when these almost dreamlike states were abducting him from the shared world, ushers in the idea of an inner universe hidden from others and explorable only by the individual who possesses it and seeks refuge in it. The use of spatial metaphors to represent the mind's proper place has an enormous impact on Western culture. Eight centuries later, Augustine's motto "Do not go out, but return within yourself, where truth dwells in man" (*Noli foras ire, in te ipsum redi: in interiore hominis habitat veritas*), represents the definitive affirmation of this topological-spatial model of the human mind.

Assuming now that Plato actually discovered (or, more accurately, created) the inner realm of the subject, we can ask whether such a philosophical achievement is not the Western equivalent of the "opening of the door of subjectivity" that Mou Zongsan attributes to Confucianism. To answer this question, we must first analyze the characteristics of this inner subjective realm. Sticking to the narrative provided by Plato, first, the manifestation of our inner space requires us to sever our relations with the external environment. Socrates withdraws from everyday life when he is lost in his thoughts, and this absenting also means isolation from the world, loss of the ability to relate to others, and even neglect of one's social responsibilities. The self-construction of the internal world has, as its premise, the disconnection between body and mind, self and others, and spirit and sensory perception of the objective world. The sensory organs represent an embodied subject's ability to "come out of self" and look out onto the universe, and they define our structural openness onto the world of life. The meditating subject seems to have a paradoxical form of acquired blindness and deafness. In the description offered to us by Plato, Socrates does not even respond when the disciples try to question him. Thus, not even the proper name, which

---

[6] In: Hannah Arendt, *The Life of the Mind*, San Diego, CA: Harcourt, 1981 (Chapter IV).

defines us in the bosom of human society, seems capable of penetrating this solitary dullness. It is therefore no coincidence that the Greek terms *idios*, which denotes what is proper to the individual, and *idiotes*, which designates one who leads a private life outside of society and public employment and is thus bent on their own selfish horizon, end up, in the evolution of language, defining the semantic field of stupidity and dullest refractoriness.

If we compare this radical shunning of all participation in the human assemblage with the teachings of Neo-Confucian philosopher Wang Yangming, the contrast becomes stark. In section 216 of his *Chuanxilu* (傳習錄 *Instructions for Practical Living*), Wang points out that *liangzhi*, that is, innate moral insight, is constantly active and dynamic. To a disciple's objection that sleepers seem to lack any self-consciousness, Wang retorts, "If it is unconscious, how is it that as soon as he is called, he answers?"[7] According to Wang Yangming, this common experience demonstrates that the mind is perpetually active because it is responsive to its surroundings, recognizes its own name, and reacts to the call of the other. In accordance with the Confucian tradition, Wang Yangming believes that the moral mind manifests itself precisely in everyday interactions, and any effort at self-elevation requires consciously completing the simplest tasks of daily life:

> As the operation of the mind, it is called the will. As the intelligence and clear consciousness of the will, it is called knowledge. And as the object to which the will is attached, it is called a thing. They are all one piece. The will never exists in a vacuum. It is always connected with some thing or event. Therefore, if one wants to make his will sincere, he should rectify it right in the thing or event to which the will is directed, get rid of selfish human desires, and return to the Principle of Nature. Then in connection with this thing or event, the innate knowledge will be free from obscuration and can be fully extended. This is the task to making the will sincere.[8]

From this perspective, dividing the body and the mind, the subjective intention, and the events in which it is exercised—the inner and the

---

7   Wing Tsit-Chan (ed.), *Instructions for Practical Living, and Other Neo-Confucian Writings by Wang Yang-Ming*, New York and London: Columbia University Press, 1963, p. 218.
8   Ibid, p. 189.

outer—into two separate domains will not only fail to realize the authenticity of the subject but, on the contrary, reveal a deficit of moral consciousness.

> A friend asked, "In our task, if we want to have this innate knowledge continue at all times, we shall not be able to deal with all the influence of external things and respond to them. On the other hand, if we go to things and deal with them, innate knowledge seems to disappear. What is the solution?" The Teacher said, "This is simply because your recognition of innate knowledge is not yet genuine, and you still separate the internal and the external. [...] If you realize that innate knowledge is the foundation and is correct, and go ahead to make a real and concrete effort, you will understand it thoroughly. When this point is reached, the separation of internal and external will be forgotten. Wherein can the mind and things fail to be united as one"?[9]

Socrates' meditative state is certainly different from that of a sleeping man, but does this difference represent a rising to a higher state or a descent into the unconscious? Sloterdijk writes,

> In fact, Socrates was on an interior journey. In some respect, we should see him as an emigrant, as the inventor of a sublime emigration. People who think as the early philosophers thought take a holiday from the common world and migrate to the alternative world that Platonic metaphysics interpreted without further ado as the transcendent world, real life, almost, in fact, the homeland of the better part of our soul.[10]

To reach the acme of this ecstatic condition, the meditating person must practice unraveling all the roots that bind them to the shared social world. Temporarily freed from material constraints, the subject turned to the inner realm does not stand in the world, that is, the subject does not exist in the world in the proper sense, bereft as they are of that "being-in-the-world" that Heidegger recognizes as a fundamental property of human existence. Indeed, this contemplative state is akin to death, reflecting, not surprisingly, Plato's idea that the body is the prison of the soul, and the practice of philosophy aims to lead the exiled and longing soul back to its own abode. In his book *The Fundamental Concepts of Metaphysics. World, Finitude, Solitude*, Martin Heidegger states that stones are *worldless*, animals are *poor in world*, and

---

9   Ibid, p. 217.
10 Sloterdijk, *The Art of Philosophy*, p. 29.

only human beings can achieve by their symbolic and manifestative capacity the state of *world-forming*.[11] We could say that the greatest danger that a purely detached and hyperuranic subject runs is that of neglecting its task of actively shaping its world-environment, ultimately becoming a mere abstract and worldless perspective point. The subject constituted as absolute spirituality and interiority risks turning to the opposite extreme, exposing to the outside spectator contemplating it, as happened to the astonished disciples before Socrates, the mere closed and refractory surface of a worldless stone.

In summary, Plato's *Symposium* lays the foundation for the concept of subjectivity in Western culture. The most important characteristic of this subjectivity is that it constitutes an inner domain. Using the metaphor of space to develop the concept of "inner being, being within," Plato gives the subject an ontological dwelling, establishing an insurmountable boundary between the inner world and the outer world. The premise for the constitution of this inner space is that the subject withdraws from any relationship with the universe outside itself, and this operation of radical isolation and detachment causes the subject to play the role of spectator rather than of participant in the world. Thus, from the very beginning, the realm of the self is presented as a kind of fortified citadel, an ideal refuge for spiritual hermitage and contemplative life.

The subject's inner world consists of an intricate network of logical relations. For Socrates and Plato, traversing this dialectical web in thought was more urgent and relevant than any connection with the "outside." This connection is not limited to the communicative interaction between the self and the other nor to the mutual adjustment between the subject and the natural environment, but it also includes the relationship between the human mind and its body. In its supreme state, the mind is freed from the disturbing effects of sentience and temporarily returns to the world of ideas to which it originally belonged. Because material reality is a prison for the human heart, the subject perceives themselves as an exile in a foreign land, and this underlying feeling determines the nature of any practice of self-improvement. The philosophical endeavor to ascend to lost perfection, because it requires a continuous exercise of self-purification from the residual conditioning

---

11 Martin Heidegger, *The Fundamental Concepts of Metaphysics: World, Finitude, Solitude*, Bloomington, IN: Indiana University Press, 1995.

of earthly life, represents a true exercise in death. As Socrates explains to his disciples in the *Phaedo*, the philosopher, at every moment of his life, aspires to be a dying person:

> All those who practice philosophy in a righteous way are in danger of it passing unnoticed by others that their genuine occupation is no other than to die and be dead. And if this is true, it would be truly absurd all one's life to care for nothing but death, to grieve for that which one has long desired and cared for so much.[12]

The philosophical proposition "I think, therefore I am" that René Descartes arrives at in his *Discourse on Method* inherits from Plato this voluntary withdrawal from the subject's own world and provides a new metaphysical basis for his inner–outer dualism. The self-intuition of the Cogito in which the self necessarily discovers itself to exist by the mere fact of occurring in thought is the conclusion of a path of systematic doubt, a true "spiritual retreat" in which the thinking subject finally discovers that it cannot doubt the existence of the doubting subject. We could say that the logical-epistemological model on which Western culture is based reaches its extreme here. Not only the basic problem of epistemology, that is, whether or not the source of knowledge is reliable, is the starting point of his *Discourse on Method*, but its outcome is the establishment of truth as a pure thought event.

What the *Discourse on Method* represents is nothing more than the autobiographical description of the contemplative self that we analyzed above. At the center of the description is a contemplative subject taking shape between two solitudes—that of the external environment and that of the domain of thought: Descartes, in his solitary and isolated room, mirrors a psychological experiment that every human can make in the inner solitude of their soul. This solitary subject proceeds in thought through the method of systematic doubt, which is like a series of concentric circles expanding from the subject to the outer world, increasingly widening the section of the real that the subject judges epistemically unreliable. Starting from traditional certainties, doubt rejects—or more precisely, brackets—the reliability of the independent existence of objects perceived with sense organs, that of the existence of the body, the exactitude of mathematics, and finally the existence of all

---

12 Plato, *Phaedo*, 64A–65A.

reality. As in the case of the contemplating Socrates, the subject, in order to seek the truth, must gradually absent themselves from the material world and from communicative interrelation with other human beings. The result of the rupture of all relations is that the subject, only when having reached the most extreme solitude, can recognize themselves reflexively and have the certainty of their own necessary existence, so that the content of the self is only the pure activity of self-reflection. The most important contribution of the Cartesian Cogito to the history of Western culture lies in having defined, in the most precise way, the boundaries of the inner world as a closed circle. It is from this solitary inner world that Western thought must now expand to the outer boundaries of the universe, to absorb or generate objective reality.

In the *Critique of Pure Reason*, Kant reaffirms that the "I," in its purest expression, coincides with the reflective activity of self-consciousness. By placing the "I think" at the apex of his epistemological system, however, Kant recognizes it as having a universal power of synthesis, that is, a role in transcendentally constituting reality itself. Post-Kantian thinkers criticize the abstract nature of this transcendental Cogito. The goal of German Idealist philosophers is to go beyond the limits placed by Kant on human cognitive capacity by asserting that the self can directly tap into reality itself by means of intellectual intuition. Since Kant believes that intellectual intuition belongs only to a divine mind, that is, one capable of creating the world that is the object of its thought, Idealist thinkers seek to deduce the entire system of knowledge from the inner dynamism of the Cogito itself, tracing the manifestation of reality in various ways back to the creative activity of an absolute ego. The objective world gradually becomes the externalization of the subject. Only when the subject, ego, or spirit grasps itself and becomes fully self-conscious, can the world acquire its authentic existence.

Then, in the Western tradition, the self alienates itself from the objective world that our senses offer, declaring it unreliable or illusory, and finally finds in its own solitary inner world the core from which reality itself derives. The process we have briefly described here is not limited to the realm of philosophy, but it has a great influence on all manifestations of culture. This solitary, self-centered worldview can have both positive and negative consequences. The consequences that we can call negative are, in my opinion, beautifully expressed in the verses of the Italian poet Eugenio Montale (1896–1981), who won the Nobel Prize for Literature in 1975:

> Perhaps one morning while wandering in glassy air,
> barren, turning around I shall see the miracle unfold:
> nothingness over my shoulder, vacuum behind
> Me, feeling the dread of a drunk.
>
> Then as on a screen, trees houses hills
> Will briskly settles for the habitual deception.
> But it shall be too late; and I will wander on silently
> Among people who do not turn around, with my secret.[13]

This poem is rich in meaning, for it shows what is the existential implication of this retreat of the human being into their own abysmal inner realm. The "person who turns around" reflects the attitude of the philosophical self who immerses themselves in contemplation and reflexively seeks themselves in their own inner mirror, only to find that faith in the reality of the world has disappeared. In Chinese thought, both Buddhist and Daoist, "embodying emptiness" is a practice of elevation to the realm of spirit. In this state of mind, however, reality does not disappear without a trace; rather, it can reveal its true face only when we have emancipated ourselves from attachment to things. In Montale's poetry, on the other hand, that of the man turning to his inner world is not a positive experience of freedom (like Zhuangzi's *free and easy wandering*) or enlightenment. The "turning man" experiences emptiness at the core of his being as barrenness and irreparable loss of the world. As in Plato's cave, what is captured through the senses turns out to be an illusion projected by our mind. Back in everyday reality, the subject carries a secret that separates them irrevocably from other human beings and condemns them to an alienating and painful loneliness, for their secret is not the discovery of the "voiceless and odorless innate moral consciousness" that Wang Yangming speaks of: the only content of their secret is the certainty of the abysmal loneliness of the human heart after its alienation from the world.

In short, in a system based on the pursuit of epistemic certainty, an ontological boundary separates the inner realm from the outer

---

13   Translation by Alexander Friedrich Richter, see https://people.maths.ox.ac.uk/ritter/montale.html

realm. In this case, internalizing means gathering the external world through the cognitive process of the mind. It is perhaps no coincidence that questions around the nature of self-consciousness have often led Western thought to await clarification from neuroscience. One of the most insurmountable difficulties facing the philosophy of mind is the impossibility of think about the interiority of the self (the *qualia*, that is, the subjective properties of experience) and the exteriority of its scientific representation together. The neural bases of consciousness that we try to locate in the brain seem foreign and ultimately incompatible with the inner side of conscious experience, the subjective properties of experience (the *qualia*). How am I able to think about the sinking of my inner life and the refractory exteriority without doors or windows of the brain that science describes to me as a single phenomenon? Perhaps in the same instant that the philosopher absents themselves from the world to sink into their secret inner domain, the world is already irrevocably lost to their thinking, and the self and reality no longer belong to each other and drift in opposite directions. It is on this ridge that Mou Zongsan proposes to rethink interiority as a transformative practice and the world as immanent to one's moral action.

The Confucian Moral Subject in Mou's Thought: Rethinking the Concepts of Interiority and Reflection

According to Mou Zongsan, how does traditional Chinese thought based on the priority of the moral mind reformulate the concept of "inwardness"? The starting point of the discussion is a statement by Cheng Mingdao, a scholar of the Northern Song Dynasty. Commenting on Mengzi's statement that "all things are already complete in us", he affirms its universal scope as follows: "'All things are already complete in oneself (萬物皆備於我)'. This is not only true of man but of things also. Everything proceeds from the self, only things cannot extend [the principle in them] to others, whereas man can."[14] The human mind and all things in the universe participate in an ontological commonality—all

---

14   Irene Bloom, and Philip Ivanhoe (ed.), *Mencius*, New York: Columbia University Press, 2009, Section 7A4.; Wing-Tsit Chan, *A Source Book in Chinese Philosophy*, Princeton, NJ: Princeton University Press 2008, p. 534.

things are one body (萬物一體). This "all things" is viewed from two perspectives. From the perspective of being, I and things are one; from the perspective of moral practice, only the human mind has the capacity to actively realize this truth by responding and resonating morally in relation to every being in the universe. Ontologically speaking, being one body, or having a common substance, does not mean sharing an undifferentiated matter nor a static metaphysical principle, but participating in a constant flow of creation through the universe. In this sense, "being one body" represents the onto-cosmological creative force. Mou calls this metaphysical efficacy the "constitutive reality of that which is heaven-given" (天命實體) or "the substance of that which is unceasing" (於穆不已之體). Both correspond to the reality that is "both being and movement" described in the *Zhongyong* and *Yizhuan* and are expressions of the universal force capable of bringing every individual to completion—the way of heaven and human nature are interconnected (天道性命相貫通). This universally effective substance not only creates all things, but it is also inherent and internal to all things as their own nature. It is worth noting that this kind of "inherence" indicates perfect ontological possession and a participation in the universal validity of heavenly principles. To be inner or inherent here means "to have possession": people possess this efficacious substance, and animate and inanimate things also possess it. According to Mou Zongsan, Cheng Mingdao's expression "all things are already complete in oneself (萬物皆備於我)" is not only true of man but of things, but it also means that not only the human heart but also the universe and every single thing possesses a "self." The "self" here does not mean that which appears in self-awareness, which pertains solely to a being endowed with awareness, but a "creative-formative core (創生中心)." Reality is not a dead reality, "only being but without dynamism"; on the contrary, it is constituted in its own interiority by an inexhaustible generating power that penetrates the whole universe.

Although the creative force of the heavenly principle penetrates and permeates all things, things in themselves do not have spontaneity (*zifaxing* 自發性), that is, they do not have the capacity to recognize in themselves the possession this force and voluntarily arouse its creativity; thus, their possession is purely potential. There must be a human mind that recognizes the meaning of things and awakens the moral creativity of the universe; otherwise, things are incapable of visibly and positively displaying their true value. As Wang Yangming writes,

> If heaven is deprived of my clear intelligence, who is going to look into its heights? If earth is deprived of my clear intelligence, who is going to look into its depths? If spiritual beings are deprived of my clear intelligence, who is going to distinguish their good and evil fortune or the calamities and blessings that they will bring? Separated from my clear intelligence, there will be no heaven, earth spiritual beings, or myriad things, and separated from these, there will not be my clear intelligence.[15]

Thus, Mou Zongsan can say that the principle of realization cannot emanate from things but is transcendent to them. The inwardness of the "being inherent in all things" is only a passive and implicit inwardness, and we can understand the meaning of "authentic inwardness" by comparing it with this implicit nature. According to Cheng Mingdao and Mou Zongsan, the difference between people and things is that people can "extend," while things cannot. Yang Zebo writes that "the so-called 'ability to extend' means the ability to bring about accomplishment by extending. Human beings have thought and can therefore develop and extend what has been given to them as a dowry by nature; they can bring their virtues to perfection and generate moral existence—this is the meaning of 'being able to extend.'"[16] In *Constitutive Mind and Constitutive Nature*, Mou Zongsan further explains, "To say that people can extend means that they are able to repeat moral creation, and they can bring out [in things] the constituent heavenly principles and illuminate them clearly and distinctly."[17]

Plants, trees, and stones cannot create morally and thus cannot absorb this creative principle as part of their own nature; the thing possesses only the nature of the principle of existence, but this nature "does not govern itself spontaneously, autonomously and self-directedly (which is the

---

15 天没有我的灵明，谁去仰他高? 地没有我的灵明，谁去俯他深? 鬼神没有我的灵明，谁去辩吉凶灾祥? 天地鬼神万物离却我的灵明，便没有天地鬼神万物了。(《传习录》第337节). *Instructions for Practical Living*, p. 257.

16 Yang, Zebo (杨泽波). Mou Zongsan "Xinti yu Xingti"; he "Cong Liu Jishan dao Lu Xiangshan". 牟宗三《心体与性体》解读：含《从陆象山到刘蕺山》(An Interpretation of Mou Zongsan's "Constitutive Mind and Constitutive Nature;" with "From Liu Jishan to Lu Xiangshan"). Shanghai: Shanghai renmin chubanshe, 2016, p. 80.

17 只是人『能推』，能盡性以推擴，故能重現一道德之創造，不能彰顯天理而使之燦然明著，而『物則氣昏，推不得』。Mou Zongsan, *Constitutive Mind and Constitutive Nature*, II, 61.

meaning of mind and dynamism) by having its own principle in itself."[18] Things do not have subjectivity, that is, they do not have in themselves an autonomous principle of actualization and concretization. Such a dynamic principle capable of unlimited extension remains external to things as it is given to them by the human mind in the act of manifesting the value of things. Through this manifestation, to use the words of Tu Wei-Ming, human mind acquires an anthropocosmic function: "Humanity is heaven's form of self-disclosure, self-expression, self-realization. If we fail to live up to our humanity, we fail cosmologically in our mission as co-creators of heaven and earth and morally in our duty as fellows participants in the great cosmic transformation."[19]

If the mind's interiority represents its structural capacity to embody the creativity of heaven and earth and extends this creative capacity to all things, giving them meaning and value, then interiority is both centripetal and centrifugal. In the Western tradition, the knowing self is constituted by the centripetal movement of withdrawing from the world to turn to one's self. According to Mou Zongsan, only by rising to the moral level does inwardness acquire a dynamic tendency to extend to the world. Unlike Plato, such inwardness does not exclude our bodies, but it embraces the mind–body totality. Cheng Mingdao explains the moral meaning of the term *bu ren* 不仁, indicating lack of humanity and benevolence, through its medical usage, in which *bu ren* are the limbs that are paralyzed and insensitive to stimuli and, in a sense, no longer belong to the rest of the body.[20] Mou Zongsan finds, in this explanation,

---

18 [⋯] 不是靠其自身之自發自律自定方向自作主宰 (此即是其心義、其活動義) 來核對其為理。Ibid., I, 90.

19 Tu Wei-Ming, *Centrality and Commonality. An Essay on Confucian Religiousness. A Revised and Enlarged Edition of Centrality and Commonality: An Essay on Chung-yung*, Albany, NY: State University of New York Press, 1989, p. 102.

20 "A book on medicine considers numbness of the hands and legs to be the absence of *ren* [true goodness]. This is an excellent description. A person of *ren* regards heaven, earth, and the myriad things as one body. They all are the person's own self. If they acknowledge themselves as the self, where do they not reach? But if these things do not belong to the self, then naturally they are of no concern to the self, which is like the absence of *ren* in the hands and legs. If one's *qi* no longer penetrates them, none of them belong to the self. It is for this reason that widely bestowing benefits on and bringing relief to the multitude are the achievements of the Saint" (醫書以手足痿痺為不仁, 此言最善名狀。仁者以天地萬物為一體, 莫非己也。認得為己, 何所不至; 若不屬己, 自與己不相干。如手足之不仁, 氣己不貫, 皆不屬己。故博施濟眾, 乃聖人之功用。). Wang Xiaoyu (王孝魚) (ed.), *Er Cheng ji*. 二程集 (Collection of the Works of the Cheng Brothers), Beijing: Zhonghua shuju, 2011,

a similarity between the body and the moral mind, whereby the ultimate meaning of *ren*, humanity and benevolence, lies in being connected to everything without hindrance or interruption (感通不礙). Taking it a step further, the full realization of the expressions "to be one body with all things" (萬物一體) or "all things are in me" (萬物備於我) lies in a human's ability to extend the sphere of their own mind-body oneness to all things, experiencing others and the universe as a sensible part of themselves. Mou often uses the terms resonance (*ganying* 感應) or sensible connection (*gantong* 感通) to express this form of moral sensibility. In *From Lu Xiangshan to Liu Jishan*, Mou summarizes this by writing that "[Wang] Yangming expresses 'making one body with all things' from innate moral consciousness (luminous consciousness), and similarly, Mingdao expresses it from being sensitively connected proper to the mind of benevolence. This is undeniably a common conception throughout Confucianism."[21] It is worth reiterating that in Mou Zongsan's thought, the term "body (*ti* 體)" can have two different connotations. By *xinti* (心體) or *xingti* (性體), we mean respectively the metaphysical basis of mind and constitutive nature, in which case *ti* 体 is not a static substance but an all-permeating creative force. In *tiren* 體認 and *tiyan* 體驗, that is, recognizing and experiencing firsthand, *ti* expresses a state of mind (*jingjie*) attainable through practical effort, in which moral solicitude embraces everything in the universe, and therefore, nothing is not part of one's body and mind. By saying that "I and the universe are one body (*ti* 體)" we merge the two meanings—the one related to moral metaphysics and the idea of mental state—expressing the mutual communication and permeation between me and the world.

We saw above that the main characteristic of the subject (other than inwardness) is reflective activity. In the moral metaphysics proposed by Mou Zongsan, does the idea of "reflection" (*fansi* 反思) have a different meaning from that of centripetal tension, self-objectification, and

---

p. 15. Translated by Daniel K. Gardner, *Zhu Xi's Readings of the Analects. Canon, Commentary and the Classical Tradition*, New York: Columbia University, 2003, pp. 58–59.

21 陽明從良知(明覺)之感應說萬物一體, 與明道從仁心之感通說萬物一體完全相同, 這是儒家所共同承認的, 無人能有異議。Mou Zongsan (牟宗三), *Cong Lu Xiangshan dao Liu Jishan*. 從陸象山到劉蕺山 (From Lu Xiangshan to Liu Jishan), *Mou Zongsan xiansheng quanji*. 牟宗三先生全集 (Complete Works of Mou Zongsan), vol. VIII, Taipei: Lianhe baoxi wenhua jijin hui, 2003, p. 225.

self-enclosure that we have seen to be dominant in Western thought? We can first consider Mengzi's famous sentence:

> The ten thousand things are all brought to completion in me. There is no greater joy for me than to find, on self-examination, that I am authentic. Strengthen your empathy and you will find that this is the shortest way to benevolence.

「萬物皆備於我也。反身而誠, 樂莫大焉。強恕而行, 求仁莫近焉。[22]

In this case, the term 反身 does not properly denote either psychological introspection (反省) or reflection accomplished with thought. In the case of introspection and reflection, the action of "turning back" (*fan* 反) implies a turning away from the external world (or, in Husserl's terminology, "putting in brackets" and "suspending" blind faith in the phenomenal world) and turning to oneself, assuming the inner self as one's cognitive object. In the Confucian tradition reconstructed by Mou, *fan* (反) has rather the meaning of "returning to the source." The universal expansion of the human heart operated in moral sensitivity is also the process of revealing the authentic value and meaning of the universe. Bringing myself to completion implies bringing all things to completion; through turning back, I go back to the origin of the co-creation of mind and world. This unity of the human heart and the universe is not the mystical contemplation of a static One but the timely practical realization of becoming one body between me and the universe.

Through this turning back to the origin (*fanshen* 反身) we come to embody the reality of authenticity (*cheng* 誠). The *Zhongyong* defines authenticity in these terms:

> Authenticity is not merely the process of making oneself complete and nothing ore; rather, it constitutes the foundation for bringing all things to completion. Making authentic the individual self is the substance of man's essential humanity, just as the completion of all other things constitutes the foundation of wisdom. This is the moral force inherent in one's inborn nature, the Way that unites the external and the internal.[23]

---

22 *Mencius*, Section 7A4, in Van Norden, *Mengzi*, p. 172.
23 Cited in Tiziana Lippiello, "Measuring Human Relations: Continuities and Discontinuities in the Reading of the *Lunyu*," *Sinica venetiana* 3 (2016), 23–40 (p. 37).

In *Constitutive Mind and Constitutive Nature*, Mou concludes the *Zhongyong* passage as follows: "Authenticity is in its essential root the fact that there is no separation between the internal and the external, that subject and object are regarded as one." [...] Of the Dao of heaven and earth he says that 'it is not separate from things, therefore the generation of things is unfathomable,' and thus, this Dao is the creative actualization of 'deep incessance,'[24] and it is also the authenticity that has neither inside nor outside."[25] "Not being separate from things" implies "not being opposed to things." Because the effort of moral practice is not a cognitive process, I and things do not confront each other in a mutual exteriority, and the real universe is not an "ob-jectum" but an absolute and universal actualization. From the point of view of perfect ontological possession, "the noumenal reality that is heavenly decree above connects with individuals below, and is possessed by them (infused in them) as nature (*xing* 性)"; however, from the point of view of moral practice, since only human beings can be morally creative in a conscious and intentional way, only they can take this noumenal reality as their own inner nature. Lu Xiangshan writes that "The myriad things luxuriate in the space of a square inch" that is, the whole universe exists in the mind, but the reason why mind and nature are internal to people is that people are capable of being self-conscious.

Such self-consciousness is certainly not the Cogito proposed by Descartes and Kant, nor is it an awareness of myself based on reflection, but it has moral value and connotations. To analyze the peculiar significance that self-awareness takes on in a moral-performance model, it is appropriate to briefly take up some of the conclusions that Mou Zongsan reaches in his *Critique of the Cognitive Mind*. This work, as we have seen, reflects Mou's interest in epistemology and logic that is central to his early research.[26] However, Mou chooses to adopt a phenomenological method, that is, one based on observation and description from within

---

24　Serina Chan writes: "This refers to the incessant transformation of heaven as lauded in the *Shijing*: 'The decree of heaven, profound and incessant!'" Serina Chan, *The Thought of Mou Zongsan*, Leiden: Brill, 2011, p. 227, n. 37.

25　依《中庸》後半部言『誠』，本是內外不隔，主客觀為一。[…] 言『天地之道』為『為物不貳，生物不測』，自天地之道即是一『於穆不已』之創生實體，而此亦即是『無內外』之誠體也。Mou Zongsan, *Constitutive Mind and Constitutive Nature*, I, 33.

26　For an in-depth analysis of Mou's youthful thinking regarding logic, see Rafael Suter, *Logik und Apriori zwischen Wahrnehmung und Erkenntnis. Eine Studie zum Frühwerk Mou Zongsans (1909–1995)*, Berlin and Boston, MA: De Gruyter, 2017.

the lived experience. The pyramidal-architectural model that Kant adopts in the *Critique of Pure Reason* is transformed here into the inner history of the cognitive self, from its original arising to its extreme limit. The limited self ultimately can only experience its own insuperable incompleteness and thus the necessity—at least theoretically—of the existence of a higher dimension. Mou Zongsan, in his later works, shifts the focus of his attention from the cognitive self to the moral-transcendent self, which alone can meet the hitherto frustrated need for perfect human self-realization. However, the examination of the concepts of "consciousness" and "self-consciousness" in *Critique of the Cognitive Mind* already lays the groundwork for his later reflection on the self.

As of now, consciousness (*jue* 覺) has four structural features: (1) it possesses spontaneity and autonomy in its own arising; (2) every manifestation of consciousness is structurally accompanied by self-consciousness because consciousness is like a lamp that, in illuminating the external world, simultaneously radiates and reveals itself; (3) to speak of consciousness is to speak of an absolute subject, a rising dynamism that continually produces itself and cannot play the role of a static and determined object of knowledge; and (4) the function of consciousness is to reveal the meaning of things, but only when the subject actively and passionately participates in the life of the world, taking care of it, can the meaning of reality come to manifestation. In short, consciousness is always also self-consciousness but in a pre-reflexive way, which precedes the distinction between the self and the thing. Consciousness has manifestative and self-manifestative capacities, and in this irreducible spontaneity and dynamism, it is an absolute subject. In this, consciousness differs from mental states because they are only a psychological reverberation that the mind can grasp and objectify. Although Mou Zongsan's analysis in this work is still limited to the level of epistemology, we are already far from the objectifying approach of modern philosophy of the mind. The concept of consciousness that Mou proposes is that of an absolute, self-generating activity that transcends and leaves behind any temporary and limited psychological formation and is already always oriented to the world, of which it constitutes the active manifestation. Given this practical involvement in the world, consciousness may already represent a conceptual bridge connecting the realm of cognition and that of morality.

In *Constitutive Mind and Constitutive Nature*, this idea takes on a more complex and more imaginative connotation. In the second volume, Mou writes as follows:

> Consciousness (*jue*) can be discussed in the terms of *gantong juerun* (感統覺潤);[27] impregnating awareness operating through responsive interconnection). This "being conscious" derives from the feelings of being uncomfortable (*bu'an* 不安), of not tolerating the suffering of other beings, of being afflicted. It is a flourishing of life, a concentration of warmth comparable to the way seasonal rain fertilizes the earth, [...] Consequently impregnating awareness points to the arousal to creativity.[28]

Within moral metaphysics, Mou establishes a relationship between being conscious and being responsively interconnected with others. Empirical knowledge is no longer a presupposition of consciousness; on the contrary, the reawakening of its creative force is linked to feelings of being uncomfortable (*bu'an*), of not tolerating the suffering of other beings, of being afflicted. These feelings in turn should not be thought of as determinants preceding consciousness but are an inner dynamism through which consciousness manifests itself.[29]

---

27 The term *juerun* 覺潤 can be interpreted in various ways. Sébastien Billoud translates it as "fecundation of thing apprehended" (Sébastien Billioud, *Thinking through Confucian Modernity. A Study of Mou Zongsan's Moral Metaphysics*, Leiden: Brill, 2012, p. 184). My interpretation is closer to the definition proposed by Rafael Suter: "The cosmological dimension of intellectual intuition Mou calls *juerun* 覺潤, 'saturating awareness.' It means that moral acts realized in intellectual intuition imbue the world with value." Rafael Suter, "Transmitting the Sage's 'Heart' (I): Unsealing Moral Autonomy-Intellectual Intuition and Mou Zongsan's Reconstruction of the 'Continuity of the Way' (Daotong)," *Philosophy East and West* 68:1(2018), 223–241 (p. 239, n. 39).

28 覺即就感通覺潤而說。此覺是由不安、不忍、悱惻之感來說, 是生命之洋溢是溫暖之貫注, 如時雨之潤。[⋯], 故曰『覺潤』故覺潤即起創生。Mou Zongsan, *Constitutive Mind and Constitutive Nature*, II, 237. Translation partially modified from Billioud, *Thinking through Confucian Modernity*, p. 184.

29 It is worth noting that to describe consciousness, Mou more often resorts to metaphors related to touch than to sight. This is not accidental when we consider that vision, unlike tactile contact, requires spatial distancing from the object. There can be no separation or obstacle between the mind of benevolence and reality *because* the flow of the constitutive mind has absolute universality, and it imbues everything. Mou points out that Cheng Mingdao himself speaks of benevolence in terms of "being one body" and consciousness in the sense of being responsive and not numb (*mamu* 麻木).

The feeling of not being able to tolerate (the suffering of others) is equivalent to the manifestation of consciousness in the moral mind. This implies that such consciousness in its original state is not limited to the interiority of the human mind, but it extends to cosmic consciousness, that is, to the universal active interconnectedness of all that exists. Such consciousness precedes the separation of subject and object, inner and outer, and external stimulus and subjective reverberation, which is instead characteristic of reflective consciousness. Self-consciousness is first awakened in the practical experience of this intolerance of others' pain, and reality, in its primal arising, already possesses a moral character, that is, a potentiality to be suffused with value and meaning. Mou's theory that consciousness is always also self-consciousness also finds its most authentic realization on the moral plane. It is only when I am practically involved in the affairs of the world that my innate moral consciousness (*liangzhi* 良知) lights up and reveals itself, proving itself. In *Constitutive Mind and Constitutive Nature*, Mou calls this giving proof of itself "retrospective verification (*nijue tizheng* 逆覺體證)." Compounds with *ni* (逆) do not indicate a reflexive return to self but have a close relationship with the concept of *zi* (自). The prefix "self-" (*zi* 自) in "self-consciousness" (*zijue* 自覺) simply means that the moral mind has its own standard and motivating factor in itself, and it does not require any heteronomous cause. If we describe the ontological foundation of this autonomy or self-legislative capacity in terms of "the (motivating) principle is internal to the human mind," however, we must emphasize the distance to free will as expounded by Kant. Horizontal systems such as the dominant one in Kant's thought, which possess, according to Mou, "being but not dynamism" interiority, imply that the mind is thought of as an enclosed spiritual space. To say that the principle is internal to the mind is therefore equivalent to saying that a relationship of containing and contained—and thus a clear separation between the two—exists between the mind and the principle.

In a vertical system, that is, in which there are both being and dynamism, the idea of inwardness is necessarily linked to that of *zi* (自). As Mou writes,

> spirit, authenticity, mind are terms having dynamic meaning, and at the same time they are principles having ontological significance. Principle indicates nothing but the self-dominance, autonomous direction,

self-regulation, and self-emancipation of the changing and inexhaustibly rich nature proper to authenticity, spirit, and mind. We can speak here of "active motivating principle" or "constitutive force of the heavenly principle."[30]

Thus, for Mou Zongsan, the subject is a dynamic interiority capable of self-emancipation and law unto itself. The subject is verb and noun inextricably intertwined. The subjective mind cannot and can never be something that can be encountered in the world, but it is the very event of the world's manifestation. The value of such an event is not primarily ontological, as is the case with the occurrence of Being (*Ereignis*) in Heidegger, nor even phenomenological, but it is a value grounded in moral practice. We could say that, for Mou, the subjective mind is nothing but the universe that, in the act of its spontaneous manifestation, acquires the dimension of "for itself" (*dui qi ziji* 對其自己). "For" (*dui* 對) does not mean to be statically placed in front of (*duimian* 對面) or opposed to (*duili* 对立) the self, but rather, it is said in the dynamic mode of corresponding (*duiying* 對應). The universe reaches the dimension of "per se" when it is saturated with meaning and moral value, and in it the originating and motivating (i.e., subjective) force is one with the objective law or pattern. The mind, through its being implicated in and morally participating in the affairs of the world, reveals itself to itself and becomes self-conscious. Thus, the "self" already contains the dynamism of resonating with the things of the world and responding and corresponding to them. The interiority of the self, therefore, acquires a new connotation, namely the normative connotation of "nothing remains outside" (*wuwai* 無外). It is the opposite of exteriority, not as the two sides of a sheet but as a structural commitment and effort to ensure that none of the things of the world are neglected and unrequited (體物不遺), and everything is for me as a living part of my own body. Interior is only that which is involved in a universal interest (from the Latin root *inter-esse*, being between), and it cannot exist apart from caring for the other and being woven vividly with the other. Internalizing reality requires

---

30 神、誠、心是活動義。同時亦即是理,是存有義。理是此是誠、是神、是心之於穆不已之易體之自發、自律、自定方向、自作主宰處。由此言之,即曰:『動理』亦曰『天理實體』。 Mou Zongsan, *Constitutive Mind and Constitutive Nature*, I, 77.

a capacity for infinite extension of my living flesh, that is, of the scope of what touches and affects me. I must make myself one body with all things, not because of rational consideration or deliberate decision but because the nature of mind is that it cannot help but feel the ten thousand things as my own body (*yi wanwu wei qiti* 以萬物為其體). As Wang Yangming states,

> the great man regards heaven, earth, and the myriad things as one body. He regards the world as one family and the country as one person. [...] (This) is not because he deliberately wants to do so, but because it is natural to the human nature of his mind that he do so.[31]

The human mind has the responsibility—or rather, is itself the lived responsibility—of awakening the cosmic mind, that is, the potential "being one body" of all that is. This creative act does not primarily have to do with the biological evolution of the mind nor with a merely aesthetic-artistic creativity; it is the creation of moral life and authentic spiritual life achieved through the turning operated by consciousness returning to the origin. Through this creation, the universe obtains not only the manifestative dimension of "for itself" but also the truth of being "in itself." Indeed, the second responsibility of the moral mind is to emancipate things from the domain of the useful and the exploitable and to look at them as an absolute finality, that is, as that "thing-in-itself" which Kant could not attain through his merely cognitive quest. Only if moral practice unveils the dimension of "returning to one's original self," of "self-enlightenment," of "retrospectively verifying by turning to oneself," then, the Kantian thing-in-itself is no longer a postulate but something that is presently manifested. Interiority, that is, subjectivity that transcends the cognitive distinction between subject and object, is absolute dynamism, the principle of actualization, and the force of realization and actualization. Although the self-improvement effort pursued through moral practice inevitably proceeds gradually, already through the single concrete moral act, I can achieve retrospective verification of my being part of a oneness that envelops everything. From a subjective point of view, we experience the luminous manifesting, dilating, and permeating everything of the one mind. From an objective point of view, the universality of the one root of all things is affirmed.

---

31 *Instructions for Practical Living*, p. 272.

As we saw above, the most serious limitation Mou sees in Kantian thought is the inability to have a complete and comprehensive view of the mind; this is due, according to Mou, to the fact that the structurally analytical and divisive model of thought prevents him from accessing the "concrete and transparent intelligence of origin" (*yuanshi er tongtou de juti zhihui* 原始而通透的具體智慧) that only the saint can embody: "In my opinion, the ultimate fulfillment of his system can only be found in the perfectly spiritual, concrete, luminous, compassionate and sincere realm of the saint."[32] Mou adds that post-Kantian idealistic philosophy, not surprisingly, tends toward the ideal of the elevation of what is human to a divine principle yet fails to overcome the logical and speculative dimension. Only the moral metaphysics that emerged in the development of Confucian thought, not abstract but performative, fertilizing, and embodied in the mind of the saint, can successfully realize this aspiration of the human to become divine. Ultimately, authentic subjectivity implies not only interiority, concreteness, and absolute activity but also the divinity and infinity potentially hidden in the human that Kant only glimpsed. The possibility of realizing the cosmic vastness of spirit through action provides a solid practical foundation for the Confucian claim that "everyone can be a saint" (*renren xie keyi cheng shen* 人人皆可以成聖).

However, how does the moral self actually manifest itself? The example we chose throughout the book, which we take up here, is Mengzi's famous saying, "When people see a child about to fall into the well, they all have a heart of fear and compassion." When I see the child about to fall into the well, the sense of compassion awakens directly in my heart. What I feel is an intense feeling of urgency, and that feeling leads me to take immediate and proactive action to save the child's life. I do not need to look for a motivating principle in my mind, because the mere occurrence of the child's situation has its own intrinsic performative dynamism. That the child appears to me interrupting my inert habitual calm does not require the mediation of a concept, nor is it necessary for me to consciously resort to my moral conscience to give meaning to what is happening, because the appearance of the child in danger is one with the manifestation of its absolute value.

---

32 我看他的系統之最後圓熟的歸宿當該是聖人的具體清澈精誠側怛的圓而神之境.
    Mou Zongsan, *Constitutive Mind and Constitutive Nature*, I, 144.

We might ask, does this absolute value belong to the child or is it a characteristic that my mind provides for them? Having absolute value is the characteristic that Kant ascribes to "things in themselves," to the noumenon, that is, to things in the original act of their creation, of their uninterrupted coming into being before entering the domain of my mind as objects of knowledge. In *Constitutive Mind and Constitutive Nature*, to denote such moral reality, Mou uses the term *zixing* 自性, the having nature of self, in which the genitive is to be interpreted as objective, that is, having the self as one's own nature:

> Nature of self, is said with respect to the individual and the reason why the transcendent foundation of moral creation can be reawakened and activated; or in general it is said with respect to the ability to make the sky, the earth, and all things in the universe of things-in-itself (making thing as thing-in-itself).[33]

If the child appears to me as a being that has absolute value, that is, as a thing-in-itself, it is because it is not an object of my knowing but a subject that has in itself, and does not receive from me, its own nature. The fact that something manifests itself as pure subjectivity means that it is not separate from me, like cognitive objects, but that is part of my own self. It is contradictory to think of a separation or individual fragmentation in subjectivity so understood. Individuals that appear separate from me I can qualify as "subjects" in a reductive sense, that is, as an active part in the subject-object dyad. The self or the "having nature of self" is subjective in a higher, practical-moral sense, whereby it is irreducibly active, creative, has in itself the source of its own begetting, and is the manifestation of the only living origin in which there is no I and you. To be on the subjective plane here means to be a thing-in-itself, that is, the absolute interrelatedness of everything and the mutual correspondence and participation of the origin. That is why the child appears to me as part of me, one body with my existence. In the oneness of the moral-metaphysical mind, every limit and boundary is already forever transcended. On the other hand, although the value of the child is ontologically "in itself," the manifestation of such absoluteness still occurs for me, that is, it is an

---

33 [⋯] 性體, 此則就其對應個體而為其所以能起道德創造之超越根據說, 或總對天地萬物而可以使之有自性 (making thing as thing-in-itself) 說, [⋯] 。Ibid., II, 21–22.

event that is given in my mind of compassion. If my selfish desires make me blindly insensitive—if I am attached to my "little self" and its exclusive identity—the child is only an incident external to the inner, enclosed world of my mind.

The there-is-nothing-external of the mind of compassion is not stated in abstract and formal terms, but it should be seen in a practical way from the meaning of "incorporating" (*ti* 體) in the expression "incorporating all things under heaven (all things in the universe)." "Incorporating" expresses the fact that "nothing can be external to benevolence" is a concrete fact. To understand this, it is necessary for the pure transcendence of the moral mind-root to manifest itself in a present and effective way in practice. Only if I authentically suffer with all things under heaven can the "nothing external" (*wuwai* 物外) of the cosmic mind be born. Mou Zongsan points out that my knowledge of this all-encompassing moral reality is not the result of normal cognitive processes but a "retrospective verification" (*nijue tizheng* 逆覺體證). The meaning of *ni* (逆) in *nijue* (逆覺), translated here as "retrospective" but which we might call "consciousness/awakening by twitching" more literally, is not the self-consciousness we attain when, after exercising our mind, we return with reflection on ourselves. As I wrote above, *nijue* is not semantically related to reflection (*fansi* 反思) but rather to "turning to self" (*fanshen* 反身), of which Mengzi says, "There is no greater joy for me than to find, on self-examination, that I am authentic" (*fanshen er cheng, le moda yan* 反身而誠，樂莫大焉); not a mere turning back of thought (*si* 思) but of the organic totality (*shen* 身) that I am—an existential and practical turning back. By freeing myself from the limitations of my selfhood, I return to my authentic and original subjectivity, that is, I experience that there is nothing external to heaven, to my constitutive nature, and to my mind; therefore, I can agree with Mengzi that "everything is accomplished in me" (*wan wu jie bei yu wo* 萬物皆備於我) or with Zhang Zai that "there is nothing in the world that I am not" (*tianxia, wu yi wu feiwo* 天下，無一物非我). As for the term "verification" (*tizheng* 體證), it is based on the moral action of embodying. In each specific circumstance, my responsibility is to embody the infinity of the mind of benevolence, and this responsibility is at the same time joy, the joy that comes from realizing my deepest inner nature. "Retrospective verification" is not an analysis aiming at certainty but an effort to cultivate the self, which the Confucian tradition often refers to by the term *shendu* (慎獨), "vigilance in solitude."

Loneliness and "Vigilance in Solitude"

We pointed out earlier that the loneliness of the contemplative subject is an inevitable consequence of the withdrawal, isolation, and rupture of all relations wrought by the subject. This state of solitude is Descartes' starting point, and through the practice of systematic doubt, it becomes the defining character of the "I think, therefore I am" that is the culmination of reflection. The vigilance in solitude (*shendu* 慎獨) theorized by Confucianism signals to us the existence of a different understanding of being alone. The loneliness of the Cogito is negative because it is founded on the progressive exclusion of everything that cannot be brought back to inner intuitive certainty. The solitude pursued by Confucians through the practice of "vigilance in solitude" (*shendu* 慎獨) is positive and revelatory of the common origin of the self and the universe. The term *shendu* (慎獨), commonly translated as "vigilance/alertness in solitude," appears both in *Daxue*[34] as in *Zhongyong*,[35] referring to the effort of causing one's will to be sincere, i.e., harmonizing inner thoughts and external behavior, even in the minute affairs. There is a hermeneutic tradition extending from Han Dynasty

---

[34] "The notion of causing one's will to be sincere means to not deceive oneself. This happens when we do things such as despise despicable fragrances and are fond of pleasant sights. These are things we naturally enjoy. Therefore, the profound person must act to *shenqidu* 慎其獨. There is no evil to which the uncultivated person, dwelling retired, will not manifest; but when he sees a profound person, he instantly tries to disguise himself, concealing his evil, and displaying what is good. When others catch sight of him, they see his inner thoughts. Of what use is his disguise? This is the meaning of the saying—'When sincerity is within, it will take shape without.' Therefore, the profound person must act to *shenqidu*." James Legge (ed.), *The Four Books*. Taipei: Yishi Chubanshe, 1971, 366–367, with modifications. Cited in Tao Liang, "The Significance of *Shendu* in the Interpretation of Classical Learning and Zhu Xi's Misreading," *Dao* 13 (2014), 305–321.

[35] "The path may not be left for an instant. If it could be left, it would not be the path. On this account, the superior man does not wait till he sees things, to be cautious, nor till he hears things, to be apprehensive. There is nothing more visible than what is secret, and nothing more manifest than what is minute. Therefore, the superior man is watchful over himself, when he is alone." James Legge (ed.), *The Chinese Classics, Confucian Analects, the Great Learning, and the Doctrine of the Mean. Volume 1*, Oxford: Clarendon Press, 1893, p. 384.

thinker Zheng Xuan to Zhu Xi, that correlates this pursue of authenticity with the idea of "dwelling in solitude." In Zheng Xuan 鄭玄 (127–c. 200) this is understood in a more concrete way, as a private place far from the pression of public judgment: "*Shendu* is to be careful over what one does in closed quarters. The uncultivated person, when in secret, thinks that his words and actions will not be seen or heard, and so he completely expends his feelings".[36] Given the tendency to stray away from ethical standards when other people are not witnessing, Zheng Xuan remarks the necessity to cultivate moral integrity even in private behaviors. Zhu Xi interiorizes this idea of a secluded private place, arguing that the inner realm is par excellence the place out of reach for anyone but the subject: "being genuine or ingenuine depends on that place that others do not know about, but the self, alone, knows. Therefore, one must be cautious of this place, and guard its incipient tendencies."[37] As Tao Liang remarks, "in comparing Zhu Xi with Zheng Xuan, the biggest difference in Zhu Xi's understanding of *shendu* is that he broadens the connotation of *du* to include psychological and internal significance."[38] Being cautious and apprehensive in the innermost realm of the solitary self means for Zhu Xi to contrast selfish desires before they sprout and are made visible in our action. This understanding of solitude bears significant analogies with the Western idea of the secluded citadel of the self which appears when I cast aside the exterior social world.

There is however another possible interpretation, which correlates solitude (*du* 獨) with the idea of incipiency and inchoateness. Transcending the psychological appraisal of *du* (獨) as the state before

---

36 Zheng Xuan (鄭玄), "The Annotation of the Book of Rites." 禮記正義. In: Ruan Yuan (ed.), *Shisan jing zhushu*. 十三經注疏 (The Exegesis of the Thirteen Confucian Classics). Beijing: Zhonghua Shuju, 1980, p. 1625.

37 Zhu Xi, *Sishu zhangju jizhu*. 四書章句集注 (Collected Annotations of the Four Books), Beijing: Zhongguo Zhonghua shuju, 1983, p. 7. "In glossing *shendu* in "Daxue" and "Zhongyong" Zhu Xi 朱熹 (1130-1200) has not ventured outside the exegetical frameworks of leisure or solitary living (閒居獨處) and sincerity propounded by Zheng Xuan and Xunzi respectively. However, Zhu is more specific in defining du as what is only known to oneself and not others (獨者, 人所不知而己所獨知之地也) (1775, 6), by which he refers to one's demeanour, personal desires and hidden agenda in one's mind). Thus, for Zhu, *shendu* is to be conscious of indecent impulses and one should curb their brooding (慎獨, 察其私意起處防之)." Shirley Chan and Daniel Lee, "*Shendu* and *Qingdu*: Reading the Recovered Bamboo and Silk Manuscripts," *Frontiers of Philosophy in China* 10:1 (2015), 4–20 (pp. 7–8).

38 Tao Liang, "The Significance of *Shendu*', p. 314.

feelings are aroused (*weifa* 未發), Mou Zongsan, dipping into Ming dynasty Neo-Confucian scholars like Wang Yangming and Liu Jishan, interpret *du* as the original state of reality. This inchoate level preceding any boundaries and divisions, is not the Nothing to which the effort of the Daoist diaphanous subject aims, but the moral metaphysical mind as inexhaustible source of life and meaning. In *Phenomenon and Thing-in-Itself*,[39] Mou correlates Wang Yangming's idea of "solitary knowledge" (*duzhi* 獨知) with Wang Jii's 王畿 (1498-1583) idea of "knowledge of the Qian" (*qianzhi* 乾知). In the *Yijing*, Qian is the first hexagram and represents the heaven as creative force. Wang Longxi states that "*Qian* leads the Great Beginning. The knowledge of the Qian is the same as the original moral knowledge (*liangzhi* 良知). It is the first disclosure of the Inchoate, the beginning of the myriad things, and do not contrapose himself to the things objectifying them. Therefore, it is solitary (*du* 獨), and since it is self-aware it is called solitary knowledge (*duzhi* 獨知)."[40]

Developing this intuition, we can say that the state of solitude (*du* 獨) is not a condition of aloneness and seclusion but is strictly related to the idea of *jigan zhenji* (寂感真機) that we described in the Chapter 4 as the imperceptible gushing forth of the manifested universe. In this nascent state of mind, subjective understanding and objective universe have not been yet divided and contraposed. Any single character of the expression *jigan zhenji* condenses the new meaning of solitude in Mou's vertical model. First of all, solitude is silence (*ji* 寂). This silence does not imply the interruption of any communication with other people, like it happens in Montale's verses, when the poet says: "I will wander on silently, among people who do not turn around, with my secret". Solitude means the silent beginning, when the divisive words of the analytical reasoning have not yet be pronounced. This refers to the original moral mind, which according to Mengzi is mind of sympathy, mind of shame and aversion, mind of right and wrong, mind of humility. In preserving the solitude, I am open to the universality of things and actively participating to the human interchange, without

---

39 Mou Zongsan (牟宗三), *Xianxiang yu wuzishen*. 現象與物自身 (Phenomenon and Thing-in-Itself). *Mou Zongsan xiansheng quanji* 牟宗三先生全集 (Complete Works of Mou Zongsan), vol. XXI, Taipei: Lianhe baoxi wenhua jijin hui, 2003, pp. 97-98.

40 *Wang Ji, Longxi Wang xian sheng quan ji*. 龍谿王先生全集 (*The Complete Works of Master Wang Longxi*), Juan 6, Shanghai: Ming shan shuju, 1882, p. 2a (*reprinted Taipei: Huawen Shuju, 1970,* p. 407).

selfish attachments, because I stay next to the pure unstoppable flow of the mind of *ren*. As Mou states, "the perfect idea of morality is having pureness of virtue unceasingly emanating from my constitutive nature (*xingti* 性體)."[41] Solitude is indeed silent resonance *jigan* (寂感) which makes possible the maximum of alertness and responsivity. *Gan* is usually translated as "perception," but in Mou's thought it does not convey the idea of a passive reception, but, on the contrary, of an active and creative participation to the joy and sorrow of the universe. Furthermore, solitude is true, *zhen* (真), i.e., the place of realization of the true and authentic subjectivity: "Confucius emphasizes *ren*, which establishes the Subject. A strong moral sense requires emphasizing the Subject. Being *ren* is my own business, as illustrated in the following quotes: «When I want *ren*, *ren* is here» (Analects, 7:30), and: «Once we can discipline ourselves to conform to propriety, the world will return to *ren*», (Analects, 12:1)."[42] This moral self-awareness is the root of subjectivity.

The solitary self-consciousness of the Cartesian Cogito is only the abstract and exterior chrysalis of the self. Only through my moral effort do I become aware of my unique responsibility to universally extend the *ren* manifested in me. Solitude is the incipient revelation of *ren*. Whereas the Cogito expresses the simultaneous emersion of the self and of the certainty of it, solitude indicates the instantaneous realization (*dunwu* 頓悟) of the onto-cosmological principle through my practical moral action ("When I want *ren*, *ren* is here"). Finally, *ji* (機 or 幾) means here the imperceptible point of intersection between my horizontal participation to an everchanging reality and the vertical intuition that the perfection of the principle dwells in me as my innermost nature.[43] Solitude (*du* 獨) is realized in this intersection as uniqueness (*dutexing* 獨特性).

41　Mou Zongsan, *Nineteen Lectures on Chinese Philosophy*, p. 452 (slightly modified version).
42　Ibid., p. 74.
43　Iso Kern point out that *ji*, in ordinary language, indicates the elastic spring for firing arrows from a crossbow, and suggests the German word *Ur-sprung* (origin, source, spring) as possible translation. See Iso Kern, *Das Wichtigste im Leben. Wang Yangming (1472–1529) und seine Nachfolger über die «Verwirklichung des ursprünglichen Wissens»*, Basel: Schwabe, 2010, pp. 469–470). Mou's metaphor of the Cereus flower (see below) perfectly depicts the idea of *Ursprung* as germinating activity and elasticity.

Uniqueness is another word for the concrete universality which Mou pursued since his early epistemologically-oriented works. What is not horizontally dispersed in fragmentary and fleeting events, but as the same time is not vertically hovering above reality like an abstract truth, possesses uniqueness. When the subject embodies the mind of benevolence, the punctual manifestation of *ren* occurs in spiritual response (*shen gan shen ying* 神感神應) to different situations, without losing its universal extension. "The cereus rarely blossoms, and when it does the blooming is completed in only one or two hours. While it is blooming, fully radiating its luster, the blossom would be filled with elasticity of life so strong that it could not help but vibrate and stir. Because intensive truths are manifested in processes with elasticity that cannot be stopped or nailed down, they possess both universality and uniqueness."[44] Extensive truths belong to the scientific domain; on the contrary, "intensive truths are related to life, and only life has intensiveness. Intensiveness pertains to life and to the Subject. Only life as the Subject can exhibit intensiveness."[45] Mou's metaphor of the Cereus flower, blooming only few times a year, provide us with an evocative image of the subject as solitary and unique. The subject, like the flower, is a living point of intersection. When this timely intersection produces itself, the incipient active force (*ji* 機) triggers the self-awakening of the subject, which vibrates[46] with the concreteness and uniqueness of its dynamism.

Wang Yangming, in his poem *Yong liangzhi* 詠良知, writes that "the soundless, odorless moment of solitary self-knowledge contains the ground of heaven, earth, and all things."[47] When there is neither sound nor smell, and emotions—anger, sorrow, and joy—have not yet manifested, we are in the nascent state, the subtlest and most fruitful spiritual realm (*jingjie*) when mind and things are woven together in the most perfect way. Here, where the creative unity has not yet produced any sensory distinction or conflict of emotions, I am in the "instant of

---

44 Mou Zongsan, *Nineteen Lectures on Chinese Philosophy*, p. 35.
45 Ibid., p. 27.
46 This vibration, in Mou's text *chandong* (顫動) and *fadou* (發抖), is akin with the trembling and shivering of the soul (*ziwo zhendong* 自我震動) when moral action is required, like in the example of the child about to fall in a well.
47 Translated by Julia Ching, *To Acquire Wisdom: The Way of Wang Yang-Ming*, New York: Columbia University Press, 1976, p. 164.

solitary self-consciousness" that only my experience can certify. The burden of this certification is the irreplaceable value of subjectivity, but solitude here is not isolation. Mou Zongsan explains that solitude (*du* 獨) is also an attribute of things:

> Where its knowledge stops and acts as the root of everything, this is the thing in its original meaning, that is, solitary. [...] The thing that I must incorporate in me so that nothing is neglected or lost is the solitude constitutive of the original thing.[48]

The thing that cannot be left behind is the thing itself, saved in the spiritual realm of moral metaphysics—no longer a usable object but an absolute end. The value of being one without any duality between me and the universe derives precisely from the original solitude, which is the innate moral consciousness as it reveals itself in practical effort, and at the same time is a creative metaphysical reality. In "moral action," my sense of compassion is awakened, and I intuitively experience that I and the other, I and the universe, are one body. Mou calls this indissoluble commonality "constitutive nature" (*xingti* 性體) and shows how it can unfold its authentic meaning only through my self-consciousness, whereby mind and nature are two inseparable sides of the same creative moral reality. If, in rational reflection, what I achieve is a pure and isolated subjectivity with no relation to the external world, on the contrary, the constitutive solitude I achieve through retrospective verification (*nijue tizheng* 逆覺體證), that is, turning back to my origin, is not a condition of isolation but the mutual correspondence and infinite relating of myself and all things.

Differences between Chinese and Western Culture: From "What Is a Self?" to "How to Become an Authentic Self?"

If we return to the starting point of this book—the question "what is the self?"—we can find that, while self-awareness seems to be a universal experience and the cognitive sciences that study the nature

---

48 [⋯] 其所之止处与作为本者即是意本之物, 所谓独也。[⋯] 所体之物而不可遗者即是此意本之物之独体也。Mou Zongsan, *From Lu Xiangshan to Liu Jishan*, p. 392.

of the self aspire for universality, their origins and development have been decisively influenced by Western culture, based on a logical and epistemological paradigm. The most important questions raised by the philosophy of mind and discussions among scientists about whether artificial intelligence can develop self-awareness unwittingly accept knowledge models shaped by Western culture.

The development of neuroscience and cognitive science has promoted research around the "self." The accelerated development of artificial intelligence has led cognitive science to use the human brain as a model to explain artificial intelligence. In public and academic debate, the question of whether self-awareness can be awakened in artificial intelligence is often addressed. One of the most popular interpretative models is the emergentist model, according to which self-awareness would be a property that "emerges" spontaneously when the number and complexity of neural connections exceed a certain threshold. The self is considered here to be a function of our knowledge and the enhancement of our ability to process information. The demands of theoretical elaboration in the scientific community determine the methods and scope of research around consciousness and subjectivity and give it a distinct epistemological character. In these discussions, the practical-moral perspective of the "self" is often ignored.[49] Western ideas based on dominant epistemological models have a decisive influence on all manifestations of culture. Although contemporary neuroscience and cognitive science are not limited to the research scope of Western universities, the dominant epistemological model in the sciences extends its influence universally. What is often overlooked is how unthinking cultural assumptions and the linguistic structures in which they are

---

49 Guo Siping (郭斯萍), in his interesting work *The Selfless Self*, contrasts the biologically-based Western psychology with the "spiritual psychology" elaborated in Neo-Confucianism. This spiritual psychology is based on the conviction that "the individual is able to transcend the biological self, and totally cast aside the little Self (*xiao wo* 小我) ruled by human yanjiu, in order to transform itself in the Great Self (*da wo* 大我), ruled by the mind of Dao, and encompassing all the world, and is able to reach the highest spiritual psychological level, in which the mind is one and the same with the universe, and it corresponds to the totality of heaven-earth-man. This level is the spiritual state (*jingjie* 境界) of the unselfish and impartial mind of benevolence (*ren* 仁)." Guo Siping (郭斯萍), *Wu wo zhi wo. Cheng Zhu lixue zhi jingshen ziwo sixiang yanjiu.* 无我之我。程朱理学之精神自我思想研究 (The Selfless Self. Research on the Idea of Spiritual Self in the Cheng-Zhu School of Neo-Confucianism), Jinan: Shandong Jiaoyu Chubanshe, 2011, p. 136.

formulated can inadvertently limit the questions we ask and give partial direction to research. Mou Zongsan, in his book *Philosophy of History*, states, about the Western epistemological model, that

> from the point of view of content, it is driven by logic, mathematics and the sciences. Put in general terms, the guiding principle is an external and abstract principle; it is the counterpart to the question "what?" on which rational understanding focuses.[50]

Mou believes that this analytical-rational spirit ends up producing a mere "intellectual subject." In contrast, Chinese culture that emphasizes moral practice, particularly Confucian humanism, demonstrates a "synthetic spirit." Such a cultural model does not emphasize abstract understanding but, rather, active moral participation and self-cultivation effort, and the resulting subject is a moral subject. We could sum up the contrast indicated by Mou between Chinese and Western culture in two different questions: "What do we mean by the term 'subject'?" and "How to exercise one's self to the point of rising to authentic subjectivity?"

Summarizing the research so far, we can say that Mou identifies three defining characteristics of the "self" or "subject" in his texts. First, the "self" is only fully realized in a vertical dimension, which means that absorbing and processing information is not the primary function of the subject. When I speak of a "self," I mean a dynamism of uninterrupted self-transcendence and a desire to ascend to a higher level of realization. Second, what unlocks the dimension of interiority is not the will to knowledge but the manifestation of the all-encompassing moral mind in my practical action. We are not talking here about moral philosophy understood as a branch of philosophical research focused on solving ethical problems, such as the conflict between will and duty; the moral mind is an individual and cosmic force that actively generates reality by revealing its value and meaning. Finally, the self cannot emerge in a state of isolation. Indeed, it is the manifestation of an interrelation and mutual commitment to moral participation between the subject and the universe. Without these characteristics that Mou summarizes in his

---

50 [⋯] 從內容方面說, 自以邏輯數學科學為主。[⋯]。則其所盡之理大體是超越而外在之理, 或以觀解之智所撲著之 "是什麼" 之對象為主[⋯]。Mou Zongsan (牟宗三), *Lishi zhexue*. 歷史哲學 (Philosophy of History). *Mou Zongsan xiansheng quanji*. 牟宗三先生全集 (Complete Works of Mou Zongsan), vol. IX.2, Taipei: Lianhe baoxi wenhua jijin hui, 2003, p. 196.

moral metaphysics, the emergence of a "self" cannot be guaranteed. The human does not reach its culmination through contemplation and reflection. Self-awareness means, first of all, an awakening to myself from selfish slumber and discovering myself woven into others and the cosmos, actualizing and instantiating in me the principle of oneness between heaven and man (*tianrenheyi* 天人合一). Recognizing that culture has a non-negligible influence on our research and adopting a dynamically comparative gaze can help us restore the wholeness of human experience. Only by intersecting the horizontal and vertical dimensions of our being can our quest advance. To quote a line from "Climbing the Stork Tower" by Tang-era poet Wang Zhihuan 王之渙:

> If you'll enjoy a grander sight,
> you'd climb up to a greater height.
>
> *Yu qiong qianli mu*
> *geng shang yiceng lou.*
> 欲窮千里目
> 更上一層樓。

Bibliography

Albahari, Miri. *Analytical Buddhism. The Two-Tiered Illusion of the Self*. New York: Palgrave Macmillan, 2006.

Angle, Stephen C. *Contemporary Confucian Political Philosophy: Toward Progressive Confucianism*. Malden, MA: Polity, 2012.

Angle, Stephen C. *Sagehood. The Contemporary Significance of Neo-Confucian Philosophy*. New York: Oxford University Press, 2009.

Arendt, Hannah. *The Life of the Mind*. San Diego (CA): Harcourt, 1981.

Arola, Adam C. "The Movement of Philosophy: Freedom as Ecstatic Thinking in Schelling and Heidegger." PhD Dissertation, University of Oregon, 2008.

Asakura, Tomomi. "On the Principle of Comparative East Asian Philosophy: Nishida Kitarō and Mou Zongsan." *National Central University Journal of Humanities* 54 (2013), 1–25.

Augustine of Hippo. *On Free Choice of the Will*. Indianapolis, IN, and Cambridge, UK: Hackett Publishing Company, 1993.

Augustine of Hippo. *The Expositions On The Psalms*, trans. by Alexander Cleveland Coxe. Altenmünster: Jazzybee Verlag, 2012.

Beretta, Paolo. "L'assoluto contraccolpo in sé stesso. La questione dell'origine tra Hegel e Derrida." *Nóema* 4:2 (2013), 22–80.

Bergson, Henri. *The Creative Mind*. Westport, CT: Greenwood Press, 1968.

Billioud, Sébastien. *Thinking through Confucian Modernity. A Study of Mou Zongsan's Moral Metaphysics*. Leiden: Brill, 2012.

Binswanger, Ludwig, and Foucault, Michel. "Dream and Existence." *Review of Existential Psychology and Psychiatry* 19:1 (1985), reprinted as: Binswanger, Ludwig, and Foucault, Michel. *Dream and Existence*. London: Humanities Press, 1993.

Block, Ned. "On a Confusion about a Function of Consciousness." *Behavioral and Brain Sciences* 18:2 (1995), 227–247.

Block, Ned, Flanagan, Owen, and Güzeldere, Güven (ed.). *The Nature of Consciousness. Philosophical Debates*. Cambridge, MA: MIT Press, 1997.

Blumenfeld, Jacob. "Hegel's Absolute Knowledge and its Many Interpretations." Unpublished Article, 2012, https://www.academia.edu/3755446/Hegels_Absolute_Knowledge_and_its_Many_Interpretations

Borner, Marc, Frank, Manfred, and Williford, Kenneth. "Pre-reflective Self-Consciousness and the *De Se* Constraint: The Legacy of the Heidelberg School." *ProtoSociology* 36 (2019), 7–33.

Brown, Kirk Warren, and Leary, Mark R. (ed.). *The Oxford Handbook of Hypo-Egoic Phenomena*. Oxford: Oxford University Press, 2016.

Bresciani, Umberto. *Reinventing Confucianism*. Taipei: Taipei Ricci Institute for Chinese Studies, 2001.

Bush, Susan. *The Chinese Literati on Painting. Su Shih (1037–1101) to Tung Ch'i-ch'ang (1555–1636)*. Hong Kong: Hong Kong University Press, 2012.

Bussanich, John. "Plotinus's Metaphysics of the One." In: Lloyd, Gerson (ed.). *The Cambridge Companion to Plotinus*. New York and Cambridge, UK: Cambridge University Press, 1996, pp. 38–65, https://doi.org/10.1017/CCOL0521470935.003

Cahiers du centre Marcel Granet—Cahier 2: Sujet, Moi, Personne. Paris: Presses Universitaires de France, 2004.

Cai Renhou (蔡仁). *Mou Zongsan xiansheng xueshu nianpu (1930–2019)*. 牟宗三先生学术年谱 (Chronology of Mou Zongsan's Life). Taipei: Taiwan Xuesheng Shuju, 1996

Castañeda, Hector-Neri. *The Phenomeno-Logic of the I: Essays on Self-Consciousness*. Bloomington, IN: Indiana University Press, 1999.

Cavarra, Berenice. "*Parousìa*: colori, diafano e luce in Aristotele e nella tradizione aristotelica." *Medicina nei secoli. Journal of History of Medicine and Medical Humanities* 32:2 (2020), 543–558.

Chalmers, David. "Facing Up to the Problem of Consciousness." *Journal of Consciousness Studies* 2:3 (1995), 200–219.

Chan, Serina N. *The Thought of Mou Zongsan*. Leiden: Brill, 2011.

Chan, Shirley, and Lee, Daniel. "*Shendu* and *Qingdu:* Reading the Recovered Bamboo and Silk Manuscripts." *Frontiers of Philosophy in China*, 10:1 (2015), 4–20.

Chan, Wing-Tsit (ed.). *Instructions for Practical Living, and Other Neo-Confucian Writings by Wang Yang-Ming*. New York and London: Columbia University Press, 1963.

Chan, Wing-Tsit. *A Source Book in Chinese Philosophy*. Princeton, NJ: Princeton University Press, 2008.

Chen Yingnian (陈迎年). *Ganying yu xinwu: Mou Zongsan zhexue pipan*. 感应与心物: 牟宗三哲学批判 (The Resonance between the Heart-Mind and

Things: A Critique of Mou Zongsan's Philosophy). Shanghai: Shanghai sanlian shudian, 2005.

Chen Yingnian (陈迎年). *Zhi de zhijue yu shenmei zhijue: Mou Zongsan meixue pipan.* 智的直觉与审美直觉：牟宗三美学批判 (Intellectual Intuition and Aesthetic Intuition: A Critique of Mou Zongsan's Aesthetics). Shanghai: Shanghai renmin chubanshe, 2012.

Chen, Xunwu. *Being and Authenticity.* Leiden: Brill, 2004.

Cheng, Zhihua (程志华). *Mou Zongsan zhexue yanjiu—Daode de xing'ershangxue zhi keneng.* 牟宗三哲学研究：道德的形而上学之可能 (A Study of Mou Zongsan's Philosophy: The Possibility of Moral Metaphysics). Beijing: Renmin chubanshe, 2009.

Ching, Julia. *To Acquire Wisdom. The Way of Wang Yang-Ming.* New York: Columbia University Press, 1976.

Churchland, Patricia. *Touching a Nerve: The Self as Brain.* New York: W. W. Norton & Company, 2013.

Clark, Andy. *Being There: Putting Brain, Body, and World Together Again.* Cambridge, MA: MIT Press, 1997.

Clower, Jason (ed.). *Late Works of Mou Zongsan. Selected Essays on Chinese Philosophy.* Leiden and Boston, MA: Brill, 2014.

Clower, Jason. *The Unlikely Buddhologist. Tiantai Buddhism in Mou Zongsan's New Confucianism.* Leiden: Brill, 2010.

Coogan, Michael (ed.). *The New Oxford Annotated Bible. New Revised Standard Version with the Apocrypha.* New York and Oxford: Oxford University Press, 2010.

Cua, Antonio S. (ed.). *Encyclopedia of Chinese Philosophy.* New York: Routledge, 2008.

Damasio, Antonio R. *Descartes' Error: Emotion, Reason, and the Human Brain.* New York: Putnam, 1994.

De Bary, William Theodore. *Self and Society in Ming Thought.* New York: Columbia University Press, 1970.

De Bary, William Theodore. *The Message of the Mind in Neo-Confucianism.* New York: Columbia University Press, 1989.

Dennett, Daniel. *Sweet Dreams: Philosophical Obstacles to a Science of Consciousness.* Cambridge, MA: MIT Press, 2005.

Derrida, Jacques. *Writing and Difference.* London and New York: Routledge, 1978.

Derrida, Jacques. *Margins of Philosophy.* Brighton: Harvester, 1982.

Eihmanis, Kaspars. *Study of Mou Zongsan's Interpretation of Laozi*. Unpublished paper delivered at Institute of Chinese Literature and Philosophy, Academia Sinica, Taiwan, http://www.litphil.sinica.edu.tw/home/news/2010051<wbr></wbr>9/20100519.htm

Ellis, Addison. "Kant on Self-Consciousness as Self-Limitation." *Contemporary Studies in Kantian Philosophy* 5 (2020), 15–36.

Elstein, David (ed.). *Dao Companion to Contemporary Confucian Philosophy*. London and Berlin: Springer, 2021.

Emilsson, Eyjólfur K, and Strange, Steven K. (ed.). *Plotinus Ennead VI.4 and VI.5. On the Presence of Being, One and the Same, Everywhere as a Whole*. Zurich and Athens: Parmenides Publishing, 2015.

Fang, Zhaohui (方朝晖). "Zhongguo wenhua wei he chengxing jingjielun?" 中国文化为何盛行境界论? (Why Is the Idea of *Jingjie* Prevailing in Chinese Culture?). *Guoxue xuekan* 1 (2020), 109–114.

Fech, Andrej. "Seeing and Hearing in the Laozi and Zhuangzi and the Question of Authority and Authenticity." *Religions* 10:3 (2019), 155, https://doi.org/10.3390/rel10030155

Fichte, Johann Gottlieb. *Fichtes Werke*, ed. by Immanuel Hermann Fichte, 11 vols. Berlin: Walter de Gruyter, 1971.

Frank, Manfred. *Selbstbewußtsein und Selbsterkenntnis. Essays zur analytischen Philosophie der Subjektivität*. Stuttgart: Reclam, 1991.

Frank, Manfred. *Selfbewußtseintheorien von Fichte bis Sartre*. Frankfurt am Main: Suhrkamp, 1991.

Frie, Roger. *Subjectivity and Intersubjectivity in Modern Philosophy and Psychoanalysis. A Study of Sartre, Binswanger, Lacan, and Habermas*. Lanham, MD: Rowman and Littlefeld, 1997.

Fung, Yiu-ming. "Wang Yang-ming's Theory of *Liang-zhi*. A New Interpretation of Wang Yang-ming's Philosophy." *Tsing Hua Journal of Chinese Studies* 42:22 (2012), 261–300.

Fung, Yu-Lan. *A Short History of Chinese Philosophy*. New York: Simon and Schuster, 1960.

Fung, Yu-Lan. *The Spirit of Chinese Philosophy*. London: Kegan Paul, Trench, Trubner and Co., 1947.

Gallagher, Shaun (ed.). *The Oxford Handbook of the Self*. Oxford: Oxford University Press, 2011, https://doi.org/10.1093/oxfordhb/9780199548019.001.0001

Ganeri, Jonardon. *The Self. Naturalism, Consciousness, and the First-Person Stance*. Oxford: Oxford University Press, 2015.

Gardner, Daniel K. *Zhu Xi's Readings of the Analects. Canon, Commentary and the Classical Tradition*. New York: Columbia University, 2003.

Gelžinytė, Brigita. "Performing Reason in Schelling and Hegel." PhD Dissertation, Vilnius University, 2020, https://epublications.vu.lt/object/elaba:74308027/MAIN

Guo, Siping (郭斯萍). *Wu wo zhi wo. Cheng Zhu lixue zhi jingshen ziwo sixiang yanjiu*. 无我之我。程朱理学之精神自我思想研究 (The Selfless Self. Research on the Idea of Spiritual Self in the Cheng-Zhu School of Neo-Confucianism). Jinan: Shandong Jiaoyu Chubanshe, 2011.

Güzeldere, Güven. "The Many Faces of Consciousness: A Field Guide." In: Block, Ned, Flanagan, Owen, and Güzeldere, Güven (ed.). *The Nature of Consciousness. Philosophical Debates*. Cambridge, MA: MIT Press 1997, pp. 1–67.

Hadot, Pierre. *Philosophy as a Way of Life. Spiritual Exercises from Socrates to Foucault*. Malden, MA, and Oxford: Blackwell Publishing, 1995.

Han, Christina. "Envisioning the Territory of the Sages: The Neo-Confucian Discourse of *Jingjie*." *Journal of Confucian Philosophy and Culture* 22 (2014), 85–109.

Han, Christina. "Territory of the Sages: Neo-Confucian Discourse of Wuyi Nine Bends *Jingjie*." PhD Dissertation. University of Toronto, 2011, https://tspace.library.utoronto.ca/bitstream/1807/29740/1/Han_Hee_Yeon_C_201105_PhD_thesis.pdf

Hegel, Georg Wilhelm Friedrich. *Hegel's Lectures on the History of Philosophy, Volume 3*. Translated by E. S. Haldane and Frances H. Simpson. London: Routledge and Kegan Paul Ltd, 1955, https://www.gutenberg.org/cache/epub/58169/pg58169-images.html

Hegel, Georg Wilhelm Friedrich. *Hegel's Phenomenology of Spirit*. Translated by A.V. Miller with an analysis of the text and foreword by J. N. Findlay. Oxford: Oxford University Press, 1977.

Hegel, Georg Wilhelm Friedrich. *The Phenomenology of Spirit*. Cambridge, UK, and New York: Cambridge University Press, 2018.

Hegel, Georg Wilhelm Friedrich. *The Science of Logic*. Cambridge, UK, and New York: Cambridge University Press, 2010.

Heidegger, Martin. *Der Satz vom Grund (1955–1956)*. Frankfurt: Vittorio Klostermann, 1997.

Heidegger, Martin. *The Fundamental Concepts of Metaphysics: World, Finitude, Solitude*. Bloomington, IN: Indiana University Press, 1995.

Heilborn, Erst (ed.). *Novalis Schriften. Teil 2, Hälfte 1*. Berlin and Boston, MA: De Gruyter, 1901.

Heinämaa, Sara, and Reuter Martina (ed.). *Psychology and Philosophy. Inquiries into the Soul from Late Scholasticism to Contemporary Thought*. New York: Springer, 2009.

Henrich, Dieter. *Between Kant and Hegel. Lectures on German Idealism*. Cambridge, MA: Harvard University Press, 2003.

Henry, Aaron, and Thompson, Evan. "Witnessing from Here: Self-Awareness from a Bodily Versus Embodied Perspective." In: Gallagher, Shaun (ed.). *The Oxford Handbook of the Self*. Oxford: Oxford University Press, 2011, pp. 228–250, https://doi.org/10.1093/oxfordhb/9780199548019.003.0010

Henry, Michel. *Philosophy and Phenomenology of the Body*. Dordrecht: Springer, 1976. https://doi.org/10.15388/vu.thesis.98

Huang, Kuan-min (黃冠閔). *Gantong yu huidang: Tang Junyi zhexuelun tan*. 感通與迴盪: 唐君毅哲學論探 (Affective Communication and Echo: An Exploration of Tang Junyi's Philosophy). Taipei: Lianjing chuban gongsi, 2011.

Hume, David. *A Treatise of Human Nature*. David Fate Norton and Mary J. Norton (ed.). Oxford: Oxford University Press, 2005.

Husserl, Edmund. *Cartesian Meditations. An Introduction to Phenomenology*. Dordrecht: Kluwer Academic Publishers, 1991.

Husserl, Edmund. *Die Bernauer Manuskripte über das Zeitbewußtsein (1917/18)* (Husserliana: Edmund Husserl—Gesammelte Werke 33). Dordrecht: Kluwer Academic Publishers, 2001.

Husserl, Edmund. *Ideas I*. New York: Macmillan, 1913.

Husserl, Edmund. *Logische Untersuchungen, Vol. II* (Husserliana: Edmund Husserl—Gesammelte Werke 19/2). The Hague: Nijhoff, 1984.

Husserl, Edmund. *Zur Phänomenologie der Intersubjektivität. Texte aus dem Nachlass. Zweiter Teil: 1921–1928*. Kern, Iso (ed.). The Hague: Nijhogg, 1973.

I Ching: The Book of Changes, tr. by James Legge. New York: Dover Publication, 1963.

Ivanhoe, Philip, and Bloom, Irene (ed.). *Mencius*. New York: Columbia University Press, 2009.

Jorgensen, John, Lusthaus, Dan, Makeham, John, and Strange, Mark (ed.). *Treatise on Awakening Mahāyāna Faith*. Oxford: Oxford University Press, 2019, https://doi.org/10.1093/oso/9780190297701.001.0001

Jullien, François. *Figure dell'immanenza. Una lettura filosofica del I Ching* [Original: *Figures de l'immanence: Pour une lecture philosophique du Yi King, Le classique du changement*]. Milan: Laterza, 2019.

Kant, Immanuel. *Critique of Pure Reason*. London: Palgrave Macmillan, 2007.

Kant, Immanuel. *What Real Progress Has Metaphysics Made in Germany Since the Time of Leibniz and Wolff?*. New York: Abaris Books, 1983.

Kantor, Hans-Rudolph. *Die Heilslehre im Tiantai-Denken des Zhiyi (538–597) und der philosophische Begriff des 'Unendlichen' bei Mou Zongsan (1909–1995): die Verknüpfung von Heilslehre und Ontologie in der chinesischen Tiantai*. Wiesbaden: Harrassowitz Verlag, 1999.

Kaufman, Walter (ed.). *Existentialism from Dostoevsky to Sartre*. Cleveland, OH, and New York: World Publishing Company, 1969.

Kern, Iso. *Das Wichtigste im Leben. Wang Yangming (1472–1529) und seine Nachfolger über die «Verwirklichung des ursprünglichen Wissens»*. Basel: Schwabe, 2010.

Klemm, David E., and Zöller, Günter (ed.). *Figuring the Self. Subject, Absolute, and Others in Classical German Philosophy*. New York: State University of New York Press, 1997.

Kosman, Aryeh. *Virtues of Thought. Essays on Plato and Aristotle*. Cambridge, MA: Harvard University Press, 2014, https://doi.org/10.4159/harvard.9780674416437

Lauer, Christopher. "Space, Time, and the Openness of Hegel's Absolute Knowing." *Idealistic Studies* 36:3 (2006), 169–181.

Lee, Ming-huei (李明輝). *Rujia yu daode.* 儒家與道德 (Confucianism and Morality). Taipei: Lianjing, 1990.

Lee, Ming-huei (李明輝). *Dangdai Ruxue de ziwo zhuanhua.* 當代儒學的自我轉化 (The Self-Transformation of Contemporary Modern Confucianism). Beijing: Zhongguo shehui kexue chuban she, 2001.

Lee, Ming-huei (李明輝). *Confucianism: Its Roots and Global Significance*. Honolulu: University of Hawai'i Press, 2017.

Lee, Ming-huei (李明輝). *Rujia yu Kangde.* 儒家與康德 (Confucianism and Kant). Xinbei: Lian jing, 2018.

Lee, Ming-huei (李明輝). *Xin ruxue lunwen jingxuan ji Li Minghui xin ruxue lunwen jingxuan ji.* 新儒學論文精選集李明輝新儒學論文精選集 (Selected Works of Lee Ming-huei on New Confucianism). Taipei: Taiwan Xuesheng Shuju, 2019.

Legge, James (ed.). *The Chinese Classics, Confucian Analects, the Great Learning, and the Doctrine of the Mean. Volume 1*. Oxford: Clarendon Press, 1893.

Legge, James (ed.), *The Chinese Classics: Translated into English with Preliminary Essays and Explanatory Notes by James Legge. Volume 2. The Life and Teachings of Mencius*. London: N. Trübner, 1875.

Legge, James (ed.). *The Four Books*. Taipei: Yishi Chubanshe, 1971.

Legge James (ed.), *The I Ching*, New York: Dover Publishing, 1963

Lehmann, Olf. *Zur Moralmetaphysischen Grundlegung einer Konfuzianische Moderne. "Phylosophierung der Tradition" und Konfuzianisierung der Aufklärung bei Mou Zongsan*. Leipzig: Leipziger Universitätverlag, 2003.

Lévinas, Emmanuel. *En Decouvrant L'Existence avec Husserl et Heidegger*. Paris: Vrin, 1949.

Lévinas, Emmanuel. *Of God Who Comes to Mind*. Stanford, CA: Stanford University Press, 1986.

Lévinas, Emmanuel. *Otherwise than Being, or, Beyond Essence*. Pittsburgh, PA: Duquesne University Press, 2011.

Lévinas, Emmanuel. *Totality and Infinity. An Essay on Exteriority*. Pittsburgh, PA: Duquesne University Press, 1969.

Lippiello, Tiziana. "Measuring Human Relations: Continuities and Discontinuities in the Reading of the *Lunyu*," *Sinica venetiana* 3 (2016), 23–40.

Lin, Ruisheng (林瑞生). *Mou Zongsan pingzhuan: xiandai xin rujia*. 牟宗三评传: 现代新儒家 (A Critical Revision of Mou Zongsan: Contemporary New Confucianism). Jinan: Qi lu shu she, 2009.

Liu, Aijun (刘爱军). *Shizhi yu zhizhi: Mou Zongsan zhishilun sixiang yanjiu*. 识知与智知: 牟宗三知识论思想研究 (Knowledge and Wisdom: A Study of Mou Zongsan's Epistemology). Beijing: Renmin chubanshe, 2009.

Liu Shuxian (刘述先). *Rujia sixiang yihan zhi xiandai chanshi lunji*. 儒家思想意涵之现代阐释论集 (A Collection of Modern Interpretations of the Meaning of Confucian Thought). Taipei: Institute of Chinese Literature and Philosophy, Academia Sinica, 2000.

Lu Xiangshan (陆象山), *Xiangshan quanji*. 象山全集 (Complete Works of Lu Xiangshan). Taipei: Zhonghua, 1965.

Lucretius Carus, Titus. *On the Nature of Things*. Oxford: Clarendon Press, 1910.

Makeham, John (ed.). *The Awakening of Faith and New Confucian Philosophy*. Leiden: Brill, 2021.

Makeham, John (ed.). *New Confucianism: A Critical Examination*. New York: Palgrave Macmillan, 2003.

Marchal, Kai. "Paradoxes and Possibilities of 'Confucian Freedom': From Yan Fu (1853–1921) to Mou Zongsan (1909–1995)." *Philosophy East and West* 66:1 (2016), 218–258, https://doi.org/10.1353/pew.2016.0001

McGynn, Bernard. "Lost in the Abyss. The Function of Abyss Language in Medieval Mysticism." *Franciscan Studies* 72 (2014), 433–452.

Meng, Peiyuan (蒙培元). *Xinling chaoyue yu jingjie*. 心灵超越与境界 (Spiritual Transcendence and State of Mind). Beijing: Renmin Chubanshe, 1998.

Meng, Peiyuan (蒙培元). *Zhongguo zhexue zhuti siwei.* 中国哲学主体思维 (The idea of subject in Chinese philosophy). Beijing: Renmin chubanshe, 2005.

Merleau-Ponty, Maurice. *Phenomenology of Perception.* London and New York: Routledge, 1962.

Merleau-Ponty, Maurice. *Signs.* Evanston, IL: Northwestern University Press, 1964.

Metzinger, Thomas. "The No-Self Alternative." In: Gallagher, Shaun (ed.). *The Oxford Handbook of the Self.* Oxford: Oxford University Press, 2011, pp. 279–296, https://doi.org/10.1093/oxfordhb/9780199548019.003.0012

Min, Shijun (闵仕君). *Mou Zongsan "Daode de xingshangxue" yanjiu.* 牟宗三"道德的形上学"研究 (Research on Mou Zongsan's "Moral Metaphysics"). Chengdu: Bashu shushe, 2005.

Morton, Timothy (ed.). *Cultures of Taste, Theories of Appetite. Eating Romanticism.* New York: Palgrave Macmillan, 2004.

Mou, Zongsan (牟宗三). *Caixing yu xuanli.* 才性與玄理 (Physical Nature and the "Profound Thought"). *Mou Zongsan xiansheng quanji.* 牟宗三先生全集 (Complete Works of Mou Zongsan), vol. II. Taipei: Lianhe baoxi wenhua jijin hui, 2003.

Mou, Zongsan (牟宗三). *Cong Lu Xiangshan dao Liu Jishan.* 從陸象山到劉蕺山 (From Lu Xiangshan to Liu Jishan). *Mou Zongsan xiansheng quanji.* 牟宗三先生全集 (Complete Works of Mou Zongsan), vol. VIII. Taipei: Lianhe baoxi wenhua jijin hui, 2003.

Mou, Zongsan (牟宗三). *Daode de lixiangzhuyi.* 道德的理想主義 (Moral Idealism). *Mou Zongsan xiansheng quanji.* 牟宗三先生全集 (Complete Works of Mou Zongsan), vol. IX.1. Taipei: Lianhe baoxi wenhua jijin hui, 2003.

Mou, Zongsan (牟宗三). "Laozi Daodejing yanjianglu." 老子《道德經》講演錄 (Lectures on Laozi's "Daodejing"). *Ehu yuekan* 334–343 (2003/2004).

Mou, Zongsan (牟宗三). "Zhuangzi 'Qiwulun' yanjianglu." 莊子«齊物論» 演講綠 (Lectures on Zhuangzi's "Qiwulun"). *Ehu yuekan* 318–332 (2002/2003).

Mou, Zongsan (牟宗三). *Lishi zhexue.* 歷史哲學 (Philosophy of History). *Mou Zongsan xiansheng quanji.* 牟宗三先生全集 (Complete Works of Mou Zongsan), vol. IX.2. Taipei: Lianhe baoxi wenhua jijin hui, 2003.

Mou, Zongsan (牟宗三). *Nineteen Lectures on Chinese Philosophy: A Brief Outline of Chinese Philosophy and the Issues It Entails.* Scotts Valley, CA: CreateSpace Independent Publishing Platform, 2015.

Mou, Zongsan (牟宗三). *Renshi xin zhi pipan.* 認識心之批判 (Critique of the Cognitive Mind). 2 vols. *Mou Zongsan xiansheng quanji.* 牟宗三先生全集 (Complete Works of Mou Zongsan), vols XVIII–XIX. Taipei: Lianhe baoxi wenhua jijin hui, 2003.

Mou, Zongsan (牟宗三). *Wushi zishu.* 五十自述 (*Autobiography at Fifty*). Taipei: Ehu Chubanshe, 1989.

Mou, Zongsan (牟宗三). *Xianxiang yu wuzishen.* 現象與物自身 (Phenomenon and Thing-in-Itself). *Mou Zongsan xiansheng quanji* 牟宗三先生全集 (Complete Works of Mou Zongsan), vol. XXI. Taipei: Lianhe baoxi wenhua jijin hui, 2003.

Mou, Zongsan (牟宗三). *Xinti yu xingti.* 心體與性體 (Constitutive Mind and Constitutive Nature). *Mou Zongsan xiansheng quanji.* 牟宗三先生全集 (Complete Works of Mou Zongsan), vols. V–VII. Taipei: Lianhe baoxi wenhua jijin hui, 2003.

Mou, Zongsan (牟宗三). *Zhi de zhijue yu zhongguo zhexue.* 智的直覺與中國哲學 (Intellectual Intuition and Chinese Philosophy). *Mou Zongsan xiansheng quanji.* 牟宗三先生全集 (Complete Works of Mou Zongsan), vol. XX. Taipei: Lianhe baoxi wenhua jijin hui, 2003.

Mou, Zongsan (牟宗三). *Zhuangzi Qiwulun yili yanxi.* 莊子齊物論義理演析 (Development and Analyses of Meaning of Zhuangzi's Qiwulun Chapter). Taipei: Taiwan shangwu yinshuaguan, 1998.

Noë, Alva. *Action in Perception.* Cambridge, MA: MIT Press, 2004.

Novalis. *Philosophical Writings.* Margaret Mahony Stoljar (trans. and ed.). Albany, NY: SUNY Press.

Novalis. *Schriften.* R. Samuel with H.-J. Mahl and G. Schulz (ed.). Stuttgart: Kohlhammer, 1965.

Palmquist, Stephen R. (ed.). *Cultivating Personhood: Kant and Asian Philosophy.* Berlin, New York: De Gruyter, 2010.

Palumbo, Pietro, and Le Moli, Andrea (ed.). *Soggettività e autocoscienza. Prospettive storico-critiche.* Milano: Mimesis, 2011.

Pang, Ann A. "Augustine on Divine Foreknowledge and Human Free Will." *Revue des Études Augustiniennes* 40 (1994), 417–431.

Pankenier David W. "A Brief History of *Beiji* 北極 (Northern Culmen), with an Excursus on the Origin of the Character *di* 帝)." *Journal of the American Oriental Society* 124:2 (2004), 211–236.

Päs, Heinrich. *The One: How and Ancient Idea Holds the Future of Physics.* London: Icon Books, 2023.

Peng, Wenben (彭文本). "Lun Mou Zongsan yu Feixite zhidezhijue de lilun." 论牟宗三与费希特智的直觉的理论 (Mou Zongsan's and Fichte's Theory of Intellectual Intuition). In: Lee Ming-huei (李明輝) and Chen Weifen (陳瑋芬) (eds). *Dangdai ruxue yu xifang wenhua: zhexue pian.* 當代儒學與西方文化: 哲學篇 (Contemporary Confucianism and Western Culture: Philosophy). Taipei: Academia Sinica, 2004, pp. 131–172.

Pfister, Lauren F. "Three Dialectical Phases in Feng Youlan's Philosophical Journey." In: Elstein, David (ed.). *Dao Companion to Contemporary Confucian Philosophy*. London and Berlin: Springer, 2021, pp. 125–157.

Pioletti, Antje Ehrhardt. *Die Realität des moralischen Handelns. Mou Zongsans Darstellung des Neokonfuzianismus als Vollendung der praktischen Philosophie Kants*. Frankfurt am Main: Peter Lang GmbH, 1997.

Plato, *Republic*, New York: Simon and Schuster, 2016.

Powell, Thomas C. *Kant's Theory of Self-Consciousness*. Oxford: Oxford University Press, 1990.

Qiyong, Guo. "Mou Zongsan's View of interpreting Confucianism by 'Moral Autonomy.'" *Frontiers of Philosophy in China* 2:3 (2007), 345–362.

Pradhan, Ramesh Chandra. *Metaphysics of Consciousness. The Indian Vedantic Perspective*. Singapore: Springer Nature, 2020.

Rae, Gavin. "Hegel, Alienation, and the Phenomenological Development of Consciousness." *International Journal of Philosophical Studies* 20:1 (2012), 23–42, https://doi.org/10.1080/09672559.2011.631147

Rajan, Tilottama. "(In)Digestible Material: Illness and Dialectic in Hegel's *The Philosophy of Nature*." In: Morton, Timothy (ed.). *Cultures of Taste/Theories of Appetite: Eating Romanticism*. New York: Palgrave Macmillan, 2004, pp. 217–236, https://doi.org/10.1057/9781403981394_12

Ricœur, Paul, *Soi-Même comme un Autre*. Paris: Seuil, 1990.

Rošker, Jana S. *Searching for the Way: Theory of Knowledge in Premodern and Modern China*. Hong Kong: The Chinese University Press, 2008.

Rošker, Jana S. "The Subject's New Clothes: Immanent Transcendence and the Moral Self in the Modern Confucian Discourses." *Asian Philosophy* 1 (2014), 1–17.

Rošker, Jana S. *The Rebirth of the Moral Self. The Second Generation of Modern Confucians and their Modernization Discourses*. Hong Kong: The Chinese University Press, 2016.

Ruan, Yuan (阮元). *Shisan jing zhushu.* 十三經注疏 (The Exegesis of the Thirteen Confucian Classics). Beijing: Zhonghua Shuju, 1986.

Sang, Yu. *Xiong Shili's Understanding of Reality and Function 1920–1937*. Leiden: Brill, 2020.

Sartre, Jean-Paul. *Being and Nothingness. An Essay in Phenomenological Ontology*. London and New York: Routledge, 2018.

Sartre, Jean-Paul. "Existentialism is a Humanism." In: Kaufman, Walter (ed.). *Existentialism from Dostoevsky to Sartre*. Cleveland, OH and New York: World Publishing Company, 1969, pp. 287–311.

Sartre, Jean-Paul. *Nausea*, translated by Lloyd Alexander. New York: New Directions, 1964.

Sartre, Jean-Paul. *La Transcendance de L'Ego: Esquisse D'une Description Phenomenologique*. Paris: Vrin, 1992.

Schelling, Friedrich Wilhelm Joseph. "Stuttgart Seminars". In: *Idealism and the Endgame of Theory. Three Essays by F.W.J. Schelling*, translated by Thomas Pfau. Albany, NY: State University of New York Press, 1944, pp. 195–242.

Scholem, Gershom. *Major Trends in Jewish Mysticism*. Stuttgart: Schocken, 1995.

Shaughnessy, Edward L. (ed.). *I Ching: The Classic of Changes*. New York: Ballantine Books, 1996

Sheng, Zhide (盛志德). *Mou Zongsan yu Kangde guanyu zhidezhijue wenti de bijiao yanjiu*. 牟宗三与康德关于"智的直觉"问题的比较研究 (Comparative Research on the issue of Intellectual Intuition in Mou Zongsan and Kant). Guilin: Guangxi shifan daxue chubanshe, 2010.

Shi, Weimin. "Mou Zongsan on Confucian Autonomy and Subjectivity: From Transcendental Philosophy to Transcendent Metaphysics." *Dao* 14:2 (2015), 275–287.

Shoemaker, Sydney. "Introspection and the Self." *Midwest Studies in Philosophy* 10:1 (1986), 101–120.

Shoemaker, Sydney, and Swinburne, Richard. *Personal Identity*. Oxford: Blackwell, 1984.

Siderits, Mark. "Buddhist Non-Self. The No-Owner's Manual." In: Gallagher, Shaun (ed.). *The Oxford Handbook of the Self*. Oxford: Oxford University Press, 2011, pp. 297–315.

Sloterdijk, Peter. *The Art of Philosophy. Wisdom as a Practice*. New York: Columbia University Press, 2012.

Sloterdijk, Peter. *You Must Change Your Life. On Anthropotechnics*. Malden, MA, and Cambridge, UK: Polity Press, 2013.

Strawson, Galen. *Selves. An Essay in Revisionary Metaphysics*. Oxford: Oxford University Press, 2009.

Suter, Rafael. "Transmitting the Sage's 'Heart' (I): Unsealing Moral Autonomy-Intellectual Intuition and Mou Zongsan's Reconstruction of the 'Continuity of the Way' (Daotong)." *Philosophy East and West* 68:1 (2018), 223–241.

Suter, Rafael. "Transmitting the Sage's 'Heart' (II): Instructing Absolute Practice—The Perfection of the Perfect Teaching in Mou Zongsan's Reconstruction of the Confucian Daotong." *Philosophy East and West* 68:2 (2018): 516–538.

Suter, Rafael. *Logik und Apriori zwischen Wahrnehmung und Erkenntnis. Eine Studie zum Frühwerk Mou Zongsans (1909–1995)*. Berlin and Boston, MA: De Gruyter, 2017.

Tang, Wenming. *Secret Subversion I. Mou Zongsan, Kant, and Early Confucianism*. London and New York: Routledge, 2021.

Tang, Wenming. *Secret Subversion II. Mou Zongsan, Kant, and Original Confucianism*. London and New York: Routledge, 2022.

Tao, Liang. "The Significance of *Shendu* in the Interpretation of Classical Learning and Zhu Xi's Misreading." *Dao* 13 (2014), 305–321.

Tao, Yue (陶悦). *Daode xingershangxue: Mou Zongsan yu Kangde zhijian.* 道德形而上学: 牟宗三与康德之间 (Moral Metaphysics: Between Mou Zongsan and Kant). Beijing: Zhongguo shehui kexue chubanshe, 2011.

Thompson, Evan. *Waking, Dreaming, Being. New Light on the Self and Consciousness from Neuroscience, Meditation, and Philosophy*. New York: Columbia University Press, 2014.

Tilliette, Xavier. *L'Intuition intellectuelle de Kant à Hegel*. Paris: Vrin, 1995.

Tu, Wei-Ming. *Centrality and Commonality. An Essay on Confucian Religiousness. A Revised and Enlarged Edition of Centrality and Commonality: An Essay on Chung-yung*. Albany, NY: State University of New York Press, 1989.

Tu, Wei-Ming. *Confucian Thought. Selfhood as Creative Transformation*. Albany, NY: SUNY, 1985.

Tu, Wei-Ming. "The 'Moral Universal' from the Perspectives of East Asian Thought." *Philosophy East and West* 31:3 (1981), 259–267.

Tu, Wei-Ming. *Spiritual Humanism: Self, Community, Earth, and Heaven*. 24th World Congress of Philosophy, Wang Yangming Lecture. N.p.: 2018.

Van den Stock, Ady. *The Horizon of Modernity: Subjectivity and Social Structure in New Confucian Philosophy*. Leiden and Boston, MA: Brill, 2016.

Van Norden, Bryan. *Mengzi. With Selections from Traditional Commentaries*. Indianapolis, IN and Cambridge, UK: Hackett Publishing Company, 2008.

Varela, J. Francisco, Thompson, Evan, and Rosch, Eleanor (ed.). *The Embodied Mind: Cognitive Science and Human Experience*. Cambridge, MA: MIT Press, 1991.

Vetter, Ferdinand (ed.). *Die Predigten Täuler*. Zürich: Weidman, 1968.

Wang, Huaiyu. "Ren and Gantong. Openness of Heart and the Root of Confucianism." *Philosophy East and West* 62:4 (2012), 463–504.

Wang Ji (王畿). *Longxi Wang xiansheng qua ji.* 龍谿王先生全集 (The Complete Works of Master Wang Longxi). Shanghai: Ming shan shuju, 1882 (reprinted Taipei: Huawen Shuju, 1970).

Wang, Keping. "Thomé Fang's Pursuit of a Cultural Ideal." *Asian Studies* 8:24 (2020), 183–207.

Wang, Xiaoyu (王孝魚) (ed.). *Er Cheng ji.* 二程集 (Collection of the Works of the Cheng Brothers). Beijing: Zhonghua shuju, 2011.

Wang, Xingguo (王兴国). *Qijie Zhong Xi zhexue zhi zhuliu: Mou Zongsan zhexue sixiang yuanyuan tanyao.* 契接中西哲学之主流：牟宗三哲学思想渊源探要 (A Confluence of the Mainstreams of Chinese and Western Philosophy: A Brief Investigation into the Sources of Mou Zongsan's Thought). Beijing: Guangming ribao chubanshe, 2006.

Wang, Xingguo (王兴国). *Mou Zongsan zhexue sixiang yanjiu: cong luoji sibian dao zhexue jiagou.* 牟宗三哲学思想研究：从逻辑思辨到哲学架构 (A Study of Mou Zongsan's Philosophy: From Logical Analysis to Constructive Philosophy). Beijing: Renmin chubanshe, 2007.

Wang, Yangming (王阳明). *Quan ji.* 全集 (Complete Works). Shanghai: Shanghai guji chubanshe, 1992.

Watson, Burton (ed.). *The Complete Works of Zhuangzi.* New York: Columbia University Press, 2013.

Wittgenstein, Ludwig. *Tractatus Logico-Philosophicus*, trans. D. F. Pears and B. F. McGuinness. London: Routledge, 1961.

Wong, Wan-Chi. "A Genealogy of Self in Chinese Culture." *Monumenta Serica* 62:1 (2014), 1–54.

Xiong, Shili. *New Treatise on the Uniqueness of Consciousness.* New Haven, CT and London: Yale University Press, 2015.

Yan, Binggang (颜炳罡). *Zhenghe yu chongzhu: Mou Zongsan zhexue sixiang yanjiu.* 整合与重铸：牟宗三哲学思想研究 (Integrating and Recasting: A Study of Mou Zongsan's Philosophical Thought). Beijing: Beijing daxue chubanshe, 1995.

Yang, Lihua (杨立华). *Guo Xiang "Zhuangzi zhu" yanjiu.* 郭象《庄子注》研究 (Research on Guo Xiang's "Zhuangzi"). Beijing: Beijing daxue chubanshe, 2010.

Yang, Yonghan (楊永漢) (ed.). *Jinian Mou Zongsan xiansheng shishi ershi zhounian guoji xu shu yantaohui lunwen ji.* 紀念牟宗三先生逝世二十周年國際學術研討會論文集 (Collected Papers from the International Conference to Commemorate the 20th Anniversary of the Passing of Mou Zongsan). Taipei: Wanjuan lou, 2018.

Yang, Zebo (杨泽波). *Gongxian yu zhongjie: Mou Zongsan ruxue sixiang yanjiu.* 贡献与终结：牟宗三儒学思想研究 (Contribution and Consummation: A Study of Mou Zongsan's Confucian Thought), 5 vols. Shanghai: Shanghai renmin chubanshe, 2014.

Yang, Zebo (杨泽波). *Mou Zongsan "Xinti yu Xingti"; he "Cong Liu Jishan dao Lu Xiangshan".* 牟宗三《心体与性体》解读：含《从陆象山到刘蕺山》(An Interpretation of Mou Zongsan's "Constitutive Mind and Constitutive Nature"; with "From Liu Jishan to Lu Xiangshan"). Shanghai: Shanghai renmin chubanshe, 2016.

Yang, Zhiyi. "Return to an Inner Utopia: Su Shi's Transformation of Tao Qian in His Exile Poetry." *T'oung Pao* 99 (2013), 329–378.

Zahavi, Dan. "Philosophy, Psychology, and Phenomenology." In: Heinämaa, Sara, and Reuter, Martina (ed.). *Psychology and Philosophy: Inquiries into the Soul from Late Scholasticism to Contemporary Thought*. New York: Springer, 2009, pp. 247–262, https://doi.org/10.1007/978-1-4020-8582-6_13

Zahavi, Dan. *Self-Awareness and Alterity: A Phenomenological Investigation*. Evanston, IL: Northwestern University Press, 1999.

Zahavi, Dan. *Subjectivity and Selfhood: Investigating the First-Person Perspective*. Cambridge, MA: MIT Press, 2005.

Zahavi, Dan. "Unity of Consciousness and the Problem of Self." In: Gallagher, Shaun (ed.). *The Oxford Handbook of the Self*. Oxford: Oxford University Press, 2011, pp. 316–335, https://doi.org/10.1093/oxfordhb/9780199548019.003.0014

Zambrano, Maria. *Verso un sapere dell'anima* [*Hacia un saber sobre el alma* (Towards a Knowledge of the Soul)]. Milan: Cortina Editore, 1996.

Zhu, Xi. *Sishu zhangju jizhu*. 四書章句集注 (Collected Annotations of the Four Books). Beijing: Zhongguo Zhonghua shuju, 1983.

Index

Albahari, Miri 60
"all things form one body" (*wanwu yiti*, 萬物一體) 235, 237
apperception (*tongjue*, 統覺) 49, 59, 76–79, 81–87, 89–93, 95–96, 101, 104, 109, 118, 193, 215, 233–234, 241
a priori knowledge 18, 21, 24, 50, 77–78, 81–82, 84, 88, 90–93, 96, 103, 105, 151, 156, 164, 193, 207, 217, 243, 256, 258, 267–268
Aufhebung (subsumption) 173, 251, 255, 268
Augustine of Hippo 197, 264, 304
authenticity (*cheng*, 誠; *chengti* 誠體) 3–4, 108, 119, 133, 143, 161, 174, 189, 230–231, 238–239, 242, 245, 306, 316–317, 320–321, 327
authentic self 7, 32, 66, 89–90, 99–100, 108, 247, 303, 331
awakening (*jingxing*, 警醒) 7–8, 29, 39, 107, 123, 161, 163, 186, 190, 202, 207, 210, 216, 244, 254, 262, 278–279, 288–292, 294–295, 322, 325, 330, 334

being (*you* 有) 148, 150, 152, 218, 231
Bergson, Henri-Louis 153
Berkeley, George 1, 76, 102
Buddhism 3, 13, 17, 93–95, 103, 114, 116, 123–124, 126, 166, 189–190, 224, 295
   Awakening of Faith in the Mahāyāna (*Dasheng qi xin lun*) 17–18, 71, 135, 190, 228
   Buddha-Nature 17
   Tiantai school 17, 114, 134, 224, 295

Cartesianism 12, 51, 58, 118, 201, 216–217, 237–238, 290, 309, 329
Chalmers, David 7–8, 45–46

Cheng Mingdao 10, 216, 229, 234–237, 311–314, 319
Churchland, Patricia 50
Cogito 49, 51, 53, 55, 57, 59, 63, 67, 118, 216, 233–234, 237–238, 290, 308–309, 317, 326, 329
cognition 45, 56–57, 70, 76, 133, 206, 247, 319
Confucianism 3, 13, 16–19, 30, 32, 35, 65, 75, 120, 123, 126, 135–136, 138, 140, 165, 168–169, 171, 173, 181, 189–192, 197, 202–203, 207, 217, 224, 238, 259, 263, 272, 301–302, 304, 315, 326, 332, 341
   School of Mind (*xinxue*, 心學) 71, 124, 190
   School of Principle (*lixue*, 理學) 124, 190, 228, 233
   Song-Ming Neo-Confucianism 16, 19, 28, 31, 65, 123, 140, 191–192, 205, 231, 302
Confucius (Kongzi) 3, 16, 28, 140, 190–191, 203, 210, 232, 301–302, 329
cosmology 14, 116, 191, 213, 217, 235, 266, 302, 312, 314, 319, 329
creativity 16–17, 23–24, 36, 64, 78, 91, 103, 120, 140, 144, 153, 169, 184, 190, 192, 205, 210–211, 213, 216, 228, 230, 236–237, 240–241, 243, 260, 262, 271, 289, 302, 312, 314, 319, 322

Damasio, Antonio 57
Daodejing 25–26, 39, 114, 117, 134, 150, 157, 161–162
Daoism 3, 8, 13, 17, 25–27, 30, 93–95, 107, 113–116, 119–122, 126–127, 129, 131–132, 134–135, 137–145, 147–148, 150, 152–154, 156–158, 161, 163, 165–170, 172–176, 178,

180–187, 189, 199, 211, 218–219, 224, 230, 259, 263, 270, 297, 302, 310, 328
  Neo-Daoism (*Xuanxue*, 玄學) 113–114, 121
Deleuze, Gilles 196, 250
Dennett, Daniel 49, 51
Derrida, Jacques 218–219, 221, 250
Descartes, René 1–2, 6, 9–10, 36, 43, 48, 51, 55, 57, 59, 63, 87, 185, 233, 237–238, 308, 317, 326
dream of the butterfly 107, 182
dynamism 6, 15, 23, 25, 28–30, 32–33, 37, 53, 55, 62, 70, 74, 78, 80–81, 83–86, 88–92, 95, 97, 99–100, 103, 105, 110, 113, 126, 128–129, 134, 140, 148, 150, 163, 178, 185–187, 190, 194–195, 197, 200, 204–205, 207–208, 210–213, 223–224, 228, 232, 235, 247, 250–251, 262, 268, 271, 273, 277, 280, 292, 295, 297–298, 309, 312, 314, 318–323, 330, 333

ego (*wo*, 我) 2, 5, 21–22, 27, 34, 43, 47–50, 52–54, 56, 65–66, 69–70, 81, 83, 88, 118–119, 134, 138, 144, 149, 155, 158, 161–162, 171–172, 174–175, 178–179, 181–185, 202, 218–220, 251, 258, 263, 266, 268, 272–273, 275, 278–281, 291–294, 309
  egological theory 90–91
  non-egological theory 47, 49, 60–62
  self-forgetting (*wang wo*, 忘我) 160, 171, 186, 277
eliminativism 45, 66
emanation (*yongxian*, 湧現) 24, 81, 86, 90, 93, 103–104, 215, 262, 283, 294–295, 329
embodiment (*tixian*, 體現; *tiwu*, 體悟) 5, 34, 116–117, 134, 139, 142–143, 150, 172, 184, 187, 219, 252, 254
emptiness 8, 117, 121, 123, 134, 142, 147, 153, 160, 165, 166, 168, 170, 178, 186, 190, 199, 249, 290, 297, 298, 310. *See also* nothingness (*wu*, 無)
enlightened moral consciousness (*zhiti mingjue*, 知體明覺) 253
enlightenment 14, 41, 66, 123–124, 224, 294, 310, 322
  instantaneous enlightenment (*yuandun*, 圓頓) 224–225, 295
Enlightenment, Age of 15
Entäusserung (externalization) 33, 269–270, 273, 275, 277
Entfremdung (alienation) 33, 273, 277, 279–281
epistemology 8, 13–14, 21–22, 24–27, 32, 41, 43–45, 51, 56, 61–62, 66–67, 69–70, 72–76, 79, 81, 86, 88, 93–94, 97–98, 100, 109, 111, 113–115, 126, 128, 137, 146, 156, 161, 165, 178, 180, 194, 216, 219, 240, 262, 296, 308–309, 317–318, 332–333
Er-innerung (interiorization) 209, 218, 279
ethics 4, 29, 31, 34–35, 40–41, 54, 116, 144, 169, 196, 198, 200–203, 220, 232, 251, 259, 287–289, 291, 294–296, 298, 327, 333
experience (*tihui*, 體會; *tiren*, 體認) 117, 140, 238, 315

fact (*shi*, 事) 261, 279
fecundating (*runze*, 潤澤) 216
Feng Youlan 15, 124–125
Fichte, Johann Gottlieb 2, 52–53, 87, 102, 110, 250
for-itself (*pour-soi*) 53, 105, 225
free and easy wandering (*xiaoyaoyou*, 逍遙遊) 107, 139, 178, 199, 310
freedom (*ziyou*, 自由) 29–31, 146, 150, 160, 172, 194–197, 199–202, 207, 215, 223, 231, 274, 279–280, 284–286, 310
free will 4, 14, 196, 198–199, 201, 220, 226, 234, 278–279, 320
function (*yong*, 用) 140, 150–151, 189, 229, 262

substance / function (*ti*, 體 / *yong*, 用) 139–140, 150, 189, 208, 227, 243, 252, 281, 315, 325
wonderful subtle function (*miaoyong*, 妙用) 152, 164, 173

Gallagher, Shaun 57, 183
gantong, 感通. See interconnectedness (*gantong*, 感通)
ganying, 感應. See resonance (*ganying*, 感應)
generativity 4, 45, 116, 158–159, 172, 192, 214, 219, 235, 249, 273, 283

Hadot, Pierre 184
Han, Christina 123
harmony 158, 161, 163, 185, 228, 245, 254, 263
heaven (*tian*, 天) 94, 143, 171, 219, 223–224, 254, 259, 334
Hegel, Georg Wilhelm Friedrich 2, 15–16, 18, 33–34, 58, 65, 136–137, 141, 145, 161, 163, 171, 173, 192–193, 209, 217, 219, 221, 224, 250–251, 253, 262, 265, 268–273, 275–281
Heidegger, Martin 3, 9, 53, 88, 115, 156, 159, 214, 232–233, 265, 284, 306, 321
higher-order theory 52–53, 85
hodological space 26, 33, 129–130, 132–133, 162, 185, 255, 270
holism 13, 16, 23, 31, 72, 80, 262
horizontality 3, 8, 12, 14, 25–29, 32, 34–35, 42–43, 62, 70, 73, 116, 120, 123, 128–129, 134, 136–138, 141, 146–148, 150–151, 155–156, 166, 168, 176–177, 180–183, 187, 193–196, 198, 200, 202, 204, 208, 210, 213, 215, 218, 221–222, 226, 228, 232, 240, 243, 247, 257–258, 260, 266–268, 270, 275, 277–278, 281, 296, 329, 334
humanity 134, 190, 221, 314–316
Hume, David 11, 15, 47, 59, 81, 93–94, 96

Husserl, Edmund 9, 21, 26, 43, 48–49, 53, 55–58, 128, 181, 239, 284–285, 290, 316
imagination 8, 23, 73, 76–78, 80, 82–84, 86, 89–91, 93, 215, 262
incipience (*ji*, 幾) 161, 210, 212–214, 220, 224, 327, 329–330
indeterminacy 186, 196–200, 210–211, 219, 297
in-itself (*en-soi*) 4, 12, 17, 29, 31, 37, 51, 53, 101, 105, 147, 165, 170, 222, 224–225, 230, 241–243, 247, 272, 280, 286, 322, 324
innate moral consciousness (*liangzhi*, 良知) 10, 143, 168, 171, 220, 238, 292, 305, 320, 328, 330
intellectual intuition 15, 17, 53, 101–103, 109, 113, 165, 257, 266, 272, 293–294, 309, 319
intentionality 26, 52–55, 58, 80–81, 101, 120, 128–129, 132, 146, 148, 151, 159, 170, 181, 244, 256, 285, 287, 290, 317
interconnectedness (*gantong*, 感通) 30, 36, 74–75, 216, 238, 240, 299, 315, 319–320
interiority 10, 13, 32, 35–37, 54, 111, 198, 232, 234, 236–242, 265, 274, 292, 303, 307, 311–312, 314, 320–321, 323, 333
introspection (*fanxing*, 反省) 56, 239, 316
intuition 10, 14–15, 17, 24, 29, 45, 53, 59, 65, 73, 76–77, 80, 82, 88, 91, 94–95, 98, 101–105, 107, 109, 113, 137, 144, 158, 165, 174–175, 185, 190–191, 215, 217, 238, 241, 257, 266, 272, 284, 289–290, 293–294, 308–309, 319, 328–329

jingjie, 境界. See state of mind (*jingjie*, 境界)
Jullien, François 213
jumping out (*tiaoqi*, 跳起) 8, 24, 83, 96–97, 104, 108, 151, 171–172, 207, 215, 222, 293

Kant, Immanuel 1, 3–4, 6–7, 13–15, 17–18, 22, 29, 37, 49–50, 53, 58–59, 71–74, 79, 81–84, 86–88, 92–93, 101–102, 114, 118, 135, 156, 164–165, 171, 178, 190, 192–193, 195, 198, 202, 204, 207, 210, 217, 231–234, 241–243, 248, 256, 261, 268, 271–272, 277–279, 297–298, 301, 303, 309, 317–318, 320, 322–324
kenosis 33, 247–254, 258, 262, 270, 282–283

lack of moral responsivity (*bu ren*, 不仁) 10, 237, 314
Laozi 113–114, 117, 134–135, 137, 139, 145–146, 161, 176, 181
Leibniz, Gottfried Wilhelm 15, 81, 84, 86–87, 105–107, 111, 115, 206–207
Lévinas, Emmanuel 34–35, 200–201, 203, 244, 250–251, 263, 282–287, 290–299
liangzhi, 良知. *See* innate moral consciousness (*liangzhi*, 良知)

Makeham, John 18
Manfred, Frank 53, 59, 88
manifestation (*chengxian*, 呈現) 4, 12, 15, 23–24, 26–27, 30–31, 34, 37, 43, 45, 47, 53, 55, 65, 73, 75–76, 80–81, 85, 89, 96, 99, 103, 105, 108, 111, 140, 142, 158–159, 169–170, 177, 184, 189, 193, 204, 206–208, 211, 221–222, 224, 230, 236, 239, 241–245, 258, 265, 278–279, 281, 286, 294–295, 297, 304, 309, 314, 318, 320–321, 323–324, 330, 333
meditation 64, 121, 123, 127, 129, 133, 141, 155, 167, 304, 306
Mengzi (Mencius) 9, 16, 19, 28–31, 161, 174, 191, 203, 212, 214, 226–227, 232, 238–239, 242, 245, 254, 299, 302, 311, 316, 323, 325, 328
Merleau-Ponty, Maurice 43, 54, 56–57
Metzinger, Thomas 49

mind (*xin*, 心) 16, 70, 220, 302. *See also* Confucianism: School of Mind (*xinxue*, 心學)
   cognitive mind (*renshixin*, 認識信) 16, 23–24, 34, 71–83, 89, 93–97, 99–105, 108, 110, 156, 182, 209, 234, 253, 295
   constitutive mind (*xinti*, 心體) 238
   discourse on mind and nature (*xinxinglun*, 心性論) 228, 272
   mind of benevolence (*renxin*, 仁心) 31, 120, 214, 220–222, 226–227, 238, 240, 244–245, 254, 272, 315, 319, 325, 330, 332
   mind of the Dao (*daoxin*, 道心) 135, 171, 182
   mind of the quiet shining (*jizhaoxin*, 寂照心) 103–105, 107–108, 110, 113, 120
   "mind that opens two doors" (*yi xin kai er men*, 一心開二門) 18, 71, 134, 228
   moral mind (*benxin*, 本心; *tianxin*, 天心; *daode ziwo*, 道德自我) 4–6, 9–11, 14–16, 18–19, 30–32, 34–35, 37, 71, 73, 75, 94, 99–101, 144, 168, 171–172, 174, 181–182, 184, 189, 202, 205, 211, 216, 225, 227–228, 230–231, 239, 241, 244–245, 247, 251, 253, 259–261, 263, 266–268, 270, 275, 277, 280–281, 288–289, 292, 294–299, 302, 305, 311, 315, 320, 322, 325, 328, 333
moral metaphysics 4, 9, 11, 13, 17–18, 28, 30, 34, 37, 70–71, 114, 163, 190, 193, 195, 198, 202–204, 213, 217, 222, 231, 238, 240, 270, 273, 296, 315, 319, 323, 331, 334
Mou Zongsan
   Caixing yu xuanli (*Physical Nature and the "Profound Thought"*) 17, 25, 114, 145, 154, 159, 171, 288
   Cong Lu Xiangshan dao Liu Jishan (*From Lu Xiangshan to Liu Jishan*) 16, 214, 238, 315

Daode de lixiangzhuyi (*Moral Idealism*) 15, 136
Lishi zhexue (*Philosophy of History*) 15
Renshi xin zhi pipan (*Critique of the Cognitive Mind*) 7, 15, 18, 22, 25–26, 29, 31, 69, 72, 74, 81, 83, 89, 92, 96, 99–100, 137, 165, 171, 178, 210, 215, 240, 262, 275, 294, 317–318, 343
Wushi zishu (*Autobiography at Fifty*) 14
Xinti yu xingti (*Constitutive Mind and Constitutive Nature*) 16, 140, 153, 187, 189–190, 195, 204, 221, 228, 234, 236, 240, 243, 272, 292, 296, 301, 313, 315, 317, 319–320, 324–325, 329, 331
Zhongguo zhexue shijiu jang (*Nineteen Lectures on Chinese Philosophy*) 3, 17, 71, 114, 122

nature (*xing*, 性) 10, 16, 31, 220, 230, 239, 317
  constitutive nature (*xingti*, 性體) 16, 238, 315, 329, 331
non-action (*wu wei*, 無爲) 131, 146
nothingness (*wu*, 無) 8, 26–27, 30, 118–121, 138–143, 145–146, 148–150, 152, 155, 157–158, 161–163, 167, 170, 172–173, 175–176, 184, 200, 211, 218–219, 231, 283, 297, 310
noumenon 4, 135, 241, 248, 286, 324
Novalis 52, 55, 137, 281

object (*keti*, 客體; *duixiang*, 對象) 3–10, 14, 21, 23–25, 27–28, 30, 42–44, 46, 48, 51–53, 56–57, 64, 66, 73–75, 77–85, 87–93, 95, 97, 110, 117, 120, 126, 128–129, 133, 140–142, 146, 149–151, 153–160, 165, 168–171, 173, 177–178, 180–182, 190, 194, 200, 204, 210, 215, 239–241, 244, 248, 250–251, 256–257, 259, 261, 266–268, 271, 273, 276–277, 280–281, 287, 289–291, 293, 298, 303, 305, 309, 316–320, 322, 324, 331
ontology 3, 7, 10, 18, 20, 24, 31–32, 34, 43, 45, 49, 51, 64, 76, 80, 84–85, 99–100, 110–111, 114–117, 120, 134–135, 137, 145, 150, 155, 164, 179–180, 189, 194, 197, 199–200, 204, 207, 211, 216, 219, 223–224, 229, 232, 235, 239, 245, 247, 249, 251, 253, 256–258, 261, 265, 267, 272, 278–280, 283–284, 286, 296, 299, 303, 307, 310–312, 317, 320–321
origin (*yuan* 元) 162, 220

perception (*jue*, 覺) 8, 74, 158, 161, 171, 213, 215, 240, 318
performativity 4, 9, 11, 22, 25–30, 32, 62, 66, 70, 72, 119, 126, 134, 155, 162, 190, 201, 203–204, 206–207, 209, 217, 235, 239–240, 242, 251, 258, 261, 279, 299, 323
phenomenology 15, 22, 26, 41, 43, 45, 48, 55, 57–58, 76, 80, 88, 128, 130, 151, 179–181, 183–186, 244, 256, 284–285, 295, 303, 317, 321
phenomenon 6, 18, 21, 29, 32, 43–46, 48, 50, 55, 57, 59, 65, 73, 78–79, 81, 84, 86, 90, 100, 135, 151, 164–165, 186, 206, 210, 213, 243, 260–261, 268, 286, 311
Plato 1–2, 36, 39, 65, 115, 135, 138–139, 162, 237, 249, 252, 303–304, 306–308, 310, 314
primordial chaos (*hundun*, 混沌) 120, 139, 162, 231, 248
principle (*li*, 理) 147

qualia 6–8, 29, 36, 46, 194, 311

reflection (*fansi*, 反思) 4, 9, 21, 23, 27, 35–36, 51–54, 57, 83, 85–88, 95–96, 105, 125, 141, 159, 167, 180, 207, 209, 233–234, 238, 251, 272, 278–279, 288, 292, 309, 315–318, 325–326, 331, 334 resonance (*ganying*, 感應) 12, 36, 70, 75, 127, 134, 144, 203, 210, 216, 220, 229, 238, 241, 260, 280, 315, 329

responsibility 12, 23, 30, 34, 37, 73, 94–95, 97–98, 125, 201, 203, 208, 237, 241–242, 244–245, 285, 291–292, 304, 322, 325, 329

retrospective verification (*nijue tizheng*, 逆覺體徵) 10, 174, 232, 241, 245, 263, 293, 320, 322, 325, 331

retrospective verification (*nijue tizheng*, 逆覺體證) 10, 174, 232, 241, 245, 263, 293, 320, 322, 325, 331

Rošker, Jana S. 20

Russell, Bertrand 14–15, 22, 145

Sartre, Jean-Paul 21, 43, 48, 51–53, 58, 130, 200–201, 284

Schelling, Friedrich Wilhelm Joseph 102, 250, 258, 265

self (*zi*, 自) 109, 111, 148, 159, 181, 243, 320

  self-consciousness (*zijue*, 自覺) 174, 225, 240, 266, 320. See also self-consciousness

  spontaneity (*ziran*, 自然) 147–148, 159–160, 164, 170, 184

self-awareness 9–10, 30, 43, 52–55, 59–60, 73, 81–82, 84–85, 87–88, 90, 92, 107, 163, 207–208, 238, 240, 285, 312, 317, 329, 331–332

self-consciousness 1–2, 8, 12, 21–22, 41–42, 44–45, 47, 50, 52–54, 56–59, 61–62, 64, 70, 81–83, 85–87, 91–92, 96, 105, 109, 125, 160–161, 163, 169–171, 173–174, 183, 192, 194, 209, 217, 222, 225, 233, 240–241, 243, 245, 248, 250, 263, 266, 276, 305, 309, 311, 317–318, 320, 325, 329, 331

self-cultivation 4, 12, 14, 16, 26, 30, 66, 116, 121–122, 124, 126, 128–129, 134, 139, 141–144, 155, 161–162, 168, 176, 185, 203, 216, 231, 237, 242, 254, 256, 281, 294, 296, 333

self-limitation (*ziwo kanxian*, 自我坎陷) 5–6, 18, 23–24, 26, 32–35, 70–71, 74, 97, 99–101, 104, 106, 108, 113, 156, 171, 173, 247–249, 251–253, 255–258, 261–263, 267–268, 273, 275, 277, 280, 283, 296–298

self-perfection 4, 10, 121, 179, 185, 187, 195, 204, 226, 245

sensibility 73, 83–84, 86, 88–89, 93–94, 96–97, 171, 178, 238, 268, 294, 315

simplicity 132, 143, 162, 169

Sloterdijk, Peter 185, 303, 306

solitude 12, 35–36, 132, 166, 299, 308–309, 326–329, 331

  vigilance in solitude (*shendu*, 慎獨) 36, 326–327

Spinoza, Baruch 194, 272

state of mind (*jingjie*, 境界) 25–27, 30, 33, 121–126, 128–129, 132–134, 138, 140, 143–144, 148–150, 153, 155–157, 160–161, 163, 169, 173, 176, 181, 184–185, 206, 238, 255, 258, 270, 296, 315, 330, 332

Strawson, Galen 49, 54, 179

subject (*zhuti*, 主體) 154, 157, 175

  subjective (*zhuguan*, 主觀) 175

  subject / object (*zhuke*, 主客; *nengsuo* 能所) 10, 43, 52, 64, 85, 89, 120, 156, 158, 177–178, 241, 257, 277, 324

substance / function (*ti*, 體 / *yong*, 用). See function (*yong*, 用): substance / function (*ti*, 體 / *yong*, 用)

suchness (*ruru*, 如如) 80, 111, 135, 145, 147–149, 159, 164, 184, 190, 224

suffering 41, 61, 213, 241, 257, 259, 291–292, 302, 319–320

Tang Junyi 16, 19, 122, 125–126

Thompson, Evan 60, 63, 66

time 6, 9, 11, 19, 23, 43, 48, 77–80, 84, 86, 89, 91, 93, 96, 99, 103, 113, 118, 126, 130, 149, 187, 189–190, 196, 200–201, 204–205, 209–210,

212–213, 220, 224, 248, 258–261, 265, 267–269, 278, 288, 295, 304, 330
transcendence 15, 23–24, 26, 28–29, 37, 85, 100–101, 134, 156, 201–202, 207–208, 227, 233, 244, 251, 260, 265, 274, 282, 286–288, 290–291, 293–295, 325, 333
trans-consciousness (*chao zijue*, 超自覺) 161, 163, 169, 171, 173–174, 266
transformation 4, 11, 13, 25, 31, 127, 129, 131, 134, 142, 146–147, 149, 155, 185–186, 190, 204, 228, 282–283, 314, 317
tremor (*ziwo zhendong*, 自我震動) 216, 230, 288–289, 293, 330
Tu Wei-Ming 13, 136, 221, 260, 314
tzimtzum (self-contraction of God) 34–35, 282–283, 286–287, 290, 296–298

universality 4, 9, 12, 15, 23–24, 30, 70, 73–74, 77–78, 98, 101–102, 104, 109, 116, 137, 144–145, 172, 186, 191, 195, 198, 206, 208, 229, 233, 235, 237, 239, 241, 245, 262, 269, 272, 276, 294, 302, 309, 311–312, 316–317, 319–322, 328, 330–332

Varela, Francisco 57
verticality 3–5, 8–9, 11–12, 14, 24–25, 27–28, 34–37, 42–43, 62, 71–72, 98, 114, 116, 120, 122–123, 126, 128–129, 132, 134, 136, 138–139, 141, 146, 155–157, 168, 173, 176, 180, 184–187, 195, 204, 208, 210, 212–213, 215, 217, 220, 222, 240–241, 247, 256–258, 260–261, 270, 275, 279, 281, 296, 320, 328–329, 333–334
vital breath (*qi*, 氣) 75, 116, 149, 233

Wang Bi 17, 114, 140, 162
Wang Yangming 118, 166, 192, 205, 211, 236, 238, 292, 305, 310, 313, 322, 328, 330
Western philosophy 16, 29, 62, 71, 86, 114–115, 135, 184, 190, 193, 282, 301, 303
Whitehead, Alfred North 14, 22, 117
Wittgenstein, Ludwig 13, 22, 44
wu (nothingness, 無). *See* nothingness (*wu*, 無)

xin (mind, 心). *See* mind (*xin*, 心)
xing (nature, 性). *See* nature (*xing*, 性)
Xiong Shili 14, 19, 165
Xu Fuguan 16, 19

Yijing (Classic of Changes) 10, 14, 31, 137, 167, 177, 204, 210, 212, 235, 254, 255, 270, 288, 328

Zahavi, Dan 43, 48, 55, 179, 180, 183
Zambrano, Maria 220
Zhang Junmai 16
Zhang Zai 3, 227, 245, 325
Zhuangzi 25, 26, 107, 113, 114, 117, 121, 127, 131, 132, 134, 136, 137, 139, 141, 142, 144, 145, 146, 147, 149, 152, 154, 160, 161, 162, 168, 171, 182, 186, 221, 222, 251, 254, 310
Zhu Xi 123, 124, 222, 228, 232, 233, 234, 260, 272, 327
zi (self, 自). *See* self (*zi*, 自)

About the Team

Alessandra Tosi was the managing editor for this book.

Adèle Kreager proof-read this manuscript and compiled the index.

Jeevanjot Kaur Nagpal designed the cover. The cover was produced in InDesign using the Fontin font.

Cameron Craig typeset the book in InDesign and produced the paperback and hardback editions. The main text font is Tex Gyre Pagella and the heading font is Californian FB.

Cameron also produced the PDF and HTML editions. The conversion was performed with open-source software and other tools freely available on our GitHub page at https://github.com/OpenBookPublishers.

Jeremy Bowman created the EPUB.

Raegan Allen was in charge of marketing.

This book was peer-reviewed by Prof. Stephen C. Angle, Wesleyan University. Experts in their field, our readers give their time freely to help ensure the academic rigour of our books. We are grateful for their generous and invaluable contributions.

This book need not end here...

Share

All our books — including the one you have just read — are free to access online so that students, researchers and members of the public who can't afford a printed edition will have access to the same ideas. This title will be accessed online by hundreds of readers each month across the globe: why not share the link so that someone you know is one of them?

This book and additional content is available at
https://doi.org/10.11647/OBP.0442

Donate

Open Book Publishers is an award-winning, scholar-led, not-for-profit press making knowledge freely available one book at a time. We don't charge authors to publish with us: instead, our work is supported by our library members and by donations from people who believe that research shouldn't be locked behind paywalls.

Join the effort to free knowledge by supporting us at
https://www.openbookpublishers.com/support-us

We invite you to connect with us on our socials!

BLUESKY
@openbookpublish.bsky.social

MASTODON
@OpenBookPublish@hcommons.social

LINKEDIN
open-book-publishers

Read more at the Open Book Publishers Blog

https://blogs.openbookpublishers.com

You may also be interested in:

Foundations for Moral Relativism
Second Expanded Edition
J. David Velleman

https://doi.org/10.11647/obp.0086

Forms of Life and Subjectivity
Rethinking Sartre's Philosophy
Daniel Rueda Garrido

https://doi.org/10.11647/obp.0259

Agency
Moral Identity and Free Will
David Weissman

https://doi.org/10.11647/obp.0197

Metaethics from a First Person Standpoint
An Introduction to Moral Philosophy
Catherine Wilson

https://doi.org/10.11647/obp.0087

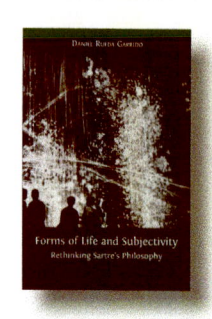